Ontology after Ontotheology

Ontology after Ontotheology

Plurality, Event, and Contingency
in Contemporary Philosophy

Gert-Jan van der Heiden

DUQUESNE UNIVERSITY PRESS
Pittsburgh, Pennsylvania

Copyright © 2014 Duquesne University Press
All rights reserved

Published in the United States of America by
DUQUESNE UNIVERSITY PRESS
600 Forbes Avenue
Pittsburgh, Pennsylvania 15282

No part of this book may be used or reproduced,
in any manner or form whatsoever,
without written permission from the publisher,
except in the case of short quotations
in critical articles or reviews.

Library of Congress Cataloging-in-Publication Data

Heiden, Gerrit Jan van der, 1976–
   Ontology after ontotheology : plurality, event, and contingency in contemporary philosophy / Gert-Jan van der Heiden.
      pages cm
   Includes bibliographical references and index.
   Summary: "Van der Heiden works largely with present-day thinkers such as Badiou, Nancy, Romano, Meillassoux, and Agamben, and examines contemporary thought as it seeks to recover a sense of the absolute, but without recourse to specifically theological underpinnings"—Provided by publisher.
   ISBN 978-0-8207-0472-2 (pbk. : alk. paper)
   1. Ontology. 2. Metaphysics. 3. Contingency (Philosophy) I. Title.
   BD311.H44 2014
   111—dc23

                                                                      2014000211

∞ Printed on acid-free paper

Contents

Preface vii
Acknowledgments xi

INTRODUCTION	**Returning to Ontology**	1
	The Contemporary Space of First Philosophy	1
	Beyond the Unifying Ground: Heidegger's Legacy	9

PART 1. CONFLICTING PLURALITIES: BETWEEN HERMENEUTICS AND MATHEMATICS

ONE	• **Mathematics and Beyond: Event, Axiom, and Subject**	29
	The Axiomatic Decision	30
	Badiou's Ontology in Discussion with Hermeneutics	34
	Subjectivity in Light of Mathematics	62

TWO	• **Hermeneutics and Beyond: Partage and Abandonment**	69
	The Structure of Signification: Metaphysical Remnants in Classical Hermeneutics	74
	From Belonging to Abandonment: Being-Toward in Nancy's Plato	78
	Koinon without *Hen:* On Hermeneutics as *Partage*	83
	Koinon without *Hen:* Nancy's Ontology of Plurality	92

THREE	• **Beyond Presupposition: Plato and Agamben**	101
	Two Platos: Mathematics versus Dialogue	101
	Supporting the Axiom	103
	An Agambian Reading of the *Parmenides*	114
	Enthusiasm of the Rhapsode and Potentiality of the Scrivener	121

Part 2. Figures of Contingency: Suspending the Principle of Sufficient Reason

Four • **Advent or Birth: Two Models of the Event** 138
Heidegger and "the Wholly Other Song of Beyng" 139
Shimmering and Shining: The Phenomenality of the Event 156
Resurrection or Second Coming: Paradigmatic Pauline Events and the Question of Faith 169

Five • **Absolute Beginning or Absolute Contingency** 185
Absolute Beginning in Romano's Phenomenology of the Event 186
Absolute Contingency in Meillassoux's Speculative Thought 204
The Contingency of the Event 222

Six • **What Can No More Be Than Not Be** 225
Remainder of Plurality, Remainder of the Event   225
Absolution, Event, and Abandonment 231
Contingency and Pure Potentiality: The Case of Agamben 240

Seven • **The Ethos of Contingency** 262
Deductive Fidelity and the Affirmation of Thought   263
Nancy's Ellipsis: The Empty Preference for Being   271
Epochē as Comportment 275
Instead of an Epilogue: Another Parmenides, Another Ending 280

Notes 289
Bibliography 318
Index 331

Preface

After the vehement criticisms of metaphysics in the twentieth century, one might say that "first philosophy" has found its place at the center of continental philosophy once again. Of course, the question of being has never truly left the scene, but serious attempts to return to ontology seem to belong mainly to the last decades. Yet, this does not mean that the way in which first philosophy is understood has not been affected by the criticisms preceding it. In fact, as I aim to show in this book, the themes and concepts of contemporary metaphysics are highly influenced by the different versions of the account of classical metaphysics as ontotheology. In this context, Alain Badiou's playful description of his own ontology as a "metaphysics without metaphysics" beautifully captures this influence: whereas contemporary thought aims and feels itself compelled to do ontology, and displays—as all metaphysics worthy of the name—a taste for the absolute, the contemporary version of first philosophy might be called an "ontology after ontotheology" and is as such a metaphysics without metaphysics. As I will show in the course of the study that follows, this means that the questions that set the agenda today aim to offer an alternative to what is considered to be the core of ontotheology.

More precisely, one may understand this "core" of ontotheology to consist in the metaphysical quest for (or presupposition of) a unifying reason or ground. This core is theological in nature because it concerns first and foremost the metaphysical concept of God. An alternative to this core will question both the unity and the ground of this unifying ground. Therefore, I propose to consider contemporary ontology in light of its efforts to offer an alternative to unity as well as to reason or ground. The first leads us to the problematic of plurality and the second to the present-day account of the concept of the event. In particular, as will become clear in the course of this book, in its quest to think being no longer from a unifying ground, contemporary ontology is an *ontology of contingency*. In fact, to think the concept of contingency is the main challenge for a thought of being today. In addition, such a transformed first philosophy also requires another comportment of thought. Leaving behind *theōria* as the contemplation of the eternal, necessary, and present entities, contemporary thought offers a number of different ways to account for the ethos of thinking that may attune us to the theme of contingency.

The task of this book is twofold. On the one hand, it aims to offer some important markers of the contemporary interest in plurality, event, and contingency, thus painting a picture of the present-day space of ontology and showing how different authors—such as Badiou, Jean-Luc Nancy, Quentin Meillassoux, Claude Romano, and Giorgio Agamben—traverse the same space by different trajectories. On the other hand, it aims to take a position in the debate of which trajectory in this space is most promising in thinking the ontology of contingency. In chapters 3, 6, and 7, my position in this debate will become most clear. First, contingency is a thought of pure potentiality and requires the absolution of all presuppositions, as I will argue with Agamben; moreover, following the striking formulation of Meillassoux, to think contingency means to think being as well as thinking in its potentiality-of-being-otherwise (*pouvoir-être-autre*). Second, this thought of contingency requires its own form of the absolute. Especially in relation to the speculative thought developed by authors such as Badiou and Meillassoux, I will argue that this absolute can neither consist in the affirmation of certain hypotheses or axioms nor in the discovery of yet another principle—the first is not capable of doing justice to the *anupotheton* of the absolute, whereas the second remains captive to the logic of the principle and the *archē*, which still belongs to the realm of the principle of reason that these authors aim to leave behind. Inspired by Agamben's attention to categories from skepticism and in a reading of Plato's

Parmenides guiding me throughout this book, I will argue that the suspension of judgment, the *epochē*, to which thought is forced by the *aporia* it encounters, offers its own fortunate passage, its own *euporia*. This passage does not lead to knowing which of the examined hypotheses is false and which is true, but rather affirms the indecisiveness of the aporia in ontological terms: of what is neither true nor false we can only say that it *can be as well as can not-be*. Thus, this formulation (as well as others like it) offers a passage to the realm of contingency as pure potentiality—what can be as well as not-be—and as potentiality-of-being-otherwise.

Acknowledgments

I would like to express my gratitude to the two referees of this manuscript whose comments helped me to sharpen some of my arguments, offered relevant references in the literature, and helped me to focus whenever my thoughts were set to wander off. I am grateful to the Netherlands Organisation for Scientific Research (NWO) for sponsoring my three-year project, *Conflicting Pluralities: Rethinking Reality in Contemporary Philosophy* (no. 275-20-022), thus giving me the opportunity to write this book.

I wrote a substantial part of this book at Boston College in spring 2012. I would like to thank John Sallis and Jeffrey Bloechl for making this stay possible and for making it such a pleasant and fruitful period. Finally, I would like to thank Ben Vedder for his support during this project in matters institutional as well as philosophical.

attracted by the question of ontology, as Hans-Georg Gadamer's and Paul Ricoeur's development of a hermeneutic ontology demonstrate.[1] Yet, what sets apart the turn to ontology in Badiou, Agamben, Nancy, and Meillassoux from this hermeneutic interest in the question of being is that it places ontology more directly in the center of our attention. Despite the many mutual differences, it makes sense to point out two shared sources of inspiration motivating philosophers to return to ontology more insistently.

First, to sketch very briefly the context from which the contemporary concern for ontology stems, the particular focus on language, discourse, and interpretation characteristic of important strands of hermeneutics and deconstruction had a serious implication for ontology: in the hermeneutic framework, our access to being is always determined by *logos*, that is, by the features of the medium *in which* being is said and understood. Therefore, a careful examination of language was a necessary detour to be able to come to ontology in the first place. In particular, this careful examination famously resulted in the hermeneutic version of Aristotle's adage "being is said in many ways," namely, "being is interpreted in many ways." Nevertheless, an analysis of this medium of our access to being does not necessarily tell us anything about the subject matter expressed in it. In particular, the multiplicity of interpretations, languages, and discourses discovered in philosophical hermeneutics does not say anything about the multiplicity or the oneness of being.

In fact, the question of whether being itself is many or one remains (necessarily) unaddressed. In the philosophical hermeneutics of, for instance, Gadamer and Ricoeur, (the meaning of) being therefore becomes a presupposed "transcendental signified," as Derrida puts it—or a regulative idea in a terminology to which Ricoeur would probably subscribe. This means that in this hermeneutic framework the meaning of being both attracts and motivates every interpretation but also remains indefinitely out of reach for the praxis of interpretation. In this context, Derrida's work has proved to be of extreme importance since he has thought this problematic to the limit: for Derrida, ontology is an intrinsically impossible project because the question of being cannot be addressed without understanding the medium in which it is said and understood. Derrida's argument is a simple one. Because our understanding of being always moves within the limits of discourse and language—we lack a "view from nowhere"—we will never be able to know whether or not being and the medium in which we speak about being are in accord with each other and whether or not language distorts being in its presentation of it. Thus, every onto-logy is necessarily affected by the possibility of an unaccounted-for disharmony between being and the medium in which it is said, such as language. The impassable possibility of such a disharmony makes the project of any well-founded understanding or knowing of being an impossible one.[2]

Yet, it is exactly in such a situation that the question of being becomes more pressing. In a medium that speaks of being without ever reaching being itself, being becomes the vanishing point, the point of attraction as well as the limit of such a discourse. Thus, it gives rise to the question of what we actually mean by being. How to return to being after this long and problematizing inquiry into the medium in which being is said? How to break the spell of language and force one's way into the question of being? For instance, how does one bridge the gap that separates the acknowledgment of the plurality of interpretations, languages, and discourses from the incapacity to address the question of whether being is one or many? In the following chapters we shall see how this return to ontology takes place and that, although in mutually different ways, present-day authors share the conviction that it is necessary to think this vanishing point itself—be it in a more speculative mode or in a revised hermeneutic mode.

With respect to the question of unity and plurality, as we shall see in chapters 1 and 2, the works of Alain Badiou and Jean-Luc Nancy exemplify this kind of critical questioning that forces its way once more into an account of being. They offer (mutually different and even conflicting) ontologies of plurality that, in turn, provide an ontological basis for the plurality of discourse and language. Only in this way is the impasse of hermeneutics and deconstruction with respect to the question of being addressed. Although I will start this book with a discussion of Badiou's and Nancy's ontologies, this does not mean that I endorse ontologies that affirm the primacy of plurality. Rather, as will become clear in chapter 3, inspired by and in discussion with the work of Giorgio Agamben, I will claim that it is only by keeping open the question of whether the one exists or not that one may arrive at a truly new understanding of the space of ontology in which we move today. The necessity of keeping this question open, as will be developed in chapters 4 to 7, has to do with the motives of *contingency* and *epochē* which, I believe, form the heart of the contemporary return to ontology.

There is a second motive shared by the contemporary protagonists of first philosophy. The works of the present-day philosophers of ontology are almost always also concerned with notions and elements from the field of social and practical philosophy. In particular, they are interested in the ontological status of praxis or action. The contemporary reflections on politics are exemplary in this regard. For instance, Badiou and Nancy hope to find a different access to the question of what politics is by rethinking its ontological basis. In this way, their efforts to rethink politics are part of a much larger movement in contemporary philosophy.

To characterize this movement, Agamben argues that one of the major problems with our treatment of politics is that we have "been losing sight of its ontological status."[3] Apparently, the realm of action has lost sight of its ontological core. Of course, this does not mean that the return to (and of) first philosophy is *in the service* of politics of action. Nor does it mean that the question of the ontological status of praxis implies that political or social philosophy itself now takes the place of first philosophy, as authors like Oliver Marchart claim.[4] By contrast, the return to ontology in light of problems stemming from political and social philosophy indicates that problems traditionally thought to belong to *practical* philosophy need to be rethought on an ontological level.

In particular, when explaining the third axis of the contemporary space of ontology, one of the major problems of contemporary thought concerns the question of *how to relate to being*—that is to say, which type of comportment or attitude is necessary to relate to being. This question arises in a context in which the theoretical attitude of metaphysics is problematized and in which attitudes that used to belong to the sphere of praxis now turn up at the heart of first philosophy in order to provide an alternative to this "theoretical" attitude.[5] This is one of the reasons why, as Agamben writes, "the problem is therefore moved from political philosophy to first philosophy."[6] In this book, therefore, I will not be too much engaged with political or social philosophy, but I will show time and again this movement to first philosophy and to an inquiry into the particular comportment or attitude of thinking to being, which is so characteristic for contemporary thought.

To gather and examine these two motivations in a more systematic way, I propose to explore the specific ontological space in which contemporary philosophers move. The metaphor of space is helpful here. Not only does this metaphor allow me to introduce the three axes that span the dimensions of this space, but it also allows me to account for the differences between the philosophical viewpoints as different trajectories in the same three-dimensional space as well as to offer the first contours of the trajectory that I consider to be the most promising, given the nature of the three axes of the contemporary space of ontology. From this metaphor, I can explain the two main goals of this book.

The first goal of this study is to map out the different axes of this space of ontology and indicate the trajectories that authors as different as Agamben, Badiou, Nancy, Quentin Meillassoux, and Claude Romano propose within this space. My guiding idea is that to understand the three different axes of this space, one should be aware of the impact of Heidegger's critique of metaphysics on contemporary continental thought. Heidegger, as is well known, characterizes (classical) metaphysics as ontotheology.[7] The contemporary space of ontology is a space that is opened up after the critique of ontotheology. In the next section I will explain that this ontotheological constitution of metaphysics means for Heidegger that metaphysics is always a quest for the unifying ground. The axes of the three-dimensional space of contemporary ontology are therefore the three axes that arise when the thought of being—onto-logy—moves away from ontotheology and its quest for the unifying ground. The three concepts or axes constituting ontology after ontotheology are: (1) the question of the existence of the one or the many, (2) the concept of the event or, as

I will prefer to name it in accordance with Meillassoux and Agamben, contingency, and (3) the particular ethos or comportment required by (or for) contemporary ontology.

The issue of plurality, as it appears in many guises, is the present-day variant of the ancient ontological question of the one and the many of which Plato already offered us a dazzling treatment in his dialogue *Parmenides*. It is characteristic for present-day philosophers to return this question to its ontological status. Echoing Agamben's words, Nancy, whose main works offer a continuous reflection of the issue of plurality on an ontological level, writes, "a first philosophy is necessary, in the canonical sense of this expression, that is, an ontology."[8]

Part 1 of this book, "Conflicting Pluralities," offers an exposition of how alternative ontologies of plurality are introduced to provide an ontological basis for the plurality of discourse and language. More importantly, this part will discuss the conflict between these alternative ontologies. Yet, these new ontologies aim to be without presupposition: being is no longer presupposed but exposed and directly addressed in these ontologies. In this sense, they are looking for an absolute. Yet, can they indeed uphold their claim to be without presupposition and to reach into the absolute? What is the importance for present-day thought to turn to such an absolute? In chapter 3, I will address these questions in discussion with the refined analyses of Agamben. In particular, in my treatment of the issue of the presupposition I will show why, out of contemporary discussions of plurality, not only the aporetic conclusion of Plato's *Parmenides* deserves renewed interest, but also another issue must arise, namely, the issue of the suspension (or *epochē*) of the principle of sufficient reason. Both of these issues guide us to the second theme and concept, namely, the event or contingency.

The notion of the "event" is omnipresent in present-day debates. In these debates it plays a well-defined role. "Event" is not a name for a simple occurrence or happening in the world. Rather, *event is a concept that is created to think an alternative to the principle of sufficient reason.* An event is an occurrence happening without reason or ground; it cannot be foreseen; it cannot be mastered; it cannot be calculated. Thus, this notion is introduced in a debate concerning the following question: Does everything that happens have a reason or a ground for its taking place, or do events happen?

It is impossible to understand contemporary thought without taking this concept of the event into account. Moreover, as I will argue extensively in part 2, since the concept of the event is created to think and characterize the space that is opened up by the suspension of the principle of sufficient reason, it is impossible to discuss this notion without discussing the concept of contingency as well. Using arguments and motives from the work of Meillassoux, Heidegger, and Agamben, I will argue that next to the quest for an absolute and the effort to think without presupposition, the concept of contingency contains the secret of the present-day interest in the event. *Ontology today is ontology of contingency.*

In addition, whereas I will follow a more standard discourse on how the speculative school differs from the hermeneutic one in part 1, I will show in part 2 that the distinction between schools becomes much more complicated when considering the notion of the event. Although the methodological differences are still very clear, the systematic treatment of the concept of the event suggests a chiasmus of schools: in addition to the well-established names of Heidegger and Badiou, I will discuss the hermeneutic-phenomenological descendant of Heidegger, Romano, who rewrites *Sein und Zeit* in light of the concept of the event, and Badiou's speculative descendant, Meillassoux, who centralizes the concept of contingency. However, rather than the opposition of Badiou and Meillassoux versus Heidegger and Romano that one might expect, a systematic discussion on the event reveals a chiasmus of schools: Badiou and Romano versus Heidegger and Meillassoux, to put it in oversimplified terms. Such a chiasmus shows how fruitful, fresh, and alive is the contemporary discussion of the event.

The third theme, comportment, should be understood as a translation of the German *Haltung* and is therefore equivalent to notions such as attitude or ethos. This theme imposes itself on us when we are confronted with the question, What is the attitude or comportment that allows us to relate to the event as well as to its contingency?

When *theōria* or contemplation is the attitude or comportment to being that marks the metaphysical tradition, what different kind of attitude does the notion of the event require? In the next chapters, I will show that this question is first raised in the contemporary discussion on human action and praxis in the following form: what is the human comportment to account for human praxis? Since contemporary thought is marked by a quest for the ontological basis of this comportment, this issue returns on the level of ontology in the aforementioned form: what is the human attitude to the event and to contingency? As we will see throughout this book, many different answers are given to this question, corresponding to the various approaches to and accounts of the event and of contingency that are given, such as Agamben's suspension and remembrance, Badiou's nomination and subjective fidelity, Heidegger's inceptual thinking, Meillassoux's speculative thinking, and Romano's understanding. All of these notions aim to capture the human attitude, allowing access to the event in its singularity and contingency.

The second goal of this study is to assess the nature of the differences between the trajectories that different authors suggest in this three-dimensional space of contemporary ontology. I will argue that one question forms the core question for a contemporary ontology. If ontotheology is the quest for the unifying ground, the basic task for ontology after ontotheology is to explore the domain of being disclosed by the suspension of the principle of sufficient reason. With Meillassoux, Agamben, and a *certain* Heidegger, I will argue that the basic category that describes being in this domain is "contingency." This means that the concepts of plurality and event ultimately have to be understood in terms of the concept of contingency and its related concept of potentiality—or as Meillassoux calls it, "potentiality-of-being-otherwise"—that form its core. To account for being in terms of contingency means also that it is approached in light of its possibility or potentiality; this means that being is understood as *that which can be as well as can not-be*. This indifference between "can be" and "can not-be" at the heart of the concept of contingency also implies, as I will argue in chapters 3, 6, and 7, that an intrinsic connection exists between the category of contingency and the ethos of thinking the skeptics introduced to philosophy: *epochē*, or the suspension of judgment on existence. This line of argument is developed in close affinity with (particular parts of) Agamben's work. Thus, this book develops its own trajectory in the space of contemporary ontology in order to do justice to the understanding of being as contingency that speaks from the suspension of the principle of sufficient reason.

Beyond the Unifying Ground: Heidegger's Legacy

As noted above, this book finds its point of departure in Heidegger's account of metaphysics as ontotheology as this account sets the task for contemporary thought to develop ontology after ontotheology, that is, an *ontology without theology*. The "without theology" of ontology becomes a more frequent and important dimension of the present-day discussion. Not only does it appear in the work of Badiou, who offers a secular account of infinity, but it also appears in interpretations of the works of philosophers such as Derrida, Nancy, and Meillassoux under the respective titles "atheism" and "posttheological."[9] This book has a clear affinity with these projects, but it aims to restrict the issue of "without theology" to ontological issues alone and to inquire into the stakes of a conception of ontology in which the concept of God is no longer used.[10]

In "Die onto-theo-logische Verfassung der Metaphysik," Heidegger paints a picture of how the concept of God enters philosophy.[11] Yet, what exactly enters the philosophical scene when this concept appears? The essay's title gives us a clear hint. Apparently, the concept of God leads to a strange entanglement of ontology and theology in metaphysics. This strange entanglement, called "onto-theo-logy," is, according to Heidegger "the as yet *unthought* unity of the essence of metaphysics."[12] As he explains elsewhere, ontotheology describes how metaphysics addresses its "guiding question" (*Leitfrage*). The guiding question asks for the "beingness of beings" (*Seiendheit des Seienden*). Notably, Heidegger distinguishes this question from the fundamental question (*Grundfrage*), which is not addressed in metaphysics and asks for "the essential occurrence of beyng."[13] In asking the guiding question, metaphysics examines what a being is as such ("*das Seiende als solches*") and as a whole or in general ("*das Seiende…im Ganzen*").[14] In "Einleitung zu 'Was ist Metaphysik?,'" Heidegger notes that this metaphysical inquiry has both an ontological and a theological orientation that can be distinguished.[15]

As ontology, metaphysics studies what all beings have in common, namely, the fact that they *are*—in some sense and in some mode or modality of being.[16] All beings thus share being, but only in the most general sense of this word. Ontology inquires into this general sense of being. The distinguishing Greek word to which Heidegger points is *koinon:* the (in-)common of beings. The German noun related to the adjective "general," and which Heidegger often uses in his discussion of the Greek *koinon,* is *das Allgemeine.* This term might be paraphrased as the "all(-in-)common," in the sense of that which *all* beings have *in common*. This determination of ontology as the inquiry into the *koinon* is still somewhat vague since it does not tell us much about the strange word that occupies the mind of metaphysicians and Heidegger alike, namely, "being." Moreover, it does not tell us what "to share being" exactly means.

So how is the meaning of *koinon* determined? According to Heidegger, metaphysics has approached this question theologically. In this context, theology does not simply concern Christian theology, but a characteristically metaphysical mode of questioning (which has also entered Christian theology). From the outset of the history of metaphysics, in both Plato and Aristotle, the ontological quest for the all(-in-)common of beings gets entangled with the quest for a highest being.[17] This is theology: it examines beings in their totality by inquiring into the highest being. Hence, combining ontology and theology is nothing but searching for the all(-in-)common by inquiring into the highest being.

To a certain extent this metaphysical approach seems to be the most natural one since it approaches beings in light of their (possible) perfection. To use an image, if we want to know what it is that all soccer players share—namely, playing soccer—it seems quite natural to examine first and foremost those who excel in it since we only truly learn what playing soccer is about when we watch Cruijff or Pelé playing. Metaphysics applies this procedure to its quest for the meaning of being. This method results in ontotheology in its most basic form.

Note that the important metaphysical motive of perfection or exemplarity, to which I refer in the above example, is not necessarily theological: it is not necessarily connected to an understanding of the being called "God." For instance, Aristotle's conception of substance can be understood as a form of perfection that does not appeal to the notion of God: amid all the meanings of "being," "substance" refers to the being that exists in an eminent sense, that exists independently of other beings. Being is said of other beings, according to the traditional interpretation of Aristotle, only in an analogous sense, since they—as accidents—depend on substance and thus refer in their existence always to what exists independently.[18] In the introduction to "Was ist Metaphysik?," Heidegger discusses the way in which metaphysics understands being in exactly these two related ways. On the one hand, in its inquiry into beings as beings, metaphysics remains on the level of beings: it always interprets being as *a* being—as spirit, as life, as will to power, as substance, and so on.[19] This inquiry always aims to find the being that exists perfectly or eminently. Yet, as Heidegger notes with a play on a metaphor borrowed from Descartes, the tree of metaphysics conceals from its own eyes the ground on which it rests and from which its roots retrieve their nourishment, namely, being itself.

On the other hand, the inquiry into beings as beings is guided by a quest for what is both most general—ontology—and highest—theology.[20] The motive of the highest is theological in the strict sense of the word, but this motive is also always combined with and cannot be separated from the metaphysical quest into the most perfect being, which is not always a quest into God, but which is always marked by the same tendency to forget being. Moreover, although the question of perfection and the question of God are different and separable in Aristotle's metaphysics, they have become inseparable in the history of metaphysics. Aquinas's thought on God as the creator of all beings, which conceives of God both as the highest and as the most perfect being since all other beings depend on their creator, provides us with an unmistakable example of the inseparable character of both questions. A typical modern example of this entanglement of the most perfect and highest being can be found in Spinoza's work: only God or nature, the name for the totality of reality, can truly be called "substance."

Let me return to the example of the soccer players. We might feel a slight unease to use this example as an analogy for the whole of being. Given the multiple ways in which being is said, as Aristotle puts it, one might wonder whether the tendency to account for being in terms of a highest one does justice to the multiplicity and the plurality in which beings are given to us. When being is determined in the first place as the (in-)common of this multiplicity, it does not only seem odd, but it also might even be reductive to approach the (in-)common of the many beings in terms of the way and the mode in which one particular being is, even if it is in an exemplary way. Clearly, this theological focus on perfection and the highest implies that reality has a certain order and that beings are placed in a natural hierarchy that has one, ultimate being as its peak.

In agreement with this latter characterization, Heidegger notes that this theological tendency to approach being and its (in-)common or *koinon* in light of a highest being means that metaphysics searches for the unity (*Einheit*) and the ground (*Grund*) of being.[21] This highest being is not only what unifies reality in its unity (the Greek *hen*), it also provides the ground or the reason for all beings. Hence, from the outset, Heidegger grants the concept of God a double role, much in line with the role the unmoved mover plays in Aristotle's *Metaphysics Lambda*. The concept of God provides metaphysics with the possibility to think the primacy of the one over the many as well as with the possibility to relate all beings back to their ground or cause. Ultimately, God is the unifying ground. The theological orientation of metaphysics combines the quest into the unifying one and into the ground. Thus, these are two of the three axes marking the space of ontotheology: oneness and ground.

From Oneness to Plurality

Let me first concentrate on the oneness at stake in this idea of the unifying ground forming the core of ontotheology. In Heidegger's "Entwürfe zur Geschichte des Seins als Metaphysik," we find the following telling quote concerning the relation between the (in-)common and the one: "The precedence of whatness brings the precedence of beings themselves in what they are. The precedence of beings establishes Being as *koinon* in terms of the *hen*. The eminent character of metaphysics is decided. The one as unifying unity becomes authoritative [*maßgebend*] for subsequent determinations of Being."[22] The metaphysical tendency to look for the unifying ground of beings, which this quote accounts for in a Platonic fashion as the tendency to privilege the inquiry into the essence of things, is a tendency that determines the *koinon*, the (in-)common, out of the *hen*, the one. What all beings share, in this Platonic form, is brought together in one being, namely, the *idea* in which all beings that share this *idea* participate. Heidegger inquires into this metaphysical relation between *koinon* and *hen* elsewhere. Consider the following quote from the *Beiträge*: "The expression 'generality' [*Allgemeinen*] is ambiguous, especially since the designation of what is thought as the *koinon* is already not based originally on what is itself seen but on the 'many,' on 'beings' (as *me on* ['nonbeing'])."[23] This quote also identifies the *idea* as "the *unifying One*."[24] Yet, what intrigues Heidegger especially is that the Platonic, metaphysical inquiry does not understand the *koinon* out of itself. Rather, as in the previous quote, it approaches the all-in-common out of the one (*idea*), or it approaches it in light of the many beings that share (in) this idea. Hence, the ambiguity of metaphysics concerns exactly the ambiguity with which it addresses the issue of generality as the in-common: either from the point of view of the one, or from the point of view of the many. Of course, if we inquire into being by examining beings and thus use beings as our medium to account for being, we have a slight problem, as Heidegger almost ironically indicates: if being should be thought in terms of *koinon* and *idea* and if this idea is the one and true being, how can you arrive at this idea when you start by examining beings that are marked by plurality and by nonbeing (*me on*)?[25]

The above quote does more than simply describe the history of metaphysics. By showing so clearly how the in-common and the many are always already understood in light of the one, it suggests that the ontological question might also take another direction, namely, one that is not theological in nature and does not privilege the one, but that, rather, aims to determine *the in-common out of itself,* or even the many as being rather than as nonbeing. Although Heidegger follows neither of these two trajectories—I will explain below why he does not do so—his description of the problem of ontology clearly leaves these two possibilities open for "ontology without theology." In chapters 1 and 2, I will expose such alternative ontologies in contemporary thought. Yet, much in line with the devastating aporia with which Parmenides concludes his dialectic examination of the one and the many in Plato's dialogue with the same name, I will show in chapter 3 why these ontologies are still problematic and why this leads us necessarily to this other issue: the suspension of the principle of reason.

Leaping from the Ground: Singularity, Event, and Contingency

I noted above that Heidegger does not follow the alternative route for ontology himself. In the framework of the *Beiträge*, it is clear why he does not do so. For him, the inquiry into the in-common and the general belongs to the guiding question (*Leitfrage*) of metaphysics. Therefore, this inquiry, which marks the metaphysical "first beginning" (*erste Anfang*) of thought, never reaches the level of the fundamental question (*Grundfrage*) that thinks the "essential occurrence of beyng." This latter essential occurrence is the subject matter for "the other beginning" (*andere Anfang*) of thought. Since ontology is the inquiry into the common and the general, Heidegger drops this notion in the *Beiträge* and claims that his own use of the term "fundamental ontology" in *Sein und Zeit* should be understood as a transitory one that forms the passage from guiding to fundamental question. This transition is also the (in)famous transition from the first beginning (*erste Anfang*) to the other beginning (*andere Anfang*) of thought. Once this passage is completed—if such a completion is possible and makes sense—the notion of ontology no longer plays any role.

When looking at this latter transition in light of his account of the *koinon* as the most general and thus empty determination of being, we may understand why Heidegger does not try to rethink the *koinon* in the *Beiträge*. In distinction to the beingness of beings, which considers being in its generality, the essential occurrence of being approaches being in its uniqueness or singularity (*Einzigkeit*). In the *Beiträge*, Heidegger frequently uses the term *Einzigkeit* to characterize the essential occurrence and the truth of being. What is at stake in the famous passage from the first to the other beginning of thought is "knowledge of the *uniqueness* of beyng."²⁶ Hence, Heidegger develops an alternative to ontotheology along the lines of this transition *from the general to the singular*. In this sense, the question of ontology into what all beings have in common—as a question into generality (*das Allgemeine*)—can no longer be of service to him. Before considering the figure Heidegger introduces to do justice to this singularity of the occurrence of being, let me note that a thought that, in contrast to Heidegger, aims to develop the concept of the in-common in a new direction has to overcome the connection between the in-common and generality; it has to show how the in-common can be thought as singularity rather than as generality. In chapter 2, I will show how Nancy offers such a trajectory in the three-dimensional space of ontology after ontotheology.

In the *Beiträge*, Heidegger proceeds differently and binds the notion of singularity not to a new interpretation of *koinon* but to the notion of *das Ereignis*, the event. In his work, *Ereignis* might be paraphrased as *the event of appropriation* in which the singularity of the essential occurrence and truth of being is thought. Hence, considered in a broader perspective, we see that he introduces the ontological category of the singular event, which allows him to think the uniqueness of the occurrence of being. If, *pace* Heidegger, we still call this ontology, it is an ontology of the event; that is, it is a thought in which being is thought out of the event.

The concept of the event provides us with an alternative to the notion of the "ground" as it is conceived in ontotheology. It is important to stress that in its everyday use, "event" does not need to mean something singular at all: our regular, everyday events, occurrences, and happenings seem to have very good reasons and grounds for their happening. In fact, Leibniz's principle of sufficient reason extends this common account of the event to reality as a whole.

chapters will be devoted to the work of Agamben, Badiou, Heidegger, Jean-Luc Marion, Meillassoux, Nancy, and Romano; there, I will show that important differences exist concerning the questions of what the event is and of what it means to *think* the event. Is (thinking) the event concerned with (understanding) the new configuration of the world to which it gives rise? Is it concerned with (drawing) the consequences of the event? Is it concerned with (experiencing) the very taking place of the event? Is it concerned with the pure possibility that forms the heart of contingency? In accordance with my analysis that the concept of the event is created to offer an alternative to the principle of reason, I will argue that ultimately the concept of *contingency* is the secret of the event. To think the event in its most primordial dimension is neither to think it in relation to its consequences nor to think it out of the very flux of its taking place. Rather, to think the event is to think contingency—as the potentiality-of-being-otherwise, to adopt Meillassoux's formulation.

The Ethos of Thinking Being

Ontotheology does not only orient thought to the unifying ground in its account of being, it also provides a particular framework for the thinking or the *logos* involved in it. From its history, we know philosophy (as metaphysics) as a *theoretical* discipline. To claim that philosophy is theoretical is not quite the same as claiming that philosophy is concerned with thinking as such. "Theoretical" is derived from *theōria*. As Hannah Arendt argues, *theōria* has a specific meaning in the history of metaphysics: it concerns the contemplation of the eternal, the permanent, everlasting presence of the highest being that the metaphysical tradition termed "God."[31] Indeed, *theōria* is the name for the practice of metaphysics, which according to Aristotle is the most pleasant and best activity of all.[32] Thus, the theoretical character of metaphysics describes the particular human comportment or attitude—ethos—that is required to think this highest being. In this metaphysical framework, *theōria* or contemplation is the highest possibility of human life, allowing the human being to relate to reality and being on its ultimate level.

Like ontotheology, every ontology requires its own comportment or attitude, its own *Haltung, Einstellung,* or ethos that marks the character of the thought or the *logos* belonging most intimately to it. Obviously, since the event concerns change and novelty and since it involves the singular, *theōria* does not provide us with a means to think an event. In its coming, an event is unexpected and unforeseeable. We do not know whether it will or will not arrive. In fact, we do not even know what it is that will or will not arrive. After its arrival (if there is such a thing) it is still not clear what exactly has arrived: how it changes the course of the world cannot be known in advance, but this can also not be known *après coup* because its effects, traces, and consequences cannot be computed either—they first need to be drawn.

Hence, if we want an ontology marked by the two axes discussed previously—of the question of the existence of the one and the many and of the event or contingency—the third axis of ontotheology, *theōria,* also needs to be revised. Trying to respond to the strange temporality and phenomenality of the event, a whole new series of notions is brought into play that should capture how we relate to an event. Next to the ones I already mentioned above, one could add notions such as hope, promise, oath, faith, fidelity, attestation, conviction, courage, and resoluteness, which are introduced in present-day thought to describe the human comportment toward the event and toward existence (often in its plurality). It is important to note that this human ethos is not simply concerned with human praxis in opposition to human being or existence. Rather, the notions that formerly were not treated in the context of a first philosophy now turn out to be nested in the heart of projects that aim to think a contemporary *ontology*. This indicates that ontology without theology might be unthinkable without a certain ethos that moves beyond the theoretical comportment of classical thought.

Yet, these developments in ontology also give rise to particular problems. One may wonder what happens to *thinking* when it can no longer be conceived as *theōria,* and when the human comportment to the event adopts the form of conviction, attestation, and declaration. Let us once more consult Arendt. She famously distinguishes between *vita activa* (*bios politikos*) and *vita contemplativa* (*bios theōrētikos*). If the event becomes a central category of ontology and the human comportment to the event can no longer be thought in terms of contemplation, does this not mean that the human comportment to the event belongs solely to the life of action, to political life? Does this also not imply that, despite my above comments to the contrary, political philosophy replaces first philosophy? To a certain extent, some of the notions I mentioned that describe human comportment toward the event seem to underline this. Conviction, attestation, and proclamation—do they not first and foremost belong to the realm of political life in Arendt's sense of the word? If conviction and faithful action describe our relation to an event, does this mean that our subjectivity—including our capacity to think—is always already in the "force field" of an event? If this is the case, what then happens to thinking and its specific *slowness*? Is thinking not characterized by nonacting because it takes its time, as if it had all the time in the world?

These latter questions also reflect a conflict in contemporary thought. To exemplify this conflict, let me refer to Badiou's "Homage to Jacques Derrida." For Badiou, "everything is submitted to a law of decision, here and now." Thus, he opposes his "metaphysics of radical opposition," which demands decisions to Derrida's "patient deconstruction of oppositions."[33] Yet, is it not possible to defend Derrida's patience and to point out that his *scholazein* forms a crucial ingredient of thinking as the capacity *to withdraw* from the "here and now," toward a nowhere that "philosophers love...as though it were a country"?[34] Or is such a defense necessarily also a defense of ontotheology, and does the power of thought to withdraw itself only belong to thought as *theōria*?

The latter quote from Arendt indicates how subtle her analysis is in this respect. It is clear from the last pages of *The Human Condition*, in which she introduces the distinction between theoretical and political life, that the notion of thinking will complicate this distinction. In her book, Arendt notes that *theōria* is not simply identical with thinking, but this does not mean that thinking belongs to the realm of politics. In *The Life of the Mind*, she proposes, by means of a beautiful phenomenological analysis, that thinking concerns a withdrawal from the world (of appearances). This is the world that we share with one another and which is therefore the world where public and political life is located and where our plurality is enacted.[35] Arendt's analysis of thinking reinforces one element of *theōria* that might too easily have been dismissed in a philosophy that takes the event, the attention to praxis and action, as its guideline. Although our capacity to think does not necessarily lead us to contemplate the eternal, it is still a capacity to withdraw from the world as the scene where all our actions take place. As such, our capacity to think shows that we are not merely actors but that we also have the possibility to be spectators and, thus, to distance ourselves—albeit briefly, tentatively, provisionally, and perhaps even incompletely—from the eventful nature of our actions and the particular forces that surround it.

The emphasis on the importance of this capacity to withdraw can be understood as an important corrective to a certain one-sidedness that tends to appear in contemporary thought. The shared focus in contemporary ontologies on the event also runs the risk of a one-sided critique of *theōria* in which the important role of thinking to withdraw from and perhaps even interrupt the "force field" of the event is easily forgotten. Yet, in order to fully explicate what is at stake here, much work needs to be done in the following chapters. In fact, it is only in chapter 7 on "The Ethos of Contingency" (and beyond anything that can be found in Arendt's work) that I will be able to argue that a contemporary version of this withdrawal of thought indeed exists. This withdrawal has nothing to do with the eternal presence of the highest being metaphysical thought contemplates. Rather, it accords with the nature of contingency itself to which the reflection on the event will guide us: what is, can also not be, and what is not, can also be. This ontological experiment on contingency asks of thinking an *epochē* of the affirmation *and* the negation of existence in order to disclose being (and thinking) in its potentiality-of-being-otherwise.

Part 1
Conflicting Pluralities:
Between Hermeneutics and Mathematics

One way to overcome the ontotheological emphasis on the one is by accounting for being in terms of plurality. Contemporary continental thought displays a number of such accounts of plurality. Yet, these conceptions of plurality are conflictual. In fact, the present-day debate is marked by two different approaches to the question of plurality that nevertheless share the effort to overcome ontotheology and are, in this particular sense, both heirs to Heidegger's legacy—despite their strong critique of Heidegger in other senses. For the sake of simplicity, I will identify these two approaches by the schools to which they belong and which I will name throughout this book the "speculative school" and the "hermeneutic-phenomenological school," respectively. Clearly, this naming does not mean that the different representatives of these schools are always in accord with each other, as will become especially clear in part 2. Nevertheless, these names do indicate a certain self-expressed affinity of those philosophers with other members of this school. Badiou and Meillassoux (and a certain Deleuze) belong to the speculative school, whereas Nancy, Heidegger, Derrida, and others belong to the hermeneutic-phenomenological school.

Throughout this book, I will be highlighting only some of the representatives of these schools. Although the choices I made in this respect are open for discussion, I would like to suggest that they since, while he aims to restore the possibility of metaphysics, he also accepts Heidegger's critique of metaphysics as ontotheology, as I will argue in chapter 1. Consequently, the speculative school's reappraisal of metaphysics includes a *rejection* of metaphysics as ontotheology. This is why Badiou uses the "paradoxical name of *a metaphysics without metaphysics*" for his own ontology—a name that is itself a playful turn of formulations of the form "X without X" that we find often in the work of authors such as Derrida and Blanchot.[7]

Meillassoux's work compels us to raise a similar issue. Analogous to Badiou's metaphysics without metaphysics, Meillassoux rejects "dogmatic metaphysics" and distinguishes between "metaphysical thought" and "speculative thought." Whereas the former pretends to think an absolute being, the latter pretends to think "the absolute in general."[8] The goal of this distinction is clear. Meillassoux embraces a form of speculative thought *that is not* metaphysical. I will offer the details of this issue in chapter 5. For now, it is important to see that the examples of Badiou and Meillassoux indicate that they *share* Heidegger's critique of ontotheology. In this sense, they are not only critics of but also heirs to Heidegger's legacy. Yet, despite their critique of dogmatic metaphysics, they also emphasize that speculative thought has the capacity to access the absolute. Thus, they strongly reject the idea that philosophy is limited by the finitude of human understanding. One of the issues to be addressed in the course of this book is whether the speculative school's taste for the absolute also has more "hermeneutic" variants.

When aiming to clarify the distinction between the speculative and the hermeneutic-phenomenological schools, one needs to address one more issue: can the qualification of the second school as a form of correlationism be maintained? In its generality, this qualification is probably difficult to maintain. Also, Harman's characterization of the whole of continental philosophy as hermeneutics—"it can be said with only a bit of exaggeration that continental philosophy has become hermeneutic philosophy"—is not precise enough for my purposes, as I will show later: it all comes down to the question of *which* hermeneutics one means.[9] We only need to point to Heidegger's continuous critique of metaphysical distinctions such as appearing versus being or subject versus object, and we only need to refer to the obsession of contemporary phenomenology with the phenomenon of otherness—that is, that which *does not* adjust itself to my conditions of existence, discourse, or knowledge but nevertheless imposes itself upon us—to see that this form of thought cannot be reduced to Kantian correlationism. Moreover, Meillassoux does not seem to be aware that the "phenomena" under discussion in contemporary phenomenology are exactly concerned with *what cannot appear*.[10] To be more precise, what is addressed under the heading of phenomenology today is mainly an inquiry into the *phenomenality* as such, that is, into that which allows ordinary phenomena to appear, but this phenomenality is exactly what remains concealed in ordinary appearance. This typical gesture of phenomenology can already be found in the opening sections of *Sein und Zeit*, where Heidegger determines the concept of phenomenon "in a distinctive sense" as that which does not show itself and is concealed.[11] In this sense, the speculative turn to being beyond appearing—if we may put it in these terms—rather seems to be a variation or an intensification of a motive that is discernible in contemporary phenomenology and hermeneutics as well. I will show this more clearly in part 2.

My efforts to complicate the somewhat one-sided accounts of hermeneutic-phenomenological thought by the speculative school are definitely not meant as a dismissal of this school or its concerns. What Meillassoux aims to say in his emphasis on correlationism is similar to the commitment we can find in Badiou's account of plurality. For the latter, plurality should be thought on an *ontological* level and should not only be thought as an effect of cultural, social, or linguistic diversity. As Meillassoux writes, not only Kant's subjectivity but especially phenomenology's consciousness and analytic philosophy's and (we might add) hermeneutics' language are "the two principal 'media' of the correlation."[12] Badiou argues that the attention to cultural and social difference exaggerates the importance of difference and plurality: plurality is not uncommon or remarkable because it is an integral dimension of reality itself; reality itself should be thought as multiple.[13] The speculative school takes this task seriously. However, complicating the distinction between schools, the hermeneutic-phenomenological school also offers important examples that respond to the task with which the reflection on history, language, and discourse in the 1960s and 1970s burdens us. The work of Jean-Luc Nancy is exemplary in this sense. For him, plurality is not only a dimension of interpretation or discourse directed to one core meaning of being. Rather, plurality belongs to being "as its constitution."[14] Nancy thinks being as plural (and singular). He also develops an ontology without theology to do justice to the fundamental plurality and singularity of being.

Hence, apparently, the speculative and the hermeneutic-phenomenological schools are both concerned with the project of an ontology without theology. Therefore, the mutual critiques and conflicts can be assessed as well as accounted for in terms of this shared concern: *To what extent is the other school capable of thinking plurality in accordance with this quest for an ontology without theology?* This is what I will do in the next two chapters. Chapter 3 will address more straightforwardly the conflicts between the speculative and the hermeneutic accounts and will show, in discussion with the work of Agamben, how another version of the question of the existence of the one and the many may appear in the wake of Badiou's and Nancy's versions of ontology.

ONE

Mathematics and Beyond
Event, Axiom, and Subject

> "The ontological decision from which my entire discourse originates is that of the non-being of the one."
> —Alain Badiou, *L'être et l'événement*

> "I maintained that philosophy had to subtract itself from the pathos of the end."
> —Alain Badiou, *Second manifeste pour la philosophie*

After introducing the themes of plurality, event, and comportment in terms of the questions with which Martin Heidegger's oeuvre confronts us, and after having pointed out the vehement discussions between the speculative and the hermeneutic-phenomenological schools in contemporary thought, it is only natural to turn to Alain Badiou and address the question of how his work offers an alternative to ontotheology: his systematic work presents us most clearly with an ontology developed in terms of the three axes of plurality, event, and comportment in his account of multiplicity, event, and subject. In this sense, not only Heidegger, but also Badiou is one of the sources of inspiration for this study: his systematic work is exemplary for the framework in which a present-day ontology may take shape. Yet, this does not mean that I simply agree with Badiou or follow his solutions. Nevertheless, his work is indispensable for capturing the discussions on the topics constituting present-day ontology: plurality, event, and comportment. To show this, I will first trace one of the most important characteristics of Badiou's conception of being and event, namely, the axiomatic decision. Subsequently, a long section follows explicating the main terms of Badiou's ontology in light of his critique of the hermeneutic-phenomenological school. This not only allows me to assess Badiou's objections to this school, but also to prepare my discussion of Jean-Luc Nancy's ontology in chapter 2. I will conclude with a critical section on the difference between the perspective of the subject and of the mathematician in Badiou's work, preparing a more critical assessment of this work in chapter 3.

THE AXIOMATIC DECISION

In the second meditation of *L'être et l'événement,* the book now famous for its idea that ontology equals mathematics, Badiou turns to Plato's difficult dialogue *Parmenides.* His interpretation starts with the following declaration and affirmation: "My entire discourse originates in *an axiomatic decision;* that of the non-being of the one."[1] In the French, this opening sentence actually begins with the words "*La décision ontologique.*" The translator's interpretative gesture to render *la décision ontologique* as "axiomatic decision" is not a mistake since it is indicative of the crucial role played by the axiom and the decision in Badiou's thought. It is clear that Badiou's declaration performatively sets aside the ontotheological preference for the one. By an inaugural decision, the primacy of oneness is overcome.

Of course, such a beginning of a book leads to some serious questions: Can one enter ontology with a decision? Does this imply that ontology today is necessarily decisionistic? If so, can one simply refute Badiou's ontology by making the opposite choice?[2] These are not rhetorical questions. This can be seen when we change our emphasis from decision to axiom. The Greek meaning of the word "axiom," as Heidegger informs us, is derived from the verb *axioō,* meaning "to value" or "to esteem."[3] We still hear this meaning in the term "axiology." An axiom thus concerns something that stands and is held in high esteem. It is not held in high esteem because a human being grants it this value by his or her will or preference, but because the axiom is something that is to be esteemed; it is not constituted but rather recognized as such. Of course, this nature of the axiom does not exclude a decision; in fact, a decision is required as well. The human being is supposed to affirm the axiom in order to follow it through to its consequences. Nevertheless, the subject and his or her decision are preceded by something that can be held in high esteem, and not the other way around. Although Badiou does not phrase it in these Heideggerian terms, he proposes an analogous way to think the order among event, axiom, and subject. In chapter 4, we will see more carefully how he does this in the second volume of *L'être et l'événement*, entitled *Logiques des mondes*.

After the decision in favor of the axiom that the one is not, Badiou turns to Plato's *Parmenides* to consider how this dialogue deals with the "dialectical consequences" of this decision. The decision is thus the starting point of this exercise. For Badiou, to begin (with) ontology and to begin a new, speculative metaphysics is to start with and from a decision in which an axiom or a hypothesis—the term Parmenides uses in the dialogue that carries his name—is posited. When speculative thought is the thought that pretends to have access to the absolute, as Meillassoux proposes, this access adopts the form of an axiomatic decision in Badiou's case. As in mathematics, the axiom opens up the space for thought and opens up the space for the philosophical consequences of this axiom. Moreover, when a decision forms the starting point of thought, this means that thought—and let me immediately term this thought "mathematical thought" to clearly show that it takes mathematics as a source of inspiration and as a model—cannot be characterized by calculation, argumentation, or deduction alone. Rather, from the outset, mathematical thought includes a decision concerning the axioms from which the "deductive fidelity" of the philosopher, like that of the mathematician, derives.[4] Obviously, this understanding of mathematical thought stands in contrast to Heidegger's understanding of mathematics. For Badiou, mathematics is not simply concerned with numbers and calculations. Rather, mathematics is concerned with axioms and with decisions affirming them. Due to this starting point of mathematics, deductions, calculations, and proofs are not simply formal operations that to this axiom's capacity to release thought from "the One." This is why it deserves to be affirmed.

Clearly, his decision affects his interpretation of Plato's *Parmenides* because it cuts the dialogue in two. He does not read or discuss it as a whole, but he enters it at the point where Parmenides goes "back to the beginning" and starts his discussion of the *other* hypothesis, "the one is not."[12] Interestingly enough, this implies *that Badiou's decision itself is never examined*. Thus, it is the *a priori* decision preceding thought and providing it with its particular orientation (see chapter 3).

Under the hypothesis that the one is not, Badiou notes that Parmenides has to conclude that even the smallest existent turns out to be many. For Plato, this conclusion can be nothing but a dream because his thought is ultimately guided by the primacy of the one.[13] Yet, as Badiou notes, these comments of Parmenides provide us with the first metaphor and "speculative dream" of infinite multiplicities.[14] It is nothing less than a prefiguration of set theory. Thus, we see why this hypothesis is so important to a thought that wants to think plurality: "the hypothesis 'the one is not' turns out to be the one which *teaches us about the multiple*."[15] In our time, the axiomatic decision for this hypothesis leads us to set theory since, as Hallward notes, "axiomatic set theory is the only theory we have that allows us coherently to think inconsistent multiplicity as such" and hence allows us to conceptualize what it means that even the smallest existent is many.[16]

BADIOU'S ONTOLOGY IN DISCUSSION WITH HERMENEUTICS

Despite the shared rejection of ontotheology, Badiou strongly criticizes Heidegger on many occasions. For him, Heidegger represents a strand of thought that has "put philosophy in the hands of the poem."[17] Thus, he relates his dispute with Heidegger and his heirs back to a distinction as old as philosophy itself: the Platonic *matheme* versus the pre-Platonic *poem*.[18] The poem and the matheme provide two different orientations to thought, and both of them are present throughout the history of philosophy. For Badiou, the late twentieth century discussion between his thought and Heidegger's is yet another version of this debate between mathematical and poetic thought.[19] Rather than arguing that the latter is a mere historical mistake, Badiou writes, "I willingly admit that absolutely originary thought occurs in poetics."[20] Nevertheless, a serious dispute and conflict is at stake between these modes of thinking concerning the question of what the *true event of philosophy* is. For Heidegger, Plato and Aristotle represent the beginning of the ontotheological paradigm in the history of philosophy. Badiou, conversely, argues that the true Greek event of philosophy is the interruption of the poem as well as the myth by the invention of the matheme.[21] This, Badiou claims, is Plato's invention.

In light of the attention for the role of myths in Plato's dialogues, not to mention the role of the poetic composition of these dialogues for Plato's thought, the latter claim obviously raises some questions. For instance, can one truly understand the true event of philosophy in terms of the distinction between Platonic versus pre-Platonic? In the next chapter on Nancy, I will show that contemporary thought also knows of another Plato than Badiou's. To be precise, I follow Gabriel Riera's essay on this matter, Badiou does acknowledge this other Plato in *Petit manuel d'inesthétique:* "It was already difficult for Plato himself to maintain entirely the maxim that endorses the matheme and banishes the poem.... Plato must himself resort to images, like that of the sun; to metaphors, like those of 'prestige' or 'power'; to myths, like the myth of Er the Pamphylian returning from the kingdom of the dead."[22] Riera connects this comment to a critique of Badiou given by Nancy's direct colleague from Strasbourg, Lacoue-Labarthe. The latter argues that Heidegger's mistake was not so much to have sutured philosophy to poetry—since, as Badiou himself acknowledges in the above quote, philosophy is impossible without a recourse to poetry—but rather to have sutured philosophy to grounding myths.[23] My own approach is clearly akin to the suggestion of philosophers such as Lacoue-Labarthe, Nancy, and Agamben to think the importance of poetry for philosophy and follow the (philosophical) expressiveness of poems and stories.[24] In particular, Nancy's work demonstrates what a systematic elaboration of such a reading of Plato offers for ontology. In particular, Nancy coins the concept of *partage,* one of the central concepts in his ontology of plurality, in conversation with Plato's dialogue *Ion*.[25] Moreover, he does so while explicating what *hermēneuein* as an activity of the poets and the rhapsodes means in the *Ion*. Thus, he presents us with another Plato. This other Plato also provides us with a concept of plurality, but not based on an axiomatic decision and without any affinity with mathematics. These two Platos and the two concepts of plurality they inspire allow me to present the aforementioned dispute between mathematics and poetics under the more precise heading of *mathematics or hermeneutics*.

To unravel this dispute and offer a first account of the difference between speculative and hermeneutic thought, I will start to reconstruct Badiou's critique of hermeneutic strands of thought. Four closely related issues forming the heart of Badiou's critique can be distinguished. These four issues also allow me to account for the most important concepts of his ontology: (1) withdrawal versus subtraction; (2) twofold plurality and conflict; (3) interpretation versus nomination; (4) finitude versus infinity.

Withdrawal versus Subtraction: On the Void

Another name by which contemporary thought often characterizes ontotheology is "metaphysics of presence." Being is thought from its inception in Greek thought as being-present. The first aspect of the dispute between speculative and hermeneutic strands of thought concerns the different ways in which Heidegger and Badiou aim to overcome this motive of presence: by means of withdrawal (*Entzug*) and subtraction (*soustraction*), respectively.

Heidegger develops a conception of the withdrawal (*Entzug*) and the refusal (*Versagung, Verweigerung*) of being to show the insufficiency of any metaphysics of presence. For him, being never simply appears. In *Sein und Zeit,* he already notes that being is the phenomenon par excellence because it is hidden, and in the *Beiträge* Heidegger argues that, at best, we can arrive at the experience that being is refused and denied to us. It is in this sense that refusal can be interpreted as a gift: we hint about being by experiencing it in its withdrawal.[26] Hence, the nonpresence of being is never simply a matter of pure absence, disappearance, or nonappearance. Rather, notions such as withdrawal and refusal indicate that, for Heidegger, being appears *in its absence,* and being appears *as refused to us.* In commenting on the difference between withdrawal and disappearance, Sallis notes, "Yet disappearance is not quite the same as withdrawal: whatever disappears is simply gone without leaving a trace of itself, whereas what withdraws may, in its very withdrawing, continue to offer some index of itself."[27] This difference between disappearance and withdrawal shows that a withdrawal is characterized by the fact that it leaves an index of itself. Clearly, for Heidegger the problems of the forgetfulness of being (*Seinsvergessenheit*) and the abandonment of being (*Seinsverlassenheit*) concern exactly this difference between disappearance and withdrawal. Typical for Heidegger's understanding of this withdrawal and abandonment in the *Beiträge* is his play with *Notlosigkeit* and *Not der Notlosigkeit.* The *Notlosigkeit*—the lack of any experience of need, want, or distress in relation to the withdrawal of being—characterizes our time: for the many, the call of being has simply disappeared. Yet, for the few this *Notlosigkeit* itself becomes a *Not*—a need, plight, want, or distress.[28] This latter need thus arises from the lack of want. Hence, for those who experience this need, being is not marked by sheer disappearance but by a withdrawal that leaves an index of itself.

Badiou aims to provide another alternative to the motive of presence in classical metaphysics. In his own variation on Heidegger's ontic-ontological difference in which being appears as nothing, Badiou calls the nothingness of being "the void." Although a certain similarity can be seen here with Heidegger's work, Badiou emphasizes that our relation to the void should not be accounted for in terms of a withdrawal but, rather, in terms of subtraction (*soustraction*): being is simply subtracted from *any* presentation, that is, it is not presented itself.[29] Rather, it is that which enables every presentation.

In terms of Sallis's distinction between disappearance and withdrawal, it seems that the void should be thought of in terms of a simple absence or disappearance that is nevertheless the source of presentation. Thus, Badiou writes, "The void is the name of being—of inconsistency—according to a situation, inasmuch as presentation gives us therein an unpresentable access, thus non-access, to this access."[30] This play with access and nonaccess to being as the access to every "situation" and everything that is "presented in a situation" of course leaves the reader wondering how one can *know* of this nonaccess. If the subtraction is complete, how can one develop a science of being?

To answer this latter question, let us first consider how Badiou interprets Heidegger's notion of withdrawal. Referring to the orientation of poetic thought, he argues that Heidegger aims to provide an intuition of being, thus offering "a trajectory of proximity" to approach being as closely as possible.[31] Apparently, despite the withdrawal of being, Heidegger's hermeneutic phenomenology aims to do the impossible and come close to being or intuit being. To account for this tendency in Heidegger's thought, Badiou depicts it in the general framework of "poetic" types of ontology: "Naturally it would be pointless to set off in search of the nothing. Yet it must be said that this is exactly what poetry exhausts itself doing; this is what renders poetry... complicit with death. If one must—alas!—concede that there is some sense in Plato's project of crowning the poets in order to send them into exile, it is because poetry propagates the idea of an intuition of the nothing in which being would reside."[32] Thus, Badiou objects to two elements in poetic thought: first of all, poetry is complicit with death. This element will be discussed below when I discuss the hermeneutic emphasis on finitude. What is important now is the second point, which also explains why poetry is complicit with death, namely, its impossible effort to *intuit* or *experience* the nothing that is being. When Badiou uses the expression "the nothing of being," he aims to say that being cannot be presented in any situation, whereas intuition and experience always aim at what is somehow (presented) in a situation. To understand these remarks it is important to recall Badiou's taste for the absolute: where poetic thought aims to intuit and experience, metaphysical thought, which for Badiou always has a mathematical core, relates to a "pure existence,...which cannot be empirically attested." In this sense, it is indeed beyond "the measure of our cognition," and our experience.[33] It is in these terms that

Badiou criticizes Heidegger. Obviously this means that, for Badiou, Heidegger still remains a captive of the main motive of metaphysics as metaphysics of presence that is "haunted by the dissipation of Presence and the loss of the origin."[34]

The role and the place of the (Greek) origin is a well-known point of discussion in the Heidegger literature. Badiou's comments repeat this point. Yet, two more refined remarks need to be added. First of all, Badiou's critique shows once more that he follows Heidegger in his critique of metaphysics: he criticizes Heidegger for not being able to find an alternative to the motive for which he, Heidegger, criticized metaphysics in the first place. Hence, it is in the name of Heidegger's own critique of metaphysics that Heidegger is criticized. Secondly, Badiou simply forgets to discuss to what extent the notion of withdrawal offers an alternative to the metaphysics of presence. In fact, Heidegger's notion of the hint or intimation (*Wink*) indicates that an "intuition" of being concerns first and foremost the index that the withdrawal leaves behind. When it makes sense to talk about an intuition or an experience in the *Beiträge*, it is the experience of the *abandonment* of being and not of being in its presence.

When pondering a bit more on this second point, another problem appears when returning to the questions I raised above: how do we know about the subtraction? Can we really think the subtraction without any index? For Badiou, the void is nothing but "the name of unpresentation in presentation" and "the void is the name of being."[35] What is a name? I will discuss the notion of nomination or naming more precisely in the next section, but let me introduce it here: the procedure of naming creates a supplement to what Badiou calls "the language of the situation." A situation is nothing but the consistent presentation of the elements that belong to a situation. The language of the situation is the language providing us with the means to refer to what is present(ed) in a situation and to formulate propositions about these elements. The procedure of naming adds a signifier to this language that, unlike the other terms of this language, has no referent in the situation itself. This is also the role played by the void as the name of being. The void as a name is such a signifier: the mark $\emptyset$ does not correspond to any element presented in the situation. Yet, when being is not presented, the mark ∅ is nothing but an *index* of being in the (extended) language of the situation; this index refers to what is beyond the situation.

This indicates that Badiou does not think subtraction as mere absence or disappearance but has to think it always in relation to a name that in the situation—for instance in the situation that is ontology or set theory—presents us with an index of being. But, then, in what sense is Badiou's subtraction truly different from Heidegger's withdrawal? At this crucial point, two typical aspects of Badiou's work need to be brought into play.

First of all, a name, since it does not have a referent in the situation, presents us with the necessity to decide between two options: *either* the name is merely an empty signifier *or* the name refers to something beyond the situation. Hence, the void is *not always already* an index of being; it might also be a mere empty signifier. This is not clear from the situation itself. Here a typical dimension of (Badiou's understanding of) mathematical thought comes into play: mathematics *performs* something; it decides on its axioms. In his effort to show what it means that ontology is set theory, Badiou analyzes what the different axioms of set theory mean. Among these axioms, one axiom stands out, namely the one that states that the empty set ∅—or the void—exists.[36] In terms of Badiou's meta-mathematical interpretation of mathematics, this axiom decides that the void is not an empty signifier but is in fact the name of being. The existence of the void is not produced by thought since the decision on this axiom orients thought and sets it in motion, as Badiou insists: "The void is not a production of thought, because it is from its existence that thought proceeds."[37]

Hence, what is truly at stake in the discussion with Heidegger is not so much the issue of whether or not Heidegger's thought remains captive to the metaphysics of presence. At this point, Badiou misrepresents his dispute with Heidegger. It is also not a matter of the distinction between disappearance or absence and withdrawal; in this respect, Heidegger and Badiou are dealing with similar problems. Rather, the dispute concerns the question of what comes first. Is the index of being *always already given as index,* or is the task of thinking *to decide that this possibly empty signifier is treated as index?* What Badiou in his emphasis on the axiomatic decision shows is that Heidegger's thought tends to forget which decision it has always already taken, namely, that the withdrawal of being is indeed not an empty signifier in our thought but concerns the withdrawal *of being*.

Moreover, perhaps this dispute does not need to lead to a rejection of Heidegger's position but might inspire another interpretation of his work, making us aware of the importance of decision in his thought. When the distinction between the *Notlosigkeit* and the *Not der Notlosigkeit* cannot be established by theoretical reason but rather requires the resoluteness of thinking in order to pursue the latter need, as Heidegger often claims, we see that thought also requires a certain ethos in Heidegger's "poetic" thought.[38] What Badiou shows here, as Derrida also often emphasizes, is that Heidegger's thought, too, derives from a decision on and an affirmation of being despite its withdrawal. One might say that it is the structure of withdrawal (or subtraction) itself that makes the comportment of pure contemplation—*theōria*—impossible since contemplation always contemplates the (eternally) present. To relate to what withdraws itself, another comportment is needed that brings into play notions such as affirmation, decision and resoluteness. As evidence that Heidegger and Badiou are concerned with a similar problematic in this sense, note that even Badiou's terminology of void and decision can be found in the following telling quote from Heidegger's *Beiträge:* "By the same token, 'void' is actually the fullness of what is still undecided and is to be decided."[39] For Heidegger, the void of being thus presents us with what is not yet decided and, hence, what still needs to be decided.

Another element of Badiou's work is at stake in the dispute between poetic and mathematical thought. This dispute concerns *the orientation that the index or the name of being opens up*. For Badiou, the withdrawal of being is approached in light of the poetic effort to provide an experience of and with being. This means that poetic thought moves from the index of being to an experience of what is indexed, namely, being. Hence, the index of the withdrawal of being is taken up in an effort to disclose being. This is why Badiou argues that poetic thought ultimately departs from the experience of the loss of the origin: the index is a trace of a more original unconcealment that is lost but still traceable in and because of the trace itself.[40]

Mathematical thought, however, does not proceed by presenting the unpresentable. By radicalizing the inaccessibility of being in the concept of subtraction, thought changes direction in its mathematical configuration. Rather than trying to overcome the subtraction of being by moving back to its origin—which is for Badiou an impossibility—mathematical thought moves in the *opposite* direction: not toward the provenance of the axiomatic decision but toward its consequences. Thus, a decision opens up the orientation of thought. Thought *does not return* to this decision in order to revoke it or examine it, but thought simply unfolds its consequences.

In particular, this applies to the project of *L'être et l'événement*: it receives its orientation from the decision that the one is not. This orientation is never questioned but, rather, followed. Taking into account that the experience of being is for Heidegger first and foremost an experience of the abandonment of being, we see that the different orientation of Badiou also leads to a different attitude with respect to the decision. For Badiou, the axiomatic decision orients thought, and thought follows the decision in all senses of the verb "to follow." For Heidegger, however, thought has the task of bringing us to "the fullness of what is not yet decided, what is to be decided." This difference in orientation is perhaps the main difference between these schools, which also affects their conception of the event.[41]

Which Plurality? Which Conflict?

My comments about the role of the axiomatic decision in Badiou's thought might be read purely metaphorically: mathematics provides us with a figure of thought to think the importance of decisions in ontology. This would be quite Platonic since Plato insists on the similarity as well as the difference between mathematics and dialectics. On the one hand, mathematics provides us with an image of how philosophy should proceed. On the other hand, however, only the dialectical inquiry beyond the axiom into what is without presupposition reaches into the Idea(s). As we already saw, Badiou disagrees with

Plato on exactly this point. For him, mathematics is not merely a figure of thought. He claims an identity. Mathematics *is* ontology. Let us see what this implies for his conception of the *conflict on existence* that accompanies his account of the many in terms of set theory.

When an account of existence is based on axiomatic decisions—such as, "the empty set exists"—a conflict concerning what counts as existing will inevitably arise because different decisions might be taken. Indeed, this happens in contemporary set theory, as Badiou notes. Constructivist, transcendent, and generic accounts of set theory exist.[42] These different accounts go back to various axiomatic decisions concerning what counts as a set and thus, in Badiou's interpretation, what counts as existing. Every decision offers a particular "orientation" toward existence. Hence, an irreducible plurality of conflicting orientations intrinsically belongs to (mathematical) thought.[43] This also indicates that thought is polemical by nature, as Badiou writes: "It is about existence itself that agreement fails to occur, as this is what had been decided upon in the first place. Every thought is polemical. It is no mere matter of conflicting interpretations. It is about conflicts in existential judgments. This is also why no real conflict in thought reaches a full resolution. Consensus is the enemy of thought, for it claims we share existence. In the most intimate dimension of thought, however, *existence is precisely what is not shared* [*l'impartageable*]."[44] This intriguing quote discusses a number of other issues concerning Badiou's critique of hermeneutics. Rather than pertaining to Heidegger, these issues relate to classical forms of hermeneutics as developed by Gadamer and Ricoeur.

A Merely Mathematical Conflict. Badiou's equation of mathematics and ontology allows him to account for thought as plural and polemic. Yet, this polemic only concerns the *mathematical* question of what a set is. Consequently, although the equation of mathematics and ontology allows Badiou to stage fundamental conflicts between different judgments on existence, these conflicts do not include and cannot address the ontological conflict between a poetic and a mathematical orientation of thought. This limitation implies that his understanding of conflicting accounts of being cannot provide us with a framework to think the most fundamental conflict in the history of thought.

This leads to the following problem. On the one hand, Badiou acknowledges poetic thought as a fundamental and fertile line of thought throughout the history of philosophy. On the other hand, he argues that the true event from which philosophy is born is the turn to mathematics. This latter claim implies that poetic thought is not a *philosophical* thought at all. This tension in Badiou's thought is due to the double function he assigns to mathematics and to which Bruno Bosteels already points when he writes that mathematics is both "the discourse of ontology" and "one subjective condition among others," one of which is art, including poetry.[45] As soon as Badiou argues that Heidegger and others suture philosophy to poetry, the obvious reply will be that he in turn sutures ontology to mathematics. When mathematics is indeed only one subjective condition among others, this requires that the conflict concerning ontology should be thought beyond the limits of mathematical thought. The dispute with poetic forms of thought cannot be accounted for in terms of mathematics: this dispute does not concern what counts as multiplicity but rather what the status of existence itself is.

Plurality, Analogy, and Unlimitedness. The second issue I want to take up in relation to the above quote concerns more directly Badiou's critique of philosophical hermeneutics. That Badiou indeed criticizes Ricoeur in this quote can be seen from the contrasts it introduces between the conflict concerning existence and the conflict of interpretations. This latter conflict refers to Ricoeur's phenomenological hermeneutics and in particular to the book that carries this title: *Le conflit des interprétations.*

Let us try to reconstruct what part of Ricoeur's hermeneutics Badiou is most likely to reject in *Court traité*. In the first essay of *Le conflit des interprétations*, Ricoeur accounts for the possibility and the limits of a hermeneutic ontology. He does so especially in distinction to Heidegger's ontology of Dasein. For Ricoeur, our access to being is always mediated by the interpretations of cultural symbols. His explorations show that different practices of interpretation exist, and they provide us with different and even mutually conflicting interpretations of the meaning of human existence. As Ricoeur puts it, "Moreover, it is only in a conflict of rival hermeneutics that we perceive something of the being to be interpreted: a unified ontology is as inaccessible to our method as a separate ontology. Rather, in every instance, each hermeneutics discovers the aspect of existence which founds it as method."[46] Hence, for Ricoeur there is a difference between ontology and epistemology. Due to the limits and the finitude of our capacity to interpret, hermeneutics cannot reach a unified ontology. Yet, at the same time, a hermeneutic ontology cannot end its inquiry with such a result—a multitude of separate, conflicting interpretations and of separate ontologies—since every inquiry into the meaning of existence is regulated by the idea that human existence is one. Therefore, the multiple interpretations need to be taken up in a dialectic regulated by the unity of being.

In this sense, we can say that Ricoeur's account of a hermeneutic ontology is indeed marked by a conflict of interpretations but also that he takes this conflict up in a movement of thinking marked by a Kantian regulative idea: thought demands that dialectics strives for "a unitary figure," a "coherent figure" of being to solve this conflict.[47] Such a dialectics is possible, as Badiou rightly suggests in the aforementioned quote, *because* Ricoeur's hermeneutics departs from the presupposition that the different interpretations *share* in the same existence. Despite all our (interpretative) differences, it is the same human existence experienced in and examined by different practices of interpretation.

This points to a difference between Ricoeur and Badiou that can be unfolded in terms of the difference between *polla* and *plēthos*, two terms Plato uses for "the many." The former term *polla*, as Badiou indicates, occurs in a dialectical relation to the one (*hen*) and presupposes the primacy of the one. For the infinite multiplicity whose dreamlike existence Parmenides encountered in his inquiry of the hypothesis "the one is not," Plato uses the latter term *plēthos*. Note that Badiou translates *polla* as plurality and *plēthos* as multiplicity.[48] In terms of the difference between plurality as *polla* and *plēthos*, Ricoeur's hermeneutics takes up the plurality of interpretations in a unifying movement of thought in dialectics; it is a form of *polla*. (This is a motive as old as Schleiermacher's hermeneutics.) Thus, it is exemplary for the dialectics between the one and the many that it ultimately subsumes the many under the one and can thus be opposed to Badiou's conception of plurality as *plēthos*, which is subtracted from the rule of the one.[49]

By focusing on the notion of *plēthos* in his reading of Plato, Badiou emphasizes the importance of the role of the unlimited in Plato's thought. He shares this attention to the unlimited nature of reality with Deleuze. The latter's understanding of the unlimited nature of reality allows me to point out another important difference with Ricoeur's hermeneutic ontology. In Plato, the unlimited is marked by a lack of measure. Due to this lack of measure, thought arrives at paradoxical and even aporetic results: something can be both bigger and smaller than something else and both younger and older, as Deleuze points out in his reading of the *Parmenides* and the *Philebus*.[50] Deleuze understands the problem of the measure in Plato in relation to the notions of idea, copy, and simulacrum.[51] The idea provides a being with a measure; something is called a "copy" when it participates in the idea and is thus measured by it. The relationship between copy and idea is not a relation of identity but of resemblance and mimesis. A measured reality is a reality that is constituted by the mimetic relation between intelligible idea and sensuous being. The simulacrum, however, complicates this picture of a measured reality. In fact, the simulacrum is not a copy, but merely appears as a copy; it is a false copy since it is dissimilar to the original idea. Thus, the simulacrum withdraws from the measure and introduces a third kind, in addition to the mimetic relation of idea and copy. Therefore, according to Deleuze, the simulacrum is intrinsically connected to the unlimited nature of being. Whereas *polla*, like the copy, is subsumed under the rule of the unity of the idea, *plēthos* and simulacrum present an alternative to this reign of the one in a conception of the unlimited.

In addition to Badiou's account of the unlimited nature of being in terms of *plēthos*, Deleuze's explication emphasizes two more aspects of the problem of plurality. First, by relating the theme of the unlimited to the problem of the simulacrum, it is immediately clear that the question of the unlimited is not unique to the speculative school, but is also taken up by philosophers such as Derrida and Nancy.[52] As I shall show in the next chapter in my reading of Nancy, this shared concern also leads to a shared critique of classical hermeneutics (and of Ricoeur's hermeneutics in particular). Second, Deleuze's account offers another understanding of the critique on Ricoeur's hermeneutic ontology. Deleuze argues that the platonic model that approaches reality as a whole out of the mimetic relation between idea and copy ultimately prepares a conception of ontology centralized on the analogy of being. The classical hermeneutic conception of a whole chain of notions, such as resemblance, mimesis, and analogy, ultimately belongs to this ontological model that understands the sharing of being in terms of "being-as," as analogy. Yet, Deleuze shows that this model of ontology remains attached to the ontotheological focus on measure and limit in its account of being. In addition, Deleuze's account indicates that the quest for an ontology of plurality (as an effort to overcome the ontotheological model) is thus a quest that aims to do justice to the *limitlessness* of being. Yet, this quest does not belong to the speculative school alone—the absence of a measure is a theme that is also present in more Heideggerian strands of thought and, more specifically, can be found in Nancy's hermeneutic-phenomenological ontology of plurality.[53]

Interpretation versus Nomination

Another crucial element in Badiou's critique of hermeneutics concerns the notions of meaning and interpretation.[54] In fact, he opposes these notions to thought as decision: mathematics, he argues, does not present any interpretation since it concerns "the real"—in Lacan's sense of the word—which is deprived of meaning.[55] How, then, is the real brought to language? To answer this question, let us turn to "*L'écriture du générique: Samuel Beckett.*"[56] In this essay, Badiou argues that Beckett's work is marked by a particular development. Whereas Beckett first embraces the model of interpretation, he later rejects it in favor of a model of nomination. This development concerns the very possibility of bringing *events* to language in poetics. "In *Watt*," Badiou argues, "the hypotheses about the incidents *are bound up in a problematic of signification*. Here we remain within an attempt of a hermeneutical type, the stakes of which are to relate, through a well conducted interpretation, the incident to the established universe of significations."⁵⁷ This quote summarizes exactly in which sense hermeneutics fails concerning "the incidents," which are here equivalent to "the events." An interpretation always reattaches the unheard of incidents to an already established "universe of significations." Instead of "universe of significations," we might also read, in the terminology of *L'être et l'événement,* "language of the situation." Rather than inventing something new—which for Badiou is the truly poetic gesture corresponding to an event worthy of this name—hermeneutics interprets the new in terms of what is already known and thus ultimately reduces the foreign to the familiar.

To a certain extent, this summary of hermeneutics is quite to the point. Hermeneutics is indeed marked by the effort to interpret what is other or foreign in terms of what is familiar and already known. One might call this *the logic and the directionality of metaphor* already at work in Schleiermacher's hermeneutics. As I argued elsewhere, this is exactly why the notion of metaphor is so important to the hermeneutics of Gadamer and Ricoeur. A metaphor transfers from the known onto the unknown by discovering resemblances. In this way, thought guided by metaphor tries to encapsulate the unknown by means of its resemblance to what is already known.⁵⁸ The innovation of a poetics guided by the figure of metaphor is therefore always an innovation that *abstracts from the outset from the singular* in order to reattach what has been discovered to the realm of already established significations.

Yet, the emphasis on resemblance does not characterize the hermeneutic-phenomenological school as a whole, as the case of Heidegger's dismissal of metaphor indicates.⁵⁹ As Derrida has convincingly shown, it is exactly the logic and directionality of metaphor to which Heidegger objects when he argues that metaphor remains within the boundaries of metaphysics.⁶⁰ The poetic word on being should not go from the familiar to the unfamiliar. It should, rather, start with the unfamiliar and the uncanny and let it provide us with a new, unheard of access to what we only thought we already knew. Hence, as Heidegger notes with regard to his famous nonmetaphor of language as the house of being, to understand what this expression means, we cannot transfer our knowledge of living and dwelling to being. Rather, being will provide us with a new understanding of dwelling.

Badiou introduces nomination or naming (*nomination*) as an alternative to interpretation. In his reading of Beckett, Badiou traces the replacement of interpretation by naming in Beckett's *Endgame*. Whereas in *Watt,* the interpreter reduces "that-which-happens" to the language of the situation, *Endgame* maintains "its character as supplement." Thus, Beckett replaces hermeneutics with naming and "naming will not look for meaning, but instead propose to draw an invented name from the void itself of what happens."[61] In contrast to the interpreter's reduction of the event to the language of the situation, naming adds something new to the language of the situation, and therefore language may preserve a trace of the event. This difference between signification and nomination is typical for Badiou's own systematic account of the supplementary character of the event:

> A signification is always distributed through the language of a situation, the language of established and transmitted knowledges. A nomination, on the other hand, emerges from the very inability of signification to *fix* an event, to decide upon its occurrence, at the moment when this event—which supplements the situation with an incalculable hazard—is on the edge of its disappearance. A nomination is a "poetic" invention, a new signifier, which affixes to language that for which nothing can prepare it. A nomination, once the event that sustains it is gone forever, remains, in the void of significations.[62]

Hence, naming is a poetic invention that fixes what is not given in our everyday situation and marks an event to which we have no access in terms of situation. Although Badiou opposes mathematics to poetics on the level of ontology, on the level of the event and the articulation of the event, he needs an account of poetics that, though not resembling the metaphorical movement in Ricoeur's poetics, does resemble Heidegger's account of the poetic word that is always concerned with disclosing the singular and the new: it is only when a poetic name is attached to the event that the latter is introduced and preserved in language.[63] The name of the event is thus truly the trace of the event in language.

The name of the event has the same status as the name of being we encountered earlier: naming produces necessarily *empty* names since they do not refer to an entity presented in the situation.[64] Yet, this theory of names does not end in their emptiness. Not all names remain empty, as Badiou insists. They have future referents that only come to pass once the consequences of the event have been drawn. Names, he writes, "*displace* established significations and leave the referent void: this void will have been filled if truth comes to pass as a new situation."[65] Naming is thus a procedure that displaces the established significations by a void in the present, but it does so in terms of a future anterior: "the void will have been filled" when the consequences of the event have been drawn. I will come back to this specific temporal mode of the name in my discussion of the role of infinity in Badiou's thought. For now, it is important to see how this affects his account of hermeneutics: when he criticizes the concept of interpretation and opposes it to naming, he ultimately dismisses one crucial notion from which important branches in hermeneutics indeed depart, namely, our co-belonging (*Zugehörigkeit*) to a meaningful tradition or context.

Understanding and interpretation depart from the always already given element of this belonging to a meaningful tradition and, by attaching the new to the already established universe of signification, return to it. Therefore, the pair "interpretation and belonging" makes it impossible to think the arrival of something utterly new. The parallel between event and void indicates that on the level of the situation, the event adopts the role of the absolute. Naming, which Badiou elsewhere identifies with *declaration,* is the procedure that allows us to access the absolute and the new.[66] Thus, it presents an alternative to the hermeneutic pair of interpretation and belonging.

Plural Infinity and the Generic

The issue of finitude versus infinity provides the fourth and final critique on hermeneutic thought.[67] This issue forms the basic dispute between the hermeneutic-phenomenological and the speculative schools, according to Badiou as well as Meillassoux. As heirs of Kant, the former school affirms the finitude and the limits of our knowledge.

For Kant, no knowledge exists without experience (*Erfahrung*); even transcendental knowledge concerns only knowledge of the possible experience *überhaupt* and not of being, substance, or any other metaphysical theme. Yet, even though Badiou acknowledges that our cognitive capacities are finite, this does not mean that the absolute cannot be "rationally demonstrated."[68] One of the driving forces behind Badiou's thoughtis how he affirms the infinite.

As Badiou writes, "As for philosophy, the aim is to finish up with the motif of finitude and its hermeneutical escort. The key point is to unseal the infinite from its millenary collusion with the One. It is to restitute the infinite to the banality of manifold-being, as mathematics has invited us to do since Cantor. For it is as a suture of the infinite and the One that the supposed transcendence of the metaphysical God is constructed."[69] This quote combines the emphasis on finitude in hermeneutics and the classical interpretation of infinity in terms of God as oneness—"the suture of the infinite and the one"—as well as the interpretation of infinity as absolute and as measure and principle of the totality of being. Thus, Badiou acknowledges that Heidegger's emphasis on finitude is set out to think ontology without theology. Yet, the Heideggerian effort is not sufficient as he fears that in Heidegger's work another divinity—the God of the poets—appears, which would introduce another theological motive in philosophy.[70] Therefore, as he emphasizes, a more banal, set-theoretical explanation of the infinite is necessary to get rid of the ontotheological notion of God and develop a truly a-theological conception of the infinite.

Finitude and Infinity. The infinite is usually connected to both the absolute and to totality. Something is called finite when it is not absolute, that is, when it refers to or presupposes something else for its own existence. This implies, as Spinoza argues, that only the totality of reality can be the infinite since everything else that exists refers to this totality for its existence, whereas this totality does not refer to anything outside itself. The primacy of finitude and the lack of a concept of infinity in hermeneutics should be understood in these terms. Also for Heidegger, everything that appears and everything that is can never be grasped as an absolute totality because it refers to what withdraws itself and to the intrinsic movement of withdrawal that is typical for being. Even being can be called finite in this sense since it presents itself only as withdrawal and as refusal.[71]

To understand Badiou's position in this debate, it is not sufficient to state that he gives a mathematical definition of the infinite as ω_0, the set of natural numbers, because in this definition there is no immediate connection to the philosophical problems of the absolute and totality. Although ω_0 is in a certain sense the "totality" of all finite sets, it is not the set of all sets. Hence, it is no candidate for totality. Also, as Badiou shows, the finite numbers depend on ω_0 rather than the other way around, so in a relative sense, ω_0 is absolute with respect to the finite numbers. Yet, it is no candidate for *the* absolute since other infinite sets exist of which ω_0 is itself an element. So let us deal with the philosophical problems of the absolute and totality first in order to return later to the specific role Badiou attributes to infinite sets.

Infinite, Totality, Absolute. Similar to all ontologies that aim to overcome the theological motive of metaphysics, Badiou will deny the existence of totality. In fact, as Meillassoux puts it, Badiou reveals *"the mathematical thinkability of the detotalisation of being-qua-being."*[72] Badiou proves that this "detotalisation" is a consequence of the equation of set theory and ontology since one of the axioms of set theory excludes the possibility of a set of all sets.[73] More precisely, the impossibility of totality is a special case of a more fundamental axiom that states in layman's terms that a set cannot have itself as an element. Although this law provides set theory with the necessary boundaries to maintain its consistency and to overcome Russell's famous paradox, this mathematical task does not inform us about the *speculative* meaning of this axiom. Let us not forget that *L'être et l'événement* is not a book in mathematics. Like the hermeneutic philosophers who cite poems without being poets themselves, Badiou quotes mathematics in order to capture the speculative meaning of set theory: "Mathematics is *cited* here to let its ontological essence become manifest."[74] Apparently, the practice of *quoting* mathematics rather than *doing* mathematics allows mathematics to present "its ontological essence." Badiou does not offer a further reflection and therefore this strange quote on the practice of quoting leaves the reader wondering what exactly this practice of quoting is and does. What is this strange interruption of the mathematical practice that allows Badiou to show its ontological import? In chapter 3, I will propose an answer to this question that turns out to be more crucial than its place in the introduction of *L'être et l'événement* suggests.

Now we need to ask: what is the *ontological* meaning of the axiom that states that a set cannot have itself as an element? When discussing Russell's paradox, Badiou notes that Georg Cantor, who at other points for Badiou is the faithful subject of the event of set theory, does not exclude sets that have themselves as elements from his theory, even though Cantor knows these sets cannot be counted. To distinguish them from transfinite sets such as ω_0, Cantor calls them "absolutely infinite." The speculative meaning of this gesture, as Badiou argues, is ontotheological since it reinstates the (metaphysical) notion of God: "Cantor's ontological thesis is evidently that inconsistency, mathematical impasse of the one-of-the-multiple, orientates thought towards the Infinite as supreme-being, or absolute." Hence, such a set is an *absolute* infinity, that is, a "supreme-being." Thus, as Badiou continues, "Cantor, essentially a theologian... wavers between ontotheology—for which the absolute is thought as a supreme infinite being, thus as transmathematical, in-numerable, as a form of the one so radical that no multiple can consist therein—and mathematical ontology, in which consistency provides a theory *of* inconsistency, in that what proves an obstacle to it (paradoxical multiplicity) is its point of impossibility, and thus, quite simply, *is not*."[75] I'm quoting these words *in extenso* for two reasons. First, they show exactly which axiom overcomes the problem of the infinite *as the absolute and as totality* in Badiou's speculative assessment of set theory: the Cantorian axiom, theological in nature, which states that transfinite sets exist, does not do this as much, but the non-Cantorian one, which states that a set cannot have itself as an element, does. This exclusion implies *that it can never be this or that set that can play the role of the absolute*. Rather, the role of the absolute can only be adopted by an axiomatic *decision* since such a decision decides which hypotheses will be taken as the first principles of ontology and thus decides on what counts as being. In particular, the (decision on the) axiom that ω_0 exists forms the absolute beginning of Badiou's conception of the infinite. Second, the above quote also gives rise to a more complicated issue. Although Badiou excludes the transmathematical from ontology by the equation "ontology = mathematics," the transmathematical is not excluded from his speculative thought, as is well known, because the event is trans-being. In fact, the comparison between Badiou's event and Cantor's absolutely infinite sets imposes itself as soon as we look more closely at how Badiou accounts for the transontological character of the event. The event does not belong to being exactly *because* it transgresses the axiom that forbids a set to be an element of itself, which is the same axiom Cantor's theological, absolutely infinite sets transgress. This follows immediately from the (nonmathematical) matheme Badiou invents for the event. An event e_x related to an evental site X is formalized as $e_x = X \cup \{e_x\}$; hence, e_x is an element of itself.[76] It is quite remarkable, to say the least, that the transgression of this axiom forms the ontotheological motive in Cantor's version of set theory but offers Badiou's account of an event beyond being! This means that Badiou's remark that it is our task "to restitute the infinite to the banality of manifold-being" does not tell the whole story: with the event, the problem of the infinite *as absolute* simply returns in the guise of something that transcends being. In particular, Badiou adds the event to his speculative interpretation of set theory. Although the event is not a set, its matheme shows that it is *like* a set; in fact, it is *like* an absolutely infinite set; it is *like* the supreme-being Badiou criticizes in Cantor; now it is separated from being since it transcends being—which, perhaps, is always a characteristic of the supreme-being.

Let me be more precise and grant Badiou two things. First, his account of ontology does indeed overcome the problem of totality in terms of an account of being as multiple. Second, the concept of the infinite in terms of transfinite sets indeed provides us with an a-theological account of the infinite. Yet, the issue of the matheme of the event causes a specific concern: what happens to the problem of the infinite *as absolute*? I already noted that axiomatic decisions have something to do with the absolute in Badiou's speculative interpretation of set theory: they open up and orient a thought. Yet, decisions go back to the acknowledgment of—in the sense of a nomination and a declaration—and the fidelity to what is held in high esteem in such an axiom. Another word for this high esteem is "event." For instance, *L'être et l'événement* is nothing but the consequence of the event that is named and declared by the formula that ontology is set theory, and the issue of the infinite is related to the Cantorian event that declares that ω_0 exists. The matheme of the event and the relation between event and decision indicate that Cantor's suggestion to call sets that contain themselves "absolutely infinite" is not so bad at all: if there is one "set" in Badiou's thought that deserves to be called *absolutely infinite*, it would be the (non-)set of the event.[77]

To summarize, infinity, totality, and absolute get their proper place in Badiou's thought by means of two axioms. The first one states that ω_0 exists and thus accounts for infinity in terms of transfinite sets. The second one states that a set cannot be an element of itself. The transgression of this axiom marks the ontotheological dimension of (a speculative interpretation of) Cantor's set theory because Cantor transgresses it *within* ontology. Badiou uses this axiom to show how ontology can get rid of the idea of *totality*, but he also uses it to transgress ontology toward the event. This means that the *absolute* is relegated to a domain that is no longer mathematical, namely, to the domain of the event; and out of this domain it retrieves its particular relation with truth, decision, and subject.

Generic Sets and Forcing. Let us now consider the technical details: what precisely does a set theoretical account of infinity offer? Obviously, the issue of infinity is not settled by the decision that transfinite sets exist. Rather, Badiou is interested in showing how the consequences of this decision provide him with a framework to think the basic structures of his notion of the subject. The notions of the generic (set) and of forcing especially aim at the heart of his ideas of the subject and of what he calls "the truth of the event" in *L'être et l'événement*. In particular, the speculative interpretation of these technical mathematical notions allows him to understand how an event, which is beyond being, can nevertheless be the impetus for a radical change of the situation by means of the faithful actions of the subject. Set theory provides the ontological structures of these subjective procedures: since the event and, consequently, the subject cannot be thought in terms of set theory, Badiou can only borrow from set theory the formal structures making event and subject possible. As a consequence, his speculative interpretation always has to deal with the difference between the perspective of the mathematician—the perspective of ontology—and the perspective of the acting subject, who is not only an inhabitant of the situation but also decides on the event. This difference has important implications for Badiou's conception of decision.

To understand this latter suggestion, we need to come to terms with a number of concepts that arise within the framework of a set theory that affirms the existence of transfinite sets.[78] We have already encountered the terms "situation" and "language of the situation," and we already saw how the procedure of naming adds a name of the event, say e, to the language of the situation. This name remains without referent in the situation S. From the point of view of the inhabitant of S, e is nothing but an empty signifier. "Subject" is, in the first place, the name of the procedure of the deciding and naming that e is not an empty signifier but rather refers to an event. For Badiou, a subject is thus always an agent that fully depends on the event: without event, there is no subject. Moreover, the subject is always divided; it is a Two. It belongs to the situation and hence does not have the same perspective as the mathematician, but the subject acts in this situation by being true to an event. As he beautifully puts it in the words of Saint Paul, the subject is a finite being that carries an infinite procedure of truth: it carries its treasure in an earthen vessel.[79] The latter formulation also indicates that the subject's *being true* to an event is not fully captured by the procedure of naming: Badiou wants to provide a model of change and wants to show how the event, next to naming, gives rise to a subjective procedure of *fidelity* to the event. This procedure is explicated in terms of the multifaceted notion of the infinite. Let me clarify this in six steps and offer a critical evaluation in the next section.

1. *Fidelity*. Fidelity is nothing but an operation by which the subject judges whether or not an element belonging to S is connected to the name of the event, e.[80] Badiou calls this procedure "enquiry."[81]

One may, of course, wonder what "connected" means here. It sounds like a highly abstract notion, especially when we think of fidelity in terms of our conviction to be true to something, but we should not forget that Badiou only aims to describe the *ontological* framework of subjectivity: he describes the subject from the distant perspective of the mathematician and not from the lived perspective of the subject itself. In ontological terms, being true to an event implies that a subject enquires the world and tries to gather those aspects that in one way or another belong (or are connected) to this event. Note that there is no rule that the subject can follow in his or her enquiries: whether an element belongs to the event or not gives in each enquiry rise to a new judgment.[82] Since the event is truly beyond the situation, the subject cannot find any reason or ground in the situation itself that would guide this judgment. In this sense, the event is like the void: it does not prescribe anything and it does not provide any knowledge; it is merely the void in the situation from which a subjective procedure is born that can change the situation. Thus, the event confronts us with a void in the situation, with something that is withdrawn from presentation, but this void is at the same time the opening up of something new. The subject is convinced that there is more to the situation than meets the eye, that is, than the situation presents: it harbors something completely new that did not yet find any expression in the situation. Naming is the first expression of it; in the enquiries, the consequences of the event are further explored and drawn.

2. *Truth of the event.* From a mathematical point of view, the enquiries of fidelity create a new set; let us call it T_s, which by definition is the set consisting of all elements of S that according to a subject s belong to e. Consequently, T_s is a subset of S. At this point, the *coup de génie* of Badiou's affirmation of the infinite can be shown. First of all, the existence of the infinite implies that situations are infinite. Consequently, S has subsets that are infinite. A subject is necessarily finite. Consequently, the subset T_s that a subject can actually create by his or her enquiries is also finite. Nevertheless, one can imagine — and here we see how Badiou adopts the mathematical point of view rather than the inhabitant's point of view — that (at infinity) *all* elements of

58   Ontology after Ontotheology

S are enquired, rendering an infinite subset *T* consisting of the union of all the subsets T_s for all possible subjects true to this particular event *e*. This infinite subset *T* of *S* is nothing but the *truth of the event*. In this sense, the subject's finite enquiries are the carriers of an infinite truth of the event. Due to his or her finitude, however, the subject can never know this. Only on a speculative level, in Badiou's account of the ontological structures of the procedures, can this be called knowledge. Here we see how the living experience of the subject is placed in light of its speculative supplement. This speculative supplement allows the philosopher Badiou to "pretend to access the absolute," as Meillassoux puts it. In this case, the absolute is the truth of the event of which the relative actions of the subject are merely a finite subset.

3. *Generic sets.* To understand what this notion of truth means in set theoretical terms, Badiou reminds us of the following. The language of the situation can *discern* certain sets. For instance, the sentence "x is a chair" can discern the set of all chairs. The concept of discernment defines Badiou's conception of *knowledge*. Our knowledge in a situation is everything that can be discerned by the language of the situation: a set (that is, in our case, a subset of the situation *S*) is knowable if and only if it can be discerned. Therefore, one would be tempted to call a sentence true if and only if it discerns a set belonging to *S*. Yet, saving the name of truth for the event, Badiou prefers to call such a sentence *veridical*.[83] To see that truth is indeed different from the veridical, we need to consult set theory once more. Recall the sentence "x is a chair." Clearly, although this sentence allows us to discern the set of all chairs in a room, it cannot discern a set consisting of a chair and a table. This latter set is said to be *indiscernible* by the sentence "x is a chair." A subset of the situation *S* is now called *generic* if it is indiscernible by *every* sentence in the language.

A finite subset can always be discerned since we can compose a sentence out of the finite list of all the names of its elements in order to discern this finite set. Therefore, the concept of the generic presupposes the concept of the infinite, as Badiou is keen to point out. (However, infinity is not enough for its existence: Badiou's discussion of Gödel's account of the constructible sets concerns exactly this issue. For Gödel, only discernible or constructable sets exist. Consequently, for Gödel the generic set does not exist. This is one of the mathematical decisions on existence mentioned above which have important consequences for the speculative interpretation of Badiou: if the generic does not exist, there is no truth of the event in Badiou's sense of the word.)[84] If a generic set exists—and Badiou follows Cohen's version of set theory, which can prove its existence under the condition of a nonconstructive account of what a set is—it cannot be *known*. Hence, a generic set provides Badiou with the formal means to think an infinite subset of the situation that cannot be known in the situation and its language. It gives a mathematical expression to the idea that something transcends the situation's encyclopedic knowledge.

Obviously, Badiou's speculative interpretation applies the notion of the generic set to the relation of event and situation. The guiding idea behind his interpretation is that an event is in every sense trans-being. The heuristic implication of this idea for the aforementioned set T, the truth of an event, is the following. An event, if there is such a thing, and fidelity, if such a procedure exists, gives rise to a subset T of S that cannot be known, that is, generic.[85] Hence, it is indeed the set theoretical account of the infinite that allows Badiou to define in which sense the event transcends both ontology and the knowledge of the situation.

4. *The future anterior of the subject's language.* Now that we know what the truth of an event is in terms of a generic set, how can this lead to a transformation of the situation? Let us first recall what we have found up to now. We have a name e without referent, which is added as a supplement to the language of the situation. Combining e with terms from the language of the situation, the subject creates a new, subjective language consisting of sentences that have neither meaning nor references in the situation itself, as Badiou writes.[86] Yet, the subject operates on the basis of the *belief* and the *confidence* that the situation can be changed radically such that these meaningless statements become veridical in the new, "post-evental" situation. Badiou describes this relation of the subject to the future situation as "future anterior": the statements that are now without meaning

consists of sentences that are *undecidable:* whether they are veridical or not depends on the extension we choose. Hence, their truth or falsity is due to a decision.

To show that this form of decision is the same as the axiomatic decision that orients thought, let me briefly indicate that the aforementioned undecidability is comparable to the one we find in Gödel's incompleteness theorems. Gödel shows that there are certain theorems that can be formulated in our formal language but that can neither be proven nor refuted given our axioms: their truth or falsity is undecidable. Therefore, if we want them to be true, we need to add them to our axioms (or vice versa: if we want them to be false we need to add their negation to our axioms).

Badiou's speculative application of this theorem is the following: the procedure of fidelity is a procedure that is part of the truth of an event and thus, in its form of generic set, determines which statements will have been veridical in the extension to which this generic set gives rise. That is, the subjective procedure of truth determines which statements will be veridical in the post-evental situation. *Knowledge (of the undecidable statements) in the post-evental situation is thus founded in the fidelity of the subject.* With the tricks of mathematics, Badiou has transformed the uncertain future into the undecidable future and shown that the latter opens up the space for a thought in which change can be effected by the subject's fidelity: the subject decides by his or her action what will become veridical. Knowledge is created by belief. When returning to the enigmatic quote connecting belief to knowledge, we understand what Badiou means. He does not make a category mistake; rather, he shows that with respect to the undecidable statements, it is fidelity that decides on its veridicality. Yet, of course, it remains to be seen whether this is convincing.

SUBJECTIVITY IN LIGHT OF MATHEMATICS

Subjective fidelity and the truth of the event form the culmination point of Badiou's speculative turn to mathematics in *L'être et l'événement.* Moreover, they show most clearly how he offers an alternative to the hermeneutic-phenomenological school while embracing Heidegger's critique of metaphysics as ontotheology. Thus, the concept of infinity allows him to develop his "metaphysics without metaphysics." Despite the finitude of all the subject's actual inquiries, Badiou interprets the subject in light of a mathematical infinity.[90] Yet, what are the limits and implications of these descriptions? Is Badiou truly capable of overcoming the ontotheological framework of metaphysics in its return to mathematics? Let me address these two questions along three lines.

One of the trademarks of the subject is the decision. It is clear that the subject lacks both reason and rule to help in his or her naming or enquiries. The model of mathematics is prominently present in Badiou's understanding of these decisions. Exemplary decisions are those that occur in mathematics, such as decisions on axioms and on undecidable statements. In light of Badiou's continual references to mathematics, the question arises concerning what role decisions actually play in mathematics.

First, to understand the importance of an axiom, one often finds the well-known example of non-Euclidean geometry: Euclidean and non-Euclidean geometry differ by the choice of one axiom. Yet, does this mean that, for the mathematician, one of these geometries is more true than the other? No. For the mathematician, Euclidean and non-Euclidean geometry live side by side and simply provide two separate geometries. Although one mathematician may work on the first geometry and another on the other, mathematics as such does not decide in favor of those geometries. Mathematics provides us with a space of thought in which the consequences of *both* geometries are explored. The idea that we should choose one of them is quite absurd from the mathematical point of view. This is also why, for the mathematician, an axiomatic choice lacks any "fear and trembling": it involves no existential choice at all. When "choosing" for non-Euclidean geometry, Euclidean geometry neither disappears nor loses its validity; it might only become less interesting for the mathematician—for instance, for the mathematician engaged in contemporary physics.

Second, a similar comment applies to forcing and generic extensions. Mathematics provides us with the space to create *all* generic extensions and study all of them—there is no need to choose in the radical sense in which the subject finds himself or herself. When the subject forces a situation by its choices, these choices destroy the possibility of other generic extensions. The subject creates another world and creates this world rather than the other. This means that while there is no real difference between generic extensions for the mathematician because all of them are possible for the mathematician, the subject is concerned with one and only one extension, namely, the one connected to the event. Specifically this *nonindifference* of extensions for the subject, which seems to be characteristic of what fidelity means in the case of a subject, disappears when we take the model of mathematics as our guideline. Consequently, the experience of "fear and trembling" is also simply obscured and effaced in this mathematical account: while this experience is a very concrete one in the case of a subject who decides on his or her life or world, the world of mathematics does not suffer from this fundamental uncertainty at work in human decisions and human actions.

This leads to another characteristic tension in Badiou's work. Again and again, when discussing subject and event, he emphasizes the *urgency* of human action.[91] Clearly, this urgency is opposed to the philosophical tendency (which Badiou discerns, for instance, in Derrida's work) to think as if one has all the time in the world and to *problematize* all forms of decisions and distinctions rather than to *make* one. Yet, neither mathematics nor mathematical practice offers a model for the urgency of action. Rather, the mathematician is the twin of the metaphysician who contemplates eternal truths: both of them think as if they have all the time in the world. Consequently, if speculative thought offers an ontological ground for the subject's praxis, a reference to mathematics cannot suffice; it requires a supplement to think the nonindifference as well as the urgency characteristic of subjective praxis.

Third, Badiou's equation "mathematics = ontology" implies that different axioms present us with conflicting conceptions of reality. Yet, although there are indeed multiple set theories corresponding to different axioms, there is not much *polemic* between these systems—simply because no space exists in which, for instance, two geometries can *struggle* with each other: another axiomatic choice simply provides another, unrelated system. How, for instance, should we conceive of a polemic between Euclidean and non-Euclidean geometry from a strictly mathematical point of view? If we argue that only one of these geometries can describe a particular physical space, a quarrel might occur since there is a *shared* concern, namely, how to describe this physical space. However, the question of this physical space does not concern mathematics. Between systems of axioms as such no conflict can occur. In this sense, Badiou's account of the conflict among the three schools in set theory—constructivist, transcendent, and generic accounts of set theory—is misleading. *Only when being is shared,* that is, when these theories claim to say something about the same being, can one argue that they have a conflict over this matter. Otherwise, their different axiomatic decisions lead to separate ontologies. Yet, Badiou argues repeatedly that being is not shared.

Hence, the following conclusion seems to be inevitable. A conflict is always over something the struggling parties are both interested in: *only if we share being might there be a conflict over being.* The mathematical model of axiomatic choice does not offer a model in which such a conflict can be thought. Thinking plurality in terms of multiplicities without relations implies that no real conflict can arise.[92] Earlier in this chapter, I noted that Badiou presents his dismissal of Ricoeur's dialogical model in terms of the dismissal of consensus. Yet, it remains to be seen whether a dialogical model of plurality necessarily strives for consensus. The next chapter on Nancy's ontology will suggest otherwise.[93]

In his speculative interpretation of forcing, Badiou argues that mathematics offers us a framework to think the future of the subject's action. In light of this argument, the issue of the *atemporality* of mathematics needs to be raised: how can one do justice to the phenomenon of the future if one describes it in terms borrowed from an atemporal discipline?[94]

Badiou saves mathematics from one of its major reductions, namely, that mathematics is identified with computations and calculations. Philosophers who point to the intrinsic connection between ontotheology, mathematics, and technology often employ this particular reduction. Yet, this connection is not the only reason to relate mathematics to ontotheology. Traditionally, mathematics provides a paradigm for metaphysics *because* mathematical objects possess the atemporality, the continuous presence, that the metaphysician looks for in its objects. This is why mathematics is always thought to be par excellence in accordance with the metaphysics of presence.

Mathematics' atemporality affects the way in which Badiou thinks the future of the subject's actions in terms of a future anterior. By generating new names, the subject "displaces established signification," as Badiou writes. This operation of displacement already positions the subject beyond hermeneutics in Badiou's understanding of the term. Yet, he is not satisfied with this more or less Derridean gesture of displacement. To overcome the unpredictability of what will happen to the empty names, Badiou brings the theory of forcing into play by which the empty names will have received referents and by which certain sentences, undecidable in the present situation, will have become veridical.[95] Approached from the perspective of the subject's finitude, this implies that the subject works under the presupposition of an "as if": although he or she cannot know it, the subject acts *as if* the empty names are not empty and *as if* the empty statements are veridical *in the future*. Yet, from the perspective of set theory, no "as if" structure is present: the subject *forces* certain undecidable statements to be veridical in the new situation. Hence, the atemporality of mathematics saves the subject from finitude and from the uncertainty of the future.

Whatever one might think of this amazing mathematical theory of forcing, it is in contrast with the basic human experience of the unforeseeable nature of the future and the unpredictable outcome of human action. By placing the actions of the subject in light of the atemporal and infinite character of mathematics, Badiou does not provide us *another* description of this experience but simply *effaces* it. For Badiou, so it seems, the subject's actions plan a future situation. This, I fear, is a highbrow variation of the model of craftsmanship that in its platonic form gave rise to the importance of the Idea in metaphysics: the world is modeled according to an Idea. Badiou affirms this interpretation of his work in *Logiques des mondes:* the life of the subject should be indistinguishable from the Idea it incorporates, springing from the event.⁹⁶ Yet, this makes Badiou's mathematical model vulnerable to the critique that it repeats the ontotheological model of metaphysics on the level of the atemporality of the metaphysics of presence, as Heidegger would argue. Thus, the dispute between hermeneutics and Badiou also concerns the issue of the temporality of the event and the subject. This dispute will be discussed in more detail in chapter 4.

A final issue concerns the question of the relation between subject and event. In *L'être et l'événement,* a human being is either a mere inhabitant of the situation or a subject faithful to an event. The mere inhabitant transforms into a subject at the very moment of declaration. This means that an event can never be described "from the outside." From the outside there is no event; naming the event means being engaged in it. Or, as Badiou puts it, one cannot represent the event but only practice it.⁹⁷ This, of course, has the strange consequence that it is impossible to *criticize* a subject's conviction. Either we are ourselves subjects and engaged in an event or we deny that this event has taken place, but in this latter case we have not yet risen to our infinite potential since we are in a state of denial that the event took place. Communication between the mere inhabitant and the subject on the issue of the event is impossible since they are as far apart as the finite and the infinite—they really share nothing when it comes to the question of whether or not the event has taken place and whether or not one should be faithful to it.⁹⁸ Critique and especially the "critical ideal of deconstruction," which was one of Badiou's main adversaries around the time of *L'être et l'événement,* is ultimately motivated by a pathos for the end and the finite.⁹⁹ For Badiou, this pathos can never reach the heights of the subject. Therefore, the faithful subject has a different pathos and is driven by "enthusiasm for novelty, active fidelity to what has come."¹⁰⁰

This, of course, leaves us with a huge question. Although the event is obviously the source of a fundamental critique of the situation, it seems impossible to criticize an event. In particular, Badiou's work lacks a subjective figure to criticize the event. This leads to the following question: can we not and should we not *think a figure of the subject that is neither a mere inhabitant nor always already engaged with the event*? Such a figure requires that one withdraws from an active engagement in the event and renders an event inoperative not in order to fall back into the situation but in order to *think* the event and one's engagement with it—just as philosophers withdraw from the world to think, to become spectators instead of actors. This latter account of thinking is beyond Badiou's account of the subject. In *L'être et l'événement,* the philosopher and his or her thinking is characterized in terms of affirmation and deductive fidelity to the event that ontology is mathematics. Yet, does this not imply that the subject of philosophy is always under the spell of the event and its (never interrogated) affirmation? How to *withdraw* from such an active engagement without falling back into either the reactionary or the inhabitant's position? That such a question cannot be posed in Badiou's system of thought does not mean that this question does not make sense. It only means that Badiou's thought is closed for this question due to his speculative interpretation of infinity and his refusal to return to and think the moment of decision. Yet, as I suggested earlier in this chapter, Badiou's conception of the void confronts us exactly with this question: if the void requires decisions, it is itself the realm of what is not yet decided; to think the void is therefore never simply to take a decision but also to think the realm in which decisions are not yet taken. This question foreshadows a comportment of thought that is marked by a withdrawal, but this is neither the withdrawal from the world, as discussed briefly in the introduction, nor from the situation; rather, it is a form of withdrawal that is necessary for thought to turn to the event in such a way that it is not always already under its spell or actively engaged in drawing its consequences, as Badiou's subject is.

Notwithstanding these critical comments to which I will return later in this study, this chapter shows that Badiou's thought is a perfect example of the present-day philosophical effort to rethink ontology after ontotheology. In fact, his work on multiplicity, event, and subject is exemplary, despite its problems, for the type of questions a contemporary ontology has to address: How to think being without privileging the one? How to think being without affirming the ground?

Two

Hermeneutics and Beyond
Partage and Abandonment

"From now on, the ontology that summons us will be an ontology in which abandonment remains the sole predicament of being."

"This text does not disguise its ambition of redoing the whole of 'first philosophy' by giving the 'singular plural' of Being as its foundation."
—Jean-Luc Nancy

Go beyond finitude toward infinity and absolute.[1] The speculative school follows this imperative, and it inspires the speculative critique of the hermeneutic-phenomenological paradigm of philosophy and its passion for finitude. Yet, is this critique justified? If so, which of the different aspects I explored in Alain Badiou's version of this critique in the previous chapter apply to which parts of the hermeneutic-phenomenological school? In the previous chapter we saw that a number of issues Badiou raises relate first and foremost to what I call "classical hermeneutics," of which Hans-Georg Gadamer and Paul Ricoeur are the main representatives. The reader familiar with the critique of classical hermeneutics by, for instance, Jacques Derrida and Jean-Luc Nancy, knows that some of the elements of Badiou's critique coincide with theirs. Hence, they provide a similar critique of classical hermeneutics *within the hermeneutic-phenomenological school.* To determine the scope of the speculative critique of hermeneutics, it is important to see which elements of this critique can be found within the hermeneutic-phenomenological school itself.

This chapter is devoted to the work of Nancy because he rethinks hermeneutics in light of an alternative ontology of plurality. In the introduction to part 1, I noted that the speculative shift from finitude to the absolute also implies a shift from discourse to being. In the previous chapter, I unfolded this shift by reconstructing Badiou's critique of Ricoeur's "conflict of interpretations": although classical hermeneutics accounts for plurality on the level of discourse and interpretations, its ontology is ultimately regulated by a Kantian idea of unity. Indeed, as Ricoeur writes in the opening essay of *Le conflit des interprétations,* his hermeneutic ontology strives for a unitary figure of being. In this respect, he might be called an Aristotelian: although being is said in many ways, it points to one (*pros hen*) core meaning. In light of this concern with classical hermeneutics, Nancy's work offers an intriguing alternative since he argues that plurality is not a feature of discourse or interpretation alone but belongs to being as such. Referring to the same passage of Aristotle, he writes, "But this plurality is no longer said in multiple ways that all begin from a presumed, single core of meaning. The multiplicity of the said (that is, of sayings) belongs to being as its constitution."[2] Nancy's agreement with the members of the speculative school that plurality should not be thought on the level of discourse alone, does not yet imply that he follows them in their turn toward the absolute and the infinite. So where are we with respect to this question? Does the hermeneutic passion for finitude indeed imply that hermeneutic thought offers no access to any absolute, or might it be possible that this thought, when turning away from its classical origin, offers another configuration of the relation between finitude and absolute?

Authors such as Martin Heidegger and Nancy are very well aware of the problems surrounding the concept of finitude. They know that finitude is usually thought of as a *privatio,* or a lack. As soon as one thinks of finitude in these terms, as G. W. F. Hegel criticized Immanuel Kant, the affirmation of finitude as well as endlessness—that is, false infinity—implies, often beyond the author's express intention, the affirmation of the superiority of the true infinity (in mathematical terms, ω_0).[3] According to Nancy, metaphysics always interprets being-finite as a privation in order to affirm the existence of a highest, supreme being. Hence, for Nancy, the conception of finitude as privation leads us immediately to the ontotheological constitution of metaphysics. To avoid this problem while according primacy to finitude, finitude itself should not be understood as privation but as the absolute of being itself, as Nancy suggests. This is why he calls his account of finitude an "infinite finitude."[4] As he notes, the real task Heidegger's thought on finitude confronts us with is *to think finitude as the absolute of being*.[5] Moreover, this finitude is nothing but the name of the end of ontotheology and its presupposition of a permanent presence and a stable being, as he writes: "*'Finitude'* designates the *end* of presence as stable, permanent, available, impassible being — as given thing and as drawn figure, as constituted myth or as established reason."[6] For Nancy, the primacy and absoluteness of finitude coincides in ontology with an account of being as plural. When beings *are* plural, that is, when their mode of being can only be understood out of their being-with one another, then none of these beings and none of their modes of being is absolute. In this context, finitude means that no being can be conceived of in its being when it is isolated from the beings with which it is. In fact, beings are never alone; they are always with others and receive their meaning from their being together with other beings.[7] Thus, finitude as absolute should not be understood as privileging "relativity," but is "absolutely detached from all infinite and senseless completion or achievement."[8] In this sense, it no longer makes sense for Nancy to distinguish a separate conception of the infinite: "Consequently, infinity is not an other essence than that of finite being; it is existence itself...as the sharing [*partage*] of finitude between all beings."[9]

Already at this point, we may identify a crucial difference between Badiou's and Nancy's ontology of the many. Although both follow Heidegger's critique of oneness, they do so along different lines of thought. Badiou follows Heidegger's critique of the generality of the in-common (*koinon*) leading necessarily to the one (*hen*). Therefore, according to him, only an ontology that thinks being as pure multiplicity can overcome the reign of oneness and generality. Nancy, however, follows another track. He departs from the primordial importance of Heidegger's conception of being-with (*Mitsein*): "That being is being-with, *absolutely*, this is what we must think. The *with* is the most basic feature of being, the mark [*trait*] of the singular plurality of the origin or origins in it."[10] Hence, Nancy answers the preeminent ontological question—what do all beings have in common?—as follows: being is in-common. However, this latter predicative should not be understood as *the* in-common, as if it would be the most general determination of all and could be understood as an Idea. Rather, as I will suggest, Nancy aims to think a *koinon* without *hen*. He aims to think the primordiality of relation and of being-in-common (*être-en-commun*). This, then, marks Nancy's relation to Heidegger's project of fundamental ontology in *Sein und Zeit:* "It is necessary to refigure [*refaire*, i.e., remake or redo] fundamental ontology (as well as the existential analytic, the history of being, and the thinking of *Ereignis* that goes along with it) with a thorough resolve that *starts from the plural singular of origins,* from *being-with.*"[11] One might be inclined to argue now that, since Nancy affirms the primacy of relatedness, he introduces yet another form of correlationism, as Meillassoux puts it. Such an argument is both correct and false, depending on which element of correlationism one emphasizes. When it refers to a certain Kantianism that claims that, due to our finite capacities to know, we cannot have access to the absolute, then Nancy's thought is not a form of correlationism. When it refers to the claim that finitude itself is absolute, that is, that beings are always related, then correlationism indeed encompasses Nancy's position. However, in the latter case, it should also be acknowledged that Nancy's work proposes yet another speculative position in Meillassoux's sense of the word: it presents us with another access to being in its absoluteness; it proposes to think neither the absoluteness of the one, nor the absoluteness of the many, *but the absoluteness of the* koinon *as singular plural.* One of the main tasks of this chapter is to analyze whether Nancy succeeds in doing this and whether we indeed have access to this absolute in the ontology of being-with.

To position Nancy in the context of post-Heideggerian thought, note that one might read "finite" as "conditioned." When doing this, one immediately sees how close Nancy is to Hannah Arendt. For her, we cannot understand the human being in terms of its essence, but only in terms of its existence, which is always a conditioned existence. Explicating the title of her famous book *The Human Condition,* she writes: "Men are conditioned beings because everything they come in contact with turns immediately into a condition of their existence.... Whatever touches or enters into a sustained relationship with human life immediately assumes the character of a condition of human existence."[12] This quote beautifully shows what "absolute finitude" means in the case of the human being: everything and everyone we encounter in the world becomes a condition for our existence. Our existence always takes place with these other beings, and vice versa, the meaning of these beings and their being can only be understood in relation to their taking place together with each other and with us. This finitude is not concerned with our finite capacity to know an infinite reality but concerns our very existence. As conditioned beings, our being is always already being-with and being-in-common with others and with other beings.

Thus, Nancy follows a different trajectory than Badiou in the space of ontology after ontotheology. Nancy is aware of this difference and therefore he sharply distinguishes his conception of plurality from Badiou's account of being in terms of unrelated multiplicities. Being-together (*être-ensemble*) is not being-a-multiple, as he explicitly states: "Togetherness, in the sense of being a substantive entity, is a collection (as in set theory). Collection assumes a regrouping that is exterior and indifferent to the being-together ('in common') of the objects of the collection."[13] This quote contrasts the indifference with which beings are together in a set with the nonindifference by which they are related in a conception of being-together.

Each of the above comments constitutes a good reason to turn in more detail to Nancy's account of being in terms of a *koinon* without *hen*. In what follows, I will pay special attention to the question of how Nancy reinterprets hermeneutics and its basic concepts. This, I suggest, does not distort Nancy's work since he coins the concept of *partage*, which lies at the heart of the conception of being-with and being-in-common, in his interpretation of the meaning of *hermēneuein* in Plato's dialogue *Ion*. Hence, not only another conception of plurality but also another version of Plato appears in Nancy's work, and I will contrast and compare these two Platos in chapter 3.[14]

THE STRUCTURE OF SIGNIFICATION: METAPHYSICAL REMNANTS IN CLASSICAL HERMENEUTICS

Badiou reproaches hermeneutics for its conservative tendencies: interpretation reduces an event to the already established universe of significations and does no justice to its newness. When trying to understand classical hermeneutics, it remains to be seen whether it makes sense to claim that it operates on the basis of an already established universe of significations. In the context of Badiou's account of the language of the situation and of knowledge, this claim implies that the interpreter reduces the event to that which one already knows. Read in this way, Badiou's image of an established universe of meaning paints a rather inaccurate picture of how classical hermeneutics relates interpretation, finitude, and tradition to one another.

In hermeneutics, the meaning tradition hands down and the meaning interpretation aims at is never of the order of an already established knowledge. Rather, interpretation is only needed when it is unclear what something means, when it is ambiguous. What we already know does not require interpretation. To capture how the notion of meaning operates in hermeneutics, we might compare it to the role of wisdom (*sophia*) for the philosopher (*philo-sophia*). In the *Symposium*, Plato famously notes that the philosopher longs for wisdom and is attracted by it. Yet, this longing for wisdom also demonstrates that the philosopher *lacks* it and is troubled by this lack. In the imaginary of the *Republic*, the philosopher longs for the idea of the Good.

The relation of the philosopher to the idea might be interpreted in two ways. In the first interpretation, the idea is presupposed as something that transcends the philosophers and attracts them in this way. Similarly, for classical hermeneutics, meaning is never established knowledge. It is, rather, presupposed as "transcendental signified" lying beyond the practice of interpretation, attracting and motivating interpretation, as Derrida writes.[15] Hence, meaning attracts interpretation, but interpretation is at the same time an *exile* trying to enter but never fully entering this meaning—like philosophers who, according to the logic of the *Symposium*, will never fully capture the wisdom they long for. This logic is also the logic of the finitude of understanding and interpretation in classical hermeneutics: due to this finitude, access to the absolute—in this case the transcendental signified—is denied to the interpreter. Hence, classical hermeneutics is guided by a version of the Platonic model expounded in the *Symposium*. Interpretation is marked by the presupposition of a meaning that lies beyond. Thus, interpretation becomes the quest that aims to "decipher a truth or an origin" that escapes and is the condition of possibility of the play of interpretation.[16]

In a similar fashion as Derrida, Nancy uses this logic to criticize Ricoeur's hermeneutics.[17] As he argues in *Le partage des voix*, Ricoeur's hermeneutics departs from an "adhesion to sense," which means that meaning is the "pre-given," the presupposition of every interpretation.[18] Hence, Ricoeur's hermeneutics is classical since it invokes a primordial belonging to meaning that precedes and motivates every interpretation: Ricoeur presupposes a "participation in meaning." This phrasing clearly indicates that Nancy also discerns a parallel between the concept of meaning in classical hermeneutics and the idea in Plato's thought: for Plato, a sensible being is knowable thanks to its participation (*methexis*) in the idea. As with Plato's idea, this does not mean that we already possess this meaning but, rather, that the permanence of this transcendent and transcendental meaning is presupposed so that texts and beings are interpretable. Hence, what is not thought in hermeneutics is this presupposition of meaning. Or, as Nancy puts it, the participation in meaning is never accounted for *but simply presupposed*. It is the philosophical *belief* from which hermeneutics departs without interrogating it: "Hermeneutic *belief* [*croyance*] in general is not anything other than that presupposition."[19]

A similarity imposes itself between Badiou's axiomatic decision and hermeneutics' presupposition of meaning. Despite the striking difference between the former's revolutionary and the latter's conservative attitude, they share something. In both cases, it is not a matter of an already established knowledge but, rather, of a conviction from which thought derives and which sets thought and interpretation in motion, offering a direction. In Badiou's case, this conviction is centered on the declaration that the event has taken place. For hermeneutics, conviction is a primordial trust or belief in the meaning that attracts it. Hence, in both cases, the point of departure of thought is marked by a belief that remains unexamined itself *because* it is the very point of departure and the presupposition par excellence of mathematical and classical-hermeneutical thought alike. I will return to this issue in chapter 3.

An important similarity between Badiou's and Nancy's critique of hermeneutics exists. Both argue that hermeneutic thought (or poetic thought, as Badiou calls it) operates on the basis of a typically metaphysical motive, namely, meaning as a lost origin that interpretation wants to retrieve but can never fully do so. As Nancy writes, "Thus the enterprise of meaning always begins by signifying the anterior or transcendent presence of a *meaning* that has been lost, forgotten, or altered, one that is, by definition, to be recovered, restored, or revived."[20] The hermeneutic and poetic wish to return to what has been lost leads Badiou to reject any idea of loss and to introduce the idea of the subtraction of being, as discussed in chapter 1.

Despite this similarity with Badiou, Nancy interprets this idea of a lost meaning differently. He notes that in its classical hermeneutic sense the loss of meaning is never complete. Ultimately, the loss of meaning is rooted in, preserved, and safeguarded by our belonging to meaning. Consequently, for classical hermeneutics, the loss of meaning is never a full loss, as Nancy emphasizes: "Hermeneutics requires...that the 'participation in meaning' is unaware of the absolute interruption." Elsewhere, he writes, "the crisis of the loss must appear only as a superficial accident."[21] Our participation in meaning can never be *absolutely* uprooted according to the classical hermeneutic paradigm. Also in this sense, classical hermeneutics does not arrive at the absolute.

At the same time, the presumed possible presence of meaning is never actualized. This means that the pre-sup-position of meaning always remains "pre" and "sup," *before* and *under* interpretation, but it is never brought to presence in interpretation itself. Ultimately, meaning can only be approached, and language only offers an approximation of the presentation of meaning. (In chapter 1, we found a similar concern in Badiou's claim that poetic thought offers a "trajectory of proximity.") Nancy retakes this logic in terms of the sign: "The goal of the sign, its *direction* [*sens*], is to lead to or to present meaning," but this goal is never accomplished; the "teleology of signifying presentation is thus bound to the ineffable."[22] Interestingly enough, emphasizing the parallel with the Platonic framework of philosophy once more, Nancy calls this movement of interpretation that always keeps the present meaning at a distance desire: "*Desire . . . is the empty signifier of the distant signified,* or of the distance of meaning." This meaning, for which interpretation longs, is called "signification" by Nancy in order to distinguish it from another, more primordial sense of meaning, namely, *signifiance* which means both signifyingness and significance: "Insofar as sense comes before all significations, pre-vents and over-takes them, even as it makes them possible, forming the opening of the general signifyingness [or significance: *signifiance*] (or opening of the world) in which and according to which it is first of all possible for significations to come to produce themselves."[23] This notion of significance will be explored below. For now, it is important to see that the desire characterizing the signifying process in classical hermeneutics is ultimately *metaphysical* in nature and mirrors, in our first interpretation of Plato's conception of philosophy, the philosophical desire for the idea. The task of a thought after ontotheology is therefore to understand "what *thinking* means when signification is exhausted."[24]

Nancy is subtle enough to note that the affinity of classical hermeneutics to this metaphysical motive is ambiguous. On the one hand, the practice of hermeneutics affirms that the significations found in the process of interpretation are "unstable and incomplete" due to their historical nature; this already points to a certain exhaustion of the metaphysical structure of signification. Yet, on the other hand, by its presuppositional account of meaning, hermeneutics also always places meaning at a distance. Thus, the "deep structure of signification is preserved."[25]

From Belonging to Abandonment: Being-Toward in Nancy's Plato

The parallel between signification and the Platonic idea shows that in classical hermeneutics the presupposition of meaning (as signification) repeats the ontotheological quest for the unifying ground. As Nancy suggests, "The metaphysical position is indeed always that of a *supposition,* in one or another of its forms."[26] Clearly, to overcome or even to examine this metaphysical remnant of hermeneutics, it is necessary to investigate — in the dialectical mode of Plato's *Parmenides* — what happens to these analyses when we do *not* affirm this presupposition of signification. We saw that classical hermeneutics starts with an absence or a loss of meaning. The aforementioned presupposition allows classical hermeneutics to think this absence and loss as a relative one. What happens to this loss when it is not approached in light of this presupposition? What is the situation of the interpreter *without* the presupposition of meaning?

Without this presupposition, it does not make sense to speak about a "loss" of meaning. Similarly, "absence" is no longer an adequate term because pure and total absence indicates that we are without relation to meaning at all. A pure absence of meaning might be compared to the totalization of the *Notlosigkeit* of which Heidegger speaks in the *Beiträge,* and which we discussed briefly in the introduction: in such a pure lack of need for being, being is not only withdrawn, but even the indices of this withdrawal are effaced. In the context of the *Beiträge,* Heidegger introduces the term "abandonment" (*Verlassenheit*) to indicate that our age is marked by a withdrawal of being, constituting the lack of need for being as the basic mood (*Grundstimmung*) of our age. Yet, abandonment also means that this withdrawal is not total or complete since "the few" still experience a need arising from this lack of want (*Not der Notlosigkeit*). They experience that our age belongs not to this or that meaning but, rather, to this abandonment of being (*Seinsverlassenheit*). Nancy adopts Heidegger's terminology of abandonment and applies it to the notion of meaning. Our situation is not marked by an absence or loss of signification but, rather, by being abandoned to sense.[27] This abandonment to sense expresses how the interpreter relates to a domain of sense that is "emptied of signification."[28] Banned from signification, Nancy suggests that the interpreter is abandoned to sense or meaning as significance.

Kafka's parable *Vor dem Gesetz* has given rise to many profound interpretations in contemporary thought because it evokes this experience of abandonment. In this story, Kafka portrays a man from the country who has no access to the law; he does not enter the door that leads into the law, and he remains standing outside, in front of the door and its guard. In this sense, the man from the country is banned from the law. At the same time, the door of the law is open until the end of the man's life, which is also the end of the story. As Derrida argues in his reading of this story, the door opens onto nothing: the law does not ask anything specific of the man from the country, and it has no particular signification to present.[29] One might also say that the law continually promises the man from the country access to it and to its demands without ever redeeming this promise. Of course, in the parable it is crucial that the man from the country waits indefinitely to get in. This renders the story its enigmatic character: if the door simply opens onto nothing and has nothing specific to demand or to present, why does the man from the country keep on waiting?

Whatever the answer, it is clear that, somehow, the open door represents a certain force acting on the man from the country and keeping him under its spell: he is and remains turned over to the law from which he is banned. As Giorgio Agamben puts it in his reading, the open door represents that the law is *still in force but without signification*.[30] It will come as no surprise that Agamben, while mentioning both Heidegger and Nancy, connects the formula "being in force without signification" to the structure of the ban and of abandonment since this structure describes what abandonment means for Heidegger: to be related to a nothing that has no particular signification but that somehow still matters and is significant. To account for the spell and the force that the law exerts over the man from the country, one might say that the law *is significant without signification*. The strange force of law the parable evokes might thus be conceived as a force that gives weight to things but cannot be understood as a particular signification since it precedes and is emptied of any signification.

I took this brief detour along Kafka's parable to sketch the philosophical context to which Nancy's conception of abandonment belongs. Nancy introduces this concept in his difficult and dense essay, "L'être abandonné."[31] In it, he reinterprets Heidegger's account of the abandonment of being. In fact, this essay offers the program for exploring the possibilities of an ontology after ontotheology: as he writes, abandonment concerns an understanding of being in which there is no place for the primacy of unity: "*Unum, verum, bonum*—all this is abandoned."[32] Moreover, abandoned being cannot be understood from the principle of sufficient reason: "Being is not entrusted to a cause, to a motor, to a principle.... It is—in abandonment."[33] Nancy uses "ban" and "abandonment" always in the following double sense: they mean banishment as well as enthrallment, exile as well as spell.[34] Clearly, "enthrallment" and "spell" are referring to the force with which abandonment apparently comes equipped, as we saw in the different readings of *Vor dem Gesetz:* the man from the country is under the spell and at the mercy of the law from which he is abandoned.

To a certain extent, the structure of abandonment laid bare in Kafka's parable is as old as philosophy itself. After all, the philosopher is banned from the idea of the Good to which he or she strives. In the previous section, I mentioned a number of times that the drawn parallel between signification and idea depend on a specific, first interpretation of the Platonic idea. It is now time to introduce the second interpretation that I promised a number of pages ago.

Nancy draws our attention to this second interpretation to account for what he means by "significance" in distinction from "signification."[35] In *Le sens du monde*, he refers to Socrates' account of the relation between the normal ideas and the idea of the Good (*agathōn*). Strictly speaking, the latter is not an idea since it is the cause of the existence of all the other ideas. Normal ideas are essences of sensible things; they offer the "look" of these things: the look of a house is granted by the idea of a house, and so on. Being beyond the essences, as Nancy writes, "the excellence of *agathōn* is without content: it concerns merely the position beyond essence, in this (non)region where it is no longer a matter of presenting itself (to oneself), but of being toward."[36] Essences have a specific content. Being beyond essence, *agathōn* (the Good) does not have a content, according to Nancy. *Agathōn* is, rather, that which makes these essences possible. It opens up the realm of ideas and is therefore not an idea itself. Drawing on the parallel between meaning and idea, we can rephrase Nancy's interpretation of Plato as follows. Whereas the ideas are of the order of contents or significations, *agathōn* is of the order of that which makes significations possible; that is, *agathōn* is of the order of significance. In contrast to the ideas that present themselves and are the presentable foreground of the Good—as Sallis puts it, or the presentation and the truth of the Good, as Nancy calls it in *Le sens du monde*—the Good itself is concerned with "being-toward" (*être-à*).[37]

Relating this back to his analyses in *L'oubli de la philosophie*, Nancy describes how metaphysics reinterprets this being-toward of *agathōn* in terms of a *reciprocal* desire and gift. Meaning, in this metaphysical sense, is nothing but "mutual fulfillment, ontotheoerotology achieved."[38] This latter term connects the philosophical *erōs* for the idea and for wisdom to the metaphysical constitution as ontotheology. *Onto-theo-eroto-logy* thus refers to the *presupposition* of meaning according to which the desire for meaning is the desire for something that can be appropriated. "It is quite precisely here that disaster strikes," Nancy writes.[39] Disaster strikes here because metaphysical desire remains necessarily unfulfilled. The gift of the Good is the gift of an excess. Consequently, it cannot be appropriated.

Yet, beyond the reciprocity presupposed by ontotheoerotology, the excessive nature of the Good provides us with an alternative task for thinking and a new way of conceiving the Platonic *erōs:* "To think sense as the in-appropriative encounter of desire and gift, as the excellence of the coming of the one toward to other, this is the task."[40] Hence, meaning in its primordial sense should not be understood as an appropriable signification but as the inappropriable. This inappropriable character of meaning is called "significance." Significance as well as *agathōn* interpreted in its inappropriability now discloses that the philosopher's mode of being is *being-toward*—a being-toward that is not founded in and cannot be understood out of a not-yet-appropriated idea or signification but should rather be understood out of the particular abandonment that characterizes *agathōn*: what is given to the philosopher always exceeds what can be appropriated. It is the task of thinking to affirm this excess: rather than striving for appropriation, the philosopher's desire "should desire essentially not to appropriate."[41] Only in this way, by being enthralled by something it cannot appropriate, can it do justice to its object.

Let us reflect briefly on the expression that is crucial here in Nancy's reinterpretation of Plato's *agathōn* and the accompanying movement of an *erōs* that should no longer be determined as a strife for appropriation but as *a desire not to appropriate:* "one toward the other." One might be inclined to read this sentence as follows: one being—the philosopher—toward another being—the idea of the Good. However, it is clear from the previous comments that the Good should not be understood as yet another idea, but it should also not be understood in Emmanuel Levinas's sense as that which is beyond being or which is the outside of being. Rather, in Nancy's reading, *agathōn* expresses that being is always being-toward (*être-à*). Although the Good is the outside *toward* which the philosopher *is,* the term "outside" should not be understood as another space, another realm (than being) or another being. Rather, the Good as the outside should be understood as a threshold that is the very disclosure toward something other. We find a similar account of the outside as threshold in the work of Agamben, whose description of the outside as threshold illuminates Nancy's account of the Good:

> It is important here that the notion of the "outside" is expressed in many European languages by a word that means "at the door" (*fores* in Latin is the door of the house, *thyrathen* in Greek literally means "at the threshold"). The *outside* is not another space that resides beyond a determinate space, but rather, it is the passage, the exteriority that gives access....

> The threshold is not, in this sense, another thing with respect to the limit; it is so to speak, the experience of the limit itself, the experience of being-*within* an *outside*.[42]

Note that the latter sentence, which determines the threshold as "the experience of being-*within* an *outside*," might be interpreted in Nancy's vocabulary as another way to address the theme of abandonment: *agathōn* is not another being that can be appropriated; it is, rather, our always being outside ourselves and being toward something else; it is ek-sistence. Thanks to the primacy of abandonment over signification, it becomes possible to experience that significations are no *archai* but refer to something else, as the ideas refer for their existence back to the Good. Abandonment interrupts the presupposition of signification by suspending significations. Thus, abandonment is not a purely negative phenomenon: it discloses "that *signification in no way yields the 'meaning' of its own production* or of its own advent."[43] This second "meaning" beyond and before signification is the realm of *signifiance*. Moreover, as Nancy's discussion of *agathōn* shows, this realm of significance should ontologically be understood in terms of *être-à*, of one-being-toward-the-other, in which both related entities are always related to the other but never in the mode of being-appropriable or in the mode of a reciprocity but, rather, in terms of a permanent being-on-the-threshold. As Kafka's man from the country is always on the threshold of a law that does not open onto a hidden signification but rather toward a compelling nothing that is significance, we cannot appropriate significance but we can nevertheless desire not to appropriate it. Such would be the second interpretation of Plato's account of the relation between *agathōn* and *erōs*.

KOINON WITHOUT HEN: ON HERMENEUTICS AS PARTAGE

To deepen our understanding of Nancy's unique position and his differentiation between *signification* and *signifiance*, I now return to *Le partage des voix*. In this essay, he coins his basic concept of *partage*—meaning at the same time sharing-in and sharing-out or dividing—by reinterpreting the Greek term *hermēneuein*. As I said before, Nancy is in discussion with Gadamer and Ricoeur in this text.

In particular, he introduces the concept of *partage* as an alternative to the classical hermeneutic presupposition par excellence, the participation in meaning.

Le partage des voix is composed of two parts. In the first part, Nancy aims to show that Heidegger's account of interpretation (*Auslegung*) in *Sein und Zeit* should not be understood in terms of a participation in a pre-given and appropriable meaning but should, rather, be understood in terms of the opening up and announcement (*Kundgabe*) of meaning. Nancy's reading of Heidegger in the first part of his essay depends heavily on the claim that the distinction between a secondary form of hermeneutics as interpretation and a primary form of hermeneutics as announcement, which stems from Heidegger's later work, can already be traced in *Sein und Zeit* and in his early lectures on the hermeneutics of facticity. Yet, in these earlier texts, Heidegger seems to distinguish interpretation and announcement as two moments of the same hermeneutics without placing them in a specific hierarchy, as he will later.[44] Nevertheless, in *Unterwegs zur Sprache*, he does make a distinction between a primordial meaning of *hermēneuein* as announcement and the more general meaning of hermeneutics as the art of interpretation. Although he is still interested in the former, primordial meaning, he prefers to abandon the term "hermeneutics" because it is intrinsically connected to the concept of interpretation (*Auslegung*).

Nancy develops his own enterprise out of this latter suggestion: whereas interpretation remains the main focus of classical hermeneutics, it is the task of philosophy to rethink the meaning of hermeneutics in terms of an announcement more primordial than interpretation. In particular, Nancy follows up on Heidegger's suggestion that this more primordial meaning of *hermēneuein* as the bringing of a message (*Kunde bringen*) and making known or announcing (*Bekunden*) can be found in Plato's dialogue *Ion*.[45] Therefore, the second part of *Le partage des voix* is devoted to an exploration of this more original meaning of *hermēneuein* by interpreting the *Ion*. In this way, Nancy aims to transform hermeneutics and create a conception of hermeneutics different from the classical one. This new conception of hermeneutics also leads to a different conception of what a dialogue is, as he indicates when explaining the way in which he reads Plato's dialogues: "the object of the *Meno*, the *Theaetetus*, the *Sophist*, the *Symposium*, in order only to cite them, is it not always likewise the dialogue or the dialogicity as such?"[46] Hence, the dialogues of Plato do not only discuss this or that theme or content, they also disclose what the nature of a dialogue is and what the essence of language as dialogue is. For such a reflection on Plato's dialogues, the *Ion* is of particular interest, as we shall see.

In the *Ion*, the verb *hermēneuein* and its related noun *hermēneus* (interpreter) apply to two figures: the poet and the rhapsode. Poets are interpreters of the gods, but not in the sense of the ones who explicate or understand the words of the gods. Rather, poets provide the gods with a voice. The poets are the voice of the gods since the latter have no voice of their own. Consequently, in this light hermeneutics is first and foremost concerned with *speaking on behalf of the other* rather than with interpretation.[47] In fact, in the *Ion*, one sees most clearly that the realm in which interpretation and understanding can take place—which is also the realm in which the words of the gods might first receive their signification—is disclosed and announced by the speech and the song of the poets. Without the poetic activity, neither a voice to be heard nor a word to be understood exists. In fact, the distinction between the disclosure of the realm of signification by the *hermēneutes* and the interpretation of the words that are spoken is distinctly present in the *Ion*. Socrates ironically notes that as long as a human has its mind "in him," he "is powerless to indite a verse or chant an oracle."[48]

The poet and the rhapsode thus do not speak with understanding but rather speak out of *enthusiasm:* the gods speak in them. They are banned from understanding these words, yet turned over to the enthusiasm that makes them sing. Thus, in the form of this enthusiasm by which the muses cast their spell over poets and the rhapsodes, the structure of abandonment becomes a determining factor in Nancy's account of this dialogue. The poet is out of his wits. He is outside of himself, and he is banned from the meaning of the words he speaks. Yet, this seemingly negative phenomenon has a positive counterpart in the enthrallment and the enthusiasm that inspire the poet to sing; he is entrusted to and abandoned to the muses.[49] (Of course, in Plato's dialogues, not only the poet or the rhapsode but also the philosopher is turned over to this form of *mania,* albeit in a different way. I will come back to Nancy's interpretation of this relation between poetry and philosophy.)

To describe the type of transmission to which the poet's song gives rise, Socrates uses the famous image of the iron rings transmitting a magnetic *power*. The poet as well as the rhapsode is like one of those rings: they do not communicate a particular signification, but *a divine power or potential* (*theia dunamis*) in which they share and in which they let their audience share.[50] This is what makes this dialogue such an attractive starting point for Nancy: in voicing divine words, the poet is banned from the realm of signification.[51] Instead of singing "out of himself," the poet speaks for the gods and is-toward the other. As Nancy writes elsewhere on the opening words of Homer's *Iliad,* "Homer does not write himself: he lets the divine voice sing. He, the poet (*aēde*), sings while he interprets the divine song."[52] Thus, the poetic transmission of a divine power offers a paradigm for Nancy's being-toward.

The rhapsode, in turn, is the interpreter of the poet; hence, he is the interpreter of the interpreter. Due to this doubling, one might be inclined to consider the rhapsode to be further away from the original, poetic inspiration and, hence, to share in the divine power in a lesser way and to communicate a lesser potential. However, as Nancy argues, this is not the case. In the *Ion,* the rhapsode never represents a form of decay or "debasement" (*dégradation*) of the divine power that originally inspired the poet. The divine potential remains intact. In fact, the rhapsode completes *the transmissibility and circulation of the divine force as such:* "the divine force is transmitted intact — but exactly as it *is to be transmitted,* and it is with the second ring that it manifests entirely this property."[53]

In this context Nancy coins his famous notion of *partage* as an alternative to Ricoeur's participation in meaning. Remarkably enough, he does not introduce it as a translation of *methexis,* but rather as the translation of *theia moira,* or divine dispensation (*partage divin*). Socrates uses the expression *theia moira* to describe how the poet receives his (limited) ability "to compose that to which the Muse has stirred him."⁵⁴ *Partage* (sharing in/sharing out) describes how the poets and the rhapsodes share in, divide, and multiply the divine power by putting their words into circulation. *Partage* is thus a form of sharing that takes place as division and multiplication. As Nancy emphasizes again and again, there is no unity of the voice of the god outside of this sharing (*partage*) of voices. The only (divine) voice that is given is the sharing and dividing of voices. This places the structure of abandonment at the heart of the sharing of voices: meaning "is abandoned to [*abandonner à*] the sharing [*partage*], to the hermeneutic law of the difference between voices, and that it is not *a gift*, anterior and exterior to our voices and our orations."⁵⁵

The primacy of *partage* does not only apply to the divine logos in the *Ion;* it also applies to divine existence: *the divine is nothing but the enthusiasm* of the poets and the rhapsodes, as Nancy writes.⁵⁶ Moreover, this enthusiasm exists only in and as its transmission and circulation; it exists only as movement from one to the other. Hence, the mode of being of the divine and of enthusiasm is nothing but being-toward, as Nancy also affirms in his account of the opening words of Homer's *Iliad*. There we see even more clearly that the poet's enthusiasm is a desire to speak. For Nancy, the opening phrase of the *Iliad*—"Sing, o goddess..."—is a testimony to the existence of the goddess, who is nothing but the *desire to speak* itself.⁵⁷ Moreover, for the *hermēneus,* this is the desire to "present the goddess" and "to let her be heard in the hermeneut's proper voice by which he convokes her."⁵⁸ This shows that the interpreter's desire to speak is the desire to speak for the other. Hence, the poet discloses in his poetic speech the ontological mode of being-toward. Here we see how the being-toward Nancy traced in his account of Plato's *agathōn* and the philosopher's *erōs* has an equivalent in his account of the poet's song, which is a desire toward the other exemplified by the poet's speaking for the other.

After this long exposition of the connection between abandonment, enthusiasm, and *partage,* it is now time to show how the notion of the poet's and rhapsode's sharing (*partage*) in a divine power offers a new, hermeneutic model of a *koinon* without *hen*.

Transmissibility and Communicability

In many texts, Nancy argues that meaning in its original sense (that is, as significance), should be understood in terms of circulation and communication. Sense is like a chain(ing) (*enchaînement*) that both relates and keeps apart the singular elements it connects.[59] This conception of sense goes back to his account of hermeneutics in light of the concept of sharing as *partage*. The figure of Hermes, who brings messages, guides Nancy's account of hermeneutics. Yet, hermeneutics' primordial communication does not concern a particular message or signification that the ones who communicate have in common or will have in common thanks to this communication. His account of the *Ion* shows that the poet only communicates the power and the potential to communicate: since the divine is nothing but the enthusiasm to communicate and to be-communicating, *the divine power or potential* (dunamis) *is nothing but communicability or transmissibility itself*. Agamben illustrates what Nancy aims at: "We can communicate with others only through what in us—as much as in others—has remained potential, and any communication...is first of all communication not of something in common but of communicability itself."[60] What poet, rhapsode, and audience have in common due to the poetic communication is not this or that signification. Rather, they are "communicability itself" at the moment of communication, and they transmit transmissibility itself. This potential to communicate is conveyed in the communication and at the moment of poetic or rhapsodic song. Also in the *Ion,* the divine *dunamis* is nothing but the poet's potential to transmit.

This difference between *having* in common and *being* in common is applied to the notion of sense: Nancy distinguishes between *having* sense, which refers to a transcendent signification, and *being* sense, or significance, which refers to a sharing that is nothing but transmission and communication.[61] It is the latter sense *that we are,* and of which Nancy speaks so often: "But we are meaning in the sense that we are the element in which significations can be produced and circulate."[62] As he writes elsewhere, "Sense is consequently not the 'signified' or the 'message': it is *that something like transmission of a 'message' should be possible.* It is the relation as such and nothing else."[63] Primordially, meaning is significance as transmissibility and communicability. To be-toward as to be-in-common is *the potential to communicate from one to the other.*

The Event of the In-Common

The enthusiasm of poets and rhapsodes exists only in the enactment of the song, that is, in the very taking place of announcement. Contrasting sense (in a primordial sense) to signification, Nancy writes: "sense is not what is communicated but *that* there is communication."[64] This quote indicates that the phenomenon of meaning is not exhausted by the famous distinction between connotation and denotation, or between sense and reference. Rather, these two dimensions of meaning concerning the meaning of what is said and the object to which it is referred both depend on language taking place. They depend on the event "*that* there is communication."

Nancy's interpretation of the *Ion* is thus a very fortunate one and goes against the grain of Socrates' ironic tone of voice in this dialogue.[65] What Socrates considers to be the deficiency and weakness of the poet and the rhapsode—they do not understand what they say—is turned into the privilege of the poetic position in Nancy's reading. In the *Ion,* the poet's interpretation is not concerned with grasping the meaning of what is said simply because the poet is not capable of this. In Nancy's reinterpretation, however, the poetic voice is the place in language where both connotation and denotation are suspended: the poetic voice presupposes neither an already given meaning that it expresses nor the existence of the objects about which it speaks. Since it is mere enthusiasm that inspires the poet, the poetic voice is the locus in language that discloses the taking place of language as the taking place of the in-common in our speech. Language is "the event of an outside," to borrow Agamben's words.[66]

Moreover, for Nancy this event of the voice is a way of addressing the other by speaking for an (other) other. Hence, what takes place in our speech is our being-outside-ourselves and our being-toward-the-other. In this sense, being-toward requires an understanding of being as event; as the example of poetic speech shows, being-toward and being-in-common is the event of being. The plurality of which Nancy is speaking here concerns a sharing that *takes place* in and as communication. A clearer difference with Badiou's conception of plurality is unthinkable: for him the event is trans-being; for Nancy, being is event.

Dialogue without Consensus

Finally, Nancy's reading of the *Ion* develops a new conception of dialogue. As noted above, the notion of dialogue guides Nancy's reading of Plato's *Dialogues*. To clarify his conception of dialogue, it is important to see first why he claims no poetics in general exists according to the logic of *Ion*.

To demonstrate that poets and rhapsodes are led by enthusiasm rather than by knowledge (*epistēmē*) or art (*technē*), Socrates points out that poets are only capable of poeticizing well in the particular style to which the muses impel them.[67] This means, as Nancy points out, that the poetic genre consists only in a multiplicity of styles. There is no general principle in poetics that would allow us to discern a poetic knowledge or even a poetic art. Apparently, a plurality of styles forms the (non-)essence of poetry. However, this does not mean that there is no poetic in-common: they share enthusiasm; they share the divine power that is equally distributed to all but that only grants a poet access to a *singular* voice, as Nancy points out: "There is then a sharing, an originary difference between genres or poetic voices and perhaps, behind the scenes, a sharing of poetic and philosophic genres. There is no general poetry, and with regards to general poetics, the existence of which has been admitted in principle, it remains undiscoverable: but it is here, of course, that it exposes itself. There are only contrasting singular voices, and the enthusiasm is first of all the entrance into one such singularity."[68] Hence, the poetic genre provides us with a model of the singular plural: the *koinon* of the multiplicity of poetic genres cannot be reduced to a general principle; it only exists in a plurality of singular styles and voices.

In this quote, Nancy also suggests that the philosophical genre shares in the poetic genre. Badiou would probably interpret this as a perfect example of the suture of philosophy to poetry marking the thought of Heidegger and his heirs: philosophy as yet another poetic voice. Yet, what does this "suture" mean? Nancy examines the implications of this suture for the composition of the *Ion*. The voices spoken and interpreted in this dialogue are those of Socrates, the philosopher; Homer, the poet; and Ion, the rhapsode. Hence, the dialogue itself is enacted as the singular plural of poetic voices. The dialogue is the linguistic locus where all singular voices *are being shared without being merged into one*. When we would ask what a dialogue is, Nancy answers, "the *dia-logue* can only be, perhaps, another name for the *theia moira*, that is to say, *hermēneia*."[69] Dialogue is the event of the sharing of voices.

With this conception of *hermēneia* and dialogue, we are no longer in the domain of classical hermeneutics. For classical hermeneutics, as Gadamer indicates, a dialogue is marked by a quest for *Einverständnis*, that is, for agreement. Literally, *Ein-verständnis* can be translated as "one-understanding." This literal translation is quite in line with the goal of dialogue, as Gadamer sees it. According to him, the partners in conversation aim to speak with a common language (*gemeinsame Sprache*) and a common formulation (*gemeinsamer Spruch*) about the subject matter they discuss.[70] For him, agreement and a common language constitute the end of dialogue. Hence, when Badiou criticizes the moment of consensus in interpretation, which I discussed in chapter 1, he points to a motive that can definitely be found in the classical hermeneutical model of Gadamer and Ricoeur. For Nancy, however, dialogue is a sharing of language in the sense of *partage*. This sharing is not teleological in nature and does not strive for agreement. In fact, Nancy agrees with Badiou's rejection of the motive of consensus, but he does not agree with Badiou that a dialogue is *necessarily* oriented toward consensus: "*Logos* is *dialogue*, but the end [or purpose] of dialogue is not to overcome itself in 'consensus'; its reason is to offer, and only to offer (giving it tone and intensity), the *cum-*, the *with* of meaning, the plurality of its springing forth."[71] Although a dialogue usually implies that we have a subject matter in common, the essence of dialogue concerns the sharing of voices: the singular plural that marks being-with-one-another in conversation constitutes the meaning that we are. Yet, when each partner in conversation speaks with a singular voice, addresses the other(s), and is addressed by the other(s), this does not mean that this speaking-together aims at a shared understanding. Their common speech might very well imply conflict and even enmity.[72] Yet, conflict and enmity presuppose that those who are in conflict are somehow related. As I discussed in chapter 1, Badiou's claim that thought is oriented by a preceding decision concerning an axiom necessarily implies that no true conflict can arise. The only real conflict that could arise concerns these axioms, but they are already decided upon in Badiou's account of thought. Between the classical hermeneutic account of thought that depends on strife for agreement and the speculative account of thought that insists on a nonrelated, nonshared multiplicity of positions, Nancy's conception of dialogue provides a model of thought that allows for genuine disagreement and a genuine conflict based on speaking-with-one-another.

Koinon without *Hen:* Nancy's Ontology of Plurality

Dialogue as the sharing of voices does not only transform classical hermeneutics, but it is also the model for Nancy's ontology of "being singular plural." In this new ontology, sharing, abandonment and sense form the basic concepts. Combining our previous results with Nancy's comments on sense and sharing in *Être singulier pluriel,* where he writes in the opening pages that "sense itself is the sharing of being [*le partage de l'être*]," we might summarize the connection between these concepts as follows. We are abandoned to the sharing of sense.[73] This means that no supreme being or master signifier transcends and structures this sharing. Therefore, the in-common expressed by this sharing is indeed a *koinon* without *hen.* Moreover, the metaphysical conception of the *koinon,* which I discussed in my introduction, abstracts from the actual existences of particular beings in order to determine what they have in common. Thus, the metaphysical *koinon* is the greatest common denominator of modes of being. Nancy's conception of *partage,* however, approaches the question of the *koinon* from a completely different angle: the koinon cannot be approached by a method of abstracting but concerns the very existence and occurrence of singular beings in their togetherness. In this sense, his ontology is an "ontology of being-with-one-another [*l'être-les-uns-avec-les-autres*]."[74]

Moreover, Nancy's account of plurality offers an alternative to Badiou's account of pure multiplicity as well as to Ricoeur's participation. Badiou does not think how singular elements are related on an ontological level, whereas Ricoeur presupposes a reciprocal relation between them. Badiou denies the possibility of sharing and dialogue, whereas Ricoeur interprets "sharing" in terms of analogy and agreement. Nancy's conception of "the sharing of singularities" (*le partage des singularités*) shows how he is capable of avoiding these two positions.[75] On the one hand, this sharing as *partage* implies that he does not affirm Badiou's claim that being is "what is not shared" (*l'impartageable*).[76] On the other hand, by emphasizing that singularities are sharing, he indicates that one being has no access to the other's; a being does not only share being with another being but is also abandoned *from and to* it. An account of analogy and agreement always presupposes a more general perspective from which we can judge whether two modes of being are analogous or in agreement.

Ex-Position versus Pre-Sup-Position

The structure of supposition and presupposition is typical for metaphysics, as we saw before. Metaphysics is marked by the act of positing something permanent underneath—sub-ject and sub-stance—that is given in advance, thus to pre-sup-pose it. Agamben's comment on Aristotle's understanding of first substance illustrates Nancy's interpretation of metaphysics. As Agamben notes on several occasions, Aristotle's account of *protē ousia* as *to ti ēn einai*—"Being-the-what-that-was"—refers to a past, to a having been (a "pre"), and indicates that the first substance was what it is. Hence, by positing substance, Aristotelian metaphysics departs from a pre-sup-position.[77] In fact, as Agamben continues, substance is "the absolute presupposition on which all knowledge and discourse are founded." However, since it remains inaccessible and cannot be said, it remains ineffable.[78]

These comments on Aristotle's *protē ousia* perfectly reflect Nancy's critique of the presuppositional structure of metaphysics, "the structure of signification," which I discussed before: signification is presupposed but it is presupposed as what can never be appropriated in language; hence, it borders on the ineffable, as Nancy also notes. This is metaphysics as ontotheoerotology.

To overcome this suppositional structure and to introduce an alternative, Nancy replaces sup- by ex- and goes from under- to out-.[79] In line with my analyses above on being-toward in Nancy's Plato, it will come as no surprise that an alternative to the structure of presupposition should be related to the notion of abandonment. Indeed, as Nancy writes in *Le sens du monde*, it is the "exposition to the abandonment of sense that makes up our lives."[80] Hence, the interruption of the structure of sup-position ex-poses us to the abandonment of meaning and abandons us to the sharing of meaning. Translated in ontological terms, this means that the existence of beings should not be presupposed as that toward which language and interpretation strives, but this existence should be understood as exposure and as exposition in which the abandonment of meaning comes to presence.[81]

To be precise, the notion of exposition combines three related but different layers of meaning: (a) exposition in the sense of being-exposed to what is other and what is to come, (b) exposition in the sense of appearing and coming to presence, and finally, (c) exposition in the sense of the German *Auseinandersetzung;* this term does not only mean dispute but also refers to the encounter and the setting apart of opinions in such a dispute.

As the first of these three meanings indicates, the turn from sup- to ex- can also be read as a turn from presupposition to *ek-sistence* as the basic character of our existence. *Ek-sistence* might be translated literally as "standing out"—awaiting what is to come, stretching out to the other—and this clearly resounds in its German form *Ausstand* and the verb *ausstehen*, which appear in Heidegger's account of Dasein's relation to its own death.[82] In *Sein und Zeit*, Dasein's own death is that which is *always* to come. It is never present for Dasein and thus Dasein can only be-toward-death as its ultimate and most extreme possibility.[83] For Heidegger, this phenomenon discloses that the mode of being of Dasein is being-exposed-to death and being-toward-death as that which is not present, has never been present, and will never be present, but is always imminent and is always to come. For Heidegger, death is thus the phenomenon of a threshold marking that Dasein is always already outside itself and is always exposed to this threshold marking its own "having-been-there."

The formulations of being-toward-death and being-exposed-to indicate an affinity of Nancy's work with Heidegger on these matters. Yet, unlike Heidegger, Nancy does not grant the phenomenon of death a privileged place.[84] Nancy's interest in plurality forms the main reason for this difference. For him, an understanding of being-toward and being-exposed-to in terms of the phenomenon of death alone misses one crucial aspect of this being-toward. This aspect can already be found in the phenomenon of being-with. Whereas death manifests our being-exposed-to by relating us to our nonbeing—we are exposed to the possibility of our nonbeing from our very birth—the encounter with other beings also manifests our being-exposed-to, albeit in a different way. Since every being we encounter is a condition for who we are, the threshold to which we are exposed in our existence is not only nonbeing but also being-other, which occurs every time and everywhere we are with others and with other beings. That is to say, at every moment of our existence. Hence, for Nancy, the singularity of our existence is not found solely (or primordially) in the phenomenon of death since singularity should first and foremost be thought in relation to the sharing (*partage*) of being. Singularity appears not in the quasi solitude of Dasein which is resolutely open to the ultimate possibility of its own impossibility, but singularity exists only in and as the sharing of singularities.

Perhaps we might say that, in this context, Nancy prefers the Heidegger who reads Friedrich Hölderlin to the Heidegger who analyses death in *Sein und Zeit*. Whereas in *Sein und Zeit* the phenomenon of death brings us to our ownmost experience of our existence, Heidegger's reading of Hölderlin interprets the dialogue or *Auseinandersetzung* Hölderlin had with the Greek poets when translating them as the only realm in which he could experience the essence of his own (German) language.[85] Thus, in this reading of Hölderlin, it is not the experience of one's own nonbeing but, rather, the experience of a foreign language and the detour along a foreign realm that allows Hölderlin to experience the essence of his own language. In line with this example from Heidegger, we might say that the first and the third meaning of exposition belong together for Nancy, who accounts for our ek-sistence as exposition in terms of the model of dialogue and of our being exposed to what is other.

The dialogical model also inspires the second meaning of exposition as appearing and coming to presence. Following Arendt's suggestion that we only truly appear in the world when we begin to act or begin to speak, Nancy adds that, consequently, every appearance is co-appearance (*comparution*): in a dialogue, our speech is never a soliloquy; it always occurs as a sharing of voices. As soon as we begin to speak we expose ourselves to the responses and words of the others, and we expose the words we speak to the unpredictable movement of a dialogue. *The movement of dialogue is thus the event of pluralizing itself.* No idea exists that could guide, regulate, master, or harmonize in advance the pluralizing occurring in human acting, speaking, and existing.

Here, the difference between Nancy and Badiou, to which I already alluded earlier, is most visible. By detaching the plural (being) from the singular (event), Badiou proposes a conception of the event as ultra-one, as "an excess-of-one."[86] Similarly, the generic set, which is the ontological form of the truth of the event, is necessarily counted-as-one in the state of the situation.[87] Hence, although the event opens up something radically new with respect to the situation, the subject's procedure is a way of letting one's life be guided by an idea and the incorporation of this idea, as Badiou puts it in *Second manifeste pour la philosophie*. In this sense, Badiou's subject is never *exposed* in Nancy's sense of the word because such an exposition implies a pluralizing. Badiou's subject, however, is not affected by a plurality but by an ultra-one. This difference between Nancy and Badiou concerning the notion of the event ultimately goes back to a different temporality and phenomenality of the event, as I will discuss in part 2.

Beyond Resemblance and Analogy

In chapter 1, I briefly discussed how speculative thought problematizes the notions of resemblance and analogy and how these notions played a crucial role in classical hermeneutics. With these concepts and the way they are used in the hermeneutic account of metaphor, mimesis, and being, classical hermeneutics aims to overcome the classical pairs such as *self and other* and *univocity and equivocity*. As Badiou and Deleuze claim, these concepts remain indebted to the ontotheological paradigm of metaphysics. They offer alternatives to these concepts in their account of the multiplicity and the univocity of being, respectively.[88] Yet, these solutions also suggest that they do not truly solve the tension with which thought has to deal when confronted with these pairs: they end up by privileging one of the two poles of the pair *one and many*. Hence, while classical hermeneutics aims to overcome these philosophical pairs in a set of concepts that runs the risk of remaining too close to the ontotheological model, Badiou's solution runs the risk of *merely* putting the metaphysical privileging of the one over the many upside down by his axiomatic decision for the many. Is such a mere reversal of metaphysics enough to overcome the metaphysical framework?

In the context of these questions, Nancy's account of plurality offers a more promising approach: he does not only aim to overcome the sheer opposition between self and other and between one and many (as the classical hermeneutical school does), but at the same time he does not do this in terms of resemblance and analogy.

In light of our previous discussions, it is not difficult to see that the notions of resemblance and analogy are indeed foreign to Nancy's work. *Resemblance* concerns that which two beings *have* in common and not their *being*-in-common as such. In its classical and medieval interpretation, *analogy* (in the sense of the analogy of being) is usually introduced in a reading of the famous passage from Aristotle's *Metaphysics* on being that is said in many ways. Although being is not univocal, it is also not equivocal, as if the multiple uses of the word "being" would indicate the homonymous character of the word.

Rather, as Aristotle points out, the different meanings of being all point to one (*pros hen*) primordial, core meaning; for instance, *protē ousia* or primary substance.[89] For this reason, the notion of analogy is usually related to the ontotheological dimension of metaphysics in the broader sense with which Heidegger uses it to describe the tendency in philosophy to interpret being as a being, namely, as that being that *is* in an eminent way, as explained in my introduction.

To illustrate the alternative Nancy's work offers, consider the following striking quote from Agamben's *Means without End:* "There are two words in Latin that derive from the Indo-European root meaning 'one': *similis,* which expresses resemblance, and *simul,* which means 'at the same time.' Thus, next to *similitude* (resemblance) there is *simultas,* that is, the fact of being together (which implies also rivalry, enmity); and next to *similar* (to be like) there is *simulare* (to copy, to imitate, which also implies to feign, to simulate)."[90] This quote introduces a distinction between *simil* and *simul.* The first term *simil* is related to *resemblance* and to *similar.* Thus, this term provides an appropriate label for the mode of being Ricoeur already described as being-as and which motivates his hermeneutic ontology: when explicating the ontological ground of poetic notions such as metaphor and mimesis, Ricoeur points exactly to this ontological mode of being-as.[91] Indeed, the word *simil* (as well as *simul*) is derived from the Indo-European root meaning "one": this affirms what I have argued thus far with the help of both Badiou and Nancy, namely, that Ricoeur's conception of being-as remains indebted to a privileging of the one.

By contrast, the term *simul* refers to "at the same time"; thus, it is a mode of "being together," as Agamben suggests above: being-one-with-the-other. In addition, Agamben's account of *simulare* meaning copying or imitating should not be understood in terms of an Aristotelian account of mimesis that originates in the concept of mimesis, but in Plato's account of this term. For Plato, mimesis implies the presence of both the original and the copy. That is, also the possibility of simulacrum is given in this notion of *simul,* which also inspired Deleuze's reflections on Plato's mimesis and simulacrum, as we saw in chapter 1. In the case of simulacrum, *simul* refers to the being-together of what appears and what is hidden: a simulacrum appears as a copy although it is not a copy.

In sum, where *simil* refers to a being-together of multiple beings regulated by a similarity between the beings, *simul* refers to a being-together of multiple beings that is not regulated in this way and, hence, allows for difference, dissimilitude, and enmity. In the example of the copy, this difference can be seen in the "copy" that may be both like and unlike the original. In the first case, the copy represents the original; in the second case, it hides the original and becomes a simulacrum.

Both notions offer us the means to think beyond the strict alternative of one or many, but they do so in different ways. *Simil* approaches the many in light of their resemblance and being-as, with the problems attached to it that I discussed above. *Simul* does not posit a resemblance between the many beings but, rather, stresses the different modes of being-together. A thought guided by resemblance and by the movement of metaphor is a thought that moves from the familiar to the unfamiliar in order to understand the unfamiliar in light of its resemblance with the familiar—it is exactly this aspect of classical hermeneutic thought that Badiou rejects since it obscures the emergence of the radically new. A thought guided by *simul*, however, keeps the possibility open that the unfamiliar remains unfamiliar and thus allows for a model in which the unfamiliar is encountered as such.

Applied to the model of dialogue, this difference reads as follows. A thought guided by *simil* is oriented toward agreement on the subject matter under discussion. A thought guided by *simul* is oriented toward the sharing of irreducible voices in the simultaneity of different speakers in a dialogue, who need not agree. Differently put, in this latter model one does not discuss, share, or communicate convictions in order to arrive at a shared conviction on the subject matter; rather, one shares convictions to pluralize them: although the convictions of both speakers may be affected and altered in a dialogue, they do not speak with one tongue or one voice at the end of the dialogue.

Dialogue is, rather, the locus in which pluralizing takes place because it brings different convictions and different voices into play *at the same time*.

In line with the above considerations, Nancy's emphasis on being-together develops an account of self and other and of the one and the many in line with the concept of *simul*. He writes: "Community is that singular ontological order in which the other and the same are alike (*sont le semblable*)."[92] The equality or likeness of self and other is not based on a resemblance but on the sharing that marks their being. This primacy of being-one-with-the-other guides Nancy's determination of both the one and the other. It does not make sense to conceive of the one in ontological terms, "unless the one, in general, is first thought in terms of with-one-another."[93] Similarly, he writes with regard to the other: "the other turns out to be *the other of the with*."[94] Thus, Nancy prefers the *we* (*nous*) over both the one and the other. "We," then, is not a collective of unrelated ones, nor is it a collective of ones that resemble one another in this or that way. "We" is the name for how the one and the other are always already at the same time together. Whereas *simil* and "being-as" mediate between the one and the many based on the model of the *analogue*, *simul* and "we" take as their model the sharing that occurs in *dialogue*.

Three

Beyond Presupposition
Plato and Agamben

> "Was philosophy not perhaps the discourse that wanted to free itself of all presuppositions?"
>
> "Are we capable today of no longer being philosophers of the letter, without thereby becoming either philosophers of the voice or mere enthusiasts?"
> — Giorgio Agamben, *Potentialities*

Two Platos: Mathematics versus Dialogue

After the long discussions of the ontological trajectories Badiou and Nancy propose, it is now time for an assessment. To what extent do these trajectories offer a valid alternative for ontotheology? In the previous two chapters, I showed how both Badiou and Nancy criticize classical hermeneutic for not being able to think the absolute and to remain on the level of language in their account of plurality. They also agree that despite the affirmation of plurality on the level of language, history, and culture, classical hermeneutics remains a captive of the ontotheological presupposition *of the one* in its conception of being. In this context, they do not only develop an alternative ontology of plurality overcoming the presupposition of the one, but they both also offer a conception of the event. Among the different notions and concepts, it seems quite clear that the event is the central category to which the quest for the absolute leads them. Thus, by introducing the concept of the event, their ontologies are not only concerned with a critique of the presupposition of the one but, rather, with the structure of presupposition as such. Ontology after ontotheology has the task to overcome this structure. Therefore, this chapter will assess their ontologies in light of the following question: what remains of the structure of presupposition in Badiou's and Nancy's thought?

In the previous chapters, I staged the difference between Badiou and Nancy as a difference between two Platos. For Badiou, the difference between the hermeneutic and the speculative schools reiterates the old distinction between the pre-Platonic *poeme* and the platonic *matheme*. A thought that takes the platonic *matheme* as its point of departure is guided by the conviction that human beings *can* access the absolute and can have access to universal truths even though they are merely finite.[1] However, Badiou's claim that the poetic orientation of philosophy is nothing but pre-Platonic is put to the test in Nancy's reading of the *Ion*. He shows that the poetic-hermeneutic account of being as plurality and *partage* is rooted in the platonic text. This difference might also be considered to be a difference between two dialogues. While the early dialogue *Ion* incites to an account of plurality in terms of dialogic sharing, the later dialogue *Parmenides* inspires to drawing the consequences from the hypothesis that the one is not and provides, as in a dream, a thought of being in terms of multiplicities.

Rather than choosing one of these two Platos, it might be more fruitful to consider why both Platos are at best partial Platos. For instance, Badiou rejects Plato's remark that philosophy in the sense of dialectics and unlike mathematics does not depart from a hypothesis or an axiom but rather aims to find that which is without hypothesis, the *anupotheton*.[2] Nancy's Plato, conversely, places us from the outset in the position of a hermeneutics that lacks understanding and is even banned from it. Yet, he can only do so by neglecting the Socratic irony with which the poetic and rhapsodic incapacity to understand is addressed. It leaves one with the question of whether understanding does not offer an important alternative to poetic enthusiasm. A third Plato, Agamben's, illustrates what implications these interpretative choices of Badiou and Nancy in their reading of Plato have for the issue of ontotheology, and in particular for the issue of the presupposition. As the motto to this chapter shows, this third Plato is concerned first and foremost with dialectics and with reaching into the *anupotheton*. Thus, I will examine where to locate dialectics between Badiou's mathematics and Nancy's dialogue.

Supporting the Axiom

Let us return to the Platonic difference between dialectics and mathematics to which I already referred in chapter 1. In the famous comment on the *anupotheton* in the *Republic,* Socrates notes that dialectics, in contrast to geometry, does not treat its hypotheses *as absolute beginnings* (*archē*) that are not interrogated further but *as hypotheses* in order to arrive at that which requires no hypothesis (*anupotheton*). Dialectics treats "assumptions not as absolute beginnings but literally as hypotheses (*hupotheseis*), underpinnings, footings, and springboards so to speak, to enable it to rise to that which requires no assumption (*anupotheton*) and is the starting-point of all, and after attaining to that again taking hold of the first dependencies from it, so to proceed downward to the conclusion."[3] Only in this way can the dialectician be certain not to have started at an arbitrary point. In chapter 1, I noted that Badiou prefers mathematics to dialectics because the dialectic quest for the true *archē* belongs to a philosophy that privileges the one over the many. Hence, Badiou's defense against the Platonic critique that his thought departs from an axiom rather than from a true beginning is simply that the quest for an absolute beginning is ontotheological. For Badiou, an absolute beginning can only be found in the event and the subject's affirmation of the hypothesis that the event has taken place. Yet, it remains to be seen whether this refutation does not overlook some essential elements of Plato's dialectics.

Dialectics in the "Parmenides"

Since Badiou starts *L'être et l'événement* with a reading of the *Parmenides,* let me first examine how the dialectical method functions in this dialogue. The *Parmenides* starts with a brief discussion between the young Socrates and Zeno on the status of Zeno's rejection of the hypothesis that the many is. Interestingly enough, Zeno discusses the consequences of the hypothesis that "the existences are many"; yet, he does not do so in order to *affirm* this axiom. Rather, as he notes, his treatise on this subject "opposes the advocates of the many and gives them back their ridicule with interest, for its purpose is that their hypothesis that existences are many, if properly followed up, leads to still more absurd results than the hypothesis that they are one."[4] Hence, from the very start of the *Parmenides,* dialectics is not presented as the deductive *fidelity* departing from the affirmation of a hypothesis; rather, Zeno's deductions aim at refuting a hypothesis. This preference for critique over affirmation can also be traced in the way the young Socrates is depicted at the beginning of the dialogue: he is not the man who convincingly embraces his theory of the ideas; quite the contrary. To Parmenides, Socrates describes his reaction when he is about to adopt this theory as follows: "when I have taken up this position, I run away for fear of falling into some abyss of nonsense and perishing."[5] These are not the words of a man of conviction but, rather, of one who fears to go astray.

Parmenides, who praises the young Socrates for his impulse toward dialectics, also notes that he should be trained more in this art since "otherwise the truth will escape you." According to Parmenides, who in the rest of the dialogue provides us with an *example* of dialectics by treating the question of whether the one is or is not, the dialectical method consists in the following: "you must not only consider what happens if a particular hypothesis is true, *but also what happens if it is not true*"—and this is exactly what he does.[6] He does not decide *in advance* on one hypothesis over the other. He examines the hypothesis "the one is" as well as "the one is not" without embracing either of the two.

From this perspective, Badiou's decision for the hypothesis that the one is not while ignoring the other (since it belongs to ontotheology), lacks dialectical rigor. Not only does the dialectical method prefer the critical approach (as Zeno indicates) to the affirmative one, but it is also not clear why the dialectical method as executed in the *Parmenides* would in itself and necessarily be a derivative of a metaphysics of oneness, as Badiou claims. In fact, there are two reasons supporting the claim that dialectics does not necessarily derive from a metaphysics of oneness. First, the primacy of the one is often related to Socrates' theory of the ideas (Badiou also does this in his critique of dialectics). Yet, Parmenides has already refuted this theory before the discussion on the existence of the one has even started. Second, and more important, the existence of the one is *under scrutiny* in this discussion—it is not affirmed from the outset. So to claim that dialectics derives from the hypothesis that the one is, is in contradiction with the fact that this hypothesis is under close dialectical scrutiny. Moreover, by questioning both hypotheses, Parmenides shows that an assumption is always an arbitrary starting point and therefore requires an examination of other assumptions in order to test the strength and explanatory value of assumptions. Thus, dialectics truly treats hypotheses as hypotheses. That is, it does not simply follow them as the mathematician does in his or her deductive fidelity, but dialectics *suspends* (to treat) hypotheses as absolute beginning. Whereas mathematics proceeds from its axioms as absolute beginnings, dialectics withdraws from the working of these axioms in order to place them under scrutiny and examine them as hypotheses.

By starting with an axiomatic decision on ontology, Badiou's *L'être et l'événement* will necessarily be caught up in the consequences of this axiom. From the critical perspective of dialectics, Badiou fixes the axiom as a premature starting point. Dialectically, one may only discover the value of an axiom—and whether it deserves to be called starting point—by placing oneself outside of its claim and appeal. Especially in light of the nuanced, modest, and argumentative way in which Parmenides examines the difficult hypotheses "the one is" and "the one is not," Badiou's ontology runs the risk of sacrificing argument to decision, dialectics to fidelity, and scrutiny to affirmation. In contrast to Badiou's claim that modesty is a sign of a thought that affirms finitude, dialectic modesty opens up a particular possibility to thought, namely, to think the hypothesis as hypothesis.[7] Although Badiou claims that even though speculative thought lies beyond our experience, its "content...can nonetheless be rationally demonstrated," one should not forget that the *ethos of decision* founds ontology as a thought for him: arguments only follow in the form of deductive fidelity.[8] Badiou's decision to read the *Parmenides* only at the place where the hypothesis "the one is not" is discussed is exemplary in this regard: his reading is guided from the outset by the decision that "the one is not," and it has no dealings with the other hypothesis.

Fidelity and Exemplarity

By invoking Heidegger's analysis of the Greek roots of the word "axiom," I noted in chapter 1 that the axiom is held in high esteem or countenance. Moreover, the axiom's countenance is not founded in a subject's assessment of it. Rather, it is the transcendental condition of a subjective decision in Badiou's sense of the word. In this sense, Badiou's axiomatic decision is not decisionistic, which is affirmed even more compellingly at the time he wrote *Logiques des mondes*. The axiom stating that "the event has taken place" does not derive its splendor from the subject. The event itself grants this axiom its splendor and this gives rise to a truth: "Every truth is dependent upon something whose existence had been totally unapparent acceding to the flush of appearance [*l'éclat de l'apparaître*]."[9] In this sense, one might repeat in relation to Badiou's axiomatic decisions what Heidegger writes on the axiom: "What has the most noble countenance [*Das im höchsten Ansehen Stehende*] composes this regard on its own. This countenance is based on its own particular look."[10] In its fidelity, the subject affirms the look, the *eidos*, or the idea of the event itself. This relation between Badiou's event and the Platonic notion of the idea is not accidental here; it is an important new contribution of *Logiques des mondes* and I will return to it below. For now, we are interested in how this esteem, countenance, and splendor of the event functions and operates in Badiou's work.

Another well-known aspect of the esteem with which an event in Badiou's sense of the word shows itself concerns the universality of the event. The claim and the appeal of the event is not limited to a certain world and not to a certain social or cultural identity, as Badiou argues upon several occasions, but it always concerns all worlds and all people—this is *"a communism of the Idea."*[11] An event lays an equal claim to everyone, that is, *every* human being has an equal possibility to become a subject to the event.

Yet, it remains to be seen how universal is this universality and what kind of appeal and claim exists in this event when Badiou argues that an event lays an equal claim *to everyone* and *in every world*. For instance, if we consider Évariste Galois's development of Galois theory, which Badiou offers as an example of an event in *Logiques des mondes,* can we truly say that this event indeed speaks to everybody?[12] For instance, doesn't a fidelity to this event require that one has at least a certain basic knowledge of mathematics in order to be able to recognize that a trace was left behind? To be more precise, the question that intrigues me here is not the question of whether or not Badiou argues that everybody can become a subject to a particular event. Rather, I'm intrigued by the precise status of this example that is introduced for Badiou's readers as an event.

The example of Galois can be extended to the use of mathematics in Badiou's work as a whole. In the introduction of *L'être et l'événement,* Badiou recalls the skepticism with which the famous mathematician Jean Dieudonné approaches his and similar philosophical efforts to claim something about (the nature of) mathematics. As Badiou emphasizes, one of the concerns of Dieudonné is that philosophers make their claims about mathematics without having enough knowledge on the subject matter.[13] While Badiou's knowledge of mathematics and set theory goes undisputed here—his explications of set theory are always clear and instructive—Badiou thinks it necessary to defend his own position, and he does so by claiming that philosophy is not ontology but, rather, metaontology. Yet, this repositioning of philosophy does exactly what Dieudonné fears it would do: philosophy displaces mathematics. Or in Badiou's vocabulary, philosophy brings mathematics into another situation and another world. This displacement brings mathematics into a situation in which the original mathematical events are no longer faithfully followed. (Such a faithful following would require deductions and would therefore be simply impossible for those philosophers who lack the mathematical expertise.) Hence, philosophers are not subjects to these mathematical events, in Badiou's sense of these terms. In their world, the original event is neutralized. Of course, this does not mean that this world lacks in events and fidelities: Badiou's philosophical work is faithful to other, meta-mathematical events such as the equation of ontology with set theory. Yet, what is crucial here is that *the mathematical event itself is interrupted and introduced in another context where it is no longer followed.*[14] In chapter 1, we saw that Badiou describes this as a form of citing. From Derrida's early work we know that citing is a form of displacement: to cite mathematics is to displace it and to graft it onto another situation and world. To grasp what this displacement does, I referred to the Galois event Badiou uses in his book: this event is displaced from its normal, evental character—no mathematical deductions are asked from the readers—and it is introduced in another context in which it is used *as example*.

At this very point a new problematic announces itself that forms the secret core of Badiou's practice of citing mathematics, which I will call *the problem of the example* for reasons that will become clear below. The contours of this problematic show themselves more clearly when we note that, for Badiou, "*it is not enough* to identify" an event by the traces it leaves behind because one "must incorporate oneself into what the trace authorizes in terms of consequences."[15] What does this "not enough" mean? Does it mean that one can identify the event in this way but, in order to make the most of it and to use the event to its fullest potential, one should become, *in addition to this identification*, a faithful subject to it? Or does it mean that one cannot even recognize an event as such without becoming a subject to it? The latter seems to be the case because for Badiou an event has no meaning whatsoever without the subjective procedures that carry (out) its truths.

If this latter conclusion is true, we are confronted with a strange tension in Badiou's systematic work and his use of mathematics. On the one hand, the event only exists for a faithful subject and is only acknowledged to exist by this subject. On the other hand, Badiou's work offers examples of mathematical events *that are not followed* in these works—in fact, they are suspended or interrupted as mathematical events—but that, nevertheless, are identified as events and provide him the means to establish systematically what an event is.

The difference between enacting the truth drawn from an event and presenting the event as event is similar to the difference between drawing the consequences from an axiom and inquiring into the axiom itself. The former is action in light of the event. The latter has bracketed the validity and esteem of the axiom for the time being, while scrutiny into the status of this axiom is taking place. To show this similarity more clearly, consider once more Badiou's use of the Galois event. While the Galois event is no longer in its original situation and does not evoke or inspire to enact a fidelity to this event—which reader of Badiou is truly concerned with the question of how to solve polynomial equations of degree five or higher?—Badiou does use it in order to present it as an example of an event.

What is an example? To answer this question and to understand what happens when Badiou uses examples, let me take a detour along Agamben's work, and in particular along his account of the example. The example, as Agamben indicates, provides us with an alternative to the logic of generality and particularity. The example is not a general rule since it is itself only a member among other members of the class of which it is an example. However, it is not a mere particular case either. When it is used as an example, it serves to exemplify the class of which it is the example. In this sense, it is set apart from the other elements of this class. In this sense, an example is no longer itself: it no longer functions as it normally functions.

To indicate what an example does, Agamben provides a number of related suggestions. First, an example is an object that shows its own singularity: "Neither particular nor universal, the example is a singular object that presents itself as such, that shows its singularity."[16] Second, alluding to Badiou's use of set theory, Agamben rephrases the particular function of the example to the set theoretical notion of belonging: "They are expropriated of all identity, so as to appropriate belonging itself, the sign ε." Hence, an example does not simply belong to this or that set, but an example exposes *belonging* itself; that is, it shows what connects the particular to the general, the element to the set. Third, in *The Signature of All Things*, Agamben furthers these reflections on what an example is: "To give an example is a complex act which supposes that the term functioning as a paradigm is deactivated from its normal use, not in order to be moved into another context but, on the contrary, to present the canon—the rule—of that use, which can not be shown in any other way."[17] To understand this quote, one should note that Agamben describes here how we learn the conjugations of a verb from a foreign language. Out of a class with the same conjugation, one verb is selected as an example in order to demonstrate the rule of conjugation of this class of verbs. Clearly, when a verb is treated as an example in this way, its normal use is interrupted and deactivated: when I consider the conjugations of *parler* to understand how French verbs ending in *-er* are conjugated, I am no longer interested in the meaning of "to speak" with which this verb is used in everyday language. Hence, to use a term as an example implies that one would suspend "its normal use." The goal of this suspension is not to transfer it to another context. In this sense, the example cannot be compared to a metaphor in which the normal use of a word is interrupted in order to use it in another. Rather, as Agamben suggests, the example suspends its normal use in order to show how this term and terms like it are used. Hence, as he puts it, when a term is used as an example, it *presents the rule of its normal use*. In sum, the example, exposing the general (rule) by means of a particular, combines two elements: the normal use of the example is *suspended* to show the *rule* of how it and other members of its class are used. Similarly, if the class is not characterized by a rule but, rather, by a form, the example *suspends* its normal use in order to present the *form* of itself and other members of its class.

Let me note for later use that the example thus provides yet another way of accounting for the displacement of the normal use of terms. In the previous chapters, I already discussed two of them: (1) In the classical hermeneutic framework, the displacement of words concerned mainly the metaphorical movement to approach the unfamiliar in light of its resemblance with the familiar. (2) In my discussion of the theory of forcing, I showed how Badiou accounts for displacement of terms from the language of the situation in terms of the future anterior: although they are still empty signifiers, they will have received a sense and a referent in the post-evental situation. To these two, I add Derrida's well-known account of the displacement at work in language as writing (*l'écriture*). This displacement opens up the realm of the to-come, the unheard of and unforeseeable dimension of what is other. Agamben's example introduces another account of this displacement of terms: the example exposes the rule of a certain use or the form of a certain class. Thus, *it presents the intelligibility of this class.* In the fourth section of this chapter, I will return to Agamben's account of the example.

For now, let me apply this analysis to Badiou's use of the Galois example. The Galois event is not treated as a mathematical event: the readers of *Logiques des mondes* are not inspired to become mathematicians themselves. Rather, using it as an example, Badiou suspends and deactivates the Galois event. However, this deactivation serves a particular purpose, namely, to show how the Galois event exemplifies what an event is. Hence, Badiou is not faithful to this event but, rather, presents it *as an event,* thus presenting us with the form of an event.

In this sense, while discussing only one comportment to the event in *L'être et l'événement*—fidelity—Badiou's systematic work requires *two* comportments: fidelity and exemplarity. Of course, Badiou is aware of the different role philosophy plays when he argues that philosophy itself is *not* a procedure of truth. As he writes in *Manifeste pour la philosophie,* truth procedures belong to the domain of science, art, politics, and love; these truths condition philosophy, and it is the task of philosophy to think how they are compossible.[18] Yet, this remark is not fully in line with his systematic work. In *L'être et l'événement,* philosophy itself is a truth procedure deriving from the axiom that the one is not.[19] Meillassoux's questions concerning Badiou's distinction between being and event can be interpreted in a similar light: if ontology derives from (a fidelity to) an event itself, is this not another event than the event that is conceptualized by means of ontology since the former event *precedes* ontology, whereas the latter one is *delimited* and *determined* by ontology?[20] I propose to understand this difference between these two events as the difference between *two comportments to the event:* fidelity to the first, which is the comportment of action, and exemplarity as a name for the second comportment. The latter comportment is different from Badiou's praxis of truth since it is the comportment of thought that renders normal action inoperative and withdraws from the claim and the appeal of the event in order to expose what an event is as well as its use.

The Platonic Idea in Badiou

Compared to *L'être et l'événement*, Badiou's attention to the Platonic idea in *Logiques des mondes* adds another element to his interpretation of Plato.[21] His recent adaptation of Plato's *Republic* presents a clear picture of how Badiou constructs this new interpretation of Plato and his dialectics. In fact, he offers us a version of the *Republic* in which the otherness of Plato's text with regard to Badiou's own thought is effaced. This most clearly happens in Badiou's "axiomatic" choice to render some of Plato's Greek terminology not in their usual French equivalents but in terms that have a specific and technical meaning in Badiou's own oeuvre.[22] Interestingly enough, the choices that are most important from a philosophical point of view concern exactly the issue I am dealing with here: what is the role of dialectics in relation to mathematics, and what is the role of the Platonic dialectical quest for the *anupotheton*? Badiou translates the idea of the Good as truth; he translates Soul as Subject; and he interprets the famous ascension in the *Allegory of the Cave* of the Soul toward the Good as the incorporation of the Subject in truth.[23] Since the Good is now equated with truth in Badiou's sense of the word, dialectics turns into the procedure of fidelity and incorporation.

In line with this "interpretation," Badiou rereads the passage in which mathematics is distinguished from dialectics in Plato's *Republic*. Although mathematics is ontology, this equality can only be known meta-mathematically, that is, philosophically. Hence, by merely providing us with the ontological side of the matter—for instance, by providing the concept of the generic set—mathematics does not yet provide us with an understanding of the generic set as the form of truth.[24] Consequently, in terms of the example of the generic set, the difference between mathematics and dialectics is presented in Badiou's version of Plato's *Republic* as the difference between, on the one hand, the mere conceptualization of the generic set and, on the other hand, the thought in which the generic set is interpreted in relation to truth; this latter element is not seen by mathematics, only by thought. In sum, in this new interpretation, dialectics is absolved from its ontotheological descent to which Badiou pointed in *Court traité*, but it pays a high price for this absolution since it is now equated with the procedure of fidelity.

The notion of the idea is subject to a similar reinterpretation. Whereas Badiou criticized it for its kinship with the one in *Court traité*, the notion of the idea returns as a concept to understand the notion of truth in *La République de Platon* and in *Second manifeste pour la philosophie*. For Badiou, Plato's idea is not concerned with the knowability or the way in which things should be seen in order to understand them. Rather, "the Idea is the mediation between the individual and the Subject of a truth," as Badiou writes, and a little later he adds: "to enter in the composition of a Subject orients our individual existence.... The Idea marks this 'entrance to truth.'"[25] This entrance to truth is concerned with the mode of acting in the sense of a subject's praxis of incorporation into this truth.

Although Badiou's adaptation of Plato's *Republic* paints a clear picture of how he proposes to understand the concept of the idea and the procedure of dialectics, it does not solve the issue I discussed above concerning dialectics in the *Parmenides*. This adaptation simply effaces this issue under its interpretative violence. When dialectics is understood as incorporation, it can only move within the wake of a hypothesis that is decided upon. Strictly speaking, there is no *anupotheton* in Badiou's reading of Plato since truth in Badiou's sense always presupposes an axiomatic decision for its existence.[26] Yet, Socrates' *periagōgē* of the soul is not in the name of a praxis that departs from particular axioms; rather, it strives for what is without presupposition; therefore, the status of axiom is not enough for Socrates.

Consequently, it is rather doubtful whether Badiou's recent adaptation still has any bearing on Plato's conception of dialectics as we saw it in action in the *Parmenides*. The Platonic dialectic method requires that one test multiple hypotheses, but this method is not acceptable for Badiou in relation to his conception of the axiom: *to "experiment" with another axiom would imply another subject*. Perhaps even stronger than before, Badiou insists that the subject is the only possible human comportment to an axiom or an event, and since a subject only exists in the realm opened up by the affirmation of an event, it is impossible to inquire into the axiom as axiom since this requires a position outside of the realm opened up by it. Thus, the theoretical comportment of dialectics is radically put aside in favor of the praxis of truth called incorporation.

To conclude, Badiou separates the realm of being from the realm of action. While he problematizes the presupposition of the one and the structure of presupposition as such on the level of ontology, he reintroduces the structures of hypothesis, universality, and oneness on the level of praxis as his latest accounts of subjectivity and truth in light of a "communism of the Idea" clearly demonstrate. Consequently, while he tackles the problems of ontotheology on the level of ontology, his awkward dualism of being and action is not capable of solving the problem of the structure of presupposition as such. In fact, since the philosopher Badiou follows the truth of the hypothesis that the one is not, the alleged dualism of being and event cannot hide that ontology itself becomes a praxis of fidelity. This, then, reintroduces the structure of presupposition on the level of ontology: every ontological claim is marked by the hypothesis that the one is not. Confronted with the possibility that this hypothesis is false, Badiou simply states that the subject should persist in its fidelity. The philosophical mood of the young Socrates as phrased in the *Parmenides* is never an option for Badiou: "when I have taken up this position, I run away for fear of falling into some abyss of nonsense and perishing."[27]

AN AGAMBIAN READING OF THE *PARMENIDES*

Before turning to Nancy, a brief Agambian intermezzo is required. Agamben shares with Nancy and Badiou a keen eye for the presuppositional structure at the heart of classical hermeneutics. In reference to the motto of the third part of Gadamer's *Wahrheit und Methode*, Agamben notes that hermeneutics presupposes language. According to him, this presupposition points to the *theological* provenance of hermeneutics since it departs from the adage "in the beginning was the word." Hermeneutics never raises the question of this beginning itself, but merely presupposes it as that which precedes and supports it.[28] Yet, invoking book 6 of Plato's *Republic*, Agamben argues that it is the task of thinking to free itself from presuppositions.[29] Discussing with Gadamer (and to a lesser extent with Derrida), he writes, "But does such a thought not obscure precisely what should be the philosophical task par excellence, that is, the elimination and 'absolution' of presuppositions? Was philosophy not perhaps the discourse that wanted to free itself of all presuppositions?"[30] A philosophy grounded in this theological presupposition, as Agamben notes, "has abandoned this task" to eliminate presuppositions; it has forgotten its Platonic origin.

Although Badiou's concept of the event problematizes the presupposition of language and tradition, the problem to which Agamben points here returns at the core of Badiou's work. The event to which thought is faithful *is always presupposed since it has always already taken place*. In fact, the subject originates in the declaration that the event has already taken place. Moreover, since fidelity is the only comportment that recognizes the event, the event is necessarily of the order of a presupposition in Badiou's ethics of truth.[31]

In the previous section, I noted the implicit presence of another comportment in Badiou's use of examples, namely, the comportment of exemplarity. As I explained, the example *interrupts* its normal use, which is always presupposed while remaining unthought, *in order to make it known* and to think it. Recalling Nancy's claim that *hermēneuein* means first and foremost announcement and *Kundgabe*, we might say that Agamben's example confronts us with a hermeneutic operation that is no longer classical but has a clear Platonic, dialectic twist. The example does not presuppose, but it makes known the rule and the form of the class of which it is a member. Thus, it does not simply follow but, rather, exposes what is presupposed. Let us further this understanding of the example in relation to the problem of the presupposition.

Philosophy wants to "free itself of all presuppositions" because every presupposition excludes something. Every presupposition has a remainder; the hypothesis "the one is not," for instance, excludes the possibility that "the one is." The Socratic philosopher fears this exclusion since it might lead him into an "abyss of nonsense and perishing." Yet, how to render such an exclusion inoperative so that we may access this remainder? Could one not suggest in defense of Badiou that, as soon as one thinks, one always follows and posits certain axioms? Is it truly possible to adopt a position in which the axiom is exposed as such?

To address these questions, let me return to the *Parmenides*. While examining the different axioms, Parmenides always departs from one particular axiom and deduces its consequences. In this sense, dialectic thought indeed follows and posits certain axioms, although it does not hand itself over to one of them in advance. Yet, if we locate thought not only on the level of this or that (stage of the) argument but, rather, on the level of the dialogue *as a whole*—or more modestly, on the level of the dialectic procedure as a whole—a different picture arises. Paraphrasing Nancy, one might say that Parmenides' dialectics as a whole does not only present us with a sharing of voices, but also with a sharing of hypotheses. After having studied the different hypotheses in which both the existence and the nonexistence of the one are carefully examined (one might even distinguish nine hypotheses) Parmenides arrives at the following conclusion: "Then let us say that, and we may add, as it appears, that whether the one is or is not, the one and the others in relation to themselves and to each other all in every way are and are not and appear and appear not."[32] This conclusion, presenting no solution of the problem but only the aporia to which the dialectic procedure has guided the interlocutors, is affirmed by Socrates to be "very true." Since this conclusion affirms neither of the presuppositions, it leaves us in an intermediate sphere between them. It only affirms that as soon as we choose either of them and put them to work in our "deductive fidelity," we get into the same serious problems because in both cases, both "the one and the other in relation to themselves and to each other" are *and* are not, appear *and* appear not. When it is true, as Socrates claims in the *Republic*, that dialectics leads us to what is without hypotheses, one may ask the following: In what sense does such an aporia of hypotheses lead us to the *anupotheton*? In what sense, to put it in

Agamben's words, is aporia transformed into *euporia*, the nonpassage into a good or fortunate passage?[33]

In light of the previous section, it is now more evident that Badiou's reading of the *Parmenides* stops too hastily and too quickly. By limiting the deductive fidelity to only one axiom, he does not only miss the other axiom; he also misses the aporetic ending. In fact, rather than missing it, Badiou refuses this aporetic ending since, as he maintains in *L'être et l'événement*, set theory presents a coherent way to think the consequences of the hypotheses that the one is not.[34] Yet, if we do read to the end of the dialogue, another picture arises. The aporetic ending of the dialogue renders both hypotheses *inoperative*. We end up in a realm in which we affirm neither of them. Yet, exactly because of this, they appear and show themselves as hypotheses. This, as Agamben maintains in accordance with Socrates' remarks in the *Republic*, is the realm of the *anupotheton*. It is the task of thinking not to affirm this or that presupposition, but to *expose* a hypothesis as hypothesis.

To understand better what happens in this aporia, let me discuss another example from Agamben's oeuvre. In *Remnants of Auschwitz*, he refers to Aristotle's argument defending the principle (*archē*) of noncontradiction in his *Metaphysics*. Although one cannot give a direct proof of this principle, those who try to refute it will necessarily contradict themselves since every effort to refute this principle by argument depends on this principle. Therefore, this principle is the "tacit presupposition" of every argument.[35] To a certain extent, Aristotle's reasoning offers the perfect means to expose one of the presuppositions of our reasoning since it makes the principle of noncontradiction explicit. Yet, Agamben wants to go one step further: he aims to render the presupposition *inoperative*, to suspend it in order to enter the domain that is not covered by this presupposition. To enter the realm in which this principle no longer applies, we need to deactivate it. Therefore, Agamben rejects Aristotle's reasoning as follows: "It suffices for the adversary simply and radically *to cease speaking*."[36] By ceasing to speak, he argues, the principle presupposed in all our (consistent) speech loses its force. In his *Metaphysics*, Aristotle anticipates this response and argues that he who refuses to reason is "no better than a mere plant," since he *does not actualize his potential* to reason and to speak. Yet, as Agamben argues, this is not exactly true: by ceasing to speak, one indeed interrupts one's communication and one's will to communicate, but one does not lose one's potential to speak or to reason. Moreover, it is only by not actualizing this potential to communicate, Agamben continues, that one shows that the potential to communicate is also the *potential not to communicate*. This latter potential not to…, which Agamben also calls *adunamia* or im-potentiality characterizes the realm disclosed by the deactivation of the principle of noncontradiction.

Before applying these considerations to my reading of the *Parmenides,* one technical clarification is needed for future purposes to identify the metaphysical context in which this discussion of potentiality and actuality comes up. Deactivation and inoperativeness, as the French term *désoeuvrement* clearly indicates, present an alternative to the metaphysical notion of *energeia,* being-at-work or actuality. Thus, these terms introduce an alternative to the Aristotelian framework of potentiality and actuality. For Aristotle, the telos of potentiality is actuality and every potentiality is marked by a privation or lack since what is potential is *not yet* actual. An alternative ontology of potentiality, as Agamben suggests, approaches potentiality beyond this negativity of the "not yet." It does so because the structure of negativity is exactly the structure of the presupposition: as long as we conceive of potentiality as *not yet* actual, it always has its actualization as its presupposition—in the form of a pre-given telos. To apply this to our example of the *Parmenides:* every dialectical analysis serves the purpose of reaching a specific telos, namely, knowledge concerning the question at hand, and in the case of *Parmenides* whether the one is or not. Agamben, on the other hand, aims to think and expose potentiality itself, and for that purpose, deactivation and inoperativeness are necessary: the regular telos of (in our case) dialectics needs to be suspended. In the example of Aristotle's defense of the principle of noncontradiction, Agamben thus says that to cease speaking is not a lack or a privation (of what a human being fully is or can be): rather, it exposes the potential not to communicate, and this potential remains even when the principle of noncontradiction can no longer be established. This example shows that Agamben's conception of the philosophical task to reach into the *anupotheton* is not concerned with finding the first *principles* of being since these are rendered inoperative in the process, as the example of the principle of noncontradiction demonstrates.

Like every aporia, the one at the end of the *Parmenides* is related to the principle of noncontradiction and to dialectics not reaching its normal and proper telos. According to this principle one of the hypotheses must be true and, normally, it is the task of the dialectic inquiry to show which of them can be maintained. Consequently, the aporetic ending of the *Parmenides* points in another direction beyond the principle of noncontradiction—not by ceasing to speak (as Agamben suggests in relation to Aristotle's argument for the principle of noncontradiction) but by reasoning excessively. The only way out of this aporia is to accept that the true goal of this particular dialogue and this particular dialectical exercise is not to find the final argument for accepting either of the two hypotheses. In fact, there are good reasons to assume that this is not the real goal of the dialogue and that the dialogue, rather, offers another, more unexpected way out of this aporia. In what follows, I present the first half of this way out of this aporia. It is only in chapter 7 that I can discuss the second half of this way out of this aporia.

Recall how the dialogue starts. Parmenides notes that Socrates needs to study dialectics more seriously to become truly at home in philosophy. In turn, wanting to learn to art of dialectics from the master himself, Socrates asks Parmenides, "Why do you not yourself frame an hypothesis and discuss it, to make me understand better?" Although Parmenides fears this task and says that he is "filled with terror when I remember through what a fearful ocean of words I must swim, old man that I am," he obliges Socrates, and he chooses an *example to demonstrate what the dialectical method is*.[37] As we know, he chooses the example Zeno and Socrates were discussing in the opening stage of the dialogue. Yet, what is to be understood better, according to Socrates' question, is not whether the one is or the one is not—it is not a matter of deciding this particular issue—but *what dialectical thought is* and how it operates.

In chapter 2, we saw that Nancy claims that Plato's dialogues are never only dialogues about this or that topic but are also always about the nature of the dialogue (*dialogicité*). *Parmenides* is a perfect example that supports this claim. As with all dialogues, it discusses a particular subject matter: is the one or is it not? Yet, it discusses this subject not only for its own sake, but to offer Socrates an example of dialectics. Unlike a normal dialectical exercise, the *Parmenides* does not aim to decide between hypotheses, but *it aims to exemplify dialectical thought*. From this perspective, the aporia is a beautiful indication of this exemplary role of the *Parmenides* since the aporia par excellence interrupts the normal course dialectics takes. If this dialogue would not end in an aporia, we might be under the impression that we reached a proper result; for instance, that "the one is." Yet, the aporia deprives us of this satisfaction. From the perspective of a normal discussion, Parmenides' exercise is futile and ineffective, and the whole discussion has to start all over again. It only shows that his excessive reasoning did not get him any clear result. Yet, exactly because this dialogue deactivates the normal functioning of dialectics, it becomes an example in Agamben's sense: it exposes how dialectical thought functions. It shows that dialectical thought is not a means in the service of an end—namely, as a way to decide whether the one is or is not. Rather, it exposes this thought as a means without end, in its pure taking place. In this way, Parmenides' dialectical exercise introduces another comportment of thought—not one that is heading for a result or a conclusion, but one that coincides with what I called the comportment of exemplarity. Only in the mode of this other ethos can dialectics be made known *itself*. In this sense, Parmenides turns out to be an excellent teacher in the dialogue that carries his name.

If we retake this issue in more classical terms, it becomes even clearer what we gain here for dialectics. From an Aristotelian perspective, the aporia blocks the passage from dialectics to first philosophy, from critical investigation of hypotheses to knowledge of what is without hypothesis. In light of Aristotle's account of dialectics, the only possible *euporia* would be the transition from dialectics to its goal; the aporia itself cannot be the goal of dialectics.[38] Against the background of Agamben's logic of the example, however, we may claim something else: this aporia or suspension of the normal course offers another *euporia* than the one propagated by Aristotle: thanks to this impassability of dialectics to metaphysics, dialectics itself becomes intelligible for us.[39] This points to another *anupotheton:* the dialogue does not offer us the truth of the examined hypotheses but, rather, discloses the intelligibility of dialectics itself.

Thus, Agamben's other *euporia* keeps the aporia disconnecting dialectics from metaphysics intact. *Pace* Badiou, this shows the importance of taking the whole composition of the *Parmenides* into account. Dialectics does not imply an (implicit) affirmation of the norm of the one in this dialogue. Rather, this dialogue shows that in order to exemplify dialectics, such an implicit affirmation is suspended and, consequently, the goal of dialectics is not found in knowledge concerning the one and the many, but it is found in its own exercise and in the dialectic practice to which the question of the one and the many gives rise. Only in this way is dialectical thought not simply put into practice, as Badiou's deductive fidelity prefers, but becomes intelligible. Only in this way, as Agamben might put it, the *Parmenides* exposes the idea of dialectics.

Enthusiasm of the Rhapsode and Potentiality of the Scrivener

To what extent is Nancy capable of overcoming the primacy of presupposition in his conception of being-toward, being-with, and being-in-common? This question is inspired by Agamben's short comment from "Tradition of the Immemorial." Referring to Nancy's work on the inoperative community, he writes, "Our time thus registers the demand for a community without presuppositions; yet, without realizing it, it simultaneously *maintains the empty form of presupposition* beyond all foundations—presupposition of nothing, pure destination."[40] Hence, although he acknowledges that Nancy's work is marked by an effort to overcome every presupposition and although his work shares some fundamental motives with Nancy's work, Agamben claims that there is still a remainder of the structure of presupposition attached to Nancy's work. The latter only succeeds in emptying every presupposition from its content but not in overcoming the presuppositional form as such: "it simultaneously maintains the empty form of presupposition." What does this critical remark mean?

Abandonment or "Being in Force without Significance"

The concepts of ban and abandonment play a crucial role in Nancy's account of *partage*. Abandonment is a form of being-outside or being on the threshold that implies that one is entrusted to that from which one is banned. In *Homo Sacer,* Agamben affirms Nancy's (and Heidegger's) analysis that this experience of abandonment marks our present-day relation to law as well as to language and tradition. Borrowing from Gershom Scholem, Agamben describes this abandonment as "being in force without significance" (*Geltung ohne Bedeutung*).[41] In fact, Agamben uses this phrase to describe how the man from the country relates to the law in Kafka's *Vor dem Gesetz,* the story I briefly discussed in chapter 2. Although the man from the country does not know what the law asks of him and what the law means, he remains captivated by the law. For him, the law is still in force although he cannot access it or understand its meaning. According to Agamben, this is what the *open* door represents in the story: as long as the door is open, the law is in force. Thus, we can read the formula "being in force without signification" in the tonality of Nancy's vocabulary (I replace "significance" with "signification" because these terms have a specific meaning in Nancy's vocabulary). Abandonment points to a situation in which tradition, language, and law are no longer meaningful but still in force, thus combining both the exile from meaning with the enthrallment that keeps the present age captivated. Our incapacity to master this ban, as Agamben puts it, marks this being in force.[42]

Yet, while agreeing with Nancy's analysis of abandonment, Agamben wishes to go one step further. Although, as he writes, "Jean-Luc Nancy is the philosopher who has most rigorously reflected upon the experience of law that is implicit in this being in force without significance," he does not provide "any way out of the ban."[43] Hence, although Agamben agrees with Nancy's characterization of ban and abandonment, he wonders whether and why the law's being in force is *impassable*. Again this is an aporia, and again Agamben is looking for a *euporia,* a fortunate way out. Why is this being in force an aporia? Is there not a way to interrupt the law's being in force?

To capture how this issue is related to the problem of presupposition and in what sense Nancy "maintains the empty form of presupposition," I will take a small detour along Agamben's dispute with Derrida concerning the interpretation of Kafka's *Vor dem Gesetz*. For Derrida the key to interpreting this story is that the open door opens onto nothing.[44] On the one hand, the nothing to which the door opens refers to the fact that neither the law nor our tradition hides a transcendental signified attracting us. The law does not demand anything, and our tradition does not conceal any specific meaning. Consequently, since no content of the law exists, we cannot enter the law. For Derrida, the door opening onto nothing implies that we can only be on the threshold of the law. In this sense, Derrida's reading beautifully represents what Nancy means with the abandonment of meaning. One might also point to the structural kinship of Derrida's reading of *Vor dem Gesetz* with Nancy's analysis of the role of Plato's *agathōn*, discussed in chapter 2: *agathōn* should not be understood as a transcendent(al) being; rather, it is the nothing exemplifying our being-toward and our being-on-the-threshold.

On the other hand, it is crucial for Derrida that the door *remains* open, that is, that the law maintains its force over us and that we remain on its threshold. In a brief comment, Agamben connects this aspect of Derrida's reading to deconstruction as a whole. For deconstruction, Agamben writes, the door is "absolutely impassable."[45] This does not only mean that we cannot enter the law, but also that we cannot pass the door in any other sense: we cannot leave it aside; *we cannot close it;* we cannot free ourselves from its spell. It is truly a nonpassage, an aporia—and this aporia is absolute. As Agamben suggests, for deconstruction to do its work, the door must be kept open and the intoxication of the text of the law must be kept in force.

Whether or not one agrees with Agamben on this particular point, it does disclose an important motive in Derrida's thought. Recall how the intoxication of what cannot be appropriated plays a crucial role in Derrida's early reflections on writing (*l'écriture*). In his famous and beautiful reading of *Phaedrus* in "La pharmacie de Platon," he notes that the conversation between Phaedrus and Socrates does not take place in Athens, where Socrates is at home; rather, Phaedrus lures him

124   Ontology after Ontotheology

out of the city and displaces Socrates. Even for Socrates it is clear that he only follows Phaedrus because he is under the spell of the speech of Lysias, which Phaedrus keeps hidden under his cloak: "But you seem to have discovered a drug [*pharmakon*] to entice me into walking outside the city. Just like dangling green branches or fruit of some kind in front of a hungry animal to lead him on, so you are likely to lead me through all of Attica or anywhere you want, simply by holding words in a book in front of my nose."[46] Commenting on this passage, Derrida writes, "Only hidden letters can thus get Socrates moving. If a speech could be purely present, unveiled, naked, offered up in person in its truth, without the detours of a signifier foreign to it, *if at the limit an undeferred logos were possible, it would not seduce anyone*. It would not draw Socrates, as if under the effects of a *pharmakon*, out of its way."[47] The movement of desire belongs to a veiled speech: "only hidden letters can thus get Socrates moving." In fact, as Derrida maintains, if "an undeferred *logos* were possible," that is, if the meaning of this veiled speech could be appropriated, there would be no spell, no seduction, and no intoxication. It is only this spell, belonging to the abandonment of meaning, that can seduce Socrates to follow Phaedrus.

This account of the desire at work in veiled speeches has one important implication for the aforementioned problem. Although there is no presupposed meaning—the door of the law opens onto nothing—the *form* of presupposition is maintained. The door opening onto nothing and the intoxication of hidden letters that want to say nothing are both figures of the empty form of presupposition that creates its own desire and movement of being-toward.

Although the intoxication of Socrates plays a crucial role in Plato's composition of the *Phaedrus*, it is of crucial importance to note that this intoxication is interrupted at the end of this dialogue. The final remarks of the dialogue clearly suggest that Phaedrus loses his spell over Socrates and that the latter is no longer under the spell of writing. Derrida interprets this passage as the Socratic restoration of the metaphysical hierarchy between spoken and written language as well as between good and bad writing. Therefore, as Derrida argues, a critique of metaphysics must remain "as if under the effects of a *pharmakon*" that marks every writing (*l'écriture*) and to refrain from separating good from bad writing, writing that bears fruit and leads to knowledge versus writing that is sterile. A similar impetus can be found in Nancy's work: to criticize the metaphysical structure of signification requires us to dwell in the realm of the abandonment of meaning, that is, in the enthusiasm and under the divine spell that mark the poet and the rhapsode.

Exactly at this point Agamben disagrees. To phrase it in terms of Plato's *Phaedrus,* Agamben disagrees with Derrida's claim that the end of the *Phaedrus,* breaking the ban of Phaedrus and of writing, is a return to metaphysics. His comments on Kafka's parable affirm this. Agamben notes that the parable ends with a statement of the doorkeeper telling the man from the country (who is about to die) that he, the doorkeeper, will go and close the door. If the open door represents the law's being in force, the closing of the door represents the interruption of the law's being in force. Another comment substantiates this idea that the man from the country does something that might be compared to overcoming a spell: "The obstinacy of the man from the country thus suggests a certain analogy with the cleverness that allows Ulysses to survive the songs of the sirens."[48] If the story is indeed told in light of this deactivation of the law's spell, one might also reinterpret the behavior of the man from the country in this light. Perhaps rather than patiently waiting to get in, the man from the country patiently waits for the door to close; as Agamben suggests, "We can imagine that all the behavior of the man from the country is nothing other than a patient strategy to have the door closed in order to interrupt the Law's being in force."[49] This indicates another comportment to the law and to writing that does not affirm the negative structure of abandonment and its related desire; rather, it affirms a comportment of waiting for the interruption of this intoxication. If God and the transcendental signified are examples of the content of the presupposition of metaphysics, the structure of abandonment represents the emptied-out form of presupposition. The affirmation of abandonment maintains "the presupposition of the nothing." Put differently, to be abandoned to the sharing (of voices, of sense, or of being), as Nancy often writes, means to rely upon and to be turned over to a presupposed nothing. It is in this emptied-out form that the structure of the presupposition remains at work in Nancy's (and Derrida's) work. Yet, another strategy is possible according to Agamben. This alternative requires that the door is not "absolutely impassable." The comportment of the man waiting suggests that the aporia, nonpassage of the law, might be transformed into a *eu-poria,* another way of passing the law by, when it closes its door—a *euporia* whereby the spell that Phaedrus has over Socrates is broken without returning to a presupposed content.

Without Enthusiasm

Agamben's essay "The Tradition of the Immemorial" suggests that for him, the problematic of *Le partage des voix* is immediately related to that of "L'être abandonné" and *La communauté désoeuvrée.* While his comment on the empty form of presupposition concerns first and foremost Nancy's concept of the inoperative community, Agamben phrases the task to think an alternative to this conception as follows: "Are we capable today of no longer being philosophers of the letter (*Buchstabenphilosophen*), without thereby becoming either philosophers of the voice or mere enthusiasts?"[50] Apparently, the voice and the enthusiasts—two central themes to Nancy's *Le partage des voix*—still maintain the empty form of presupposition. Before explicating what kind of critique this implies, it is necessary to indicate first how Agamben understands the concept of the voice.[51]

The notion of the voice plays a crucial role in his account of the metaphysical conception of language. According to Agamben, metaphysics has always discerned in (human) language something as the *human* voice. This human voice is characterized by a double negativity: it is *no longer* a mere animal voice or sound, but also *not yet* a signification. He illustrates this with an example borrowed from Augustine's *De trinitate.* There, Augustine reflects on his encounter with the word *temetum,* which by that time was a dead word in Latin that used to mean wine or intoxicating drink.[52] When one hears such an unfamiliar, dead word, Augustine notes, one is aware that one does not hear a mere animal sound, but neither does one have access to its meaning. What one experiences here, in between a mere sound and a grasped meaning, is the word's *pure intention to signify*. Thus, the suspension of significations opens up the realm in which the human voice offers itself to be experienced as a pure intention to signify. This distinction between the intention to signify and the actual signification of a word presents us with Agamben's analogue of Nancy's distinction between *signifiance* (significance or signifyingness) and *signification*. Hence, Agamben's "human voice alone" is equivalent with Nancy's significance. As Augustine's *temetum* indicates, the realm of the human voice alone only presents itself when the normal use of language and the realm of significations is interrupted: when we do not understand the meaning of the word but are aware that we encounter a human word, we experience this human voice.

Agamben argues that Nancy's analysis of abandonment does not yet fully overcome metaphysics since it maintains the empty form of presupposition, and Agamben's understanding of the human voice — as the analogue of Nancy's significance — affirms this. Augustine introduces the dead word *temetum* to offer an example to help us understand *what* we love in our desire for knowledge. According to Augustine, one cannot love what one does not know. Therefore, one cannot love the object that one strives to know; hence, what is loved is nothing but desire itself, that is, the process of coming to know itself. Translated in the terminology of signification: one does not love the meaning of the word *temetum* but, rather, the intention to signify what one encounters when one reads or hears such a dead word. Obviously, Augustine's example repeats an old Platonic motive that Nancy also discovered in his analysis of Plato's *agathōn* as being-toward: not the idea of the Good, but its being-toward the good is most important; not the signification of *temetum*, but its pure intention to signify. Hence, for Agamben, Nancy's account of being-toward and significance discloses *the realm of the human voice* presupposed by metaphysics.

This analysis provides us with the key for understanding Agamben's quote on the philosophers of the letter and of the voice. For him, the main contribution of Derrida, who is a philosopher of the letter, as well as Nancy, who is a philosopher of the voice and of the enthusiasts, is their demonstration of the "negative foundation" of metaphysics. However, demonstrating the hidden core of metaphysics is not yet the same as overcoming it, as Agamben explicitly says in relation to Derrida: "he believed that he had opened a way to surpassing metaphysics, while in truth he merely brought the fundamental problem of metaphysics to light."[53] The nothing onto which the door of the law opens returns here in the form of the negativity at the heart of language and metaphysics: *no longer* animal voice, *not yet* signification. Both, the nothing as well as the negativity, are examples of the negative foundation of metaphysics. For Agamben, this "negative foundation of metaphysics" is nothing more than the structure of presupposition: everything that is refers back (or forward) to something else to account for its existence.[54] Therefore, to overcome the structure of presupposition, philosophy "must find an experience of speech that *no longer presupposes any negative foundation.*"[55] This raises the question of what such an experience of speech might be.

As noted in chapter 2, Agamben has a keen interest in the themes of communication and transmission. Nancy is not as concerned with the communication of this or that message or meaning as he is with the communication of *communicability itself;* or, in the terminology employed in "The Idea of Language," he is concerned with saying *sayability itself.*[56] For Agamben, this communication is related to the comportment of exemplarity: by deactivating the normal use of language, he hopes to expose communicability itself.

Phrased in these terms, it is obvious that both Nancy and Agamben are heirs to Heidegger's account of language in *Unterwegs zur Sprache*. In our ordinary use of language, we always speak about this or that topic; thus, we bring it to language, as Heidegger says. Yet, although it is presupposed in our everyday speech, language *itself* is never brought to language. Therefore, it is the task of thinking to do so.[57] Agamben's and Nancy's reflections on communication and transmission take on this Heideggerian task. Whereas Nancy treats this issue in terms of the nature of dialogue, as discussed in chapter 2, Agamben relates it to the problem of the presupposition: "*The task of philosophical presentation is to come with speech to help speech, so that, in speech, speech itself does not remain presupposed but instead comes to speech*. At this point, the presuppositional power of language touches its limit and its end; language says presuppositions as presuppositions and, in this way, reaches the unpresupposable and unpresupposed principle (*arkhē anypothetos*) that, as such, constitutes authentic human community and communication."[58] In this quote, Agamben interprets the Heideggerian task in Platonic terms as the task to think the *anupotheton*. This task requires that the presupposition of language be said *as presupposition*. This means that normal language is deactivated in order to show language in its sayability, communicability, and knowability.

For Agamben, this is also the role of the Platonic notion of the idea. Traditionally, the idea is interpreted as a being different from the sensible being of which it is an idea. To go from the sensible being to the idea in which it partakes would thus be a movement from the sensible to the intelligible world. For Agamben, conversely, the idea is not another being besides the being of which it is the idea; it is the same being, but now considered as the being *itself*. Hence, a displacement takes place here from the being to the being *itself*, but this displacement is a "movement that transports the object not toward another thing or another place, but toward its own taking-place—toward the idea."[59] Hence, the idea or the thing *itself* is not another "object presupposed by language" next to the thing of which it is the idea, but rather it is "that *by which* the object is known, *its own knowability*."[60] Hence, the taking-place of the object mentioned in the quotes above concerns the event in which a being is made known *in its intelligibility or knowability*. One should note here the strong equivalence between this interpretation of the Platonic idea and his account of the example.[61] The displacement by which a mere sensible being in its ordinary use becomes an example—a singular being that exposes the rule of its use or the form of its existence—is the displacement by which a mere sensible being becomes a singular being exposing its idea or knowability.

Here we see how Agamben and Nancy, despite their shared interest in communicability and transmissibility, part ways in their accounts of this communicability in terms of their understanding of the Platonic idea. Nancy's account of Plato's *agathōn* as the mere movement toward... is not sufficient for Agamben because, although Nancy no longer presupposes another being toward which we move, the ellipsis in "movement toward..." represents the empty form this presupposition maintains in Nancy. Thus, he fails to grasp how Plato's idea is concerned with disclosing the knowability of a being, the rule of its use or its form.

Finally, let me discuss this difference between Agamben and Nancy in terms of the "mere enthusiasts" Agamben wants to avoid. What does it mean not to become mere enthusiasts? To answer this question, let us return to Plato's *Ion* and ask: who exposes the poetic activity in the *Ion*? In Nancy's account the poet is exposed to divine enthusiasm. His account of being-toward, abandonment, and communication derives from this form of exposition modeled on poetic enthusiasm. Indeed, in the *Ion*, the divine power makes the poet and the rhapsode sing. Yet, it is neither the poet nor the rhapsode who *exposes* this power; it is, rather, Socrates who demonstrates the poetic nature of their *hermēneuein*.

Surely, Nancy would not deny this. In fact, he even writes that philosophical discourse is characterized by the fact that the philosopher is better "*in the domain of the other*" and is concerned first and foremost with the *truth* of this other domain, although the philosopher cannot master this other domain.[62] Yet, Nancy also suggests that philosophy shares in the genre of poetry, that is, shares in the modality of enthusiasm. Moreover, since Socrates enacts every voice—of the poet, the rhapsode, and the philosopher—Nancy even suggests that Socrates may be considered as the main enthusiast whose character exposes most clearly the sharing of voices. However, *pace* Nancy, the *Ion* paints a picture of Socrates as one who is not enthralled by the poets nor the rhapsodes nor the divine power by which they speak. This is in line with the *Republic*, in which Socrates says that he used to be intoxicated by Homer's poetry in the past "by the upbringing we have received." Yet, while he does not deny that he might still be vulnerable to this intoxication, he has found a way to "force" himself "to stay away from" the intoxicating poetry. The philosophical prose (*logos* without meter) against this intoxication is his incantation to render the poetic, divine power inactive.[63]

Hence, even when Socrates enacts the rhapsodic role in the *Ion*, he is neither an enthusiast nor does he make anyone else enthusiastic in the way poets and rhapsodes do. Therefore, his enactment is *not* the enactment of the normal rhapsode who brings his audience under the spell of the divine power that moves him. Rather, Socrates' enactment *exemplifies* the rhapsodic activity, in Agamben's sense of the word. He enacts another comportment toward Homeric poetry: not the rhapsodic one that presupposes enthusiasm, but the exemplary one that exposes what rhapsody and poetry is. Thus, Socrates exposes rhapsody in its knowability, but this requires the suspension of poetic enthusiasm.

Despite Nancy's attention to the interruption of signification and interpretation, his analysis requires a second interruption: the poetic enthusiasm needs to be put out of action in order to show the form of poetry.[64] Consequently, to understand the difference between Nancy and Agamben, "everything depends on what is meant by 'inoperativeness,'" as Agamben writes in *Homo Sacer*.[65] He adds, "the only coherent way to understand inoperativeness is to think of it as a generic mode of potentiality."

Whereas Nancy selects the rhapsode as the figure to exemplify inoperativeness, Agamben chooses Melville's creation Bartleby, the scrivener who, after appearing first as a very diligent albeit somewhat bleak copyist of laws, soon changes his conduct toward the lawyer for whom he works. With the famous phrase "I would prefer not to" as an answer to his employer's requests, he first interrupts the normal functioning of the lawyer's office and at a certain moment even "decided upon doing no more writing."[66]

Agamben's preference for Bartleby is especially provocative in light of the striking analogy between rhapsode and scrivener.[67] The scrivener is to the author what the rhapsode is to the poet. Copying is to writing what reciting is to speech. The rhapsode is the one who maintains the divine power in force by handing it down and whose activity is in the service of communicating this divine power. Similarly, the copyist is the one who repeats what was once written.[68] Yet, Bartleby is the clerk who gives up writing. This gesture interrupts the apparent automaticity with which the rhapsode actualizes his potential to sing whenever the gods are in him. Bartleby's preference not to copy renders the transmission of any power by means of this copying inoperative. Thus, he *suspends* the actualization of the writer's potential. The rhapsode is enthralled and taken away by the divine power. Bartleby is involved in a more "dry, husky sort of business" and discloses his potential to read, to hear, to repeat and to copy *as mere potential*.[69] He does so by deferring the actualization of this potential. Thus, Bartleby shows that his potential does not exist by the grace of something else and that it refers neither back nor forward to a divine or other presupposed power. He exposes his own potentiality beyond every presupposition.[70]

At this point, prematurely, I interrupt my reading of Agamben and his preference for Bartleby, the angel of potentiality, as Berkman calls him.[71] The reason is that this notion of potentiality brings us into the heart of the discussion of the second axis determining contemporary ontology. Therefore, we first need to explore this second axis before we can return to Agamben's interpretation of Bartleby as the angel of potentiality and contingency.

PART 2
FIGURES OF CONTINGENCY: SUSPENDING THE PRINCIPLE OF SUFFICIENT REASON

Despite the many ways in which present-day philosophy introduces, defines, and locates the event, it is possible to discern a shared concern in the different concepts of the event that are created today. Although I acknowledge that it is always risky to depart from one quote of one particular author to capture a range of concepts, let me offer Jean-Luc Marion's description of the phenomenon of the event to enter this shared concern: "Actually, the event appears in effect as other phenomena, but it is distinguished from objective phenomena in that it does not result from a production, which would deliver it as a product, decided and foreseen, foreseeable according to its causes and as a consequence reproducible following the repetition of such causes. To the contrary, in happening, it attests to an unforeseeable origin, rising up from causes unknown, even absent, at least not assignable, that one would not therefore any longer reproduce, because its constitution would not have any meaning."[1] In opposition to what Marion calls "objective phenomena," that is, the products of a Kantian transcendental subject, the phenomenon of the event surpasses the boundaries such a subject sets on the object. The event is *not* produced and hence *not* known; rather, to account for the event means to attest to an unforeseeable origin. Moreover, the event is *not* decided upon if such a decision means to ground the event in the act of a subjective will. Conversely, the event requires its own comportment, which Marion calls "attestation" and which Badiou identifies as subjective fidelity and which is different from a knowledge of its causes. Hence, if we use the phrase "to account for," as I did in the previous sentences, it concerns a mode of accounting that involves an attesting affirmation rather than a knowledge of the event's happening. The event is *not* foreseen according to its causes; in fact, these causes might be unknown as well as simply absent. As a consequence, it is also *not* reproducible since something can only be reproduced when we know its causes and may repeat them. Hence, the event can only be discerned *when the principle of sufficient reason is suspended*.

In only one quote Marion gathers these characteristics of the event: out of reach for the modern, transcendental subject; unforeseeable and unknowable in terms of its causes; therefore requiring its own mode of "subjectivity" or comportment; and thoroughly singular. Each of these characteristics returns in one form or another in present-day continental accounts of the event. In this sense, the event is a highly technical term; it is an ontological category that does not simply refer to "everything that happens." The phrasing "everything that happens" might still refer to something that is subject to Leibniz's principle of sufficient reason as one of its versions reads: *nihil fit sine cause*—nothing happens without a cause; that is, everything that happens has a reason for it to happen. Yet, in Marion's terms, only "objective phenomena" are subject to this principle. The phenomenon of the event, however, cannot be understood as objective phenomenon and, in fact, introduces a new ontological category that can only be explored when we suspend the principle of sufficient reason and its implications.

Inspired by Heidegger, I already noted in the first chapter that Leibniz's principle goes hand-in-hand with the metaphysical, ontotheological conception of God. "As the first existing cause of all beings, God is called reason," Heidegger comments, and he adds that God as the unifying ground of all beings exists if and only if this principle is valid.[2] Therefore, an alternative to ontotheology requires the *suspension* of this principle—to leap away from this principle and from this ground, as Heidegger puts it in *Der Satz vom Grund*, playing with the double meaning of the German *Satz* as proposition and leap. Marion's quote suggests that this suspension leads us to the category of the event—as it already did in Heidegger's work.

By approaching the concept of the event in light of the effort to develop an ontology after ontotheology, a number of different developments in contemporary thought become clearer. First, it shows how and why in the speculative school Badiou's reflections on the event are concerned with the same ontological issue as Meillassoux's absolute rejection of the principle of sufficient reason. Second, it explains why contemporary phenomenology does not only feel the need to pluralize Heidegger's fundamental ontology of Dasein, as Nancy does, but also feels compelled to rethink this fundamental ontology in light of a phenomenology of the event. Varying on Heidegger's conception of Dasein, Marion reshapes Heidegger's fundamental ontology in terms of the primacy of the gift, and Dasein becomes the *adonné*, the one to whom is given. Similarly, Marion's student Claude Romano rethinks fundamental ontology by replacing Dasein with *l'advenant*, the one to whom happens. Finally, and most importantly for this study, the turn to the event shows that the speculative school and the hermeneutic-phenomenological school are both motivated by a similar concern. To capture this concern, consider the following remark by Meillassoux: "If every variant of dogmatic metaphysics is characterized by the thesis that *at least one* entity is absolutely necessary (the thesis of real necessity), it becomes clear how metaphysics culminates in the thesis according to which *every* entity is absolutely necessary (the principle of sufficient reason)."[3] In its classical and dogmatic form, metaphysics' quest for the unifying ground is always also the quest for a being that "is absolutely necessary." This quest to ground reality in necessity culminates in a metaphysics that claims that every being is absolutely necessary. This latter necessity is captured by the principle of sufficient reason. Hence, the quest for a realm in which this principle no longer applies is, in fact, a quest for an ontology that no longer presupposes the primacy of necessity. In fact, as this second part demonstrates, it is a quest that aims to think reality in terms of its fundamental *contingency*. "Event," I will argue, is thus also the name for the primacy of contingency in contemporary ontology, and this primacy can only be discovered by a suspension of the principle of sufficient reason. This particular name—event—to address the issue of contingency also indicates that the emphasis on contingency is carried by a particular question: how to think the possibility and the arrival of something radically new and unforeseen as an absolute aspect of our reality?

At the same time, this shared concern suffers the same fate as the common focus on the problem of the unity of being I analyzed in the first part of this book. Despite a shared impetus to suspend the principle of sufficient reason, contemporary ontologies develop two different trajectories in the realm opened up by this suspension. Also the axis of the event of the three-dimensional space of contemporary ontology gives rise to two contrasting trajectories and even opposing orientations.

Clearly, in light of the previous chapters, one might be tempted to describe these two orientations once more in terms of the difference between the two schools and their respective methods: Badiou's and Meillassoux's speculative accounts of the event versus Heidegger's, Nancy's, Marion's, and Romano's hermeneutic-phenomenological accounts of the event. Obviously, this methodological difference is visible in the discussion of the concept of the event and the principle of sufficient reason. Yet, as I will argue in the next chapters, to approach the issue of the event in terms of the methodological affinities among authors obscures the real struggle of orientations that takes place in the present-day conceptualizations of the event. Where the methodological division suggests the following pairing: Badiou and Meillassoux versus Heidegger and Romano, a systematic account of the discussions concerning the event suggests that a chiasmus of schools is taking place when we try to understand the different conceptions of the event: Badiou and Romano versus Heidegger and Meillassoux. This chiasmus of schools does not confuse the discussion; rather, it shows how fresh and alive these discussions are. Whatever specific methodological approach one may adopt toward the problems that confront ontology today, one has to deal with the same problems although they may be traversed by different trajectories. More importantly, because representatives from different schools sometimes share a similar trajectory, varying approaches do not simply lead to opposed trajectories; rather, they lead to complementary analyses of the similar trajectories promising a more fertile interaction between approaches.

In chapter 1, I briefly announced the two different trajectories in a reflection on the event. I did so in the following temporal terms: the difference between these two trajectories is the difference between being *after* and being *before* the event, between *following* the event and *awaiting* the event in its imminence. There are important reasons why this focus on the primacy of the past or the future of the event marks a real dispute over the event in contemporary thought, which will become clear in the next chapters. Chapter 4 covers this problem in terms of a discussion between Heidegger and Badiou, whereas chapter 5 places it in light of the work of two contemporary philosophers, Quentin Meillassoux and Claude Romano. Romano provides us with a hermeneutic phenomenology of the event for which the phenomenon of birth is exemplary, while Meillassoux considers the speculative consequences of an ontological rejection of the principle of sufficient reason and introduces a speculative variation of Heidegger's *Sein-können* ("potentiality-for-being") as *pouvoir-être-autre,* "potentiality-for-being-otherwise." In chapter 6, I will retake the issues of chapters 4 and 5 in terms of Agamben's ontology and return to my interrupted interpretation of Agamben's reading of *Bartleby, the Scrivener* in order to discuss how the question of contingency is addressed in this reading.

Four

Advent or Birth
Two Models of the Event

> "The as yet unnamable which is proclaiming itself
> and which can do so, as is necessary whenever a birth
> is in the offing, only under the species of the nonspecies,
> in the formless, mute, infant, and terrifying form of monstrosity."
> —Jacques Derrida, *L'écriture et la différence*

> "One wishes to say: 'listen, if this thought is still fully to come,
> let us return to see when at least a part of it will have come!'"
> —Alain Badiou, "L'offrande réservée"

Without any doubt, Badiou and Heidegger are two of the most influential philosophers for rethinking the conception of the event today. For both, the event concerns "the revolutionary," that is, the singular and unheard-of new beginning, a radical change of thought and reality.[1] Moreover, they both introduce the concept of the event as an alternative to the ontotheological motive of metaphysics. Nevertheless, as I suggested before, their conceptions of the event follow different and at times incompatible trajectories. This chapter proposes to understand these differences systematically under the heading of the difference between birth and advent as two models for thinking the contingency of the event.

Heidegger and "The Wholly Other Song of Beyng"

According to Heidegger, the principle of sufficient reason forms the very heart of ontotheology and the metaphysical conception of God. As Heidegger claims, this God exists if and only if the principle of sufficient reason is valid: "God exists only insofar as the principle of reason holds.... But the first cause is God. So the principle of reason holds only insofar as God exists. But God exists only insofar as the principle of reason holds."[2]

Therefore, as I argued before, the quest for an alternative conception of ontology is necessarily an examination of the realm that is disclosed by the *epochē* of this principle. For Heidegger, as I will argue, this realm is determined by the concept of the event as *Ereignis*. This is not a straightforward claim when considering his lecture series on the principle of reason: although concepts related to *Ereignis* such as appropriation (*Zu-eignung*) play an important role in *Der Satz vom Grund*, the notion of the event itself is not significantly present, if it is present at all. Yet this does not mean that the concept of the event is simply absent. As Petra Jaeger, editor of the *Gesamtausgabe* edition of *Der Satz vom Grund*, reports in her epilogue, Heidegger wrote the following sentence in the margin of the address added to the lecture series: "The address '*Der Satz vom Grund*' is an attempt to emplace being through discussion in the event."[3] This comment implies that Heidegger's interpretation and transformation of the principle of sufficient reason in the course of the address is concerned with relocating being. Hence, ontology undergoes a significant transformation—a transformation so significant that Heidegger even prefers to abandon the term "ontology" for the thought opened up in this transformation: the suspension of the principle of reason withdraws being from the realm of this principle and discloses the realm of the event in which being is now "emplaced." Since this connection between suspension and event is not accounted for in *Der Satz vom Grund*, I will read this lecture series in light of some crucial and thematically connected passages from the *Beiträge*.

Changing Tonality

The importance of the principle of sufficient reason for philosophical thought as well as for the human relation to reality cannot be overstated. The "principle of reason" (*Satz vom Grund*) is the "fundamental principle" (*Grundsatz*) of ontotheology: since the principles and propositions developed in both philosophy and the sciences respect and presuppose the principle of reason, this latter principle is the basis for all of them: "The principle of reason is the ground/reason of principles. The principle of reason is the ground/reason of the principle."[4] Moreover, this principle is the very element of the human relation to reality: we live and think according to this principle; this means that, when we encounter beings, we look for the grounds, reasons, and causes of these beings. This relation to the world finds its culmination in the scientific attitude: the principle of sufficient reason is the element par excellence of scientific reason.[5] Philosophically, this human attitude to reality is determined as representation (*Vorstellung*). As subjects, humans relate only to what they can represent, that is, as the German terminology more clearly indicates, to what they can put in front of them—*vor sich stellen*—so that it stands there *securely* and secured as object (*Gegen-stand*); only in this way can humans grasp this object and its existence. Only that of which we know the causes and reasons stands securely in front of us. In this specific sense of the word "representation," the modern philosophical account of the human comportment to the world is stamped by Leibniz's account of the principle of sufficient reason.[6] This also implies that this principle is the principle of *ontology* since it determines what does and does not count as a being. According to this principle, everything that is and everything that happens has a sufficient cause and reason for its existence and occurrence, respectively. Therefore, only those beings and occurrences of which the grounds and reasons can be provided count as beings. "Every *being* (*as being*) has a *reason*." In the modern framework, only objects count as beings. Consequently, everything that is has its reason of existence, its "why," as Heidegger puts it: "Nothing is without a why."[7]

Playing with this latter formulation, Heidegger famously contrasts the principle of reason with the famous words of the mystic Angelus

Silesius, who writes that "the rose is without why: it blooms because [or while; *weil*] it blooms."[8] For the human whose relation to reality is stamped by the principle of reason, the Silesian messenger communicates *nothing* since the messenger discloses something about the rose that cannot be captured within the boundaries of this principle. As Heidegger claims, the principle only applies to the rose when we put it in front of us as "object of our representation," but it does not apply to the rose as it "stands alone" and "simply is a rose."[9] *Pace* Meillassoux, who claims that Heidegger is a strong correlationist relating being back to the thinking human being, Heidegger clearly suggests here that there is a mode of being of the rose that does not depend on our representation of it. Thus, it is independent of the way we normally, by following the principle of reason, relate to it. Angelus Silesius's words suggest that we have the possibility to *relate otherwise* to the rose, that another comportment or attitude toward being and beings is possible. We may relate to beings in such a way that we *let them be* rather than that we subsume them under the principle of reason. To let the rose be means here to consider the actual taking place of the rose's blooming and flourishing, which is without reason. What the principle of reason considers to be nothing turns out to be nothing less than the being of the rose itself, according to Heidegger's interpretation of the hint given by the Silesian messenger.

Strictly speaking, when Heidegger introduces this example in the fifth hour of his lecture series, he does not yet have the means to fully understand this hint. Therefore, Angelus Silesius is truly a messenger who brings a hint and a word from a realm that still needs to be opened up: it is still covered in mist and as if behind a veil (*Nebel*); the new realm is dawning and shimmering in the words of the messenger, but not yet shining out of itself.[10] In this sense, the messenger's hint is performative. It is a word that does something. It punctures the domain of the principle of reason and pluralizes reality by the announcement of a mode of being that cannot be subsumed under the unifying gesture of this principle.

In the course of the lecture series, which is truly on-the-way (*unterwegs*) in Heidegger's sense of the term, the messenger's hint from beyond the principle of reason motivates and orients the next step in this course, namely, the suspension and deactivation of this principle. This is the only hope for reaching into the realm from which this hint comes and to which it hints. In this sense, the hint opens up a space of transition and transformation to which the rest of the lecture series is devoted. In the text, this transition takes place by a shift in tonality attuning us to a new reading of the principle of reason. This new tonality, as Heidegger calls it, gathers being and reason and shows that the principle of reason *conceals* a particular saying of being (*Sagen vom Sein*) that cannot be identified in or by the principle's manifest statement (*Aussage*) about beings.[11]

This shift in tonality, as Heidegger makes clear, cannot simply be *deduced* from the principle of reason when read in its usual tonality. It should, rather, be conceived as an interruption of this usual tonality. It requires a discontinuity, namely, a leap (*Sprung*) away from the ground, that is, an *Absprung*.[12] This leap away from the quest for reasons makes an inquiry into the *essence* of reason (*Wesen des Grundes*) possible. One should not underestimate the consequences of this shift in tonality. The principle of ground forms the heart of ontotheological thought and affects our comportment to beings, our mode of speech, and our philosophical thinking. It requires that we express our understanding in statements and propositions, allowing us to grasp the reasons and causes of beings and occurrences. However, the saying of being that is heard in the second tonality is of a different nature; the change in tonality brings us "into another manner of speaking."[13] Hence, this change affects our attitude to being as well as our manner of speaking and thinking: "This requires nothing less than that the manner of our thinking transform itself." This transformation also displaces metaphysics since, in this transition, "metaphysics loses the rank of the normative mode of thinking."[14]

Before explaining in more detail what this leap is and how it transforms thinking, let me first show how this transition is systematically connected to themes from the *Beiträge*. The latter text also speaks of a transition and transformation of thinking, namely, from the first beginning (*der erste Anfang*) of thought to the other beginning (*der andere Anfang*). The first beginning concerns the history of metaphysics characterized by the guiding question about the beingness of beings, as I explained in the introduction. For Heidegger, this guiding question is a truly *ontological* question. However, as ontological question, it does not yet reach the fundamental question concerning "the truth of beyng" (*die Wahrheit des Seyns*) and "the essential occurring of beyng" (*die Wesung des Seyns*).[15] This is why he argues that the other beginning cannot be called ontology. Even the fundamental ontology developed in *Sein und Zeit* does not attain the fundamental question. Fundamental ontology, as Heidegger understands it in the *Beiträge*, is therefore transitional in nature. Whereas "normal" ontology operates on the basis of the guiding question without addressing it *as question,* fundamental ontology does let the guiding question appear as question. Hence, while fundamental ontology *prepares* the shift toward the other beginning, it does not yet complete the leap into the fundamental question.[16]

The other beginning is first and foremost concerned with the *Ereignis* since "the essential occurring of *beyng*" is nothing but this event. By drawing a parallel between the shift of tonality from *Der Satz vom Grund* and the "turning in the event" (*Kehre im Ereignis*) that marks the transition from the first to the other beginning, one may conclude that the suspension and the deactivation of the principle of sufficient reason discloses the realm in which the event as *Ereignis* is thought—as the note in the margin of the lecture "*Der Satz vom Grund*" already indicated. A new tonality is found so that "the wholly other song of beyng resounds."[17]

Leaping into a Wholly Other Song

Let us deepen this comparison between *Der Satz vom Grund* and the *Beiträge* to understand how the former's shift in tonality and the latter's transition from the first to the other beginning affect *thinking* and the place of metaphysics. In both texts, Heidegger emphatically states that there is no place for metaphysics in the enactment of the leap: "In the domain of the other beginning, there is neither 'ontology' nor any 'metaphysics.'"[18] Yet—and one should keep this subtlety in mind whenever one reads this type of sentence in Heidegger's work—this does not mean that the realm to be disclosed by the new tonality and in the other beginning is a realm that is unrelated to metaphysics or ontology. This new realm is *not* separated or isolated from metaphysics.

It is exactly at this point that Heidegger brings out the figure of the leap. A leap into a new realm always needs an old domain to leap away from. As both *Der Satz vom Grund* and the *Beiträge* argue, the leap is a leap-away-from (*Absprung*), and metaphysics is the domain one leaps away from (*Absprungsbereich*).[19] Metaphysics does not remain untouched in this transition, and it is not simply left behind in this leap-away-from.[20] Rather, the mode of thought disclosed by the leap makes the domain of metaphysics "surveyable in a different way than before." That is, the leap provides us with a new way of understanding metaphysics.[21] This new way of surveying metaphysics is not an additional or secondary effect of the leap and the mode of thinking the leap opens up. Rather, it is an essential element that shapes this other mode of thinking.

In sum, Heidegger combines two statements on metaphysics. On the one hand, "*every sort* of metaphysics is and must be at an end" for the other beginning to take place. On the other hand, the expression "the end of metaphysics" does not mean that "philosophy would be done with 'metaphysics.'" Rather, as he continues, "'metaphysics' in its essential impossibility must now for the first time play over to philosophy, and the latter itself in the same way must play over to its other beginning."[22] The mode of thinking that belongs to the other beginning can only be disclosed in and as a new contemplation or reflection (*Besinnung*) on ontotheology and the history of metaphysics.[23]

To capture the meaning of this contemplation (*Besinnung*), note that Heidegger distinguishes between "historical reflection" (*geschichtliche Besinnung*) and "historical consideration" (*historische Betrachtung*).[24] Whereas the latter concerns a "kind of cognition" employed in the historical sciences in order to describe the past, reflection as *Besinnung* examines the meaning [*Sinn*] of happenings (*das Geschehende*) and "the meaning of history."[25] In this context, happenings do not refer to everything that goes on around us. It is a qualified notion for Heidegger. Historical reflection can only take place "where history is grasped creatively and co-formatively—in the creation of the poet, the architect, the thinker, the statesman."[26] Only such poetic, architectural, philosophic, and political creations deserve to be called true happenings or events. Heidegger develops this idea in particular in relation to the thinker and the creative happening or revolutionary beginning that marks true thought. The reflection on the history of metaphysics is integral to the other beginning, but it does not simply coincide with it. Let us therefore consider what thinking is in the other beginning (or the new tonality) according to *Der Satz vom Grund* and the *Beiträge*.

In *Der Satz vom Grund* Heidegger describes how thinking changes in the shift of tonality: Thinking (*Denken*) becomes memory (*Andenken*) in the sense of *Gedächtnis*.[27] Thought as memory is directed toward the history of metaphysics, but it is not a remembrance of this history that collects the insights, propositions, or systems handed down to us. It is not concerned with the past as *das Vergangene,* as Heidegger puts it. It is, rather, concerned with the past in the sense of *das Gewesene,* that which has been. This is a past that continues to work in the present. It affects our present by granting us "inexhaustible treasures." He describes this granting of "treasures" in terms of *schicken* and *entziehen*.

The verb *schicken* means "to send," "to distribute," and "to arrange"; it is often translated as "to destine" in order to capture the close connection to the word *Geschick* (fate or destiny). Heidegger plays with the similarity between the words *Geschick* and *Geschichte* (history) to account for the historicality of being: the history of being concerns the way in which being is destined to us, distributed and arranged for us. Yet, in its destining, the destining or sending itself (*das Schickende*) withdraws (*entziehen*) itself. For instance, in the principle of sufficient reason, being is sent to us as ground and reason, but being is itself hidden in this giving. This means that the principle does not disclose being but only presents a statement about beings. In the leap, however, this structure of *Geschick des Seins* and *Entzug des Seins* is unconcealed: it is the change of tonality that allows us to hear in the principle of reason a saying of being, according to Heidegger.[28] Thinking as *Andenken* (memory) is concerned with this particular thought of being: it contemplates how, in the history of metaphysics, being is sent to us in its withdrawal. In this sense, thought reflects on the structures that make the history of metaphysics possible. Obviously, this means that thought requires the history of metaphysics since this history is the "subject matter" (*Sache*) of its contemplation. Yet, this does not make this contemplation itself metaphysical: the reflection on this history is enacted in and as the leap away from metaphysics.

Let us combine this analysis from *Der Satz vom Grund* with one of the aforementioned quotes from the *Beiträge* in which Heidegger states that thought does not simply leave metaphysics behind but has to show *why* another beginning is necessary by first establishing the "essential impossibility" (*Wesensunmöglichkeit*) of metaphysics. Indeed, *Der Satz vom Grund* provides an account of this essential impossibility of metaphysics, as can be seen in the following argument. Being beyond metaphysics, thinking as *Andenken* shows how being is thought *in metaphysics*. We could also say that, by deactivating metaphysics, thought shows how metaphysics works and how it is *philosophy*, that is, a thinking of being. The combination of *Geschick* and *Entzug*—disclosed by thought as *Andenken*—indicates that in metaphysics, being can only be disclosed out of concealment; this concealment is itself the source of the disclosure of being. Hence, differently put, metaphysics can only be a thought of being on the basis of an *indispensable remainder* with respect to its own understanding and interpretation of being: without such a remainder as the source of the disclosure of being, no metaphysics is possible. The "essential impossibility" of metaphysics today becomes clear as soon as we become aware of the fact that modern thought exhausts exactly the concealment of being. *In fact,* since metaphysics approaches being along the lines of the guiding question, *it is exactly the principle of sufficient reason that marks the disappearance of the "last remainder of the concealment of being"* since this principle states that there is nothing beyond the realm of beings and their reasons or grounds.[29] This is why metaphysics has become essentially impossible at the end of the modern era; it has lost its source and can therefore no longer accomplish its original task, namely, to think being.

Note that this analysis of the essential impossibility of metaphysics shows the particular Heideggerian meaning of the phrase "the end of metaphysics." This meaning should be taken into account when we consider Badiou's and Meillassoux's efforts to revive speculative and metaphysical modes of thinking. Although this appears to offer a huge contrast to Heidegger, the speculative versions of Badiou and Meillassoux also depart from Heidegger's analysis of metaphysics and share his insight that we can no longer think being in terms of the principle of sufficient reason. By thinking the history of metaphysics, thought as leap also opens up a "wholly other" alternative to the guiding question. This second dimension of the leap aims to do justice to the original motivation of metaphysics to think being, although it does so in a wholly other way.

Before discussing this second dimension of transitional thought, let me return briefly to the negative structure of metaphysics I discussed in chapter 3. Agamben uses this terminology to describe how philosophers such as Nancy and Derrida, when claiming to overcome metaphysics, are actually only bringing "the fundamental problem of metaphysics to light."[30] Now, after this discussion of Heidegger, we can see more clearly how to understand Agamben's statement. Heidegger's analysis of the role of concealment in the metaphysical thinking of being supports Agamben's claim. Metaphysics indeed operates on the basis of a fundamental negativity that makes metaphysics possible as a thinking of being. Heidegger's concept of *Geschick*, or destiny, to account for the history of metaphysics shows this most clearly. In the *Beiträge*, he writes that the abandonment of being (*Seinsverlassenheit*) is the destiny of the first beginning. In his later essay "Zeit und Sein," he explains what this might mean and why it describes the law or the destiny of the history of being.[31] This history is marked by a plurality of sendings (*Schickungen*) in which being is sent to us. Yet, this plurality is abandoned to a law or destiny that gathers all these sendings together: all of them belong to and occur out of a primordial withdrawal of the sending (*das Schickende*) itself, namely, *Ereignis*. Moreover, since this withdrawal remains concealed and unthought, metaphysics operates on the basis of a fundamental negativity: its destiny, that is, the essence and the law within which the history of metaphysics takes place, is the withdrawal of the event that destines and gives being.

Hence, Heidegger's analysis affirms Agamben's conception of the fundamental negativity of metaphysics. Yet, it also refines Agamben's statements. (1) Although metaphysics operates on the basis of an unthought remainder or "negativity," as Agamben calls it, Heidegger notes that this remainder is *exhausted* in the history of metaphysics. The necessity to overcome metaphysics is thus not found in its negative structure as such, but in its historical inconsistency: *metaphysics needs a remainder to think being, but it annuls this remainder in the historical process of its thought*. This is why metaphysics can no longer meet its own intrinsic demand to think being. (2) The effort—undertaken by Heidegger and Derrida in their own way—to make this exhaustion visible cannot simply be called metaphysical, as Agamben does, since it requires a position on the threshold of metaphysics, leaping outside of it. Obviously, Agamben knows this. In fact, it is the reason why the concepts of inoperativeness and deactivation play such an important role in his thought: only by interrupting the normal functioning of metaphysics can its negative structure be shown—but this is itself no longer simply metaphysical. (3) Therefore, it is impossible to maintain that Heidegger's (as well as Derrida's) thought remains *fully* indebted to this negative structure of metaphysics. Heidegger's account of an alternative in the other tonality and the other beginning is not necessarily bounded by or to this negative structure of metaphysics. Rather, what is preserved is the original motivation of metaphysics to think being. Yet, as the notion of *Vordenken* shows, to which I will turn now, the retrieval (*Wiederholung*) of this motivation leads to the advent of a wholly other thought—"wholly other and nevertheless the same," since it continues the same task of thinking to think being but in a wholly other way.[32]

Let us return to the question of thinking in *Der Satz vom Grund*. The other thinking, *Denken*, of being is not only *An-denken* or memory; it is also *Vor-denken*. In the German, a *Vordenker* is a thinker who prepares something. Similarly, for Heidegger, *Vordenken* is thinking that prepares something new that has not yet arrived and has not yet been born but is in the process of arriving; in *Vordenken*, thinking is in the time of advent, awaiting and preparing the birth of something it cannot predict, calculate, force to come, or master. Although *Andenken* and *Vordenken* cannot be separated since they concern one and the same thinking, one might say that *Vordenken* is that aspect that *relates thinking to the advent of the wholly other beginning of the thought of being:* "That into which the leap anticipatorily [*vordenkend*] leaps is not some region of things present at hand into which one can simply step. Rather, it is the realm of what *first approaches* as worthy of thought. But this approach is also shaped by the traits of what has-been, and only because of this is it discernible."³³ Thinking leaps into a realm that is still in preparation and confronts it with something that is worthy of thought (*denkwürdig*) but is also still in the process of approaching. Yet, this advent is co-shaped (*mitgeprägt*) by the characteristics of what has been (*das Gewesene*). This indicates how Heidegger understands the connection between *Andenken* and *Vordenken*. Both dimensions of thinking are disclosed in and by the leap out of metaphysics. While thinking reflects on what has been—that is, the history of metaphysics—thinking is also confronted with the unthought (*das Ungedachte*) of what has been. This unthought is not left behind in the leap. Rather, it is exactly *what is worthy of thought* and thus calls for *Vordenken;* it requires a preparatory thought to advance into this unthought concealing the essence of metaphysics as well as the other beginning.³⁴

Heidegger's analysis of the word *Grund* in the last hours of his lecture course *Der Satz vom Grund* offers an exemplary demonstration of this interplay between *Vordenken* and *Andenken*. First, he shows the different transitions the notion of reason undergoes in the history of metaphysics and how this notion marks our relation to being: contemplating this history leads us back from the German *Grund* via the Latin *ratio* to the Greek *logos*. As he notes, these terms have irreducibly different meanings. At the end of this reflection, Heidegger concludes: "But being and ground/reason are...the concealed fullness of what first comes to light in the *Geschick* of being as the history of Western thinking."³⁵ In line with the whole lecture course, this conclusion indicates that being and reason belong together in the history of metaphysics: being gives itself as reason or ground throughout this history. Yet, this conclusion also means that being does not give itself as reason in one particular meaning. By showing the different meanings of *logos, ratio,* and *Grund,* thought as *Andenken* discloses the hidden abundance and the unfolding plurality of senses with which being is destined and sent to us as reason in the history of metaphysics.

Second, the new tonality with which Heidegger reads the principle of reason confronts us with a particular unthought. It is not enough to think the plural ways with which being is sent to us as reason. It is also imperative to think the co-belonging of these different meanings, that is, the law or the rule that allows us to think how being can be given as reason or ground in so many ways. In terms of Heidegger's notions of *Schickungen, das Geschick,* and *das Schickende,* one might say that the co-belonging of being and reason is the law or the destiny that gathers together how being is sent to us in metaphysics: although each of the different sendings (*Schickungen*) sends being in a different sense of reason, being is nevertheless always sent to us in connection to reason. Yet, this destiny (*Geschick*) itself depends on something that remains concealed in the phrase that being and reason belong together, namely, that which sends (*das Schickende*). Thinking has a very precise task—to bring this concealment into the open.

One exemplary term that shows how this task is enacted is *Ab-Grund,* meaning abyss as well as absence (*Ab-Wesen*) of reason and ground. The new tonality in which the principle of reason is heard discloses being as *Ab-Grund.* Yet, this new tonality does not simply confront us with another turn or another sending in the history of being. Rather, the concept of *Ab-Grund* refers us to the concealed realm of *das Schickende* out of which being is given in its co-belonging with reason. It is not my intention to analyze the notion of *Ab-Grund* in all its subtleties and difficulties; I only want to indicate two aspects of this notion that are crucial for the context of this study.

First of all, if *Abgrund* is the term that Heidegger uses to describe the provenance of the co-belonging of being and reason in metaphysics, this implies that this co-belonging itself is abyssal: *it is contingent and without reason.* Hence, although thinking as *Andenken* contemplates how being is destined to us in its co-belonging with reason or ground, this thought invites and prepares a thought that thinks this abyssal co-belonging *itself.*

Second, the notion of *Ab-Grund* brings once more to mind the important figure of the leap-away-from (*Ab-Sprung*). In addition to *Andenken,* which thinks the co-belonging of being and reason, the hyphen in *Ab-Grund* suggests that thought as *Vordenken* prepares a leaping away (*Absprung*) from reason (*Grund*). This means not only that it leaps away from all the different meanings of reason or ground—*Grund, ratio,* as well as *logos*—with which being is sent to us in the history of metaphysics, that is, in the first beginning of thought, but also that it leaps away from the co-belonging of being and reason. When the abundance of the destiny or sending of being (*Seinsgeschick*) unfolds plural, singular ways in which being is *Grund, Ab-Grund* prepares a thought before or outside of this co-belonging of being and reason—an outside that is at the same time a turning into the abyssal provenance of this co-belonging.

In the *Beiträge,* we see a movement similar to the one we just discussed from *Der Satz vom Grund.* In the *Beiträge,* the turning in the essential occurrence of "beyng" is also the turning in the essential occurrence of reason or ground (*Wesung des Grundes*), and Heidegger names this occurrence *Ab-Grund.*[36] In the new tonality with which *Andenken* hears the principle of reason, *Sein* and *Grund* resound together. In the logic of the *Beiträge, Ab-Grund* and *Ereignis* resound together in the other beginning. Hence, the suspension of the principle of reason opens up the abyss and the event alike.[37] As preparing another thinking of being, *Vordenken* is a thinking whereby an ontology dawns in which being is thought as abyss and event.

In the *Beiträge,* the terms *Andenken* and *Vordenken* do not play the same role as in *Der Satz vom Grund.*[38] Nevertheless, this text offers a clear account that defines thinking in the other beginning. Heidegger leaves no doubt as to the particular task of this thinking, which he calls "inceptual thinking" (*das anfängliche Denken*): "all that matters for thinking is the meditation [*Besinnung*] on the 'event.' "[39] How does thinking accomplish such a task? Like *Andenken* and *Vordenken,* inceptual thinking is not only engaged in the *preparation* of the other beginning but also in an *interpretation* of the essence of the first beginning. In this sense, Heidegger's reflections on inceptual thinking prefigure the double determination of thought as *Andenken* and *Vordenken*. In fact, in the *Beiträge*, he uses the figure of the *Auseinandersetzung* to describe how inceptual thinking relates (to) both the first and the other beginning: "Thinking of beyng as event is inceptual thinking, which prepares the other beginning by confronting the first one [*als Auseinandersetzung mit dem ersten Anfang*]."[40]

Auseinandersetzung could literally be translated as "setting apart." In the above quote it is aptly translated as "confronting," but its semantic value also includes "discussion," "exposition," "dispute," and "encounter." In chapter 2, I argued that Nancy's use of the term "exposition" also includes the meaning of *Auseinandersetzung*: we encounter and are exposed to beings other than us, and we receive our own being from this exposure. Heidegger uses *Auseinandersetzung* in this sense on several occasions. A striking example can be found in his reading of Hölderlin from 1942, where he uses this term to describe Hölderlin's translations of the Greek poets Sophocles and Pindar.[41] This translation, as Heidegger notes, is a historical dialogue (*geschichtliche Zwiesprache*) in which Hölderlin aims to name the essence of the German language. Apparently, Hölderlin has no immediate access to this essence. Only in and through the exposition to and encounter with a foreign language can this essence be found.

In the case of Hölderlin, the Greek language of the famous poets provides him with the necessary means to appropriate his own language. The foreign language is not only other than one's own language, but it is also the provenance (*Herkunft*) of the appropriation of one's own language. Only in the enactment of this encounter can a foreign language become such a provenance. At the same time, Heidegger insists that this dialogical encounter does not mix up the two languages. The Greek and the German languages are kept apart because this historical dialogue lets each language be in what is its own (*das Eigene*): the languages are neither merged nor mixed up. Consequently, the figure of *Auseinandersetzung* describes a dialogical movement that does not strive toward unification. Rather, the foreign partner in conversation remains foreign because the German language does not assimilate it. As such, it is and remains the foreign provenance of what might be called the true event of this translating dialogue: the poet is exposed to a foreign language in order to appropriate the essence of his own language. Thus, what takes place in the encounter with the foreign language is nothing less than the poetic equivalent of what the *Beiträge* calls *Ereignis* in the context of thought: the encounter with a foreign language is the poetic event that appropriates the essence of the poet's own language.

This explication of Hölderlin's poetic confrontation helps us to interpret how *Auseinandersetzung* characterizes inceptual thinking in the *Beiträge*. In the *Grundprobleme der Philosophie*, which is a course closely connected to the *Beiträge* in theme as well as in time, Heidegger uses the term "historical confrontation" (*geschichtliche Auseinandersetzung*) to characterize the encounter and dialogue between the first and the other beginning.[42] In line with Heidegger's interpretation of Hölderlin's translating dialogue with the Greek poets, the *Beiträge* understands the confrontation that marks inceptual thinking thought as a historical dialogue (*geschichtliche Zwiesprache*), albeit this time it is a dialogue of thinkers and not of poets.[43] While maintaining the irreducible difference between the first beginning and the other beginning—remember that there is no place for any form of metaphysics in the other beginning, according to Heidegger—the other beginning is nevertheless exposed to the first beginning. Heidegger describes this encounter as the retrieval of the first beginning in order to unfold the other beginning: "*inceptual* thinking is necessary as a confrontation between the first beginning, which is still to be won back, and the other beginning, which is to be unfolded."[44] The distinction between retrieving or winning back and unfolding anticipates the distinction between *Andenken* and *Vordenken*. Indeed, inceptual thinking requires an encounter with the first beginning to accomplish its main task: the original appropriation of the history of metaphysics prepares the other beginning as "the *turning in the event*."[45] Hence, the retrieval—here used in the double sense of winning back and repetition (*Wiederholung*)—of the first beginning does not belong to the first beginning. In its inquiry into the essence of metaphysics, inceptual thinking is already preparing the other beginning.[46]

Hence, we may conclude that *Der Satz vom Grund* and the *Beiträge* offer similar conceptions of thinking. Nevertheless, our reading of the *Beiträge* also offers something that *Der Satz vom Grund* does not and which is essential to the questions guiding this study: it presents a detailed description of inceptual thinking as a *comportment* to the event. It will not come as a surprise to anyone familiar with Heidegger's work that the crucial notion that captures this comportment is *Verhaltenheit*, of which Heidegger writes that it "determines the style of inceptual thinking in the other beginning."[47] The first beginning of philosophy had its own basic disposition (*Grundstimmung*), namely, *thaumazein* or wonder (*Er-staunen*).[48] Yet, since "*our* basic position toward beings is not any more and never again will be that of the first beginning..., the basic disposition can no longer be the one of wonder."[49] The other beginning has its own basic disposition and style, for which Heidegger chooses the name *Verhaltenheit*.

Which style and ethos does *Verhaltenheit* express? In German, this word is related to *Haltung*, which simply means "ethos" or "comportment," as well as to *sich verhalten*, which means to behave or to comport in a particular way. Clearly, it is related to the adjective *verhalten*, which does not simply mean comportment in general but, rather, refers to a controlled, restrained, or careful comportment. This is why *Verhaltenheit* is often translated as "restraint." Yet, such a translation remains a mere substitution of words if we do not enter the realm of thinking to which it belongs, so let us consider more closely what Heidegger means by *Verhaltenheit* as the basic disposition of inceptual thinking.

First, while introducing three basic moods (*Grundstimmungen*) at work in inceptual thinking—shock (*Erschrecken*), restraint (*Verhaltenheit*), and diffidence (*Staunen*)—Heidegger immediately adds that the middle term is the middle, the milieu, and the center (*Mitte*) of the other two. In fact, as he continues, shock and diffidence "characterize with more explicitness what *originally* belongs to restraint."[50] Hence, *Verhaltenheit*, understood in its originary (and not in its common or traditional) sense, captures these three basic moods as well as the comportment they disclose.

Second, this comportment is understood in immediate relation to the preparatory mode of inceptual thinking. Heidegger explicates *Verhaltenheit* as "the pre-disposition [*Vor-stimmung*] of readiness [*Bereitschaft*] for the refusal as gift."[51] Hence, to prepare (*vor-bereiten*) in the mode of inceptual thinking, thinking is to be attuned to a predisposition (*Vor-stimmung*) to a preparedness (*Bereitschaft*) for the refusal (*Verweigerung*) of being.[52] Apparently, the real gift of inceptual thinking is not so much something we can appropriate, possess, or grasp, but it is the refusal of something—namely, being. In this sense, *Verhaltenheit* may indeed be called a restraint: it holds back in order not to prematurely appropriate being; thus, it is also a preparedness to endure and hold out the refusal of being. *Verhaltenheit* describes an attitude or comportment toward being when being is refused to us, that is, when abandonment marks our relation to being.

Third, in the fourth part of the *Beiträge,* entitled "The Leap," Heidegger unfolds the meaning of this comportment further in terms of the difference between the first and the other beginning. This difference confronts thinking with the necessity of a decision: *either* one remains bound to the end of the first beginning, *or* one is prepared "to initiate the other beginning, i.e., to be resolved toward its long preparation."[53] While the first beginning is the domain from which inceptual thinking leaps away, the other beginning does not offer the same solid ground: it requires a long preparation and the thinker's comportment should be one of being *resolutely* prepared for it. The term "resoluteness" (*Entschlossenheit*), which Heidegger uses in *Sein und Zeit* to describe how Dasein should relate to its disclosedness (*Erschlossenheit*) for its own potentiality-of-being (*Seinkönnen*), returns here to characterize the nature of thought's preparedness for the other beginning.

Combining these three aspects of *Verhaltenheit,* one might say that *the comportment of thinking* to the event is *a resolved preparedness to prepare* the event. Yet, one might wonder, why is it necessary to position oneself on the side of the advent of the event? Why not wait, as Badiou suggests in the quote I used as an epigraph to this chapter, until at least a piece of it has actually come? For Heidegger, the advent of the event corresponds to the possibility of the event, and as I shall argue later, to the event as possibility. In the introduction, I referred to Heidegger's play with the words *Notlosigkeit* and *Not der Notlosigkeit* in the *Beiträge*. The *Notlosigkeit*—the lack of any experience of need, want, or distress in relation to the withdrawal of being—characterizes our time in which the concealment as the source of the disclosure of being is exhausted and nothing remains but beings and their reasons or grounds to be. Yet, at the same time, something happens to this *Notlosigkeit*. It becomes a *Not* itself—a need or a distress. This "need arising from the lack of need" (*Not der Notlosigkeit*) is a very strange need since it does not correspond to an actual need.[54] It is merely an acute invitation or appeal—a *Nötigung*—to "an other sort of questioning."[55] In this sense, this strange need is a *hint* disclosing the *possibility* of another beginning and another mode of questioning.[56] By attesting to the possibility of the event, the event is announced and heralded by its advent. The event thus belongs in "the time that remains," in which a birth is announced but has not yet taken place. In chapters 5 and 6, I will continue these explorations of the importance of the notion of the possible, but first I will confront Heidegger's model of advent with Badiou's model of birth.

Shimmering and Shining: The Phenomenality of the Event

When expressing his worries concerning the Heideggerian notion of *alētheia*, Nancy argues that these worries all go back to Heidegger's phenomenological approach. "In a sense," he writes, "phenomenology speaks of nothing but that: appearing. But it still irresistibly convokes us to the pure presence of appearing, to *seeing*." Therefore, phenomenology "does not yet sufficiently touch on the *being* or the *sense* of appearing." As Nancy concludes, this means that phenomenology does not "open sufficiently to the coming of sense, to sense as a coming."[57] The problem Nancy confronts us with in his singular vocabulary is the following: while appearing "results" in the presence of a phenomenon that is available for the phenomenological gaze, the being of appearing or presencing itself is not fully available for this

Advent or Birth   157

gaze since it includes a "coming" that "is infinitely presupposed" by phenomenology.

As soon as we realize that "event" is the name for this being of appearing and coming—that is, the name for that which makes the appearance of the phenomenon possible—we also see that Nancy's comments concern first and foremost the tendency in present-day thought to account for the event in phenomenological terms. (Unlike Heidegger's, Nancy's questions seem to concern primarily philosophers such as Marion, Romano, and Chrétien.) Indeed, in the course of his arguments, he points to the problematic consequences of a phenomenological account for our understanding of the concept of the event. By privileging appearing, "some value of scintillating phenomenality remains invincibly attached" to the event and to our understanding of "the surging forth or surrection of being."[58]

In a long footnote accompanying these concerns, Nancy argues that Badiou and Heidegger share this particular relation between truth and event. Referring to Badiou's account of truth and event, he claims, "One is, at bottom, on a Heideggerian register, that of '*Das Ereignis trägt die Wahrheit* = die Wahrheit durchragt das Ereignis' (the event carries the truth = truth juts out through the event)."[59] Nancy worries about the role truth plays in relation to the event, especially as the right-hand side of the equation expresses. As the left-hand side states, the event carries truth. This means that the event precedes truth and makes it possible for it to happen. Described in this formal way, both Heidegger and Badiou would agree with it: the event is indeed prior to truth. Also, Nancy does not seem to have any problems with this formulation. Yet, as the right-hand side indicates, this implies that truth penetrates—or pierces and punctuates, as Nancy suggests—the event fully. This penetration, as Nancy goes on to explain, can take place in two possible ways. One way is that (a) the event is fully appropriated by truth. Since truth is appearing in this context, this means that the event scintillates with "a constitutive self-evidence." Clearly, what troubles Nancy here is that this dimension of "constitutive self-evidence" reinstates the motive of presence, which is part and parcel of ontotheology as metaphysics of presence. The other possible way is that (b) nothing takes place but "the incisive, empty truth." Since nothing offers itself to be understood in such an event, the only way to penetrate this event is by "an inaugural *decision*." Nancy argues that both of these possibilities for truth penetrating the event can be found "mixed and intermingled in Heidegger without excluding a third source."

Nancy's suggestions are in accordance with the question concerning the relation between Heidegger and Badiou I raised above: (1) The attention to a decision that is not decisionistic or voluntaristic indicates an important similarity between Heidegger and Badiou. How can we differentiate between these two positions? Nancy's account adds two more questions to this first one. (2) He argues that we can find another similarity on the level of the way in which they discuss the phenomenology and the truth of the event. Is this true and, if so, how do they differ in their account of the phenomenology of the event? (3) Beyond the double motive of truth penetrating the event, Nancy suggests a "third resource" for the event in which it is not fully penetrated by truth. What would such a resource be, and can it be traced in the work of Heidegger or Badiou? This section is devoted to these three questions.

Hint and Trace: Two Appearances of the Event

I will first discuss the issue of the appearance of the event. Is there indeed something like "constitutive self-evidence," a pure scintillation by which the event gives itself, as Nancy suggests? How should we think the relation between event and appearance in Badiou and Heidegger?

The previous section already provided us with the material to answer these questions in the case of Heidegger. There, I showed that the figure of the hint (*Wink*) explains how Heidegger thinks the event as that which is to-come. The time of the event is truly the time of advent. The hint heralds the coming of the event while deferring and suspending its actual arrival. This account of the *time* of the event has an immediate consequence for the *phenomenality* of the event. Clearly, the event in its advent is never simply present. Rather, it is only announced as that which is to-come. What is present and what already appeared is only the hint, the herald, and the announcement of the event. Yet, in their appearance they refer beyond themselves. They refer to what is yet to come and what is neither seen nor touched; the hint calls for preparation and resolved preparedness.

In this account of the Heideggerian event as advent, Nancy's description of the way in which truth and appearing penetrate the event is less convincing. The event is not given in or as "constitutive self-evidence." While one might call the hint to be constitutive of the time of the event, the hint is not *self*-evident since it does not refer to itself but to a nonevident event *that is to-come*. In this sense, a hint as Heidegger understands it is never a trace. A trace always refers to what has already passed by and to what precedes it temporally—even if the trace refers to an immemorial past, as Levinas and Derrida suggest. Perhaps poetically, a hint might be called a trace *of the future*.

How about Badiou's concept of the event? Is there a "self-constitutive" truth or appearance of the event in his work? Can truth indeed penetrate the event to such a degree that it constitutes it? *Logiques des mondes* seems the proper text to answer these questions since Badiou develops an objective phenomenology in this work, the goal of which is to explain how worlds of appearances and relations are constituted.[60] While *L'être et l'événement* shows how the event interrupts the structure of being, *Logiques des mondes* develops a slightly different conception of the event in order to show how the event overthrows the structure of appearing in a world and installs a new one—and is in this sense trans-appearing and not only trans-being. The event, one can immediately conclude from this summary, *cannot* be studied in a phenomenology in the strict sense since it does not appear. Yet, the occurrence of an event has serious implications for the way in which objects appear in the world. Despite important differences, this is the analogy between *L'être et l'événement* and *Logiques des mondes:* in the first book, the event cannot be presented in the situation but does affect the post-evental situation; in the second book, the event cannot appear in a world but does change the structure of appearance of this world.

Let us zoom in to understand more precisely what is going on in the transition from *L'être et l'événement* to *Logiques des mondes*.

Using the sophisticated language of mathematical category theory, Badiou first develops in books 2, 3, and 4 of *Logiques des mondes* the formal structure of appearing: what does it mean for objects to appear in a world? These structures are developed in order to introduce a formal account of the event that overthrows this structure of appearing because it does not respect the laws of appearing. In fact, the ontological law transgressed by the event is the same as in *L'être et l'événement:* a "site" is defined by the mathematical impossibility that a set belongs to itself.[61] Yet, in terms of appearance this transgression can take on different forms—three, to be precise—and only one of them is worthy of the word "event." Hence, despite important analogies, *Logiques des mondes* offers a different definition of the event than *L'être et l'événement* does. Before explaining why Badiou changes his definition, let me provide it and discuss its implications for the scintillation Nancy fears to be at the heart of the event.

According to Badiou's formal account of the world, every world—which is the term in *Logiques des mondes* that substitutes the word "situation" used in *L'être et l'événement*—has an order of appearance and, derived from it, an order of existence.[62] Some elements exist more than others. In fact, as Badiou proves in his formal framework, every world has an element that exists *minimally*. This element is said to *inexist*.[63] Now, by definition, an event changes the order of appearance in a world such that the element that inexisted before exists maximally after the event.[64] Badiou calls this particular element that changes from pre-eventual inexistence to post-eventual maximal existence *the trace of the event*. Although the event itself cannot appear since it transgresses the laws of appearance, it grants a scintillating existence to its trace. Thus, the trace of the event is the event's glory and scintillation (*éclat*): the element that has a "past without glory" is now a "maximally intense existence."[65]

In chapter 3, I argued that Badiou's conception of the axiom depends on the splendor and esteem that come from the event itself and is not granted to it by a subject. Although this argument was developed as a consequence of Badiou's explicit statement in *L'être et l'événement* that the subject is preceded by the event, the actual systematic treatment of the relation between subject and event does not really allow us to draw that conclusion. In fact, in *L'être et l'événement*, the existence of the event is only given with the subjective declaration of this existence. There does not seem to be any room to introduce a splendor or esteem that comes from the event itself and that is somehow given prior to the subject as that which inspires and motivates the subject. So how can Badiou substantiate his claim that the event precedes the subject? *Logiques des mondes* repairs this systematic flaw—and this is the reason Badiou changes his definition of the event: the subject does not only relate to the event in its nonpresented and nonappearing nature, but the subject responds to the trace of the event, which is an *objective* scintillation of the event toward which the subject is oriented. That is to say, it is the *trace* of the event where we can find the systematic place of the esteem and splendor of the event in Badiou's work: the trace refers back to the event since its scintillating existence is granted to it by the event that drew its glory from the trace's past mere inexistence.

What are the consequences of this discussion for Nancy's concerns? Strictly speaking, the event is not given with a "constitutive self-evidence" since the event does not appear. Yet, it is also clear that the particular glory with which the trace appears constitutes the splendor of the event for the subject who declares it.[66] In *L'être et l'événement*, Badiou writes, "the entire effort lies in following the event's consequences, not in glorifying its occurrence."[67] He is of the same conviction in *Logiques des mondes*, where he writes, "It is not enough to identify a trace. One must incorporate oneself into what the trace authorizes in terms of consequences. This point is crucial."[68] Even though it is not enough to glorify the occurrence of the event to become a subject, the identification of the event by its trace is nevertheless a necessary ingredient of becoming a subject. This scintillating value of the event is so important for Badiou that he adopts it in the very definition of the event.

The concepts of trace and hint capture the *temporal* difference between Badiou's event and Heidegger's event: Badiou's trace is left behind by an event that has already occurred, while Heidegger's hint awaits and prepares an event that is still to come. The previous considerations show how this temporal difference converts into a *phenomenal* one. Both Heidegger and Badiou argue that the event does not appear. Hence, when considering the phenomenal difference of their conceptions of the event, one should note that the expression "phenomenality of the event" should not be understood as an objective genitive but rather as a subjective genitive. The event gives rise to a specific form of appearance of an intermediate, either hint or trace, by which it appears indirectly itself.

Badiou's trace scintillates and shines. This shining demonstrates with maximal clarity its own birth as the objective consequence of an event. In chapter 1, I raised some questions about the relationship between the atemporality of mathematics and the motive of presence and the metaphysics of presence in Badiou's thought. Here, we see how the phenomenality of the event and its elaboration in terms of the trace of the event in *Logiques des mondes* reiterates the suggestion that the motive of a shining presence remains invincibly attached to Badiou's account of event and subject.

By contrast, the Heideggerian hint does not shine. It only shimmers; it announces the dawning of another beginning and prepares the event of its occurrence. The phenomenal nature of the hint refers to an event that is not present. Rather, to phrase it in the words of Nancy, the "coming into presence of being takes place precisely as non-arrival of presence."[69] This shimmering without a visible sun repeats the Platonic gesture we also found in Nancy: thought is preparatory in nature and awaits that which it cannot force to come.[70]

Announcement and Declaration: A Double Proclamation of the Event

Although I have already discussed at length that neither Heidegger nor Badiou embraces a form of decisionism or voluntarism in their account of the comportment toward the event, the notion of decision does play an important role in their understanding of comportment to the event. To study their understanding of notion more closely, note that for both of them, a decision has a particular linguistic form. One might say that for both of them, the decision consists of and goes hand in hand with a *proclamation* of the event that inaugurates the subject's and the thinker's comportment toward the event, respectively. However, this proclamation takes on two different forms, namely, declaration and announcement, respectively.

In chapter 1, I already discussed Badiou's conception of naming and nomination. "Declaration" is a synonym for this act of naming. It is a performative act: by the utterance "the event has taken place," it is declared and decided that the event has taken place. The previous analysis of the trace of the event specifies the nature of this performative act and shows in which sense it is indeed inaugural. In fact, strictly speaking, in the context of *Logiques des mondes* the utterance "the event has taken place" is no longer enough to fully capture the performative dimension of this utterance. The trace of the event can be discerned objectively since it shines with great clarity in its maximally intense existence. Hence, one can identify an event and that an event has taken place by simply following its trace. Yet, this identification does not yet constitute a subject. One can also formulate this as follows: while this identification is a necessary condition for the subject, it is not a sufficient condition for the subject. Hence, the utterance "the event has taken place" can also be understood as a phenomenological description of the trace and an identification of the event by means of this description. Therefore, if we still want to keep the performative dimension of "the event has taken place" and understand this utterance as a declaration, we should understand it as *the performative that inaugurates the subjectivity of the one who utters it* and which is founded on the clarity with which the event has left its traces. Here we see most clearly how the decision at work in the declaration is inaugural but not decisionistic. It is not decisionistic since it is not related to an empty and unmotivated truth that is constituted by the decision itself. Rather, truth is understood as an idea of the event. The decision inaugurates the becoming-subject of the human being who utters the (full) declaration, "the event has taken place and I become part of the incorporation of its truth." Whereas the birth of the event is objectively identifiable, the subject's comportment toward this event can only be inaugurated by a decision.

Hence, in comparison to *L'être et l'événement*, *Logiques des mondes* introduces a conception of the subjective comportment that does not coincide with the mediate appearance of the event. Whereas in the former case, only one comportment can be distinguished (since there is no event without the subjective affirmation and declaration of it), the introduction of the trace of the event allows Badiou to understand the decision *not* to be faithful to the event as a subjective comportment to the event as well—although these forms of comportment suffer from one deficit, namely, that they ignore what shines most clearly: the reactive subject ignores the trace of the event and the *obscure* subject "reduce[s] to silence that which affirms the event."[71] Badiou's symbols for these three subjective comportments to the event affirm this difference concerning the trace of the event: what distinguishes the formula of the faithful subject from the ones of the reactive and the obscure subject most strikingly is the negation sign, ¬, appearing in front of the symbol ε for the trace of the event in the formulas for the latter two comportments.[72] Clearly, this implies that these three comportments are not equal. While the event asks for a subjective response, the latter two subjective figures ignore what this event objectively offers as its unmistakable trace in a world.

We may conclude the following. Whereas the declaration indeed inaugurates the subject and thus marks the decision for one of the subjective figures, the faithful comportment finds the certainty and ground for its choice in the scintillation of the event's trace: the reactive subject simply denies this objectively given trace, whereas the obscure subject obscures it in name of an imaginary collective. To phrase it in the terminology of universalism that Badiou also embraces, the trace of the event is equally given for everyone, and this is why all subjective figures have to relate to this trace—either affirming it or disaffirming it. In this sense, the faithful subject's conviction cannot be understood as an opinion: there is no plurality on the level of the event, only universalism and shining clarity. Hence, even though the event itself is contingent and singular, it is a singular universal and not a singular plural. In this sense, the faithful subject does not suffer from this contingency because the event opens up a universal idea for it to follow. Yet, the price to pay for freeing the subject from its contingency and to offer it a solid ground in the event is very high: it implies an irresolvable dualism of being and event as well as of appearing and event, and the structures of ontotheology, overcome on the level of ontology and phenomenology, are restored on the level of the subject's praxis.

Moreover, despite the fact that Badiou acknowledges more than one subjective comportment in *Logiques des mondes*, he still offers no place for the comportment of exemplarity, which would be a comportment that does acknowledge the event but suspends the subject's praxis in order to understand what an event is in its contingency. I shall come back to this in the following chapters.

When considering Heidegger's account of the linguistic utterance that accompanies the decision he speaks of in the *Beiträge*, one can trace two similarities with Badiou. First of all, decision has nothing to do with a decisionistic subject; it has nothing to do with a choice (*Wahl*), as Heidegger writes.[73] Nevertheless, the decision inaugurates the mode of thinking in the other beginning. Heidegger interprets this inaugural dimension of the decision as follows. When discussing the notion of decision (*Entscheidung*) he hyphenizes it as de-cision (*Ent-Scheidung*), thus emphasizing the "cision," that is, the separation and the parting of the ways (*Scheidung*) of the first and the other beginning; a de-cision is a bifurcation point in thinking. As Heidegger explains, "de-cision [*Ent-Scheidung*] refers to the sundering [*das Auseinandertreten*] itself, which separates [*scheidet*] and in separating lets come into play for the first time the ap-propriation [*Ereignung*]."[74] Hence, the decision is a form of sundering (*Auseinandertreten*) that is at work in inceptual thinking as the setting apart (*Auseinandersetzen*). It is only by sundering and setting apart from the first beginning that the other beginning lets the event come into play in the thought of "beyng." This event is, as Heidegger continues, the event of the appropriation of "the belonging to beyng of the human being." It is this de-cision that is the ground for the numerous decisions that mark the difference between the first and the other beginnings and that Heidegger enumerates in section 44 of the *Beiträge*.

This brief analysis immediately pinpoints the difference between Heidegger's and Badiou's accounts of the decision in relation to the event. Whereas Badiou's event provides the subject's decision with a clear, shining ground to decide, Heidegger's decision does not have such a ground. Rather, Heidegger's decision has the task of disclosing the realm in which the event can be announced. Thus, the contingency of the event also affects thinking and the thinker's comportment to it. Since the event is still to come, the de-cision of thinking and of the thinker is part of the preparation of the event. By sundering from the first beginning, the de-cision clears and paves the way for the event to come. Hence, the de-cision does not *by itself* make the event happen. The de-cision and the decisions to which it gives rise are, rather, part of the resolved preparedness by which the event is awaited and prepared. Yet, neither thinking nor the thinker has any certainty whatsoever of the success of this preparatory work. The contingency of the event's coming is at the same time the contingency of thinking. Although thinking resolutely prepares the coming of the event, its preparatory work may, but just as well may not, disclose the event.

One might be tempted to attach the concept of contingency to the notion of history and historicity: metaphysics is the history of being; that is, it does not tell us the necessary and eternal story of being, but it tells us the story of how being is sent to us in its historicity. Yet, this historical aspect is only one side of the meaning of contingency: the first beginning is a contingent beginning; it could have been otherwise—this concerns the contingency of what has been. Thinking is not only *Andenken* of what has been, but it is also a *Vordenken* into what is to come. Similarly, there is not only a contingency of what has been but also of what is still to come. The preparatory orientation toward the other beginning confronts us with another dimension of contingency that concerns the future and that remains invincibly attached to the preparatory work of thinking: thinking may or may not enter the realm of the event. Since thinking always relates to the event as advent and since thinking never fully experiences the birth of the event, this "may or may not" statement indicates that thinking remains preparatory in nature. Here, one may ask whether this Heideggerian "may or may not" indicates a (subtle) difference with Agamben's "can or cannot," which marks his account of pure potentiality discussed in chapter 3.[75] I will return to this issue in chapter 6. For now, it is clear that the contingent character of thinking as *Vordenken* implies in Heidegger's case a pure *im*potentiality (which might be the same as what Agamben calls "the impotent possibility"): thinking cannot actualize or force the event to come.[76] This leads to a striking difference from Badiou's conception of the decision. Because the birth of the event (which is itself contingent) has already taken place, neither the subject's decision nor its faithful comportment to the event is marked by the contingency that is attached to Heidegger's conception of thought as well as decision. The birth of the event is a solid ground for the subject who does not worry over the question of whether the event will happen, but only over the question of how to be faithful to it. This removes the core experience of contingency from the subject's comportment to the event.

The type of performativity with which Heidegger's de-cision goes hand in hand is the *announcement,* which is the primordial hermeneutic activity for Heidegger.[77] An announcement does not predicate anything. Rather, as we saw in our analysis of *Der Satz vom Grund* earlier in this chapter, the announcement suspends the first beginning of thought and the common tonality with which the ontotheological principle par excellence is heard. It announces a thinking of being that has not yet arrived but to which it nevertheless hints. So what kind of word is this announcement of the event in light of the contingency it confers on thinking? How is the event given in this performative hint or intimation? Although neither thinking nor the thinker can force the event to happen, it is obvious that both thinking and thinker affirm the advent of the event in their resolute preparedness to prepare the event. In fact, even though one might be tempted to differentiate between a future (actual) event and a heralding announcement anticipating this event, Heidegger's account of announcement does not simply respect this structure and will never understand the event in terms of a future present. In this sense, it might be better to say that the announcement of the event *is* the event of announcement for Heidegger.

To capture what this latter phrase means and to address the question of whether it contradicts the order between announcement and event that I discussed earlier—the announcement hints to an event that is still to come—let us reconsider once more Heidegger's account of the leap in *Der Satz vom Grund*. The figure of the leap (*Sprung*) as leap-away-from (*Absprung*) seems to imply that thinking leaps to another shore and another realm and that this new realm is both at stake and presupposed for the leaping to take place. Yet, Heidegger always takes great care not to approach thinking in terms of such a new shore. Thinking does not belong to another domain that can be reached only after the leap. Rather, thinking is the very enactment of the leap (as leap-away-from) itself; according to Heidegger, it is thinking only in and as the leap itself.[78]

The phrase "the announcement of the event is the event of announcement" should be understood along the same line as the figure of the leap. The announcement hints at and thus draws us out of the first beginning and the common tonality of ontotheology's fundamental principle. In this sense, the announcement invites us to consider this principle in another tonality, to listen to this principle in its deactivation: it approaches the statement that says that all beings have a reason for their existence *as not* being operative. This announcement of the event is the event of announcement; that is, the announcement itself punctuates the domain of the first beginning, thus showing the possibility of another thinking. This is also what allows Heidegger to maintain the contingency of this other thinking: as possibility, it may arrive, but it may also not arrive.

These reflections on declaration and announcement as Badiou's and Heidegger's understanding of the subject's and the thinker's comportment to the event, respectively, clearly show that the crucial difference between these two philosophers ultimately concerns the question of the contingency of the event. For Badiou, this contingency only means that although the event has taken place, it did not take place out of necessity, and one may add that its implications are not drawn out of necessity. Yet, we are only related to the event insofar as its trace shines and a universal appeal has opened up. In this sense, it is difficult not to say that the subject's comportment is grounded in and finds its reason in the splendor with which the event presents its trace. For Heidegger, however, the contingency of the event, understood as "it may *and* may not happen," permeates the comportment of thinking fully. Thought, in its preparedness to prepare the event, is enacted as and out of this contingency—"it may *and* may not happen." This explains also why, as Badiou puts it somewhat ironically, not even a piece of the new thinking and the event has arrived: only by enacting a preparedness, the event and its corresponding thought truly suspend the principle of sufficient reason.

Resurrection or Second Coming: Paradigmatic Pauline Events and the Question of Faith

After this systematic explanation of the difference between Heidegger's and Badiou's understanding of the event and comportment to it, I turn to their readings of the letters of Saint Paul since these readings offer a common ground for a comparison of their systematic conceptions and allow me to apply the systematic insights to a particular reading. Nowadays, Paul's letters are at the center of philosophical reflection in continental thought. In this section, I am not so much inspired by the contemporary discussions surrounding them, nor am I interested in a complete account of these readings. Rather, my interest is triggered by three circumstances.

First, it is surprising that Badiou can trace the main structures of his systematic work in Paul's letters. Whether it concerns the structure of the event, of the subject who is true to the event, or of the universalism springing from an event, Badiou finds all of them in Paul. The same is valid for Heidegger's reading. His Paul prefigures some of the basic categories of *Sein und Zeit*, as Critchley convincingly shows; in particular, it prefigures his analysis of being-toward-death.[79] Hence, despite obvious differences, both Badiou and Heidegger discern a philosophical potential in Paul's letters resonating with their own philosophical projects. In fact, Badiou identifies this philosophical potential as the potential to criticize ontotheology: "Paul prescribes an anticipatory critique of what Heidegger calls onto-theology."[80]

Second, both Heidegger and Badiou find this potential in particular events that form the heart of the Christian experience of life to which Paul introduces us in his letters. Obviously, when these philosophers find their own philosophical conceptions prefigured in Paul, one should be careful whether they are imposing their own vocabulary on these letters. When considering the central role attributed to notions such as faith, fidelity, conviction, resoluteness, and preparedness to describe the comportment to an event, both Heidegger and Badiou seem to be true heirs of Paul. Faith determines the human comportment to the Pauline event and allows the Christian believer to have access to it, as both Heidegger and Badiou note. Even though neither Heidegger nor Badiou considers himself to be a believer in this sense—they explicitly distance themselves from the *content* of Paul's faith—they both maintain the *form* of the believer's comportment toward the event, and they both keep the terminology of faith, introducing, perhaps, as Critchley beautifully calls it, a "faith of the faithless."

Third, among all these affinities, one particular difference stands out. Paul's letters offer more than one event: Badiou and Heidegger identify a *different* event as the *characteristic* event of Christianity. This difference exemplifies their different conception of the event.[81] Therefore, I start my discussion with this third point.

For Badiou, the event par excellence defining Christianity in Paul's letters is the Resurrection of Christ. Paul, Badiou writes, "reduces Christianity to a single statement: Jesus is resurrected."[82] In fact, this event summons the faithful to their own identity, which they find in faith alone: "Resurrection summons the subject to identify himself as such according to the name of faith (*pistis*)."[83] Thus, Paul offers us a formal framework of how to be true to one's convictions and of how to carry out the consequences of the event declared by the statement, "Jesus is resurrected." For Badiou, as we saw, the nature of the event is that it has already taken place and thus it inspires us to faithful action. These features return in the Christ-event he discerns in Paul's letters: by the time of Paul's conversion, the Resurrection has indeed already taken place—at least, according to Paul. This is why the Christ-event and its declaration are paradigmatic examples for Badiou.

For Heidegger, on the contrary, it belongs to the nature of the event that it is still to come and that one should be prepared for its coming in expectation, as we saw in our analysis of his later work in the *Beiträge* and *Der Satz vom Grund*. This different orientation does not mean that Paul's letters do not offer Heidegger a paradigmatic event. In fact, for Heidegger, Paul offers another paradigmatic event: next to the resurrection, he focuses on the parousia, or the second coming of Christ.[84] For Heidegger, this is the event *par excellence* that shapes the Christian experience of life and its temporality.[85] The early Christians lived in the continual expectation of the second coming of Christ. Hence, with the birth, death, and Resurrection of Christ, the real event of Christianity that shapes Christian *life* has not yet taken place.[86]

One should not misunderstand this "not yet" character. It is not a modification of the present. The "not yet" does not primarily indicate an occurrence that will take place in a future present. Such an account would miss the particular character of the parousia that marked the life of Paul and his fellow Christians.[87] Rather, Heidegger's analysis of the parousia is a prefiguration of his analysis of death in *Sein und Zeit*. Like the phenomenon of death for Dasein, Heidegger insists that the to-come character of the *parousia* should be understood in relation to the particular comportment of Christian life to which it gives rise. The expectation of the parousia determines the temporality and the enactment (*Vollzug*) of life.[88] This is exactly why Paul dismisses the inquiry into the time and the date of Christ's return as a false question. When stating that nobody knows the answer to this question and that "the day of the Lord comes like a thief in the night," Heidegger's Paul indicates that the importance of this return is not founded in a future present but in the way the parousia affects the enactment of Christian life now, in this very moment.[89]

This structure of the parousia runs parallel to Heidegger's well-known account of death in *Sein und Zeit*. Death is never present for Dasein but is only given as an inevitable and imminent possibility, of which we nevertheless do not know the time. Yet, not knowing when we die does not point to the limitation of human understanding. Rather, it is a consequence of the primordial meaning of death. Death is not a future present; it is, rather, an imminent possibility accompanying every moment of our existence. In fact, this imminent possibility is Dasein's most own (*eigen*) possibility. In his lectures on

Paul, the parousia plays this role: the enactment of early Christian life originates from the *imminent possibility* of the parousia.

Let me examine the difference between these two paradigmatic events—Badiou's Resurrection and Heidegger's second coming of Christ—in more detail along two lines of thought.

Paul's Meontology

For both Badiou and Heidegger, an intrinsic relationship between event and nothingness exists, which Critchley quite accurately calls their "meontology."[90] For Badiou, the event is nothing from the perspective of the situation. For Heidegger, the event is nothing from the perspective of the principle of sufficient reason. Yet, in each of Heidegger's and Badiou's cases this means something differently, as can also be traced in their reading of Paul. In this sense, I don't agree with Critchley, who places both Badiou's and Heidegger's meontology under the heading of Paul's *hōs mē*. In fact, when referring to the famous *hōs mē* passage in 1 Corinthians 7:29–32, Critchley writes, "To say that this is an over-determined passage in recently published interpretations of Paul is an understatement. It plays a crucial role in Heidegger's reading of Paul, as we will see presently. But it is an equally pivotal passage for the interpretations of Taubes, Badiou, and Agamben."[91] Yet, the *hōs mē* passage does not play a role in Badiou's reading at all; he does not refer to it. Badiou's meontology stems from another passage (1 Cor. 1:28), which Critchley should know since he quotes it.[92] As opposed to what Critchley claims, this passage marks a crucial difference with Heidegger's (and Agamben's) reading of the *hōs mē* passage, as I will show, but I wish to begin first with Badiou's meontology.

As I discussed in the previous section, *Logiques des mondes* defines the event by its overthrowing of the order of a world's appearance to such an extent that what inexisted before exists maximally after the event. Badiou's reading of Paul prefigures this eventful transformation from nonexistence to maximal existence. More precisely, the fact that such a transformation is announced in Paul's letters exemplifies their potential to criticize ontotheology, as Badiou writes, "The most radical statement in the text we are commenting on is in effect the following: 'God has chosen the things that are not (*ta mē onta*) in order to bring to naught those that are (*ta onta*).' That the Christ event causes non beings rather than beings to arise as attesting to God; that it consists in the abolition of what all previous discourses held as existing, or being, gives a measure of the ontological subversion to which Paul's anti-philosophy invites the declarant or militant."[93] The event brings to naught the things that are. Repeating this, Badiou writes later in *Saint Paul*, "The ontology underlying Paul's preaching valorizes nonbeings against beings, or rather, it establishes that, for the subject of a truth, what exists is generally held by established discourses to be nonexistent, while the beings validated by these discourses are, for the subject, nonexistent."[94] By the same movement that robs the things that are from their existence, the event grants existence to the things that are not (or are considered to be not in the discourse that prevails in the situation). Put in the terminology of *Logiques des mondes*, the event disrupts and restructures the world of appearances by bringing the inexistent to maximal existence. Similarly, as the theory of forcing from *L'être et l'événement* indicates, the faithful subject restructures the situation in accordance with the truth belonging to this event. Hence, the choice for the Resurrection as the paradigmatic event is the choice for the model of birth and beginning as the model of the event: with the event something new has begun and something new has been born. One might say that everything appears in a new light due to this unforeseeable, singular, and utterly new beginning. Yet, this should be understood in a very strong sense of the word: the objective order of appearing itself has changed and the axioms structuring a situation are overthrown; the world is restructured in accordance with the event and its truth.[95] As opposed to what Critchley claims, Badiou's account of the Christ event is not based on "anguished vigilance" at all; this experience of contingency is erased from his account of the subject, as we saw before in our systematic treatment of his work.[96]

In the case of Heidegger, the question of the not and the negation also plays a role, but he comes across this question by means of the aforementioned passage of the *hōs mē*, meaning "as (if) not," which is also crucial in Agamben's reading of Paul.[97] Paul uses this phrase (in 1 Cor. 7) to depict how the Christians should live. Although the order and figure (*schēma*) of this world will pass by, the parousia is to-come and the existing order of the world has not (yet) passed by.[98] Paul combines these two aspects. On the one hand, as long as the early Christians are awaiting the second coming, the order of the world stays the same and there is no reason to change it. Therefore, Paul explicitly advises the people from the community of Corinth to "stay as they were" before their conversion (1 Cor. 7:17). Those who are married should stay married. There is no reason for them to change their actual state. Yet, on the other hand, the expectation of the parousia does and should change the people's *comportment* to this order of the world. Even though everyone should stay as they were, Paul adds that those who have a wife should have her *as not* (*hōs mē*) having her; those that weep should weep *as not* weeping; and those that rejoice should rejoice *as not* rejoicing. Heidegger explains this as follows: "Christian life is not straightforward, but is rather broken up: all surrounding-world relations must pass through the complex of enactment [*Vollzugszusammenhang*] of having become, so that this complex is the co-present, but the relations themselves, and that to which they refer, are in no way touched."[99] Hence, all worldly relations are lived as if they were insignificant. In this sense, the enactment of life anticipates and prepares the *parousia*. Yet, paradoxically, this enactment leaves these worldly relations completely unaltered and unaffected. One may be tempted to describe this situation in the following paradoxical form: everything changes while everything stays the same.[100] To understand what Heidegger's Paul means here, one might also put it as follows. One may think that a new comportment to reality should (cor)respond to a certain "objective" change in reality. But this is not the case. No actual alteration in the order of the world or in the positioning of a human being in this world can be a sufficient or necessary condition for adopting the new comportment to the world expressed by the word "faith." This new comportment has nothing to do with transforming the figure of the world since it describes a withdrawal from the normal order of the world: "The significances of life remain, *but a new comportment* [Verhalten] *arises.*"[101] "At issue," Heidegger writes, "is only to find a new fundamental comportment [*Grundverhalten*] to it."[102] One might also say that this new comportment renders as inoperative the believer's everyday comportment to the world. While the significations of life remain the same, they are no longer significant to the believer. The *hōs mē* formula expresses that the one who adopts this attitude does not transform the world but simply withdraws from the appeal of the order of this world and awaits the ending of this order. Christian life prepares for the coming of Christ and the end of the present figure of the world by its specific enactment of *hōs mē* that characterizes this life.[103]

It might be helpful to refer again to the analysis of death from *Sein und Zeit*. To understand Dasein's authentic potentiality-of-being (*eigentliches Seinkönnen*) is to understand its being-toward-death (*Zum-Tode-Sein*). In this context, death is the analogue of the end of the present figure of the world: what we encounter in the world can no longer be encountered once we are dead. The purifying role of death can now be understood as follows. In its everyday existence, Dasein understands itself out of something in the world—some entity or some position it holds. For instance, to use Paul's example, Dasein understands itself in its everydayness as being married. Yet, by doing so, Dasein misses its own potentiality-of-being and its own existential possibility (*existenzielle Möglichkeit*).[104] Death, however, interrupts this everyday understanding because it announces a mode of (non)being in which the relations to the positions out of which Dasein understands its own being are all deactivated. In death, Dasein is no longer married. In this sense, being-toward-death invites Dasein to an understanding of itself that does not require a change in its ontic or innerworldly situation—it can remain married—but it no longer understands its own mode of being out of this married state: while being married, it understands itself as (potentially) not married. For Dasein, not the significations of everyday life but its existential possibility is most significant: the former are contingent, and to understand one's own potentiality-of-being is to understand the very contingency of one's existence. The *parousia* plays exactly this role in Heidegger's account of the experience of Christian life. Everything that is and every position we hold will pass by—there is no eternal order of the world; its order is contingent and awaits its passing. Therefore, for the Christian to understand his or her own existence, it is necessary to be in or to hold this or that position—to be married, to weep, to rejoice—*as not* being in it or holding it.

It was already noted that the *hōs mē* passage plays an important role in Agamben's reading of Paul. His interpretation of this formula may clarify what is at stake for Heidegger. Although we maintain our position as husbands and wives, for instance, this position is performed in a significantly different attitude. To understand this different attitude, Agamben analyzes the word "vocation" (*klēsis*), or calling.[105] Although we were called to be husbands and wives in the world's present order, the *parousia* confronts us with another calling, as Agamben notes: "The messianic vocation is the *revocation of every vocation*."[106] Moreover, he immediately connects this revocation at the heart of the Christ-event to the problem of *potentiality*—Heidegger's "existential possibility" and "potentiality-of-being." Though the comportment of the early Christians toward the *parousia* renders the order and the figure of the world inoperative, this deactivation "gives potentiality back to them."[107] The early Christians are expropriated from everything they possess and every position they hold by the *hōs mē*, but at the same time it grants them "a generic potentiality [*potenza*] that can be used without ever being owned."[108] Hence, according to both Agamben and Heidegger, no new world order is at stake in Paul's letters. Rather, the *parousia* discloses a new comportment toward the world in which the world and the positions we hold in it *become potential* or are returned to their potentiality. In these latter formulations, we see how different Heidegger's Paul is from Badiou's Paul, a militant wanting to change the world.[109] In line with Heidegger, Agamben understands Paul's *hōs mē* formula as follows: "The messianic does not simply cancel out this figure [*schēma* of the world], but it makes it pass, it prepares its end. This is not another figure or another world: it is the passing of the figure of this world."[110]

Believing, Knowing, Thinking

Despite their different accounts of what is the paradigmatic Christ-event in Paul's letters, Badiou and Heidegger seem to agree on one point: in Paul's letters, faith (*pistis*) is the privileged comportment to the paradigmatic Christ-event. One might even suggest that, since neither Badiou nor Heidegger adopts the particular belief in the Christ-event, they secularize the Pauline notion of faith in their own systematic work, thus offering a "faith of the faithless," as Critchley suggests. Nevertheless, although they reject the specific content of Christian faith, they seem to retain its emptied-out form as a worthwhile remainder of this faith to rethink the human comportment to the event.

Fidélité and *fidèle*, the terms Badiou coins to describe the comportment of the subject drawing the consequences of the event, indicate how much the subject is modeled according to the Pauline notion of *pistis*: the militancy of the believer is (formally) integrated into Badiou's systematic account of the subject. In fact, we can go one step further. In line with his conception of mathematics as a thought (*pensée*) in *Court traité*, his conception of thought adopts the militancy of the believer when he writes that thought is always a matter of deciding on existence and, subsequently, to faithfully drawing conclusions from it.[111] Yet, what does it mean for thought when the only relation to the events that constitute it is formed by the comportments of declaration and fidelity? Can we truly claim to be *thinking* when we behave like a religious believer or a political militant in the service of some higher truth? Does Badiou's work not run the risk of effacing one crucial aspect of thought, namely its *withdrawal* from the world and from the event and its deactivation from any enthusiasm in order to *think* both world and event? These questions arise when one realizes that Badiou not only addresses questions of praxis or politics, but also of first philosophy, of ontology, and the nature of thinking. This makes it less convincing that faith and its derivatives should be located at the heart of thought.

A similar question may be raised in relation to Heidegger's work: In which sense does Pauline *pistis* prefigure thought and, if it does, what does this mean for thought? In Heidegger's case, these questions may be answered along two lines of thought.

First, Heidegger's work clearly states in which sense faith *does not* prefigure thought. Three examples show this. The first example stems from *Phänomenologie und Theologie,* in which Heidegger discusses this issue in connection with religious faith, which means, in this case, Christian faith. The point of departure is the question of the relation between phenomenology and theology. He argues that Christian theology is a science because it shares with the other sciences that it departs from a *positum,* a positively given being. In the case of theology, this positum is the revelation of and faith in "Christ, the crucified God," or more precisely, the mode of existing that Heidegger calls "*Christianness.*" Among the sciences, theology occupies a singular place because its *positum* "arises *not from* Dasein or spontaneously *through* Dasein, but rather from that which is revealed in and with this way of existence, from what is believed." In this sense, theology departs from a positum that is *held to be true without any reason;* it requires revelation and faith, as Heidegger notes: "One 'knows' about this fact only in believing."[112] In exactly this sense, faith is a mortal enemy of philosophy and phenomenology, and faith does not need philosophy.[113] Therefore, faith does not prefigure thought; in fact, it has nothing to do with it.

The second example can be found in *Das Anaximander-Fragment.*[114] There, the issue of faith enters the scene when Heidegger characterizes the status of his translation of Anaximander's fragment. He distinguishes the way in which he encounters this fragment in a translation by thinking (*Denken*) from both a scientific translation and a translation based on faith (*Glaube*). He concludes, "Faith has no place in thinking."[115] Here, faith does not refer to Christian faith but, rather, to the trust one puts in the authoritative translations of Anaximander's fragment. Rather than following the scientific method or the authority of established translations, thinking paves its own way toward a translation of the text by a "historical dialogue" (*geschichtliche Zwiesprache*). Thought requires of the event an encounter and a discussion (*Auseinandersetzung*) with the fragment that is to be translated. A thoughtful translation (*Übersetzung*) can only be enacted when the translator is transferred (*übersetzen*) to the realm of openness out of which the original spoke—neither scientific method nor authoritative translations can force this transferal into the realm of significance of the original text; they can only force a *transmission of the significations without the original realm of significance*. In this sense, faith does not prefigure thought.

The third and final example comes from the *Beiträge* and brings into play a more complicated account of faith. In section 237, Heidegger discusses the distinction between faith and knowledge. Of course, in the background a third notion plays a crucial role, namely, inceptual thinking and its turning to the essential occurrence of *beyng*. Heidegger compares thinking both to an "orginary belief" (*ursprüngliches Glauben*) and an "essential knowledge" (*wesentliches Wissen*).[116] On the one hand, he explains that believing is commonly understood as "deeming true that which utterly withdraws from all knowledge." In this sense, belief is *not* "essential knowledge"; this form of believing is not thinking. On the other hand, knowledge is commonly understood as scientific knowledge, which depends upon the principle of sufficient reason. Thus understood, Heidegger writes, "essential knowing is obviously not a 'knowing,' but rather a 'believing.'" Consequently, thinking is originary belief.

While faith and knowledge understood in a common sense are both insufficient for grasping what thinking is, they offer the possibility of saying something about inceptual thinking when used in contrast to the common meaning of the other. In this context, Heidegger writes that those who question the event *are* the "the original and proper believers."[117] Thus, we find in this brief passage from the *Beiträge* that the value of an originary believing forms the very heart of inceptual thinking. To distinguish this faith from the faith that deems something to be true, Heidegger understands originary faith as the persistence (*Ausharren*) in the extreme decision (*die äußerste Entscheidung*) that characterizes the comportment of inceptual thinking in its resolute preparedness to prepare the event: "To be sure, this originary belief is not like an acceptance of that which immediately offers support and makes courage superfluous. Instead, this belief is persistence in the extreme decision."[118]

Second, the distinction between a faith that deems something to be true and an originary faith implies that Heidegger's work leaves room for a notion of faith that does not operate on the basis of a *positum* and shares a deep affinity with his notion of thinking. This implies that the notion of faith continues to work in Heidegger's account of thinking as the comportment to the event. What does this mean for his conception of thinking?

To answer this question, let me take a detour through Agamben's reading of Paul, which is very close to Heidegger's in many respects.[119] Agamben distinguishes between two forms of believing, namely between believing "that Jesus is the Messiah" and believing "in Jesus Messiah." Agamben explains this difference in terms of a difference between the Gospels and Paul's letters. The Gospels try to show that Jesus—the man with this name, who lived such and such life, while doing this and that—*is* the Messiah; the Gospels thus aim to establish a proposition. Paul, however, is not interested in the vicissitudes and historical circumstances of Jesus' life. He merely believes in Jesus Messiah. On the one hand, the former form of believing is a propositional attitude in which something is predicated on the subject "Jesus." The latter, on the other hand, is a performative, a "*performativum fidei*," as he writes, that is, a performative enacted by faith.[120] The absence of the copula in this latter form of believing indicates that there is no predication or proposition at the heart of Paul's faith: it is the self-proclamation of faith.[121]

Agamben goes on to describe the faith proclaimed by Paul as follows: "I only believe in Jesus Messiah; *I am carried away and enraptured in him, in such a way that 'I do not live, but the Messiah lives in me'* (Gal. 2:20)."[122] Paul is "carried away" by Christ; he is "enraptured in him." In fact, as Paul writes, he no longer lives. Instead, he finds a foreigner in himself who lives in him. In light of my discussion in chapter 3, Agamben's use of words should make us a bit suspicious: while Paul's faith is indeed concerned with deactivating the present figure of the world, it does so in the name of a higher enthusiasm and a higher drunkenness called faith. Is this, then, from a systematic point of view not an exact copy of the position of the poet and the rhapsode in Plato's *Ion*, which I analyzed as the exemplary "presuppositional form without content" in chapter 3?

It is quite remarkable that Agamben does not address this issue in *The Time that Remains*, which is why I will show how an earlier comment on Paul by Agamben can actually be applied to this exclamation of Paul that Christ lives in him. I will demonstrate that the question of retaining the form of faith while emptying out the specific content, as both Badiou and Heidegger do in their readings of Paul, indeed places us in the same context of the "presuppositional form without content."

In chapter 3, I briefly discussed the issue of the human voice in Agamben's work. I did so in relation to Augustine's use of the dead word *temetum*. Yet, Agamben offers another example in the same context, namely, one borrowed from 1 Corinthians 14 in which Paul discusses the practice of glossolalia, of speaking in foreign tongues.[123] Here, as Agamben emphatically points out, Paul understands glossolalia as the practice in which I no longer speak, but a foreign voice speaks *in me*. Hence, Agamben discerns here the same structure as the one he finds in Galatians 2: I no longer speak but a foreign voice speaks in me; I no longer live, but Christ lives in me. How does Agamben analyze this specific structure in relation to 1 Corinthians 14? Clearly, the foreign voice speaking in me implies that the words I speak are no longer my own. I am expropriated from my words and their meaning. In this sense, the experience of glossolalia interrupts the normal functioning of language as a communication of meaning. Yet, this deactivation expropriates language in such a way that it does not return the capacity to speak *to Paul*. It is not Paul who speaks but, rather, a foreign voice in him.[124] As in the case of the poetic and rhapsodic song in the *Ion*, when speaking in tongues, the speaker is carried away with an enthusiasm that inspires his voice, but which does not give the pure potential to speak back to him since it refers its speech back to this enthusiasm that elicits this speech.

The passage from Galatians 2:20 that the Messiah lives in Paul may be read in a similar way. As the foreign voice interrupting the normal functioning of language, faith interrupts the normal order of the world and of our lives. Yet, as the foreign voice referring poetic and glossolalic speech back to a preceding enthusiasm that elicits this speech, faith does not give life back for the believer's own free use: not Paul lives, but Christ lives in him. In terms of the problems discussed in chapter 3, we can now interpret what it means that the *form* of faith is kept in Paul's proclamation: *it maintains the form of presupposition as enthusiasm,* but it does not give the presuppositioned—life or language—back to the one who has the potential to live or the potential to speak. Thus, Pauline faith confronts us with the same problems as the poetic and rhapsodic speech we found in Nancy's reading of the *Ion* since it proceeds on the basis of "being carried away" and "being enraptured" by a foreign force, voice, or life. This means that the Christ-event does not consist in giving a pure potentiality back to the human being; one can only relate to this event *by and in faith*. Just as poets and rhapsodes voice the divine voice, the believer enacts Christ's life. Whereas Agamben sees this in his earlier discussion of 1 Corinthians 14, he misses this dimension in his book on Paul and in particular in his discussion of Galatians 2:20; in fact, he relapses into the structure of the form of the presupposition he criticizes in Nancy.

Whereas the *hōs mē* structure provides us with an example from Paul's letters of how to render a structure inoperative and of how the order of the world is deactivated, the context of faith places it in light of the Messiah living in me and not in light of human life itself. It is here that Agamben, the author of *The Time that Remains,* needs to be corrected by Agamben, the author of *The End of the Poem:* although the fruitfulness of the *hōs mē* passages needs to be acknowledged, Paul's ending in faith leaves us in the midst of the problems of the empty presupposition. Yet, where does this leave us with respect to Heidegger's account of thinking—after all, this was the question inspiring the detour along Agamben.

First, one might respond to the above analysis that for Heidegger, Paul's exclamation that Christ lives in him is simply part and parcel of the *positum* of faith. Therefore, Heidegger would suspend it as he suspended the specific content of the parousia: only by suspending the particular expectation of Christ's coming, the structure of this expectation becomes available for a phenomenological analysis as a possibility of Dasein's existence. Yet, this is exactly Agamben's concern with the "presuppositional form without content" discussed extensively in chapter 3: Heidegger empties out the content of faith but maintains its form and thereby introduces a pure negativity—where Paul finds the Messiah—to which language and life refer back.

Second, in more general terms, contemporary readings of Paul are motivated by the effort to develop alternatives to ontotheology. Yet, although Paul's letters deactivate important structures of ontotheology, as we saw most clearly in the analysis of the *hōs mē* structure, his account of faith repeats the structure of presupposition. Although faith provides an alternative to forms of understanding and knowledge that presuppose the principle of reason, it does not offer a model for thinking or understanding that fully deactivates the structure of presupposition. As long as the structure of presupposition is maintained, the experience of contingency, which forms the ultimate motivation of contemporary thought to turn to the concept of the event, is under threat. In this sense, we may say that faith and conviction, while stemming from the deep experience of contingency, also efface, obscure, and even deny the primacy of contingency in their own ways. We already saw what this implies in Badiou's case: the subject's conviction is grounded in the scintillation of the event. This effaces the deep human experience of uncertainty connected to any form of contingency in favor of a "mathematical heroism," as Badiou writes.[125]

Similarly, though Heidegger explicitly aims to maintain the experience of uncertainty with which contingency confronts the human being, one should also note that the empty form of presupposition haunts and threatens the primacy of contingency in his work. As long as being is presupposed, it seems as if thinking has already decided on the event's taking place. Heidegger's expression "the voice of being" ("die Stimme des Seins") is in this sense the exemplary locus in his work where Agamben's concerns regarding the empty form of presupposition must be raised.[126] When the voice of being always already resounds, is this not a foreign voice speaking in the thinker? Is this not the ontological version of Paul's glossolalia that places a nonhuman origin of language at the heart of human language and a nonhuman voice at the heart of human language?

In conclusion, although Heidegger's work testifies to an awareness of an originary contingency, there is always another motive discernible in it as well. To phrase it in terms of the voice of being, pure contingency would imply that the voice of being may *and* may not be heard and that being may *and* may not call. Yet, this other motive is always also present: his work is only possible because the thinker has *already* heard the voice of being, thus effacing the radical contingent possibility that being *may not* call. This other motive effaces a radical contingency.

How subtle this problem is in Heidegger's work can be seen in the distinction between the lack of need (*Notlosigkeit*) and the need arising from the lack of need (*Not der Notlosigkeit*), to which I have already referred a number of times. This distinction operates as follows. On the one hand, the lack of need indicates how in our era the voice of being may also not be heard since the lack of need is nothing but the lack of hearing the voice of being. Thus, Heidegger suggests that the voice of being may also not call. Yet, on the other hand, this potential not to call is neutralized by the specific hierarchy in which this lack of need is placed. The need arising from the lack of need is higher and more valuable than the lack of need since the former is a sign of thinking and the latter a sign of thoughtlessness. Moreover, it is clear from this hierarchy that human thinking is elicited by a call from *another, alien* voice and, thus, not returned back to its full potentiality but rather to an empty presupposition. As I will discuss in chapter 6 and chapter 7, this is the reason why Agamben raises the question of the empty presupposition also in relation to Heidegger's work. First, however, we will turn to another version of the discussion between Badiou and Heidegger concerning the concept of the event and its contingency in contemporary thought.

Five

Absolute Beginning or Absolute Contingency

> "Advent *ex nihilo* this presents itself as the concept
> par excellence of a world without God,
> and for that very reason it allows us to produce
> *an irreligious notion of the origin of pure novelty.*"
> —Quentin Meillassoux, "Excerpts from *L'inexistence divine*"

This chapter furthers the different trajectories developed in Heidegger's and Badiou's conception of the event, but it will do so in terms of the work of Claude Romano and Quentin Meillassoux. From a methodological point of view, Romano's work provides us with a phenomenology of the event that remains very close to Heidegger's fundamental ontology. Yet, he follows the model of birth much more than the model of advent, as his insistence on absolute beginning indicates. The work of Meillassoux, however, is concerned with providing an alternative to the principle of sufficient reason. Although he clearly follows Badiou's speculative method, his systematic solution seems to be more close to Heidegger's account of the event, especially when looking at it from the perspective of the advent proposed in the motto to this chapter. Thus, in relation to the thought of Heidegger and Badiou, Romano and Meillassoux offer us a chiasmus of method and thematic: whereas Romano explores a hermeneutic model of an event that has always already taken place, Meillassoux is concerned first and foremost with a speculative version of an event that may take place as well as not take place.

Absolute Beginning in Romano's Phenomenology of the Event

In his essay "L'événement ou le phénomène advenant," after his characteristic description of the event as unforeseeable and incalculable, which I cited in the introduction to part 2. Marion goes on to ask how an event can be a phenomenon. How is the event accessible for a phenomenology in the strict sense of the word, and how does it show itself? To illustrate the difficulty of this question, he refers to Heidegger's analysis of the phenomenon of death in *Sein und Zeit*.[1] For Heidegger, this phenomenon prefigures the structure of the event. Marion, however, suggests otherwise. As long as we conceive of the event *as a passage,* death cannot be the exemplary phenomenon of the event in phenomenology. He explains this in the following striking and convincing way: "If death passes in me (supposing, by the way, that a phenomenon were to appear in this passage), as I die with it, I *can never see the event in it*.... My death does not place me thus before any effectivity, any passage, but before a simple possibility."[2] Nancy's comment that phenomenology ultimately privileges the sense of seeing (which I discussed in the previous chapter) applies perfectly to Marion's work: only an event that somehow gives itself to be seen in a phenomenon can be an event for phenomenology. The problem with the phenomenon of death is that it does not truly happen *to me*. It merely passes me by and leaves me aside (*passer sur moi*). Therefore, it neither places me before nor after its passage; it only places me before its *possibility*.[3] Marion's distinction is not at odds with Heidegger, who claims that, although it is certain that my death *will* take place, this taking place does not give itself *as taking place,* but only *as imminent possibility.* Hence, the issue between them is whether or not death exemplifies the phenomenological structure of the event. For Marion, phenomenology requires that an event give itself as passage and as happening.

Yet, Marion adds enigmatically that this does not mean that my death is not an event. In fact, he writes, "it is very likely a question of a pure event, but too pure to show *itself* and therefore also to give *itself* as a perfect event."[4] This strange distinction between a pure event and a complete or perfect (*parfait*) event gives rise to many questions. For now, let me interpret it in terms of the crucial difference between *passage* and *possibility*. A complete event requires that the one *to whom* it happens be present throughout its taking place (otherwise the event cannot give itself as event to him or her). Therefore, death cannot be a complete event. Yet, at the same time, death is granted the status of *a pure, all too pure event*—so pure that it erases and effaces the phenomenological subject or *adonné* (the one to whom is given), as Marion terms his version of Heidegger's Dasein. Whereas the complete and perfect event gives itself as passage, the pure, all too pure event of death can only give itself as imminent possibility *because* it effaces the experiencing, understanding, and thinking entity relating to the phenomena. The difference between passage and possibility thus mirrors the difference between two types of event—the perfect event and the pure event—of which the former is the true phenomenological event. The latter, on the contrary, is the vanishing point of the phenomenological conception of the event pushing, one might say, phenomenology beyond its proper limits and inviting it to address something as event that neither gives nor shows itself as event. I will return to this strange difference later in this chapter.

Let us first consider the following. If death is not the exemplary event, which event is? As Marion rather promptly asserts, the evental phenomenon par excellence is *birth:* "Birth—I am considering here the phenomenon that shows itself truly in the mode of what gives itself, the properly evental phenomenon."[5] This, of course, immediately raises a second question: Is my birth indeed given to me as event in its taking place? The answer to this question is not straightforward. In fact, one may suspect that it could be negative. I do not have any recollection of my birth, and if I understand my birth as the event in which I came into existence, my birth is an immemorial past for me.[6] My birth has passed by and it has *always already taken place* as soon as it gives itself to me. As such, it is, of course, inscribed in the very heart of my existence, but its taking place seems to be beyond or, rather, before me. Marion raises these objections and claims that they do not affect his understanding of birth as phenomenon, so what does he mean when he affirms that birth is "the properly eventual phenomenon"? The rest of this first section is devoted to answering this question, but I will do so by means of the work of Marion's student Claude Romano. In the text I quote here, Marion not only refers to Romano's impressive study *L'événement et le monde*, but also Romano offers in his study a more comprehensive elaboration of the relation between event and birth than does Marion in his lecture.

Romano's Concept of the Event

As we have seen in chapter 2, Nancy reworks Heidegger's *Sein und Zeit* in light of the primacy of the existential of being-with in order to offer an account of the plurality of being in terms of this existential. Romano's two-volume study on the event, *L'événement et le monde* and *L'événement et le temps,* does something analogously. This study rewrites *Sein und Zeit* in light of the primacy of the event for human existence. In the introduction to the first volume, Romano claims that Heidegger's fundamental ontology reduces the eventual character of Dasein's existence.[7] He also immediately reveals the cause of this reduction: Heidegger's analysis of death. This analysis presupposes a problematic distinction between dying (*Sterben*) and the factical (*faktisch*) event of ceasing to exist (*Verenden*). Only death as dying discloses Dasein's existence. The distinction between *Sterben, Verenden* and *Ableben* has been criticized more often: can one truly separate these three phenomena so clearly in the death of a human being?[8] Romano's critique, however, claims something new: Heidegger effaces and reduces the eventual character of Dasein's being by withdrawing the factical event of death from the analysis of dying. Moreover, Heidegger is not capable of capturing the true eventual phenomenon that inaugurates existence and grants existence to Dasein, namely birth.[9]

Among the different motives guiding Romano's reading of Heidegger, the true dispute concerns Romano's structural disagreement with Heidegger concerning what counts as event. Romano's two-volume study demonstrates how this exemplary event determines his conception of the event. Let me discuss his rich account in four steps.

1. Being and Event. Whereas Heidegger's ontology focuses on the primacy of Dasein's existence and being-in-the-world, Romano aims to show that the concept of the event is directed toward something older than and prior to being: "'Earlier' than Being is the event by which it *occurs.* Having priority by right over Being, which it establishes, and of which it alone is the condition, such an event 'is' not.... Preceding my existence is the impersonal event 'one is born.' This governs any understanding of the human adventure, as an opening to events by which 'Dasein'—let us call it thus for the final time—*advenes* to itself and has a history."[10] The event is earlier and older (*plus vieux*) than being since being suddenly and unforeseeably occurs due to an event. Clearly, this means that an event *is not*. To understand what being means here, one should remember that we are in the context of Heidegger's fundamental ontology. Being concerns first and foremost the existence and being-in-the-world of Dasein. In accordance with this primacy of the event over being, Romano renames Dasein with the neologism *advenant*. This word is derived from the verb *advenir*. Although *advenir* is etymologically related to words like *avent* and *avènement*, there is a semantic difference: *advenir* simply means "to happen" or "to occur," whereas *avent* and *avènement* are better translated by the English "advent," which captures the meaning of coming, drawing near, or approaching as in *l'avènement du Messie* (the coming of the Messiah). Hence, Romano pairs *événement* in the first place with *advenant* and *advenir* and only secondarily, as we will see, with *avènement*, and his analysis aims to be a "phenomenological hermeneutics of the *advenant*." Finally, he refers to human existence as the human *adventure*, which is also etymologically related to the verb *advenir*.[11]

To characterize the event, Romano notes the following. In the first place, the event introduces, unlike a mere occurrence or fact in the world, something completely new that cannot be understood in terms of the world we inhabited before the event took place. The event changes the order of appearance in a world. Second, the event suddenly arrives out of nothing, out of a pure void. The event is a "pure beginning from nothing," he writes, "the event, in its an-archic bursting forth, is absolved from all antecedent causality." Hence, also for Romano, the realm of the event requires the suspension of the principle of sufficient reason: "With an event, one can only say one thing: it has its cause in itself; that is, strictly speaking, it has none."[12] Third, as a consequence, the event and what it introduces cannot be understood in terms of the significations and even the significance, in Nancy's sense of the word, that structured the previous world: an event interrupts and overthrows the previous horizon of meaning and discloses a new one.

We traced these particular aspects of the event also in Badiou's thought. Yet, Romano does not understand them in terms of a duality of being (or appearing) and event, as Badiou does. Although an event is indeed beyond being and beyond the world for Romano, this means that the event is a *condition* for being and the world. An event is not, as Romano writes, "inscribed *in* the world but instead *opens a world* for the *advenant*." To understand what this means, we should read this sentence in light of its Heideggerian background. Dasein understands innerworld entities (as well as our own being) because of the possibilities it projects (*entwerfen*) out of the situation in which it is thrown. The notion of the event precedes and alters this structure of project and thrownness; the event "reconfigures the possibilities that precede it and signals the advent of a new world for an *advenant*." Or, as Romano puts it a few pages later, "the event *reconfigures* the world for the one to whom it happens"; it introduces "into my adventure a radically new *meaning*... and thus modifies all my previous projections." Hence, Romano introduces the concept of the event to show that our existence is not thrown in a world "once and for all." Rather, events throw our existence in a reconfigured world and make the new possibilities of this world possible. "*After* an event's bursting forth, things will never again be the same as *before*," he writes. The post-evental world can no longer be understood in terms of the pre-evental world. Rather, the new reconfiguration of possibilities opened up in the post-evental world place the pre-evental world under critique.[13]

2. *Three Temporal Dimensions.* In order to understand how this conception of the event relates to the ones I discussed in the previous chapter, consider Romano's account of the *temporality* of this event—or, rather, of the event as temporalizing. Since a world begins in and as an

event, an event does not take place in time. Rather, as Romano suggests in another adaptation of Heidegger's *Sein und Zeit,* the event temporalizes time in three dimensions: "moment, always-already, and future."[14]

(a) Since the world is disclosed in and by the event, the temporal mode of the moment—the fullness of time in which the event happens—seems to have a certain primacy. As Romano writes, "the event should establish a beginning that is preceded by nothing and that proceeds from nothing."[15] It is in a sudden moment that this "absolute beginning," being without cause and beyond the principle of reason, introduces something utterly new in the world we inhabit.[16] Occurring in *"the nothing of the moment,"* the event is both "a hiatus" and "a dehiscence of time." It is a hiatus since it punctures and tears apart the time and the horizon of the old configuration of the world. Yet, this interruption is also the sudden disclosure of a new time and a new horizon of the world, from which comes the reference to "dehiscence": in one moment, the event opens up a new sense as a piece of fruit suddenly bursts open and offers its seeds in one instant. Similarly, in one moment, the event offers new possibilities to the human being for understanding and interpreting the world. This moment is emphatically called "the event of the event."[17]

This sudden, brilliant, and splendid bursting forth of a new fertility for the understanding and the *advenant*'s life already refers to the paradigmatic example of birth. However, the term "dehiscence" is used not only in a botanical but also in a medical context. In the latter context, it describes the sudden reopening of a surgical wound. This reopening is not a sign of fertility or of a new beginning, but it is usually the way in which the patient is exposed to an extreme danger. Rather than being a sign of fertility and birth, dehiscence can also be a sign of an imminent death.

(b) While the event's happening privileges the moment, the event is not accessible in or as this moment, as Romano acknowledges; it is "only accessible as such according to a delay and an original displacement."[18] To understand why he claims this, one should be aware of the hierarchy between being and event. Although in a different context and in a different discourse, we are here in a similar situation as the one we found in Badiou's account of the event in relation to the subject. For him, the event always precedes the subject because the subject is nothing but a comportment to the event that has taken place. In Romano's case, the event relates to the *advenant*. Obviously, the *advenant* is not a subject in Badiou's sense, but it shares one remarkable structural feature with the Badiouan subject: it is constituted by a comportment to an event *that has taken place*. In Romano's hermeneutic-phenomenological terms, this means that the *advenant*'s existence (or adventure) and being-in-the-world is constituted by an event that precedes it. Hence, the original delay of which the previous quote speaks is due to the fact that appearance and accessibility are always *for the advenant;* being for the *advenant,* it requires a world. Since existence originates in an event, the appearance of the event for the *advenant* requires that the event has already taken place.[19] Hence, the event can only appear as having always already taken place. When the event makes itself known to the *advenant,* "it has always already taken place as such."[20]

Thus, *while the event necessarily takes place as or in a moment, it appears only as already having taken place*. Although Romano does not put it in these terms, we find here once again the structure of the trace at the heart of the event. The event never appears in the fullness of its taking place to the *advenant*. Rather, this appearance always refers back to the immemorial past of its taking place, "long before." Nevertheless, as Romano insists, this is not a diminished, distorted, or inadequate appearance: to appear as always already having taken place is the event's "absolute evidence"; this is the event's "scintillation without genesis."[21] We also came upon this motive of the scintillation (*éclat*) of the event by means of its trace in Badiou's *Logiques des mondes*. The event's taking place is not accessible in its instantaneity. However, *rather than bringing a hint of its coming*, it leaves a trace that shows with the greatest clarity *that an event has taken place*. Only in this way, thanks to the delayed appearance of the event with absolute evidence, Romano can conclude that the event "always already carries the seal of the irremediable."[22] Thus, despite important differences, Badiou's and Romano's accounts of the event share the following feature: *the human comportment to the event should be understood out of the primacy and the absolute evidence of the event's having taken place.* It will come as no surprise that the phenomenon of birth is indeed paradigmatic for such a conception of the event as well as for the human comportment to it.

(c) Finally, the temporal dimension of the future comes up in relation to the question of hermeneutics and interpretation—hence also in relation to the *advenant*'s comportment to the event. While the event intervenes in the world with a new sense, this sense is not simply and fully captured by its sudden appearance. Although this "sense is (always already) his" (that is, of the event), it confronts the interpreter with an endless task.[23] This temporal mode can thus only be properly understood in connection with understanding. Let us therefore turn to this issue of understanding, which is the term Romano uses to describe the human comportment to the event.

3. *Understanding an Event.* The term *advenant* indicates that the human being is "the very opening to events in general." As Romano suggests, this openness is itself "the event that is constantly underway of my own advent to myself from the events that happen to me."[24] To describe how the *advenant* relates to events, he introduces his evential version of Heidegger's existential of the understanding (*Verstehen*) as follows: "Understanding is the primary attitude, prior to any other, in which an *advenant* constantly holds himself and by which he always relates to all that happens to him: a prereflexive and pretheoretical comportment that is inseparable from the way in which an *advenant* ceaselessly advenes to himself [*s'advenir*]."[25] As in Heidegger's existential analytic of understanding, Romano argues that the first attitude to the event is not a theoretical one. It is also not a faithful acting or praxis, as Badiou argues. Rather, the *advenant*'s primary comportment toward the event is understanding (*compréhension*). Hence, not Dasein's being but the event and especially the event of the happening of its own existence is the subject matter of the *advenant*'s understanding. In particular, this implies that the understanding is not guided by a familiar "horizon of preceding meaning." As the event is an absolute beginning, it can only appear as

completely incomprehensible in such a pre-given horizon. Evential understanding aims to understand exactly that which punctures and overthrows such a pre-given horizon: the dehiscence of an absolutely new sense that changes the horizon of significance irremediably. Therefore, although understanding is still described in terms of a projection toward interpretative possibilities, these latter possibilities do not stem from an already given world. Rather, it is the event itself that makes these interpretative possibilities possible.[26]

Hence, although Romano does not dismiss the notions of sense, meaning, and significance as Badiou does, he does introduce a distinction between world and event that is reminiscent of Badiou's resistance to the classical hermeneutic notion of sense. For Romano, to inhabit a world is to presuppose a horizon of sense. That is, not only does this world come equipped with its particular significations, but these significations refer back to a horizon of significance that carries them and makes them possible. In fact, this significance constitutes the world we inhabit. The event, however, interrupts this horizon of significance. This is why he writes, in a somewhat anti-Nancyan fashion: "*the significance of the world appears instead to be insignificant for understanding the meaning of a genuine event.*"[27] The event is the absolute beginning of significance. However, since significance is the element of understanding—no understanding can take place outside of this element—understanding operates on the basis of "a structural delay": its element is not the significance of a *prior* world, but the significance of the *posterior* world disclosed in and by the sudden occurrence of the event.[28]

Although Romano's theory does not offer us anything that resembles in the least Badiou's theory of forcing, as discussed in chapter 1, it does make sense to read Romano's account of the event as a hermeneutic-phenomenological elaboration of a similar intuition that the significance of the event should be understood from the *future anterior*. Romano compares the way in which an event changes a world and its significance with a truly innovative work of art, which "cannot really be understood in its singularity except from the posterity to which it gives rise, the refashioning it brings about in the forms, themes and techniques of its period. A work of art cannot be understood within the artistic context in which it is born, which it necessarily transcends if it is an original work."[29] The sense disclosed by the event cannot be understood in the context of its occurrence, but its sense is only made manifest by the posterior world to which it will have given shape. Whereas the event is meaningless in the context in which it occurs, it *will have received* a meaning in the future in the form of the changes it brings about in "forms, themes and techniques," as the example of the work of art suggests. The event restructures the context of works of art. That is, the event can only be understood from a future anterior: its sense is the significance that the posterior world *will have received*.[30] Understanding an event is the project toward the interpretative possibilities that this posterior significance offers. In this sense, this posterior significance is the element in which the evential understanding dwells. Of course, this significance is not (yet) accessible for the understanding—an event can only be *understood retrospectively*—yet this significance is always already the event's significance and always already implied as the element in which every effort of the *advenant* to understand themselves and their world takes place.

For Heidegger, the projection of understanding toward certain possibilities makes these interpretative possibilities possible in the first place. As Romano writes on this account of understanding: "The possibility of the possible...would then mean its *making-possible* by a primordial projection." Yet, in line with his previous discussion, he insists that the projection's making-possible moves itself within a given horizon of the world and conforms itself to the possibilities this horizon offers. Only an event can disclose a world and, thus, reconfigure the possibilities its horizon has to offer. This means that the event introduces another form of making-possible (*possibilisation*), "more originary than making-possible by a projection."[31] The reconfiguration of the horizon of the world makes possible the possibilities this horizon offers to understanding.

As Romano adds, it remains to be seen whether this more original making-possible can still be called a "possibility." In light of the projection of the understanding, this making-possible confronts the *advenant* with an im-possibility, that is, with something that does not proceed from a capacity or potential of the *advenant* but is rather *given* to him or her. The *advenant* cannot anticipate the event's making-possible since the latter *gives* the *advenant* the possibility of projection and anticipation gratuitously and without reason since it discloses the world and its horizon of sense.[32] Here we see once more, but this time from the perspective of understanding, why it is crucial for Romano that the event appears as having take place: *the human comportment to the event presupposes the event's having taken place since the event makes the making-possible of understanding's projection possible.*

4. The Paradigm of Birth. Before assessing the different aspects of Romano's conception of the event more critically, let me conclude this discussion by showing how the above refers to the phenomenon of birth as both the *paradigmatic* and the *original* event. Romano understands the event as the reconfiguration of the possibilities of a world. This suggests that there is already a world that is disclosed *differently*. Yet, there is one event, "the first event," that cannot be understood as a reconfiguration of the world in the strict sense of the word since this first event discloses the world for the first time. This is the true origin and absolute beginning of existence. For the *advenant*, this event is its birth.[33] In fact, Romano can only maintain that the event precedes being since the *advenant*'s existence and its particular modes of being-in-the-world originate in the event of its birth. In discussion with Heidegger, for whom being-in-the-world is one of the conditions of Dasein's being, he notes that being-in-the-world is itself conditioned by the birth of the *advenant*.[34]

This primacy of birth over existence can best be illustrated in terms of understanding. Whereas Heidegger's understanding consists of the possibility of Dasein disclosing its own authentic (*eigentlich*) potentiality-of-being, Romano argues that there is one phenomenon that cannot be appropriated by understanding because its own possibility and making-possible depend on it: the project of understanding always refers back to the nonappropriable disclosure of a world by the event. The phenomenon of birth testifies to "a radical powerlessness with respect to this primary event" at the heart of Dasein's potentiality-of-being.[35] This incapacity mirrors Romano's account of the event as im-possibility. The terminology developed in this context reminds us of Levinas's famous description of the other: "Birth is, in itself, opening to a past that is 'older' than any past that can be taken over, a past that has never been present for the *advenant*"; this is why birth appears as "strictly *immemorial*."[36] This terminology accentuates that birth, the origin of existence, can never be appropriated by understanding: in this sense, it is heterogeneous to it.

Yet, despite its heterogeneity to understanding, birth never threatens the execution of understanding in any way. Rather, birth forms an inexhaustible and excessive source of meaning for understanding and confronts the *advenant* accordingly with an endless task of interpretation that transcends its finitude: "In all understanding, I am exceeded by the excess [*surcroît*] of meaning that precedes me immemorially from my birth, which is arrayed on each and every occasion starting from interpretative possibilities that are not made possible by me, and which makes all appropriation an infinite task, transcending the horizon of death and my own finitude."[37] Hence, the infinity Badiou locates in his mathematical conception of the generic set and that forms the heart of the truth procedures of art, science, politics, and love is relocated by Romano and placed at the heart of human existence. Hence, the birth of a new truth in Badiou's sense of the word does not just offer human life the capacity to transcend its finitude in fidelity to an infinite truth; rather, for Romano, the birth of every human being confronts him or her with an infinite meaning that transcends the finitude of human life and understanding. Apparently, the giving of birth is richer than the taking of death. These lyrical statements determine the meaning of birth as being the paradigm and origin of all events: "birth is what determines the meaning of all other events." This means that every other event is *as* birth, confronting the *advenant* with a rebirth. As Romano continues, this means that birth grants the *advenant* the "*capacity to undergo* an event, at the risk of a radical transformation of [its] possibilities."[38] Yet, it remains to be seen what kind of *risk* this is when all these other events are ultimately grounded in the first event and when the first event confronts the human being with a semantic plenitude transcending even the horizon of his or her death.

Origin, Excess, and Contingency

To assess Romano's phenomenology of the event fully, many issues ought to be addressed. I will limit myself to the question most important for the main line of inquiry in this study: How does Romano's model of birth affect the concept of the event? I address this question by treating three issues: origin, excess, and contingency.

1. The Event of Birth as Origin. When reading Heidegger's *Sein und Zeit*, one cannot avoid the impression that, as soon as one confronts Dasein, one encounters an always already *matured* human being. The early stages of human life do not seem to interest Heidegger. In light of the typicality of *Sein und Zeit*, Romano's attention to the fact that Dasein's being-in-the-world is conditioned by something that precedes it and from which it originates seems to be quite to the point: can one truly describe and understand the structures of our being-in-the-world without taking its provenance into account?

It remains to be seen whether the notion of birth *alone* is enough to capture Dasein's coming of age. Obviously, our life is unthinkable without our physical birth. Yet, the evential birth, as Romano calls it, cannot simply be this physical birth since, as physical entities, we already existed before our mothers actually gave birth to us. Hence, our physical birth, though a beginning, is not our absolute beginning. Of course, Romano would immediately reply that one should not confuse factual and evential birth. Yet, it is highly doubtful whether his understanding of the event as beginning and birth can be strictly separated from our everyday understanding of factual birth as the beginning of a new life. In light of this, one should ask two questions: how can evential birth be qualified as *absolute* beginning, and how is it possible to understand it as *one, singular, original* event from which human existence or adventure and the events that constitute it originate?

For Romano, birth is the absolute origin of a world and an existence. Since the birth of the *advenant* is the sense of all other events that happen to it during its existence, one can only conclude that the sense of birth captures and *gathers* the sense of every event that occurs in its wake. The risk in every event to transform the horizon of meaning is ultimately nothing other than the adventure that originates from birth. In this sense, every event occurring to a human being refers back to the original event and unfolds the excessive meaning of this one origin. Formally, this reiterates the motive of oneness in terms of the event. Remarkably enough, we also saw this in Badiou's account of the event: whereas he overcomes the primacy of oneness on the level of being, he reintroduces it on the level of the event as the ultra-one.

Because birth discloses a world and makes understanding possible, it conditions the structures that Heidegger considers to be those of our existence. Yet, Romano's account of this conditioning is not very convincing: does our birth indeed disclose a world? Can we truly say that a human being is in a world and understands interpretative possibilities in a world at the earliest stages of its existence? For Heidegger, this would be unthinkable. For instance, a child needs to learn how to speak. As is well known, one cannot account for Dasein's being-in-the-world in terms of attunement (*Befindlichkeit*) and understanding (*Verstehen*) alone; discourse (*Rede*) is "existentially equiprimordial" with these two. Romano agrees with Heidegger on this point. In particular, he claims that the "in-fans advenant" does not yet have the capacity to speak as its own possibility. This possibility is only given to it in the evental moment it begins to speak.[39] Here we find an odd movement in Romano's study. On the one hand, the *advenant* always already has the capacity to understand since understanding is the first comportment of the *advenant* toward an event. This suggests that understanding is disclosed by and in birth. On the other hand, this comportment is equiprimordial with discourse and thus it is, strictly speaking, only "operative" when the *advenant* begins to speak. The expression "in-fans advenant" makes sense if (factual) birth is the origin of the *advenant;* there is a stage in life during which a human cannot yet speak. Yet, this expression does not make sense if the concept of *advenant* implies understanding and, with that, discourse: to begin to speak is not a reconfiguration of the world, but it discloses the world for the first time. Consequently, one has to conclude from this internal analysis of Romano's phenomenology that there is not *one* original event that conditions and discloses the *advenant* and its world *for the first time*. The origin of the *advenant* is multiple and consists of at least two different sources or two different "factual" events: birth and beginning to speak. Moreover, as soon as we leave the analysis of Romano's phenomenology aside and try to understand more clearly what it means to begin to speak, many other problems impose themselves. To begin to speak is a highly complicated development in human life. For instance, it is not clear at all that we can say of this event that it happens in one moment. At what point do we call the child's babble speech? Is there one event during which the capacity to speak actualizes itself, or does it correspond to a complex chain of events?

2. *The Excess of the Event.* The event confronts understanding with an excess of meaning. This is another feature that Romano's phenomenology of the event shares with Badiou. In fact, I would suggest that Romano offers a hermeneutic-phenomenological account of what Badiou phrased in mathematical and speculative terms. For Badiou, the event is the birth of a procedure of truth. He captures the infinity of this truth in terms of the generic set, as discussed in chapter 1. In this sense, the faithful subject transcends its own finite life by becoming the carrier of an infinite truth. Romano's model of birth gives rise to a similar structure, but now in terms of an excess of sense. The birth of the *advenant* is the origin and source of the meaning of the *advenant*'s world. This source is excessive (*surcroît*): it is always richer and more abundant than that which the *advenant*'s finite life and understanding can encompass. Thus, according to Romano, it is the source of an *infinite* sense.

One might wonder whether this hermeneutic-phenomenological account of an infinite sense does not propose a more viable alternative to Badiou's mathematical account of infinity. In chapter 1, I described in which sense the reference to mathematics runs the risk of reiterating the metaphysical motive of presence. The hermeneutic-phenomenological approach does not run this particular risk, while it does propose, like Badiou's work, the conception of an absolute beginning that interrupts the previous universe of signification and introduces an infinity that is not affected in any way by the finitude of either human existence or human understanding.

Nevertheless, although Romano's analysis is not affected by the motive of presence in the same way as Badiou's analysis is, his notion of excess is not unproblematic and invokes another motive that is closely connected to the motive of presence, namely, the motive of fullness and richness. The best way to show this is by briefly confronting this conception of the excess of meaning with Derrida's understanding of excess. The reason to select Derrida here is inspired by Marion's remark in the context of the essay on the event I quoted above to introduce Romano's work: "The origin, which refuses itself, does not nevertheless give itself in penury (Derrida), but indeed in excess, determining in this way the regime of all givens to come."[40] For Marion, the event is an origin that gives its semantic richness in abundance, and he argues that in Derrida's thought, the origin gives itself in penury or deficiency. This, of course, is a rather peculiar way of representing Derrida's point of view. For Derrida there is no origin, so we cannot say that, according to him, the origin would give itself in penury. In fact, this account of Derrida's point of view tends to obscure the philosophical issue at stake between him on the one hand and Marion and Romano on the other.

This issue consists of two elements. First, for Derrida there is never one origin; when we go back to how something came about, we always find a multiplicity of origins. I already pointed out that Romano's conception of the event of birth tends to privilege the unity of an origin. Secondly, and closely related to this, one should consider the issue of excess itself. As soon as Marion and Romano speak of an event that gives itself in excess, they always qualify this excess as an excess *of sense*. This implies the following. Sense exceeds understanding, but it exceeds it in such a way that it makes it possible and in no way threatens the enactment of understanding. Sense and understanding are thus in perfect accordance with each other. Sense, one might say, is always a *tamed* excess of understanding. Yet, if we conceive of the event as sheer dehiscence and excess, the bursting open of dehiscence might very well be the tearing apart of understanding *as such*. These are the true stakes of the discussion with Derrida. Why is the excess of the event over understanding not of such a nature that it interrupts not only this or that understanding of the world, but understanding as such? Why does the event as excess offer something that harmonizes and fits so well with understanding?

Let us transform these provocative questions into arguments. For Romano, the event is the condition of the possibility of understanding. However, since understanding cannot appropriate the sense of the event, it is also its condition of im-possibility; in the event, understanding finds its limits. In this particular case, being a condition of impossibility has two implications, as one might clarify along a Derridean line of argument: (a) If the event truly exceeds the understanding, the understanding cannot determine this excess in advance *as sense*. According to Romano, understanding is our primary comportment toward the event, so we simply do not have the means to determine the event as an excess *of sense*. We never know in advance if the excess of the event *does not destroy* our capacity to understand. (b) Consequently, Romano's claim should be rendered in a more modest form, namely, in the form of a conditional. The event and its excess are a condition of possibility for the understanding *if* they give sense. Only then, they provide the understanding with the "upon which" of its projection. This formulation clearly demonstrates the other possibility in which the excess makes the understanding impossible: if the event does not give sense, its dehiscence simply bursts the texture of the understanding. (Although Romano also calls the "making-possible" of the event an "im-possibility," this only means that this making-possible is not a possibility of understanding; he never goes so far as to say that the event might interrupt the capacity of understanding itself and make it impossible.)

This proves that the antithesis of excess and penury proposed by Marion cannot be maintained. Rather, a Derridean analysis shows that the *promise* of sense with which the event gives itself can never be separated from its *risk* of tearing apart understanding itself. This risk is not a tamed one. The event does not only expose the *advenant* to the risk of a full transformation of its particular horizon of meaning; it also exposes the *advenant* to the risk of losing its capacity to understand. Recall that Marion distinguishes between a pure and a complete event, between death and birth. The risk of losing one's capacity to understand happens and becomes reality in such a pure event. The complete event is one that is in perfect accord with understanding; it gives itself and shows itself as an excess of sense. This is the event of birth. The pure event, on the other hand, cannot give itself as such since it is "too pure." Death can only be experienced as possibility. More precisely, it can only be experienced as the possibility *of impossibility*. This Heideggerian phrasing is not a play on words. The event of death can only be understood as the possibility that interrupts our capacity to understand and to be. The model of birth propagates a tamed excess in which the event gives itself as pure semantic fullness, enhancing human life as the life of understanding. This model marginalizes the pure phenomenon. Yet, the choice for this model is a mere presupposition of Romano's phenomenology. The event can never be known as a pure semantic fullness. As soon as one suspends this presupposition, another phenomenon imposes itself: the pure event in which the ultimate risk takes place.

3. *Event and Contingency.* Both Badiou and Romano understand the event as an absolute beginning to which the human being relates once it has taken place. Whether it is fidelity or understanding, in both cases human comportment concerns the *aftermath* of the event's taking place. Clearly, this aftermath is for Badiou and Romano the most important contribution of the event: for both of them, although in two different discourses, human comportment is engaged in acting or understanding in accordance with the new figure and order of the world that the event has opened up. This world is a posterior world that will take shape in acting and understanding, respectively.

Hence, of both birth and event one might say, in Shakespeare's famous words, "what is done cannot be undone."[41] At this point we see most clearly how a determination of the event as absolute beginning moves away from the determination of the event as contingency since the relation between event and contingency concerns exactly the taking place of the event. Once the event has taken place—and it has always already taken place in human understanding—it is irremediable and irrevocable.[42]

Thus, in these accounts, the human comportment toward the event does not experience the fundamental contingency that characterizes the event, namely, that it can also not take place. In Badiou's case we saw this most strikingly in his account of the objective, scintillating trace of the event: there is no denial of the event that can efface the absolute evidence with which its trace shines. This, actually, is quite odd since the concept of the event is introduced to provide an alternative to the principle of reason as the main principle of ontotheology. The concept of the event is created to provide an alternative to *necessity;* this alternative is traditionally known as contingency. Thus, one might expect that the event is first and foremost *the event of contingency* and that the human comportment toward the event is first and foremost concerned with experiencing, understanding, or thinking contingency. By putting the notion of the event at the heart of ontology, the notion of contingency becomes the absolute core of ontology. Therefore, the model of absolute beginning needs a supplementary model that thinks absolute contingency.

Absolute Contingency in Meillassoux's Speculative Thought

The work of Quentin Meillassoux offers such a model. In the following quote, Meillassoux does not only establish the intrinsic connection between event and contingency, but he also indicates how, according to him, his thought of contingency is related to Badiou's thought of the event:

> The term "contingency" refers back to the Latin *contingere,* meaning "to touch, to befall," which is to say, that which happens, but which happens enough to happen *to us.* The contingent, in a word, is *something that finally happens*—something *other,* something which, in its irreducibility to all pre-registered possibilities, puts an end to the vanity of a game wherein everything, even the improbable, is predictable. When something happens to us, when novelty grabs us by the throat, then no more calculation and no more play—it is time to be serious. But what is most fundamental in all this—and this was already one of the guiding intuitions of *L'être et l'événement*—is the idea that the most powerful conception of the incalculable and unpredictable event is provided by a thinking that *continues to be* mathematical—rather than one which is artistic, poetic, or religious.[43]

The second part of the quote propagates a conception of the event that is close to Badiou's. Rather than poetics, it is mathematics that offers us a proper concept of "the incalculable and unpredictable event." Hence, in the discussion between hermeneutics and mathematics, Meillassoux considers himself to be on the side of mathematics. In addition, he seems to affirm that the subject's serious fidelity, as Badiou develops it, is the proper attitude one can have toward the event.

Yet, this alleged closeness to Badiou cannot hide the fact that Meillassoux's own project is of a different nature. The first part of the quote indicates in a nutshell how we should understand his "essay on the necessity of contingency," as the subtitle of *Après la finitude* reads. Although the attention to the concept of the event in contemporary thought and in Badiou's work in particular leads us in a variety of directions, the heart of the matter is an ontological one. Essentially, the renewed interest in the concept of the event concerns a major change in ontology: what the ubiquitous attention to the event asks us to account for is that *contingency constitutes the heart of our understanding of being*. This issue, and this issue alone, inspires *Après la finitude*. This is also why I consider this book to be very important, despite the many critical questions that I will raise below.

This particular focus of *Après la finitude* implies two fundamental differences from Badiou. First, Meillassoux does not accept Badiou's dualism of being and event. The event is not trans-being. Rather, as contingency, it forms the heart of ontology itself.[44] In this sense, while heavily criticizing Heidegger, Meillassoux seems to be closer in certain respects to the German hermeneutic phenomenologist than he wishes to acknowledge. One may capture this similarity and difference as follows. Meillassoux creates a concept of contingency in a discussion that rejects the principle of reason. Meillassoux thinks that the belief in this principle is still operative in ontology today: "The contemporary belief in the insolubility of metaphysical questions *is merely the consequence of the continuing belief in the principle of reason*—for only someone who continues to believe that to speculate is to seek out the ultimate reason for things being thus and so, also believes that there is no hope of resolving metaphysical questions."[45] Here we see in a nutshell why, according to Meillassoux, the hermeneutic-phenomenological school is not capable of truly solving the problems of present-day ontology: this school does not take its own suspension of the principle of reason seriously enough since it does not apply it to speculative thinking. As he puts it, as long as to speculate is understood as "to seek out the ultimate reason for things," ontology is incapable of finding another way of "resolving metaphysical questions." Meillassoux's way of criticizing hermeneutics fits very well in the present-day discussion: he criticizes hermeneutics—and Heidegger's hermeneutics in particular—in the name of a theme that hermeneutics introduced into philosophy in the first place. Note that Meillassoux describes the "without reason" that arises when the principle of reason is (in his case) dismissed and the "ex nihilo" with which something occurs when this principle no longer applies in terms of *advent,* as the prepublication of *L'inexistence divine* indicates.[46]

In relation to Badiou, the second difference concerns the role and the place of subjectivity Badiou develops. Meillassoux is not interested in this notion at all in *Après la finitude*. Although he claims that as soon as "novelty grabs us by the throat...it is time to be serious," he is not concerned with such a novelty or the type of fidelity this novelty demands of us in Badiou's account. For Meillassoux, *contingency concerns possibility and not passage*. Unlike Marion and Romano, Meillassoux is not interested in the passage of the event as the birth of a new world. He only aims to show that we can think contingency as the possibility that things *can be otherwise*.

Even from a very general understanding of Meillassoux's work, it is quite curious to see that he professes his allegiance to Badiou and criticizes Heidegger without interruption in *Après la finitude*. What I will claim in this section and against the vein of Meillassoux's vehement critique, is that his account of contingency as the potentiality-of-being-otherwise (*pouvoir-être-autre*) should be understood as a radicalization of Heidegger rather than of Badiou.[47] Already *pouvoir-être-autre* suggests such a reading since it is an immediate reference to Heidegger's important term *Seinkönnen* or potentiality-of-being from *Sein und Zeit*.

Correlationism as a Critique of the Hermeneutic-Phenomenological School

One of the most problematic aspects of *Après la finitude* concerns its effort to get rid of the hermeneutic-phenomenological school *in one blow* by characterizing all of it as "strong correlationism." Since I'm interested in establishing a relation between Meillassoux's account of contingency and Heidegger's conception of the event, it is necessary to demonstrate first in which sense Meillassoux's claim that Heidegger is the exemplary strong correlationist goes astray. So let us first follow his line of argument in the first three chapters of *Après la finitude* and comment on it.

Meillassoux introduces the term "correlationism" to characterize and criticize philosophy after Kant, as I already indicated in part 1. Kant's famous distinction between *phenomena* and *noumena* and his conviction that we cannot *know* the things in themselves but only as they appear to us implied a huge transformation of the philosophical inquiry as a whole. Due to Kant, one can only know of the *correlation* between knowing and beings as they appear to us; we cannot know how beings are in themselves. For Meillassoux, correlationism is the extended version of this Kantian correlation of thinking and being: "By 'correlation' we mean the idea according to which we only ever have access to the correlation between thinking and being, and never to either term considered apart from the other."[48] Philosophy no longer has access to being in itself, to the absolute, but limits its claims to the correlation of thinking and being. Capturing phenomenology and analytic philosophy in one grand sweeping gesture, Meillassoux claims that twentieth century philosophy is nothing but such a form of correlationism by the phenomenological focus on consciousness and the analytic focus on language: thought only has access to being in and through the media through which it is given to us and through which we are directed to it.[49] Let me assess this idea of correlationism along two lines of thought.

1. Reading Heidegger as Correlationist. To exemplify and criticize the correlationist attitude of philosophy, Meillassoux contrasts the way in which contemporary phenomenology describes the givenness of the world—Heidegger's *es gibt* and Marion's *donation*—with the problem of "ancestrality." The latter term refers to the reality that preceded the human race and even the existence of life as such. This is, for instance, the reality at stake in problems such as dating "the accretion of the earth."[50] Meillassoux claims that such a reality cannot be properly thought in a correlationist framework.

Of course, when reading from a Heideggerian point of view, the reader is a bit surprised: what happens to the ontological distinction between being and beings and to the distinction between thinking and (scientific) knowledge? By definition, correlationism concerns the metaphysical relation between being and thinking, but it will now be assessed in terms of the Kantian relation between beings and (scientific) knowledge. Let us keep this question in mind when we see how Meillassoux proceeds. Confronted with the question of whether or not knowledge shows us how things are in themselves and thus describes a state of affairs before they even could be given *to* or *in* a human thought, Meillassoux claims that the correlationist would respond as follows: "being *is not* anterior to givenness, it *gives itself* as anterior to givenness."[51] This raises the question of who would respond in this way. Since Heidegger is considered to be the exemplary correlationist for Meillassoux, one might expect that the author would inquire into what Heidegger actually says about results from the natural sciences. Since Meillassoux does not give us any such inquiry, let me provide one quote from Heidegger's *Sein und Zeit*: "That before him, *Newton's* laws were neither true nor false cannot mean that the beings which they point out in a discovering way did not previously exist. The laws became true through Newton, through them beings in themselves became accessible for Da-sein. With the discoveredness of beings, they show themselves precisely as the beings that previously were."[52] For Heidegger, in statements from the natural sciences we are not dealing with being but with beings about which something is asserted. He is very clear: the beings discovered by Newton's *did* exist previously, and they become accessible "in themselves"—and not merely as beings *for us*—thanks to Newton's discoveries. In addition, this quote involves Heidegger's account of truth: he wants to show how truth as correspondence is founded in truth as discoveredness. A scientific law or theory is called true (*wahr*) when it corresponds to a state of affairs in the world. However, this form of truth requires that we have this law or theory at our disposal in the first place. Since they are not given in a platonic *topos ouranios*, laws and theories first need to be discovered, and these beings first need to be disclosed *as they are*. Therefore, truth as correspondence is founded in truth as discoveredness.

This quote from *Sein und Zeit* is not an anomaly in Heidegger's work. In this context, his account of the statement as *logos apophantikos* offers another striking example. A statement does not present us with a representation of a being—that is, not with an object—and not even with a meaning. Rather, statements "let beings be seen from themselves."[53] This conception of the statement criticizes and rejects a conception of language or consciousness as media in which we represent beings and by which we lose access to the beings as such.

According to Meillassoux, mathematics allows us "*to discourse about the great outdoors; to discourse about a past where both humanity and life are still absent.*"[54] This means that, thanks to mathematics, scientific theories disclose a world that stretches out far beyond what we can and even could have experienced since it concerns a reality that precedes the origin of human life. Heidegger would easily agree with this and simply add that without these theories we would not have access to them. Moreover, he would add that these theories by which we discover the beings in our world that existed long before humans came to inhabit the earth, tell us something about their specific mode of being—which he calls present-at-handness (*Vorhandenheit*)—but Heidegger never claims that this mode of being is imposed on them; it is simply their mode of being. But this is also exactly the problem for Heidegger, as is well known: how to think other modes of being if we want to capture everything in the language of mathematics, which privileges the mode of being of present-at-handness?

Naturally, much more can be added to this brief discussion on the status of the natural sciences. What is at stake for me, however, is that it indicates that the identification of Heidegger as an exemplary correlationist is questionable in light of the issue of ancestrality. To a certain extent, Meillassoux is aware of this issue. Before he offers his only, unique example of Heidegger's correlationism, he notes that

Heidegger criticizes the Kantian effort to think beings as objects; that is, he criticizes Kant exactly for treating beings as correlates of the subject. Yet, Meillassoux insists that Heidegger remains an heir to Kant, and it is exactly the concept of *Ereignis* that would prove this. *Ereignis* articulates "the co-belonging (*Zusammengehörigkeit*) of man and being," as he writes in reference to *Identität und Differenz*, and he continues: "Thus, the notion of *Ereignis*, which is central in the later Heidegger, remains faithful to the correlationist exigency from Kant."[55]

In light of my discussion in this study so far, this is a highly intriguing remark since *Ereignis* is exactly the concept of the event Heidegger develops for understanding the characteristics of an ontology arising from the suspension of the principle of reason—the same principle that *Après la finitude* rejects and replaces by the principle of unreason. Thus, *Ereignis* is indeed the concept in Heidegger's work that needs to be studied in order to understand the relation between the hermeneutic and the speculative schools on the issue of the possibility of a contemporary ontology.

Since these are the high stakes in his passage of *Après la finitude*, let us consider how tenable Meillassoux's claim is. Is *Ereignis* truly "the correlationist exigency from Kant" to which Heidegger responds in *Identität und Differenz*? It is not evident at all that the answer to this question should be affirmative. In *Identität und Differenz*, it is not Kant but Parmenides who guides Heidegger's account of the co-belonging of being and thinking. He introduces the term "co-belonging" to interpret (and affirm) Parmenides' famous phrase that being and thought are the same. Especially in light of the analysis of strong correlationism that follows in Meillassoux's book, one would definitely like to see a proper analysis of why it is the Kantian correlation rather than the explicitly discussed fragment of Parmenides that guides Heidegger's account of co-belonging: for Meillassoux's account of strong correlationism culminates in the claim that strong correlationism does not affirm Parmenides' adage that being and thinking are the same but, rather, implies that "*being and thinking must be thought as capable of being wholly other*."[56] It is very strange and also not very convincing to see that the only example of strong correlationism Meillassoux actually finds in Heidegger's later work is borrowed from an essay in which Heidegger so obviously thinks the exact opposite of what would characterize strong correlationism, namely, a rejection of Parmenides' adage. Of course, for Heidegger, thinking is capable of another beginning. In this sense, Heidegger's work might be said to be directed to a wholly other mode of thinking. Yet, this thinking is not wholly other than being; rather, it addresses the question of being differently and no longer shares in the presuppositions of metaphysics, that is, in the principle of reason.

Let me draw the mildest possible conclusion from the above discussion: Meillassoux does not really prove what he promises to prove. Therefore, I will not pursue this line of inquiry. Rather than continuing to read Meillassoux's discussion of (strong) correlationism as an account of Heidegger's thought, I will follow the systematic problem he addresses under the heading of strong correlationism and make only some side-notes on its relation to Heidegger's thought.

2. Metaphysics and the Absolute. His systematic account of correlationism brings us immediately back to the main questions of this study. Correlationism, as Meillassoux indicates, is to be understood as a critique of metaphysics. He notes that this means that it concerns a critique of the principle of reason since this principle forms the heart of the metaphysical quest for an absolute being: "metaphysics culminates in the thesis according to which *every* being is absolutely necessary (the principle of sufficient reason)."[57] Meillassoux agrees with correlationism that this principle is untenable; and in this sense speculative thought is indeed an heir to Kant as well as to Heidegger.[58] Thus, Meillassoux places himself in the same philosophical space as correlationism, which is a space guided by the question of how to develop an alternative to this principle. Yet, within this space, he chooses a different trajectory than the correlationists do.

Correlation is introduced in opposition to the absolute; that is, correlationism is the strand of thought that in its critique of metaphysics criticizes every attempt to think an absolute; it is a "*de-absolutizing*" thought. This is elaborated in two basic correlationist theses: (a) everything we engage with is a correlate of thought and never a being in itself; (b) this correlation is not an absolute itself.[59]

Hence, the world and everything that we encounter is a correlate of thought. Yet, since this correlation cannot be an absolute, we can never know whether the way in which the world is given to us is necessary or contingent. Although the world is given to us, and although we can describe the world in accordance with this givenness, we do not know "why the correlationist structure has to be thus." Although we can describe the principle of causality that rules over the relation between beings, we can neither deduce its necessity nor know its contingency. This undecidability between necessity and contingency is coined "facticity" by Meillassoux, and he distinguishes it from contingency: "For if contingency consists in knowing the potentiality-of-being-other of worldly things, facticity just consists in not knowing why the correlational structure has to be thus."[60] Hence, whereas contingency concerns a positive knowledge—something is contingent if we *know* it can be different—facticity concerns a lack of knowledge. It is this facticity that marks the correlationist conception of the givenness of the world and that marks the finitude of thought in the correlationist conception of it: since correlationist thought depends on correlation as a *factum brutum*, it cannot think this fact itself. Consequently, Meillassoux goes on to explain, correlationism can also not exclude the possibility of something that is "wholly other" than the world or thought. Note that Meillassoux uses the term "wholly other" as a name for the unthinkable. This is the heart of facticity: "what is operative in facticity is not knowledge of the actual possibility of the wholly other, but rather our inability to establish its impossibility." This latter inability to establish the impossibility of the wholly other forms the heart of his conception of strong correlationism: "Thus, the strong model of correlationism can be summed up in the following thesis: *it is unthinkable that the unthinkable is impossible.*"[61]

This summary reveals the intrinsic limitedness and finitude of strong correlationism. Since it is unthinkable that the unthinkable is impossible, strong correlationism is always haunted by the impossibility of showing in thinking that the unthinkable does not exist in itself. Apparently, Meillassoux seems to suggest, this is why the wholly other so often appears as a theme in contemporary hermeneutic-phenomenological philosophy.

Can we indeed trace such a suggestion in the work of, say, Levinas, Heidegger, or Derrida? Meillassoux's account implies that their thought encounters, despite itself, its own limits in relation to the wholly other. Moreover, if Meillassoux is right, they cannot discuss or think this subject matter, since the wholly other is the unthinkable itself. Yet, the theme of the wholly other is present in the thought of all three of them. While Levinas's language often seems to indicate that the wholly other is beyond ontology and beyond thinking, Heidegger's and Derrida's accounts are more subtle and philosophically more viable in this respect. For Heidegger, the wholly other is *by definition* inaccessible to metaphysical thought—or, as he often simply calls it, "philosophy"—since it concerns the other of metaphysics. Nevertheless, the term "wholly other" itself refers to thinking (*Denken*) rather than to the unthinkable: "wholly other" qualifies the other beginning and the beginning thought, which is a thought of the event. In this sense, the notion of the wholly other does not correspond to the unthinkable as such for Heidegger, only to what is metaphysically unthinkable, that is, what is unthinkable in a mode of thought that presupposes the principle of reason.

3. The Principle of Noncontradiction. The final issue I want to address in Meillassoux's characterization of strong correlationism concerns the principle of noncontradiction. Meillassoux explains that the correlationist use of this principle is in line with what we saw before. For the correlationist, this principle is only of thought: we cannot think something contradictory; yet, since it is "unthinkable that the unthinkable is impossible," we cannot conclude that being in itself is not contradictory.[62] Meillassoux's speculative alternative, on the contrary, argues that this principle is true and can even be derived from its basic conviction that there are no necessary beings. The argument Meillassoux uses is actually quite simple, and its validness depends on the question of whether one accepts the following claim: if a being is contradictory, then it *is* (since it is a being) and it *is not* (since it is contradictory). If we accept this reasoning to be more than a sophism, Meillassoux can continue his proof as follows. If such a contradictory being ceases to exist—that is, "is not"—it will "change" into itself because it already is not. Consequently, it cannot not be; that is, it is necessary, and this is in contradiction with the assumption that no necessary being exists.

I do not want to go into the many questions that this particular argument raises. I only want to point out that Meillassoux offers a slightly misguided account of how contemporary thinkers deal with the problem of the excluded third (rather than the law of noncontradiction). They do not claim that the law of noncontradiction holds for thinking but might not be true for being in itself. Everything depends here on the question of how one exactly understands the operation of negation (or "reverse," as Badiou calls it).[63]

Since Meillassoux does not give any examples in his abstract discussion of correlationism, one can only guess which references, authors, and arguments he is thinking about. Therefore, let me provide a characteristic example of how the principle of the excluded third is contested in contemporary thought. Once more, the present-day readings of the letters of Saint Paul are instructive. In *Saint Paul*, Badiou argues that "Jew" and "Greek" are the names of the discourses that together constitute the language of the situation Paul inhabits.[64] Hence, in this situation, Jew is the opposite of Greek and Greek is the opposite of Jew. Consequently, in light of the principle of the excluded third, Paul's formula "neither Jew nor Greek" is empty and cannot have a reference. Yet, for Badiou this "neither Jew nor Greek" is not empty but discloses Paul's universalism, which is *added* to the situation. Although disagreeing with Badiou on the matter of Paul's universalism, Agamben also claims that this "neither Jew nor Greek" is not empty; rather, it discloses what he calls "the remnant," a concept to which I will return in the next chapter.[65] These examples do not only show in which form the principle of the excluded third is *not* accepted as a principle of thought, they also indicate that this nonacceptance is intrinsically connected to the issue of the event: if the event can indeed introduce something new in the situation, this new element—Badiou's universal man or Agamben's remnant—cannot be captured by the principle of the excluded third that describes the whole of the situation: according to this principle, the set describing the whole of the situation equals the set Jew ∪ Greek, but the set Jew ∪ Greek does not present this new element. Meillassoux does not only refuse to discuss the particular way in which contemporary thought plays with this principle in its intrinsic connection to the concept of the event, he also does not address the way in which his own conception of contingency, to which I will now turn, requires a similar "rejection" of the principle of the excluded third: the absolute new that may arrive in a situation is not an element of the set composed by the formula "A ∪ not-A" to which every element of the situation belongs, whatever the set A is (and, of course, if the principle of the excluded third is valid in the accompanying logic).

Contingency as the Potentiality-of-Being-Other

To provide an alternative to both the metaphysical quest for an absolutely necessary being and to the correlationist de-absolutization of thought, Meillassoux's speculative alternative aims to "*uncover an absolute necessity that does not reinstate any form of absolutely necessary entity.*" Moreover, in accordance with the problem of ancestrality, this speculative alternative should be able to show "that thought can think what there must be when there is no thought."[66] Since the most important principle of metaphysics is the principle of reason, this alternative should be sought in the rejection of this principle, as Meillassoux writes: "The ultimate absence of reason, which we will refer to as 'unreason,' is an absolute ontological property, and not the mark of our finitude of our knowledge. From this perspective, the failure of the principle of sufficient reason follows, quite simply, from the *falsity* (and even from the absolute falsity) of such a principle." Hence, in the speculative version Meillassoux proposes, the failure of the principle of reason is not due to the incapacity of thought to reach being in itself but concerns the very question of being. While beings appear to be ordered according to this principle, behind this principle a more chaotic reality is found: "there is no reason for anything to be or to remain thus and so rather than otherwise."[67] Note that this refers to Leibniz's well-known formulation of the principle of reason to which also Agamben refers: there is a reason why something is rather than is not. Reason, as Leibniz's formulation states, provides the ground for the "rather than" of "being-thus-and-so rather than being-otherwise." As soon as this principle is removed, the ground for the "rather than" disappears and everything is placed in light of its possibility-of-being-otherwise, as Meillassoux writes—or its potentiality, as Agamben calls it.[68]

As I have shown, Heidegger does not consider the suspension of the principle of reason to be the consequence of the limitedness of human knowledge. Rather, it is the jump away from the realm over which this principle rules that allows us to think being in the first place. In this sense, Meillassoux and Heidegger agree that the inoperativity of this principle is necessary for understanding being. Since the destining of being is in no way necessary for Heidegger, one cannot say that the meaning of being "remains the same" for him. In fact, his account of *logos, ratio,* and *Grund* indicates how even the co-belonging of being and reason with which being is destined to us in the history of metaphysics, is susceptible to change and takes on different meanings in this history.

Yet, at this point, a subtle difference between Heidegger and Meillassoux announces itself. Whereas Heidegger, in relation to the principle of reason, speaks in terms of a *suspension* and of a jump away from the domain in which this principle reigns, Meillassoux's break with this principle is much more direct: rejecting the principle of reason, he posits the principle of unreason or contingency. Suspension is another operation that he is positing. Contingency is the absolute that the speculative philosopher discovers, and he defines it as follows: "*The absolute is simply the potentiality-of-being-otherwise* [pouvoir-être-autre] *as such.* ... The absolute is the possible transition, devoid of any reason, of my state towards any other state whatsoever." Contingency is the potentiality of reality of being otherwise. Recall that the speculative alternative to correlationism should show "that thought can think what there must be when there is no thought." To account for this latter possibility, he notes that the possibility of being otherwise includes the possibility of the *abolishment* of thought. Thinking contingency includes thinking this particular possibility of what lies beyond the end of thought. As he writes, "we are able to think...a potentiality-of-being-other capable of abolishing us, or of radically transforming us." Or, he continues, to think contingency "*harbours the possibility of our own non-being.*"[69] Despite the difference between suspension and positing, Heidegger and Meillassoux do share a focus on the advent rather than the birth. The concept of the event that stems from Meillassoux's account of contingency places the emphasis on the future rather than on the past since it is exemplified by the end of thought as pure possibility rather than by any birth that has already taken place.[70] This difference between birth and death also allows us to reinterpret the difference between facticity and contingency to which Meillassoux points in his book. The model of birth, as we found it in both Romano and Badiou, necessarily favors a form of facticity: the event addresses us not in its contingency, in its possibility to be there when we are not there, but in its *always already having taken place*. It gives itself in this way only *for* us, that is, for the *advenant* and the subject, respectively. For both Romano and Badiou, the concept of the event does not make any sense without either the actual presence of the *advenant*, who responds to the possibilities the event offers to understanding, or the subject who carries out the consequences of the event. In both cases, the disappearance of the human being renders the event completely ineffective. Consequently, there is no event without *advenant* or subject, respectively. To think the event in accordance with Meillassoux's conception of contingency, on the contrary, one needs to develop a conception of the event that exceeds thinking and human life to such an extent that it needs to be thought as their possible abolishment. Hence, in opposition to the event as absolute beginning, which privileges the having taken place of the event, the event as absolute contingency implies the possibility of the end of human thought and human life. In this conception, the paradigmatic event can never be birth. *Rather, in thinking absolute contingency, thinking thinks the possibility of its own end;* this is "a *pure possibility;* one which may never be realized."[71] In this sense, it is not only the concept of potentiality-of-being-otherwise that brings Meillassoux close to Heidegger, but also his understanding of contingency in light of a possible end or radical transformation—of our thinking existence.

Meillassoux's Indebtedness to Heidegger

Let us examine this similarity between Meillassoux and Heidegger a bit more closely. For both Meillassoux and Heidegger, contingency concerns a possibility that *may or may not happen*. From a structural point of view, it seems quite clear that Meillassoux's understanding of contingency is closely related to Heidegger's conception of (authentic) death and the access it gives to our proper potentiality-of-being. Not only does Meillassoux's explication of contingency as the potentiality-of-being-other clearly refer to Heidegger's potentiality-of-being, but also his distinction between an absolute and an empirical contingency seems to be borrowed from *Sein und Zeit*. He defines absolute contingency as a pure possibility of which we do not know when or whether it will actualize itself; empirical contingency, however, is a "perishability" of beings that will occur sooner or later.[72] This distinction is exactly the same as Heidegger's between an authentic and an inauthentic understanding of the certainty (*Gewißheit*) of our death. In everydayness, Heidegger argues, the certainty of death is only an empirical one. We are only empirically certain that our lives will end at a certain moment in time.[73] Yet, authentically, this certainty of death gains a completely different meaning. In its focus on the empirical certainty of death, "the they covers over what is peculiar to the certainty of death, *that it is possible in every moment.*"[74] Authentic death is marked by another certainty, namely, the certainty that death is possible every moment. Meillassoux's conception of absolute contingency repeats this certainty, but he rethinks it on the level of being. The certainty or necessity of contingency is exactly that the world *can* change. In the form of this contingency, it affects thought. In thinking absolute contingency, thought is *always necessarily* thinking the possibility of its own end that may and may not actualize.

In addition, we need to return to Meillassoux's distinction between facticity and contingency. For him, facticity describes our uncertainty about the fact whether the way in which the world is given to us is necessary or contingent. (By contrast, contingency concerns our positive knowledge that the world can be otherwise.) The term "facticity" seems to refer to Heidegger's use of this term (*Faktizität*) in *Sein und Zeit*, where it is closely related to his account of Dasein's thrownness (*Geworfenheit*). Yet, for Heidegger, these concepts do not concern the mere givenness of certain circumstances of the world. Authentic understanding in light of death as the "not-to-be-bypassed," pure possibility of Dasein requires the suspension of all ontic circumstances. In his account of facticity, Meillassoux forgets what we could call the *hōs mē* structure at the heart of Heidegger's analysis of death. In authentic understanding, Dasein relates to every circumstance in its world as not being the case. As Heidegger indicates, death is a "nonrelational possibility" that singularizes (*vereinzelt*) Dasein. It disconnects Dasein from others and from other beings in order to understand its own being as potentiality-of-being.[75] In this context it becomes clear that neither thrownness nor facticity culminates in the insight that the world and all beings in it are given to Dasein in an unexplainable way. Rather, both categories concern Dasein's being-thrown in its ultimate possibility, namely, its potentiality-of-being. Dasein exists as pure contingency, that is, as pure possibility.[76] Consequently, Heidegger's facticity is closer to Meillassoux's contingency than the latter is willing to admit.

One may object to these arguments that speculative thought claims something about being rather than about the human being. Doesn't Meillassoux distance himself from *Sein und Zeit* and especially from its fundamental ontology? Yet, Heidegger's development displays a similar transition.[77] He turns away from fundamental ontology to demonstrate how it is anchored in the contingency of being as such. This contingency is thought as *Ereignis*, which is why Meillassoux's short reference to *Ereignis* in *Après la finitude* is both important and disappointing, as we saw above. Therefore, let us try to understand more precisely how Meillassoux distances himself in argument from Heidegger's account of the contingency of being.

First, one might locate this distance in terminology: *Ereignis* is called "wholly other," whereas Meillassoux does not use this term in his account of absolute contingency. In fact, this term seems to provide Meillassoux with the means to distance himself from Heidegger when he describes his work as a thought of the wholly other.[78] The reason why Meillassoux refrains from using the term "wholly other" seems to be quite simple: although it is the name for the unthinkable, Meillassoux also relates this term always with a certain inarticulate conception of (the unthinkable) God.[79] Yet, God is not a synonym for *Ereignis* in Heidegger's work. Rather, the relationship between human beings and Gods *depends* on being, and consequently on *Ereignis*, because the latter is the event that also changes how we think the gods and how we think the human being.[80] Moreover, since for Meillassoux absolute contingency concerns the pure possibility of reality being unforeseeably and unpredictably other, why doesn't he say that it concerns the possibility of being wholly other? What is the philosophical pertinence of limiting this term to a vague conception of God or gods? Indeed, absolute contingency implies that reality is a "hyper-Chaos," as Meillassoux puts it; hence, it implies that everything can be wholly other but can also remain the same.[81] At this point, the only difference between what he calls correlationism and absolute contingency is that absolute contingency rules out the possibility that reality is not contingent, whereas correlationism leaves this option open. Yet, to say that Heidegger's work leaves room for the option that reality may not be contingent is a strange, if not to say distorting, way of summarizing a thought that aims to think contingency in the form of the event.

Second, one might argue that Meillassoux rejects the concept of *Ereignis* since this notion involves a form of appropriation: the event consists exactly in the appropriation of the event by thinking. Does this not reintroduce the correlation Meillassoux criticizes so heavily? Yet, everything depends on the question of how we interpret the notion of appropriation in Heidegger's work. As we saw, the thought thinking the event is also always a form of *Vordenken*. It is a *preparatory* thinking since it cannot *actualize* contingency as pure possibility; it can only prepare it and suspend any decision on whether the event will or will not happen. This is why Heidegger also states in the famous passages from "*Zeit und Sein*" that the event is not only a form of appropriation but also that expropriation (*Enteignis*) belongs to the event (*Ereignis*).[82] The appropriation of being as contingency and as pure possibility implies that thought cannot force or actualize anything concerning this possibility.

Third, to affirm the similarity between Heidegger and Meillassoux concerning the issue of contingency and the reproach of the wholly other that would lurk in the form of a certain conception of God in Heidegger's work, let us simply turn to the question of God. In its refusal of both the metaphysical God as the unifying ground of reality and the religious God as the wholly other, *Après la finitude* discusses the question of God only in terms of what is to be rejected.

In order to understand how Meillassoux thinks the notion of God and its inexistence in more positive terms, we need to turn to his essay "Spectral Dilemma." In this essay, he argues that the question of the existence of God is highly urgent. The urgency of the dilemma "either God exists, or he doesn't" stems from our wish to do justice to the many people who died horrible deaths in the twentieth century.[83] He puts this dilemma in the following striking terms. On the one hand, our wish for justice seems to require that God exists. How otherwise will justice be done to the departed? On the other hand, if God exists, God has allowed these atrocities to take place. Since this is in contrast to our conception of God—God would never allow these atrocities to take place—the only conclusion left is that God does not exist. As Meillassoux writes, "Thus the dilemma is as follows: either to despair of another life for the dead, or to despair of a God who has let such deaths take place."[84] To find a way out of this dilemma, he uses the principle of absolute contingency to introduce a conception of a God that "inexists" but is nevertheless possible.[85] Hence, he introduces "the possibility of a God still to come," and in line with his conception of contingency this concerns a possibility both "*contingent* and *unmasterable.*"[86] This means that we cannot predict or force this God to come; we can only state that this God's coming may or may not happen. For Meillassoux this provides a way out of the dilemma because it combines "the possible resurrection of the dead" with "the inexistence of God."[87] (Once more, this indicates the typical difference between Meillassoux and Badiou. For Badiou, the event concerns the transformation by which an inexisting element starts to exist maximally. For Meillassoux, however, this transformation is thought as possible and *never* as actualized.)

Whatever one might think of this dilemma and its solution—I find it both elegant and highly thought-provoking—I would like to point out that this inexistent God that *can* come and inexists *in* and *as this possibility*, provides us with a conception of a God that is neither the metaphysical unifying ground nor the religious wholly other: the existence of the first follows from the principle of ground, whereas the inexistence of the second cannot be demonstrated in the strong model of correlationism. Yet, to invoke the resemblance with Heidegger once more, although Meillassoux claims that Heidegger develops a thought of the wholly other and thus introduces a notion of God of which we cannot demonstrate the inexistence, one might wonder whether Heidegger's notion of the last god, which he develops in the *Beiträge*, is really so different than the one Meillassoux proposes here. When Heidegger uses this term of the last god, it concerns an entity that requires and depends on the event and its temporal structure. The following quote describing the "essential occurring" (*Wesung*) of the last god is typical in this respect: "The last *god essentially occurs* in the intimation [*Wink*], in the intrusion and the remaining absent [*Ausbleib*] of the advent. The last god is not the event itself and yet is in need of the event as that to which the one who grounds the 'there' belongs."[88] The intimation or hint (*Wink*) marks the essential occurring of the last god. As I explained in chapter 4, a hint is not a trace of an event that has already taken place. Rather, it announces what is still to come. The same terminology returns here to describe how god "is": it does not exist in actuality, but it is given only in and as the announcement of what *may* come. In the intimation or the hint, the last god arrives, but only in "the remaining absent of the advent," as Heidegger writes. This is corroborated by the quote above: the last god is in need of the event. This god depends on the imminent possibility of what may (and may not) come.

THE CONTINGENCY OF THE EVENT

I have argued that Romano and Badiou, despite important differences, both conceive of the event in terms of its having taken place. The human comportment or relation to the event, which Badiou terms "fidelity" and Romano terms "understanding," is in both cases always *après coup*. This means that although the event is *contingent in itself*—meaning that it also might not have taken place—the human being can never experience it in its very contingency, if we mean by the latter the experience that the event *can also not take place*. In Romano's work, in which birth is the exemplary event, this is evidently the case: my birth is always *presupposed*. Without being born, I would not exist. The contingency of the event can only be known as "I might also not have been born" and never as "I can also not be born." That is, the event departs always from the actuality of the event. The previous chapter arrived at a similar conclusion in relation to, especially, Badiou's *Logiques des mondes:* every subjective affirmation or rejection of an event is preceded by the scintillating trace the event left behind. As *presupposed* in its having taken place, the event can no longer give itself in its contingency. One might also say that the event is the negative ground for the comportment of the subject to it: it is a *negative* ground because the happening of the event cannot be experienced as contingency in the strong sense of the word of what may and what may not take place. Hence, if the event is thought as the absolute beginning that makes the human comportment to it possible in the first place, this thought does not think the contingent essence of the event: what matters in such an account of the event is not whether it is contingent or necessary but simply that it has taken place, and since it has been done, it cannot be undone.

Considered from this angle, Heidegger's and Meillassoux's works offer substantially different approaches. Heidegger is concerned with the event in its contingency, that is, the taking place of the event is not presupposed but is prepared in and by thinking. Meillassoux is mainly concerned with the question of contingency, namely, with the potentiality of the world to be otherwise. The actual occurrence of such a change would, of course, be an event in the strong ontological sense of the word as developed in present-day thought, that is, as an occurrence to which the principle of reason does not apply. This concern with contingency, I would conclude, also gives shape to his questions with respect to the *phenomenological* givenness of being. Hermeneutic phenomenology as such is not the problem, I would suggest. What is the problem is every account of the event that hides and obscures the experience of contingency from which the theme of the event in contemporary continental thought stems, namely, that it may *and* may not happen and that it may *and* may not give.

Yet, there are important differences between Heidegger and Meillassoux, and my considerations in this chapter are definitely not meant to identify or conflate their work. For instance, the similarities do not extend to Meillassoux's efforts to account for ancestrality or for the stability of physical laws with probability theory. Moreover, one should not forget the difference in method. In particular, I would like to repeat one striking difference. In chapter 4, I described Heidegger's approach to the principle of reason as a suspension of this principle and an investigation of the realm opened up in and by this suspension, which allows him to enter the realm of the void: "By the same token, 'void' is actually the fullness of what is still undecided and is to be decided."[89] Hence, by affirming neither the principle of metaphysics nor any other principle, this other realm is disclosed. Meillassoux, however, is strictly speaking not as interested in exploring what it means to suspend the principle of reason. Rather than an *epochē* of this metaphysical principle, Meillassoux simply alters principles and posits the principle of unreason. This seems to imply that, although being changes in character—first it was determined by the principle of reason, now it is understood in terms of the principle of unreason— the corresponding thinking does not change. For Meillassoux, thinking used to be speculative (since also metaphysics is a brand of speculative thought) and it remains speculative. This makes one wonder why *Après la finitude* maintains that being is *thought* differently—in fact, that it is the very core of being to be capable of being different—without accounting for thinking as potentially different. Meillassoux excludes thinking from this ontological change although he affirms Parmenides' adage that being and thought are one.

Six

What Can No More Be Than Not Be

> "To be capable, in pure potentiality, to bear the 'no more than' beyond Being and Nothing, fully experiencing the impotent possibility that exceeds both—this is the trial that Bartleby announces."
> —Giorgio Agamben, *Potentialities*

In light of the previous two chapters and their conclusions about the different concepts of the event in contemporary thought, it seems natural to turn to the work of Giorgio Agamben—and not so much to his work on the event itself but, rather, to his work on potentiality and contingency. These concepts in Agamben's work form an important hinge between Heidegger's event and Meillassoux's contingency.

Remainder of Plurality, Remainder of the Event

In chapter 3, I argued that Agamben criticizes the role of the presupposition and its empty form in contemporary thought. He does so in light of the Platonic *anupotheton*, what is without presupposition and hypothesis. For him, Plato invites us to think the *absolute*, but this need not be an absolute being; rather, as Agamben suggests, philosophy thinks the absolute by way of absolving thought from all presuppositions. This "'absolution' of all presuppositions" is the true task of philosophy according to Agamben.[1]

Looking back on our discussion of the methodological difference between hermeneutic-phenomenological and speculative thought, Agamben's work offers a unique position in this debate. He shares with Meillassoux the conviction that, despite the contemporary rejection of dogmatic metaphysics, it remains the task of philosophy to think the absolute, that is, *to think beyond all presuppositions.* Yet, Agamben's work offers a much more subtle and nuanced account of Heidegger's heritage than Meillassoux's too rough account of this heritage. Thanks to Agamben's approach, the ambiguities of Heidegger's heritage with respect to the theme of absolution become clearly visible, as I will show later in this chapter.[2] In addition, this approach promises a solution to some of the issues that haunted Meillassoux's appraisal of contingency, without losing the latter's focus on the absolute. This focus on the absolute (and, as far as I am concerned, not the sometimes curious flirtation with mathematics in the form of set theory and probability theory) constitutes the indispensable contribution of speculative thought to contemporary ontology.

In chapter 3, I already analyzed what the effort to absolve from all presuppositions means for the concepts of plurality developed in contemporary thought, such as Jean-Luc Nancy's conception of plurality and Alain Badiou's conception of multiplicity. Such an exposure discloses what remains unthought in a thought that departs from a particular presupposition or hypothesis. Therefore, this exposure discloses *what is other than* the presupposed (since it *suspends* the presupposition). This implies that this suspension is itself a pluralizing—it opens something other than what is already taken into account by the hypothesis. Moreover, this pluralizing cannot be subsumed under a concept of plurality that depends on the given hypothesis. Hence, this suspension gives rise to an *other* pluralizing. Combining this with the results of the previous two chapters, in which I argued that the realm disclosed by the suspension of the principle of presupposition is the realm *of the event,* one might suggest that this other pluralizing is what contemporary philosophy terms "event."

To a certain extent, this latter suggestion is affirmed by Badiou's work since it offers a dualistic version of this order between multiplicity and event: the event reorganizes (the consistent multiplicities in) the situation. Nancy, however, would be less willing to allow for such an order between plurality and event since plurality as *partage* concerns the very taking place of this sharing. In this sense, the plurality of being as "being singular plural" is nothing but the event of this taking place. Therefore, he would not recognize an event outside of the concept of plurality or pluralizing that he develops. Our analysis of Nancy's conception of dialogue in chapter 2 forms the main reference for this: for him, the movement of dialogue is the event of pluralizing itself. Nevertheless, as Agamben points out, this conception of both event and plurality is attached to a certain understanding of abandonment: the pluralizing of being—including our own being and thinking—is abandoned to this movement of sharing. We will need to take a new look at this analysis of abandonment to capture what conception of the event Nancy's interpretation of abandonment implies.

Continuing this issue of the presupposition from our discussion of plurality to our discussion of the event in the previous two chapters, we may now also see why Badiou's and Romano's conceptions of the event are intrinsically problematic. Whether it concerns the comportment of fidelity or of understanding, the event is always already the presupposition for this human comportment to it. The ethos and praxis belonging to the event can only be enacted *because the event has always already taken place*. Of course, this particular focus allows them to concentrate on the aftermath of the event: as Marion and Romano argue, it is not the event itself but only the transformations of the world to which it gives rise that can be understood; similarly, Badiou argues that what matters to us, the subjects of an event, are only the consequences that need to be drawn from this event. This also implies that they are more interested in the actual changes to which an event gives rise than in thinking the nature of the event itself. Nevertheless, a simple difference exists between the changes that take place and the category of the event due to which they can take place. At this point, Nancy's terminology is quite apt for describing Badiou's and Romano's accounts of the comportment to the event: the human being is *abandoned to the event* for its subjectivity and its understanding, respectively. The human being has only *après coup* access to the event and is entrusted to it for its subjectivity and understanding.

Yet, if the concept of the event is introduced in order to think the suspension of the principle of presupposition, how can the event's having taken place be presupposed? Here we see why the problems of presupposition and contingency are intrinsically connected in relation to the event: *the presupposition that the event has taken place implies the effacement of the contingency that the event can also not take place.* This shows that the critique of Badiou's and Romano's concept of the event, as I developed it in the previous two chapters, is ultimately concerned with the absolution of all presuppositions. Also, the above reflections suggest that this absolution—our version of the absolute—also requires us to think the event in its contingency.

In addition to Badiou's and Romano's concept of the event that departs from the hypothesis that the event took place and in addition to Heidegger's concept of the event as what is to come, one should consider the possibility of a conception of the event in its *very taking place*. As my work in chapter 2 and the above comments suggests, Nancy's work on *partage* as the taking place of sharing being invites us to explore another conception of the event. Moreover, this account of the event in its very taking place goes hand in hand with a particular conception of contingency. Following Jacques Derrida's striking interpretation of Nancy in *Le toucher, Jean-Luc Nancy*, one might capture the type of contingency that speaks from this analysis of the event in its very taking place by the figure of the touch. For each being, Nancy argues, being is singular, but this singularity only occurs in and as the event of its singular *touching* of other beings. Etymologically, such a figure of contingency makes sense since contingency comes from the Latin *contingens* and *contingere,* meaning to happen, to occur, as well as to touch.[3] The contingent is that which touches us and, thus, contingency is related to contact and to the spatial figure of contiguity. Of course, this spatial model is a fruitful one for a thought that aims to think how beings can share being without fusing into one: contiguity describes a form of contact that does not unite the two beings that touch. Thus, we might suggest, Nancy's work offers us a conception of contingency as the very event of touching, the contact and communication taking place now, at this very moment.

What are the implications of the figure of the touch for such a conception of contingency? A touch depends on an immediate presence, here and now, of that which is touched. Only if the surface I touch with my fingers is contiguously there with my hand can I touch it. As soon as there is a spatial or temporal distance, no actual touch can occur.[4] In fact, as Husserl already argued in *Ideen II,* there is a qualitative difference between the sense of spatiality arising from the touch in its exploration of the surface it touches and the sense of spatiality that depends on a distance beyond the reach of the actual touch. These different forms of spatiality find their analogue in the ontological interpretation of the figure of the touch. While being-in-touch-with-other-beings is an integral part of how I am—and how any being is—the possibility that I am *not,* that is, that I am out of touch with everything there is and that I necessarily leave everything *in-tact* or untouched in such a situation, cannot be thought in a conception of contingency that depends on the figure of the touch. In this light, the phenomenon of my own death forms a limit case of such a conception of contingency since my death separates my ability to touch from the necessity to leave things untouched when I am no longer. Can we truly be touched by (our own) death except in the mode of a possibility in which we can never actually exist, here and now? Hence, as in the case of Marion and Romano as discussed in the first section of chapter 5, death cannot be a complete event in Nancy's model of the touch.

The latter example indicates that, although this conception of the event in its taking place goes hand in hand with a specific concept of contingency that is in fact experienced in the sharing of being, this concept of contingency does not capture the pure possibility as the basic dimension of contingency to which Meillassoux and Heidegger are oriented. A thought of the touch cannot grasp the possibility of being-out-of-touch and the possibility of *leaving intact what may come.* This shows the contrast with, for instance, Meillassoux for whom contingency is connected to a thought that can think what there must be when there is no thought.[5] This forms the heart of his struggle with the different modes of givenness as developed in phenomenology: what if there is a form of reality that is left untouched by thinking since it concerns a reality in which thinking either is no longer or is altered radically? Guided by this question, we may interpret Meillassoux to connect his concept of contingency to a mode of thinking that is out of touch with the world, that is, in which the world is not given. This is why, for him, contingency concerns the potentiality-of-being-not as well as the potentiality-of-being-otherwise. Clearly, for Meillassoux, this critique on givenness is not only a critique on Nancy and Marion. Despite their shared focus on the potentiality-for-being(-other), the question of givenness also separates Heidegger and Meillassoux: how to think the giving (*es gibt*) of the event characterizing Heidegger's *Ereignis* in relation to Meillassoux's critique of phenomenology. Up to now, I neglected this issue, but I will deal with it in the next section. First, I will conclude the analysis of the three main types of event discovered in contemporary thought.

Neither the conception of the event derived from the figure of the touch (Nancy) nor the conception of the event as pure possibility (Meillassoux and Heidegger) is subject to the objection I raised against the concept of the event that departs from its having taken place (Romano and Badiou). Yet, the former two are different. Whereas the focus on the touch captures more strikingly the experience of the taking place of the event here and now, Heidegger and Meillassoux develop a keen conception of the experience or the thought of contingency as the experience or thought of what may and may not take place. This difference can also be captured as follows: in its actual taking place, the event does *not* offer the experience that it may or may not take place; it simply takes place. The possibility of its not taking place is removed from the experience that undergoes the happening of the event—in this sense, this experience is truly *abandoned to* the happening of the event and *abandoned from* the possibility that event can also not take place; we are only left with experiencing the sheer positivity of its occurring to which we are entrusted but which we cannot understand. In this sense, the concept of the event arising from Nancy's thought also should be understood out of the concept of abandonment that plays such a huge role in his work.

Thus, our analyses of the effort to think the event out of its having taken place, or out of its sheer taking place, indicate that the two resulting concepts of the event leave a certain unthought remnant. This remnant is taken up in the third concept of the event. This remainder is the *contingency* of the event, that is, its intrinsic possibility to take place as well as not to take place.

Absolution, Event, and Abandonment

The reflections in this chapter so far lead to a variety of questions: What is Agamben's version of the absolute? How to understand Heidegger's attention to the event's gift of being—"*Es gibt Sein*"—in light of Meillassoux's critique of the primacy of givenness in phenomenological strands of thought? What is the difference between Nancy's and Heidegger's conceptions of the event when for both the issue of the event only comes into view due to the abandonment of being (*Seinsverlassenheit*)?[6] Although these questions may seem to be unrelated at first sight, they are part of one complex.

Although Nancy inherits his account of abandonment from Heidegger, their elucidation of the problematic of abandonment is not identical. In fact, Heidegger's understanding of the relation between abandonment and event holds something in store for us that cannot be found in Nancy's interpretation of abandonment. Moreover, Heidegger's understanding of these themes will elucidate my claim in the previous chapter that contrary to what Meillassoux argues, Heidegger's *Ereignis* should be understood as an absolute rather than as a correlational notion. To substantiate this claim, I need to clarify what I mean by absolute and distinguish it, as Heidegger does too, from other conceptions of the absolute such as Hegel's.[7] Moreover, it is imperative to address the issue that seems to disprove my claim: Does the *giving* of the event—the *Es gibt*—not simply prove that Meillassoux's interpretation of Heidegger as a correlationist—but not a *strong* correlationist—is right? This section is devoted to unfolding this complex of questions concerned with the relation between absolution, event, and abandonment in Heidegger's thought and its relation to Agamben's project.

To access this complex, I first turn to one dense page in Heidegger's "*Zeit und Sein*."[8] Heidegger argues that the abandonment of being is the destiny (*Geschick*) of the first beginning of thought. Essentially, metaphysics operates on the basis of a fundamental negativity: the event in which being is destined (*schicken*) to us remains concealed in metaphysics. In "*Zeit und Sein*," the event's destining is understood as the event's *giving* of being (and of time) that lets being be present (*Anwesenlassen*).[9] The "essential impossibility" of metaphysics, as I argued in chapter 4, consists in the fact that metaphysics drains this concealed source of being in its effort to think being as pure self-transparency. For Heidegger, Hegel's account of the absolute, and in particular of "the absolute self-knowledge of absolute spirit," is the culmination of this metaphysical outcome of the history of being. This Hegelian absolute constitutes the end of metaphysics since "the last remainder of the concealment of being disappears" in this enterprise.[10] Obviously, in this Hegelian sense, Heidegger's thought resists any form of absolute thought. Moreover, since the turning to the event is a turning to the event's giving and destining of being, this turning is a turning toward the primordial giving that Meillassoux discovers at the heart of correlationism. So where does this leave us with the issues of absolute and (cor)relation?

Although Heidegger's thought is not absolute in Hegel's sense, the turning to the event may nevertheless be called absolute in another sense. The abandonment of being is the *Geschick*, the destiny of the first beginning of thought, and the event marks the fundamental negativity of the different sendings (*Schickungen*) of being in its history (*Geschichte*). Yet, when destiny and history are characteristics of a thought that depends on the abandonment of being, a thinking *turning to the event* can only be "unhistorical" (*ungeschichtlich*) and "without destiny" (*geschicklos*), as Heidegger writes.[11] One may already be inclined to call such a unhistorical thought and its destining without destiny (*Schicken ohne Geschick*) an absolute thought. This inclination can be translated into a more precise conception of what we are naming "absolute" here.

The abandonment of being as the destiny of metaphysics is indeed an abandonment in the sense of the word explained in chapter 3.

Obviously, Nancy and Agamben inherit this notion from Heidegger. From the previous analysis, it follows that the abandonment of being is also an abandonment of the event. The event is not only withdrawn from metaphysical thought, but it is also metaphysics' unthought presupposition: metaphysics is entrusted to and at the mercy of the different sendings by which the event destines being. In his essay "*Se*" in which he deals with the same page from "*Zeit und Sein*" as I do here, Agamben calls thought absolute when it *absolves* and performs an *absolution* from the relations and presuppositions by which it is bound.[12] Applied to the concept of abandonment, this means that thinking is to absolve abandonment from its negativity, that is, to absolve it from the "empty form of relation" that binds it.[13] In the context of Heidegger's account of the event, absolution should thus refer to a change of thinking in which (the thought of) being is no longer bound to the *destiny* of metaphysical thought, that is, no longer bound to and turned over to the *hidden withdrawal* of the event. And, indeed, this is what Heidegger aims to think: rather than presupposing the event and *being exposed to* the event—as metaphysical thought is—thought *exposes* the event by bringing the history of the event's withdrawal to an end: the turning to the event "is equivalent to the end of [the event's] withdrawal's history."[14] Thus, thought absolves and frees itself (as a thought of being) from the withdrawal of the event *that constitutes the negativity of metaphysics* in order to expose this withdrawal.

This negativity of metaphysics is indeed, in Agamben's terminology as developed in chapter 3, an *empty form* of presupposition since (1) it relates (the thought of) being to a presupposed event that remains out of reach for metaphysical thought, and (2) it does so by an empty presupposition since Heidegger does not offer any *content* or *law* that describes how the event sends being; the only characteristic Heidegger offers and that gathers the different sendings in the one destiny of metaphysics is the event's withdrawal; it is the mere fact that the event (as well as its withdrawal) does not give itself to be thought. Only when thought turns to the event is this presupposition examined and the thought of being absolved from this empty relation.

In *Homo Sacer,* Agamben interprets this absolution of abandonment in terms of the change that takes place in the relation between being and beings as Heidegger describes it in the *Beiträge*. As noted before, Heidegger argues that the guiding question, in which being is understood *out of* its relation to beings, needs to be transformed into the basic question in which being is understood *without* any relation to beings. Of course, this latter effort is not easy to grasp at first: What does it mean to inquire into being without beings? It implies the end of ontology as we know it, since ontology addresses the question of the being of beings. Why does Heidegger think it necessary to approach being in light of the event and to place the event at the heart of this renewed ontology? The reason, Agamben clarifies, is because in the history of being, "Being [is] *in the ban* of the being."[15] The guiding question presupposes that to think being is to think the being of beings. Yet, at the end of its history, metaphysics is led to the idea that there are beings *and nothing else.* This shows why the relation of being and beings as the point of departure for an inquiry into being leads to an abandonment of being: not only is (the thought of) being at the mercy of what beings allow us to understand, but since beings are now understood in terms of the idea that there are *only* beings and nothing else, beings offer nothing to understand about being. This is indeed, as Agamben writes, "Being's abandonment *to* and *by* a law that prescribes nothing."[16] The guiding question, marking and motivating ontology, prescribes nothing at the end of the history of being. Therefore, as long as the guiding question guides our inquiry into being, we are left with nothing but the empty form of the relation between being and beings that has no meaning of being to offer.

At this point, Agamben makes an unexpected shift. He suggests that the abandonment of being is not necessarily bound to the destiny of metaphysics. Absolved from this destiny, a thought of being would open up in which abandonment is "truly experienced as such." In this sense, for Agamben, the full truth of Nancy's claim that abandonment is the sole predicament of being can only be understood if we "push the experience of abandonment to the extreme."[17] While this suggestion aims to radicalize the experience of abandonment, Agamben's discursive strategy is slightly confusing here since it introduces abandonment in a second, different meaning. In the context of *Homo Sacer,* abandonment first describes the structure of the empty form of relation or presupposition; this is simply the definition of abandonment, of which Nancy and Heidegger offer their versions. This first abandonment is to be absolved by thinking. As Agamben writes again and again, philosophy cannot be satisfied with recognizing the structure of abandonment; it should absolve it. This corresponds perfectly to Heidegger's account of the abandonment of being as the destiny of metaphysics. Yet, Agamben also suggests terming the absolution of abandonment with the same term "abandonment." What is gained by this discursive strategy?

One might consider this strategy as an effort to clarify Heidegger's turning to the event. Agamben's doubling of abandonment corresponds to a distinction in Heidegger's work between the abandonment of being as the destiny of metaphysics and the concealment (*Verbergung*) intrinsic to the event and with which "the attention of thought is concerned" when it turns to the event.[18] This concealment at the heart of the event should guide our understanding of the absolving nature of Heidegger's thought. In Heidegger's own explication of the difference between his *Ereignis* and Hegel's absolute, the notion of finitude plays a crucial role, as is well known. Finitude is not meant as merely a dimension of human thinking, as Meillassoux seems to presuppose in his characterization of correlationism in *Après la finitude*. Finitude in relation to the event is not even meant as a characteristic of all history. Whereas the end of history leads Hegel to the infinite and the absolute, Heidegger's end of the history of metaphysics does not disclose the dimension of the infinite but rather of the *finitude of the unhistorical* event. Whereas for Hegel this history becomes transparent for the absolute spirit in its absolute self-knowledge and necessity, Heidegger's exploration of the event discloses an absolute concealment at its core. The finitude of the event is thus nothing else but another name for the movement of concealment intrinsically belonging to the event. Unlike the forgetfulness of being at the heart of metaphysics, this concealment is not a withdrawal that is withdrawn from us. In this sense, it is *without* negativity. Heidegger's reference in *"Zeit und Sein"* to the Greek term *lēthē* to grasp the meaning of this concealment is most significant in this respect.[19] For him, as I argued elsewhere, *lēthē* is the provenance of *alētheia*.[20] That is to say, every unconcealment of being refers back to this basic form of concealment that does not give. Clearly, the event is that which gives being (its *es gibt*) in the history of being. Yet, an exploration of this giving requires that the gift be suspended and bracketed (*epochē*). Only this suspension of the empty presupposition of metaphysics makes thought attentive to the concealment out of which may be given (as well as not be given), but which does not actually give. Hence, in thinking concealment, the thought of the event thinks the giving as well as the nongiving of the event as the event's pure potentiality: it can no more give than not give. Thought turning to the event is thinking this unhistorical potentiality. Obviously, this aspect needs to be discussed in more detail since it brings us to the heart of the matter in our discussion with Meillassoux, namely, the role of the event's giving in Heidegger's thought.

Concealment, as Heidegger writes, is the "movement most proper to *Ereignis*." This Heideggerian concealment inspires Agamben's use of the term "abandonment" in its second meaning, that is, abandonment absolved from any destiny and relation. This is what Agamben calls "simple" and "pure abandonment," and it should be understood as an adaptation of Heidegger's use of *lēthē*, or simple concealment: "Rather what takes place is simply a movement of concealment without anything hidden or anything hiding, without anything being veiled or anything veiling—pure *self-destining without destiny*, simple abandonment of the self to itself."[21] Agamben interprets this movement as "pure *self-destining*." What does this mean for Heidegger? If we suspend all sendings (*Schickungen*) by which being is given, the taking place of the event's giving of being is no longer presupposed; this is the very unhistorical nature of the event itself. Differently put, it is also no longer solely the movement of the event as it destined this history that is to be thought, but it is also the movement of the event that sends being potentially otherwise or even of the event potentially *not* sending being at all. This latter option of not sending being might be considered a limit case. Nevertheless, Heidegger reflects on this option in "*Zeit und Sein*" when he writes of the event, "*Ereignis* is in itself *Ent-eignis*." Hence, if Agamben's reference to self-destining is meant as an interpretation of Heidegger, self-destining means that the event destines itself as *Ent-eignis*, ex-propriation. Rather than merely translating it as ex-propriation as is usually done and bringing into play the chain of propriation and appropriation, which has often been problematized in the literature on Heidegger, one should also emphasize that *Ent-eignis* is used here as an immediate reference to simple concealment, which is the realm of nongiving that constitutes the withdrawn core of every unconcealment and giving.[22]

Let us try to grasp this strange occurrence of nongiving in the giving of the event more precisely. In the lecture course *Parmenides*, which is one of the main references for Heidegger's understanding of *lēthē* as simple concealment, he employs the verb *vorenthalten* to name this nongiving of concealment.[23] As soon as we put a hyphen in it—"*vor-enthalten*," as Heidegger does—we see immediately why he uses this verb.[24] Concealment is that which contains (*enthalten*) in advance (*vor-*) what *may* be given. This interpretation suggests the following more precise description of the experience of concealment or *lēthē*: the concealment at the core of the event is not so much concerned with giving or nongiving as such but, rather, with the event as the *possibility* of giving. As a possible giving and as a possible destining, the event is also always the possibility of nongiving or giving differently. According to the logic explored in chapter 4, we may now conclude that the realm of simple concealment is the realm out of which can be-given and can also not-be-given. Concealment thus refers to the event as potentiality, which in turn is another name for the contingency Heidegger thinks in his notion of *Ereignis*: the event may and may not take place, it may and may not give. This is the very nature of the other beginning in which the event itself is to be thought: this other beginning is always to come because the event it aims to think is itself potentiality and contingency. The wavering and hesitating gestures that belong to a thinking of which restraint is the basic mood correspond to the primacy of potentiality in the concept of the event—the event is the potentiality to take place and not to take place.

Clearly, this interpretation brings Heidegger's account of the event very close to Agamben's understanding of potentiality and contingency. I will turn to this topic in the next section to establish the proximity between Agamben and Heidegger more significantly. Before doing that, let me enumerate the results of my analysis for the discussion with the speculative school.

First, the alleged opposition between the speculative return to metaphysics and Heidegger's proclamation of the end of metaphysics obscures the stakes of both speculative and Heidegger's thought. For the latter, the end of metaphysics is always the end of the history of metaphysics. Consequently, as we saw, the event is unhistorical and is an absolute since it absolves itself from the historical epochs in which being is given. Thus, Heidegger's event is without any doubt "after finitude" in Meillassoux's sense of the limitedness of human understanding.

Second, though unhistorical, Heidegger's event is finite. This finitude concerns the simple concealment of the event, its *Ent-eignis*. In light of this determination of the event, Meillassoux's attention to *Ereignis* as a form of co-belonging of being and thinking is to the point, but also one-sided. To put it in Heidegger's words, the mood that motivates the inquiry into the event is not the "jubilation of belonging to being [*Seinszugehörigkeit*]," but rather the "shock [*Erschrecken*]" that lies concealed in this jubilation that "brings the abandonment of being into the open."[25] This shock pushes thinking beyond the mood of wonder, which is the basic mood of the first beginning of philosophy, "to dwell in its *ēthos*," which Heidegger calls *Verhaltenheit*.[26] Hence, rather than a form of co-belonging, it is the experience of abandonment and the absolution it demands that are at stake in his turning to the event. As long as the event is thought as co-belonging *alone,* a speculative reading only scratches the surface of Heidegger's understanding of the event. In particular, it forgets to interpret those aspects of Heidegger's event that mirror rather than oppose the experiment Meillassoux undertakes when he argues that thought has as its task to think being when being *is no longer (or not yet) given*. For Meillassoux, this means to think contingency or *the potentiality-of-being-otherwise*. Yet, this focus on contingency is more analogous to Heidegger's focus on the contingency of the event than Meillassoux seems to appreciate. In accordance with my results in chapter 5, the difference between these two philosophers concerning their conception of contingency is methodological. This methodological difference will be discussed in chapter 7.

Third and finally, despite Badiou's and Meillassoux's apparent aversion to Heidegger, their critique of twentieth century thought as a thought that only thinks the problem of language (not to mention consciousness) is also an invitation to reread Heidegger. Philosophical hermeneutics as well as deconstruction interpreted the later Heidegger first and foremost as a profound thinker of language. Although Heidegger's work indeed contains beautiful reflections on the role and the essence of language and on the deep affinity between thinking and poeticizing, and although the hermeneutic and deconstructive readings of Heidegger offer many insights in these themes, these particular readings also have a tendency to efface and obscure the ontological stakes of Heidegger's later work.[27] It is the important contribution of the speculative school to return to questions of ontology. Despite its particular combative tone and sometimes distorting way of questioning Heidegger, their contribution also contains an invitation, perhaps against their intent, to reinterpret texts such as the *Beiträge* and "*Zeit und Sein*" in light of the ontological issues Heidegger addresses therein. More generally, present-day philosophy and its representatives such as Nancy, Agamben, Badiou, and Meillassoux make clear how important Heidegger's analysis of ontotheology and the alternative he pursues in his account of the event are for understanding how and why the themes of plurality and event determine the ontological agenda today. In this sense, I fully subscribe to Nancy's words when he writes that Heidegger's conception of the event "remains undoubtedly to be appropriated by a thought of today"; the analyses in this section and the previous chapters are meant to contribute to this appropriation.[28]

Contingency and Pure Potentiality: The Case of Agamben

I return to my interpretation in chapter 3 of Agamben's reading of *Bartleby, the Scrivener,* in which I presented Agamben's Bartleby as an alternative to Nancy's version of the rhapsode Ion who is abandoned to the enthusiasm that makes him speak. For Agamben, I suggested at the end of chapter 3, Bartleby is an angel of contingency: he announces being as contingency.

The Story of the Divine Scribe

To understand what Melville's story has to say on the issue of contingency and potentiality and how it fits with the context of this book, let me first describe the philosophical context in which Agamben situates Bartleby. This will allow us to grasp Agamben's version of the essence of ontotheology, which he phrases in terms of the pair consisting of potentiality and actuality as well as their complex relation.

Agamben develops his conception of potentiality in discussion concerning Aristotle.[29] In his essay on Bartleby, he focuses on the occurrence of this notion in Aristotle's *Peri Psuchē*. Since it is the task of the soul to know and understand the form of beings that it encounters, Aristotle argues that it cannot have a form of its own since such a form would deform the forms of the beings the soul aims to know. Therefore, the soul must be a pure potentiality to know. To grasp this pure potentiality, Aristotle famously compares the soul to a *grammateion,* a *tabula rasa* or a writing tablet "on which nothing is actually written" so that everything *can* be written on it.[30]

Departing from this figure, Agamben tells in a few dense pages how the story of potentiality unfolds in the history of philosophy and theology. In the course of this history—from Aristotle to medieval thought—the pure potentiality of writing, which is first only a figure for the intellect, becomes a figure for creation because "every act of creation... is an act of intelligence," and vice versa. Moreover, creation itself is founded on the creating acts of a creator who is thought to be "absolutely without potentiality" since this creator is pure actuality.[31] Thus, the story that started with the pure potentiality of the soul is succeeded by a (hi)story in which this potentiality is subsumed under the pure actuality of the creator as the divine scribe. As Agamben suggests, the theologians discussing this divine scribe try to "drive all experience of potentiality from the world."[32] Whereas the concept of the divine scribe aims to first subsume potentiality under actuality and eventually even expel potentiality altogether, Agamben's story suggests a more complicated relationship between potentiality and actuality: metaphysics is built upon the presupposition of potentiality in every actuality. In terms of the vocabulary developed before, potentiality is the negative source of metaphysics for Agamben.

This story of the divine scribe and its relation to the figure of writing raises many questions. For instance, does an intrinsic connection between the idea of the demiurge or creator and the figure of writing exist in the history of philosophy? In addition, related to the relationship between actuality and potentiality, one may wonder whether Aristotle is a proper accomplice. For instance, are Aristotle's famous comments in *Metaphysics Lambda* from which the traditional hierarchy between actuality and potentiality is deduced not a perfect counterexample to Agamben's effort? Of course, he would not deny these passages, but he does argue that when taking other passages of Aristotle on the notion of *dunamis* into account, a more complicated picture arises "for the reader freed from the prejudices of tradition."[33] As he often reminds us, the secret of Aristotle's conception of potentiality is that it is not only a potential to... but also always a potential not to... (*dunamis mē*...), to which he also often refers as "impotentiality" (*adunamia*).

One passage from Aristotle to which Agamben refers in three different texts—his essay on Bartleby as well as *Homo Sacer* and "On Potentiality"—concerns the definition of *dunamis* from *Metaphysics Lambda*. Usually, this definition is translated as follows: "A thing is capable of doing something if there is nothing impossible in its having the actuality of that of which it is said to have the potentiality."[34] Agamben, however, translates it as: "A thing is said to be potential if, when the act of which it is said to be potential is realized, there will be nothing impotential."[35] Hence, the "impotential" (*adunaton*) receives in Agamben's translation a different emphasis and meaning than it usually does. Rather than defining possibility in terms of "there is nothing impossible" for it to be actualized as the common translations are, Agamben suggests that this definition of *dunamis* states what happens to the potential not to...in the actualization of a potentiality: in the actualization of a potentiality, the potential not to...is set aside. To actualize is a "nullification of the potential not to be," that is, "when nothing in it is potential not to be and when it can, therefore, not not-be."[36] Yet, as he adds, this "nullification" of impotentiality is a particular form of *preserving* the potential not to...in and on the level of actuality: "To set im-potentiality aside is not to destroy it but, on the contrary, to fulfill it, to turn potentiality back upon itself in order to give itself to itself," and "the potentiality to not-be *preserves itself* as such in actuality."[37]

The combination of nullifying and preserving immediately reminds one of Hegel's concept of sublation (*Aufhebung*) in which the preceding stage of the dialectical process is both canceled and preserved on a higher level.[38] Yet, in Agamben's more genealogical (and nonteleological) approach, this combination should be understood as abandonment, or "sovereign ban," as *Homo Sacer* puts it. Although the terminology developed in *Homo Sacer* to understand the relation of the ban seems to belong to political philosophy—as the use of concepts such as the state of exception and the sovereign suggests—Agamben argues that it is concerned with an *ontological* issue.[39] For instance, he translated the notion of the sovereign ban—to be entrusted to a sovereign who decides on the state of exception—into ontological terms to describe the relation between potentiality and actuality. When arguing once more that Aristotle is the crucial philosopher since his thought "bequeathed the paradigm of sovereignty to Western philosophy," he does not refer to Aristotle's *Politics*. Rather, he refers (once more) to *Peri Psuchē* since this text confronts us with yet another aspect of Aristotle's conception of *dunamis*. For Aristotle, as noted before, the soul has the potential to know every form. Yet, it does not lose this potential when it actually knows something. It preserves its potential to know in an unaltered way even in its actual knowing. As Aristotle writes, "Hence it is wrong to speak of a wise man as being 'altered' when he uses his wisdom, just as it would be absurd to speak of a builder as being altered when he is using his skill in building a house."[40]

Thus, while setting aside the potential not to know or the potential not to build in the actual knowing or building, this setting aside does not alter either the knower or the builder. Their potential to know and to build remain at their free disposal. Agamben discerns the structure of abandonment in this relation between actuality and potentiality as follows. The potentiality to know or to build is presupposed by every act of knowing or building, but this potentiality is also set aside in the very moment of the act of knowing of building itself. This relation between potentiality and actuality forms the heart of what Agamben calls the sovereign ban, and, beyond Aristotle's use of it in a psychology, he extends this relation to ontology. As before, he can do so as soon as one accepts the connection between the act of the intellect and the act of creating as it has been developed in metaphysics:

> For the sovereign ban, which applies to the exception in no longer applying, corresponds to the structure of potentiality, which maintains itself in relation to actuality precisely through its ability not to be. Potentiality (in its double appearance as potentiality to and as potentiality not to) is that through which Being founds itself *sovereignly,* which is to say, without anything preceding or determining it...other than its own ability not to be. And an act is sovereign when it realizes itself by simply taking away its own potentiality not to be, letting itself be, giving itself to itself.[41]

The notion of the sovereign is most often understood as a theological-metaphysical heritage: the true ruler of the world is also its creator. Since metaphysics is usually, in a Heideggerian tone of voice, understood as the thought that gives priority to presence and actuality, one would be tempted to understand the sovereign as pure actuality. Yet, in line with this genealogy of the divine scribe discovering the secret of potentiality at the core of the metaphysical account of the creator and its actuality, Agamben argues that the metaphysical heritage does not simply consist of depicting the sovereign in terms of actuality alone but, rather, as *a sovereign relation between actuality and potentiality.* To put it in terms of the concept of creation, which Agamben uses in "Bartleby, or On Contingency," the demiurge and divine scribe are no longer thought as *pure* actuality since they presuppose the relation of the sovereign ban between actuality and potentiality.[42]

Differently put, what exists or what *is* in actuality, is *in the ban of the sovereign potential to create and not to create;* it is banned from and entrusted to this sovereign potential for its existence in actuality.

Thus, Agamben's reinterpretation of the notion of the sovereign in terms of the relation between actuality and potentiality leads to a different understanding of the theological motive in ontotheology. In its effort to understand being out of a highest being, *metaphysics does not simply affirm the pure actuality* of this highest being, but *rather brings into force the relation of abandonment between actuality and potentiality.*

In this context, Agamben also reads Aristotle's text that might count as the best counterexample to this analysis in this light: *Metaphysics Lambda,* in which the unmoved mover is introduced as a pure actuality that causes every movement, changes its appearance as soon as one interprets it in light of what Aristotle writes on divine thought. Divine thought cannot think nothing since there is no dignity in thinking nothing, as Aristotle remarks.[43] Moreover, it cannot think something since this would imply a movement, and every change is a "change for the worse" for a being that is already highest. Therefore, divine thought can only think itself.

This reading shows one crucial aspect of Aristotle's divine thought. Since it is without movement, divine thought is necessarily without beginning; it is an eternal being-in-act. Yet, to be without movement *also demands* that thought (not being nothing) is a pure potentiality in the sense of pure matter: as soon as thought would have a form of its own—that is, *offered some particular content to be thought*—thought thinking itself would again turn out to be a movement.[44] In this sense, *the divine relation of thought thinking itself is an empty relation between the actuality and the potentiality of thought.* To put it in Agamben's terminology, if we consider divine thought to contain the secret of the role played by the pure actuality of the highest being that is said to characterize ontotheology, we may conclude the following about the ontotheological constitution of metaphysics. Divine thought is *the zone of indistinction* between actuality and potentiality in which the *empty* difference between actuality and potentiality *is nevertheless maintained* in the form of an empty relation: although it has no content, the pure potentiality of thought—its being pure matter—is presupposed in and by the act of divine thought as that to which it is turned. Thus, divine thought is the locus where the relation of abandonment between actuality and potentiality appears at the core of the reflections on a highest being.

Hence, for Agamben following a Heideggerian line of thought, the experience of abandonment and of the sovereign ban is nothing but a secret of ontotheology that appears to us at the end of metaphysics. In "the jubilation of belonging to being" as presence and actuality, a "shock" occurs that "brings the abandonment of being into the open" and discloses it as the very destiny of metaphysics, as Heidegger writes.[45] Therefore, as Agamben adds, it is the task of philosophy as ontology to find a "way out of the ban."[46]

Let us consider this interpretation of ontotheology more precisely. The divine scribe is no longer simply pure actuality, but its main characteristic—analogous to the capacity of the soul to know *everything*—is, rather, its sovereign potentiality to create everything according to its own will. What does it mean that being is characterized first and foremost by its capacity to sovereignly actualize its own potentiality to be? In particular, what does this tell us about the relation of sovereign potentiality to what exists in actuality, about the capacity of being to actualize itself sovereignly? That is, what does it tell us about abandonment (as the destiny of metaphysics)? The answer to this latter question is as simple as it is baffling (and perhaps confusing). Since abandonment means that this sovereign potentiality is not immanent to what exists (is-in-act), but is, rather, outside of it, the sovereign act in which such a potentiality is actualized does not only change that which is in actuality, but this change cannot be foreseen, computed, or mastered in terms of what is in actuality. For what is in actuality, the sovereign actualization represents an event and an exception in the strong sense of the word, namely, something that cannot be grasped in terms of the principle of sufficient reason.

Yet, does such an analysis not confuse the order between event and principle of reason? Is the event all of a sudden also present in a thought that maintains the principle of reason? In order to see what happens here and why the structure of the event (or a simulacrum of it) appears in ontotheology, we need to be more precise. The sovereign act is *only* an event in terms of what is-in-act. Strictly speaking, there is a ground for the sovereign act, namely, this actualization itself. Hence, what is-in-actuality is banned from this ground and is turned over to it in the strongest sense possible: whatever exists exists due to this sovereign actualization of being. Thus, similar to our statement that metaphysics is marked by a fundamental negativity, we may say now that despite the fact that the sovereign act is an event for what-is-in-actuality, it has a negative ground.

This consequence of Agamben's analysis of ontotheology gives a particular twist to the analyses I pursued in the previous chapters, which are all concerned with the relation between the suspension of the principle of reason and the concept of the event. If we follow Agamben's analysis of the abandonment at the heart of ontotheology, we see how the principle of reason remains operative as an empty principle with respect to the sovereign act that can only appear as the empty ground for what is-in-actuality. Yet, an empty ground is not yet an abyss (*Ab-Grund*). Consequently, one should not only distinguish between two forms of abandonment—as negativity and as pure abandonment, as explained in the previous section—but one should also distinguish between two concepts of the event: the first one remains indebted to ontotheology since it relates the event to an empty, negative ground from which it is abandoned and to which it is entrusted; the second one conceives of the event as a true abyss (*Ab-Grund*).

Agamben's analysis of the sovereign act contains one more important element. If we want to know what kind of ground this negative or empty ground is, we need to be aware that the sovereign act of being *presupposes* the potentiality of being. The structure of the ban between actuality and potentiality presupposes potentiality, which is also the potentiality not to be. If the sovereign act and its accompanying sovereign ban is the secret and the destiny of ontotheology, the philosophical task to break this ban is the task to expose this potentiality not only as the presupposition of its actualization but also to expose it *as such*, that is, *without its actualization*. Agamben's distinction between abandonment as the destiny of metaphysics and pure and simple abandonment, which I introduced above, thus corresponds to the difference between potentiality as the presupposition of the sovereign act, and potentiality without actualization, maintaining its potential not to be. This latter potentiality is simply another name for contingency, as Agamben makes clear: the contingent is that which can also not be, that is, maintains the potential-not-to-be.

To identify the philosophical task par excellence as the task of thinking being as a potentiality without actualization, that is, as pure and absolute contingency, may appear as a highly abstract task. Therefore, to get a better understanding of what this task includes, the next two subsections are devoted to showing how this task relates to other efforts in contemporary thought, and how Bartleby is engaged with this task according to Agamben's interpretation of *Bartleby, the Scrivener*.

Impotentiality: A Dispute between Agamben and Heidegger?

In perhaps more simple terms than Agamben's sophisticated reasoning, it is not difficult to see why present-day philosophy is bound to find itself face to face with the problem of actualization in its critique of ontotheology. As soon as the principle of reason as the principle of causality in its broadest sense—that is, not only as the principle of efficient causes—is suspended, the model Aristotle proposes in *Metaphysics Lambda* to understand actualization in terms of a final cause is robbed from its core. In this teleological model, the suspension of the principle of reason equals the erasure of the cause that explains the movement of actualization. Thus, this suspension confronts us with an actualization that is no longer grounded in the actuality of a final cause, and which therefore can only refer to the potentiality that precedes it. Moreover, rather than being its presupposition, actuality is at best the effect of this movement (which, perhaps, no longer deserves to be called actualization when actuality is no longer its *causa finalis*).

In light of this framework, Heidegger's famous claim in the opening sections of *Sein und Zeit* that potentiality (*Möglichkeit*) is higher than actuality (*Wirklichkeit*) appears as a predecessor of Agamben's conception of the task of contemporary philosophy to think actuality and actualization not as presupposition but out of potentiality itself, that is to say, to think potentiality as that which *may also not actualize itself*.[47] This latter formulation refers us immediately to the central phenomenon by which this task is adopted in *Sein und Zeit*, which is the same phenomenon prefiguring the event, namely, the phenomenon of death.[48] The phenomenon of death confronts Dasein with its ultimate possibility by which Dasein has access to its authentic potentiality-of-being. When introducing this possibility, Heidegger first proves why it is not another instantiation of Aristotle's teleological model of actualization: there is no actuality causing this potentiality of Dasein to actualize itself.[49] In fact, this ultimate possibility *can never actualize itself*. In Heidegger's famous words, the possibility at the heart of the phenomenon of being-toward-death is "the possibility of the impossibility" (*die Möglichkeit der Unmöglichkeit*). This possibility of Dasein's impossibility is not simply the possibility that, on a certain day, Dasein or "being-there" will have deceased and no longer be there. Rather, it is the possibility that cannot be actualized since Dasein is and exists only *as this possibility*. As Heidegger writes, "As possibility, death gives Dasein nothing to 'be actualized' and nothing which itself could be as something real [*als Wirkliches*]. It is the possibility of the impossibility of every mode of behavior toward..., of every way of existing."[50] In his interpretation of Heidegger's analysis of death in *Apories*, Derrida strikingly argues that this possibility of the impossibility understands the "possible *as* impossible," that is, the possible as what can not-be.[51] Thus, the expression "the possibility of the impossibility" exemplifies what I called in chapter 4 the *hōs mē* structure at the heart of Heidegger's understanding of the phenomenon of death: every relation (*Bezug*) to the world and its concerns is enacted (*Vollzug*) as what can also not be.[52] Without effacing the differences between Heidegger's earlier and later work, we can state that this comportment toward what is is a prefiguration of what he later will call *Verhaltenheit*, or restraint. Rather than enacting one's life in accordance to the relations in which we stand, restraint holds back from such an enactment and understands these relations in light of their potential not to be.

When it is true that Heidegger's analysis of the phenomenon of death prefigures Agamben's analysis of a potentiality without actualization, one complicated issue now needs to be raised against the background of my comments on the relation between Agamben and Heidegger in the previous two chapters. There, I noted that Agamben objects to the *negative* structure Heidegger introduces both in *Sein und Zeit* and in his later work in the form of the voice of conscience and the voice of being, respectively. (Note that I am only interested here in the structure of potentiality Heidegger introduces in the phenomenon of death; I will not address the issue of being-a-whole, to which this analysis of death also aims and which authors such as Agamben and Derrida heavily criticize.[53]) As is well known, the voice of conscience appears in *Sein und Zeit* from section 54 onward. So, where does this leave us, and what happens in the course of one section in *Sein und Zeit*? Is the phenomenon of death a form of negativity, or does it provide a way out of this negativity?

To answer this question, one should turn to Heidegger's assessment of his own account of death. At the end of section 53, he argues that it only offers him the *ontological* possibility of an authentic comportment to death. According to his distinction between existential and existentiell, section 53 belongs to the level of an existential project that demonstrates an existentiell *possibility* but does not yet demonstrate that this possibility is indeed a *factical* possibility. As his analysis in section 31 argues, a project (*Entwurf*) never projects free-floating possibilities but only *thrown* possibilities, that is, possibilities that are rooted in Dasein's facticity.[54] Therefore, the ontological possibility of section 53 requires a supplementary phenomenon that grounds this ontological possibility in Dasein's facticity.[55] Heidegger introduces the voice of conscience as this supplement. This is the voice that attests to—that is, makes known and demands—the possibility of an authentic potentiality-of-being.

This problem can also be rephrased in terms of the (in)famous distinction between authenticity and inauthenticity.[56] Since Dasein understands itself first and foremost in an inauthentic way, there should be a phenomenon in Dasein's facticity that explains how it can be *called* from an inauthentic to an authentic existence. This is the task of the voice of conscience. Heidegger famously argues that this call is silent and does not convey any particular meaning or message. In this sense, it is an *empty* call. This characterization of the voice of conscience corresponds with his interpretation of authenticity: *Eigentlichkeit* does not require any change in Dasein's ontic situation but only a different comportment to it. The call of conscience requires a comportment other than everydayness or inauthenticity; the similarity to the structure Heidegger discovered in Paul's letters and which we discussed in chapter 4 is striking.

The distinction between authenticity and inauthenticity allows us to understand Agamben's claim that Heidegger's analysis of death is marked by a fundamental negativity. For Heidegger, authentic being consists of a specific comportment of Dasein to its own being and to all the relations or behaviors toward the world, namely, *as the potentiality to not-be*. That is to say, to be authentic means for Dasein to relate to its own being as contingency. Yet, this comportment is not simply and always already given; rather, it requires *another* comportment of Dasein to itself as exemplified by the call; the call is a condition of possibility and the supplement of the possibility of impossibility. This has three implications. (1) First, this means that this ontological possibility is hidden for Dasein. Being inauthentic, Dasein has no access to its own contingency. It is banned from being authentic. Therefore, the call is necessary to make authenticity known. Note that this does not mean that authenticity is given before this announcement. Rather, the call itself, by its announcement of authenticity, divides Dasein into two modes of being—authentic and inauthentic. Authenticity presupposes the call. (2) Second, by this division, the call gives itself as a call that "comes *from*" Dasein (in its authenticity) "and yet *over*" Dasein (in its inauthenticity).[57] This is why Heidegger compares this voice, although it comes from Dasein, to "an *alien* voice": it is foreign to Dasein in its inauthenticity.[58] Since this foreignness of the voice is without content (as the call is), the division as well as the relation between authenticity and inauthenticity is an empty one. A voice that calls in silence and does not communicate any particular meaning only introduces such an empty relation; it does not change anything in Dasein's worldly circumstances, only in the way Dasein *is* (in) these worldly circumstances. (3) Third, the call does not only make known (*bekunden*), but it also makes authenticity known so that it calls Dasein out of its inauthenticity; more precisely, the call demands (*fordern*) this. Only because of this demand may Dasein find the impetus to get out of its inauthenticity. Of course, this means that Dasein, in the mode of being in which it finds itself (that is, everydayness), is entrusted to and at the mercy of this demand that makes another mode of being known as its authentic mode of being. These three elements of the call demonstrate that the voice of conscience introduces a structure of abandonment between Dasein in its inauthenticity, which is the mode of being in which it always already finds itself, and its authenticity. In particular, Dasein is placed in a relation of the ban to the possibility of the impossibility, which is death.

To capture what this structure of abandonment means for the notion of the voice and the call, let me take a small detour along Franz Kafka's parable *Vor dem Gesetz*. According to Agamben, this parable confronts us with a similar problem as the one we discern in the notion of the voice. As I noted in chapter 3, the man from the country from Kafka's story is placed in a relation of the ban to the law since he is banned from the law (he is outside of it), but he is still under the force and spell of this law (he is still at its mercy). According to Agamben, this being in force of the law is represented by the fact that the door of the law is open. Now, Agamben objects to those readings of the story that claim that the key to reading this story can be found in the insight that the law demands *nothing* from and makes nothing known to the man of the country. Yet, to demand (the) nothing is not the same as not-to-demand. The man from the country is banned from the law since the open door suggests an inside, a position within the realm of the law. To demand nothing means that no particular demand is to be found in the law; this is exemplified in the story by the open door that opens onto nothing (according to Derrida's reading). Of course, this implies that in Kafka's story, the law demands in such a way that its demand cannot be fulfilled. In this sense, it *seems* to represent a "pure" potentiality—by demanding nothing in particular, the law may demand everything—that cannot be actualized.

As I understand it, the core of Agamben's disagreement with these readings of Kafka's *Vor dem Gesetz* (and of his remark on deconstruction as a whole in the same chapter of *Homo Sacer*) concerns the difference between demanding nothing, represented by the open door of the law, and not-to-demand, which is represented by the closure of the door at the end of the story. A law that demands nothing in particular is a law that may potentially demand everything since its structure of demanding—its being in force—remains intact. Yet, *the potentiality to demand everything does not include the potentiality not-to-demand.* On the contrary, in Agamben's conception of potentiality as a potentiality not to..., the potentiality to demand is conceived differently, namely, as the potentiality not to demand; this is a potentiality *that does not maintain* its pure demanding (in the form of the demanding of nothing to which the man from the country is subjected in Kafka's story) but opens the possibility of not demanding, that is, of closing the door of the law—a possibility announced at the very end of the story. Recall that potentiality in this sense as the potentiality not to...allows Agamben to relate potentiality to contingency—similar to Meillassoux's conception of contingency as the potentiality-of-being-otherwise.

By analogy, we may apply this discussion of Kafka's story to Heidegger's conception of the voice of conscience and the position of abandonment in which it places Dasein with respect to its authenticity. Like the law that demands nothing in particular, the call of conscience that calls for nothing in particular *does not* include the possibility of not-to-call. Although the call does not call anything in particular, *it cannot not-call.* Not-to-call is excluded from Heidegger's analytic of Dasein because the actual enactment of the call is the condition of possibility for a factical grounding of the "ontological possibility" of an authentic being-toward-death in the facticity of Dasein. Departing from the distinction between authenticity and inauthenticity, Heidegger cannot consider the phenomenon of the call in light of its potentiality-not-to-call since this call is the necessary supplement that offers the factical ground for the disclosure (and the demanding) of this distinction. While we may not hear the voice of conscience, or while we may neglect its demand, it is impossible for Heidegger that the voice of conscience does not call.[59] Hence, the mode of pure potentiality, announced in the possibility of the impossibility, is not absolute since it is entrusted to the calling of the call.

Consequently, no pure potentiality of the call itself exists since such a potentiality would include the potential to call *as well as the potential not to call*. In particular this means that the call and the voice of conscience introduce not only the empty presupposition at the heart of *Sein und Zeit*, but also threaten the primacy of contingency since Dasein's potentiality-of-being depends on an alien voice that always calls. Hence, on the one hand, Heidegger's analyses of death and its "possibility of the impossibility" are meant to think a potentiality without actualization, moving toward a thought of contingency; on the other hand, these analyses require and depend on the voice of conscience that reintroduces the empty relation of the ban at the heart of the possibility of the impossibility. Hence, Dasein does not return to its pure potentiality but to a potentiality that depends on this other voice; this, as Agamben's analysis suggests, problematizes the primacy of contingency in Heidegger's work. If the voice of conscience or the voice of being always calls and cannot not-call, contingency is threatened as the basic realm of reality. This implies that our understanding of Heidegger as a philosopher of contingency, as developed in chapter 4, remains marked by a fundamental ambiguity caused by the role of the voice of being. I will draw the final conclusions from this analysis in chapter 7.

Decreation and Revocation: Bartleby's Experiment

How does Agamben offer an account of a potentiality without actualization that does not suffer from the same drawbacks as Heidegger's analysis of death? The title of the third section of "Bartleby, or On Contingency" reads "The Experiment, or On Decreation."[60] The experiment of Melville's *Bartleby, the Scrivener* is an experiment on being, as Agamben writes: "Not only science but also poetry and thinking conduct experiments. These experiments do not simply concern the truth or falsity of hypotheses, the occurrence or nonoccurrence of something, as in scientific experiments; rather, they call into question Being itself."[61] The task of literary and philosophical experiments is to call being into question. It is clear from this quote that the expression "calling being into question" implies that being is not presupposed but rather interrogated. In light of the divine scribe,

Melville's story conducts an experiment that *suspends* the understanding of being as creation.

Indeed, Bartleby is a counterfigure of the divine scribe, as Agamben develops it in the first part of his essay and as I discussed above. Rather than repeating and thus affirming the act of writing as the act of creation, Bartleby gives up writing. He no longer affirms and repeats what came into existence by the sovereign act. In this sense, Bartleby is engaged with *decreation,* as Agamben suggests, that is, with the deactivation and deactualization of creation; it takes back what is actualized into potentiality. In the imagery of the story this means that the written letters are no longer repeated. Rather than copying the letter already written, the scribe returns to the *grammateion,* the writing tablet on which nothing is actually written. As Agamben states, Bartleby "has become the writing tablet" by giving up writing; "he is now nothing other than his white sheet."[62] But what does this mean?

The reason for Bartleby to give up his work is not truly clarified by the story's narrator. Only at the end does he suggest that it might have something to do with Bartleby's previous job at the Dead Letter Office. Letters that could not be delivered to their intended addressees find their final destination at this office. The narrator concludes his story with the impression this office must have made on Bartleby:

> Dead letter! does it not sound like dead men? Conceive a man by nature and misfortune prone to a pallid hopelessness, can any business seem more fitted to heighten it than that of continually handling these dead letters and assorting them for the flames? For by the cartload they are annually burned. Sometimes from out of the folded paper the pale clerk takes a ring:—the finger it was meant for, perhaps, moulders in the grave; a bank-note sent in swiftest charity:—he whom it would relieve, nor eats nor hungers any more; pardon for those who died despairing; hope for those who died unhoping; good tidings for those who died stifled by unrelieved calamities. On errands of life, these letters speed to death.[63]

For Bartleby, letters are not only the "cipher" of creation—as the divine scribe who is also the creator of the world—rather, "undelivered letters are the cipher of joyous events that could have been, but never took place," and Agamben continues: "On the writing tablet of the celestial scribe, the letter, the act of writing, marks the passage from potentiality to actuality, the occurrence of a contingency. But precisely for this reason, every letter also marks the nonoccurrence of something; every letter is always in this sense a 'dead letter.'"[64] Hence, Agamben argues that Bartleby's motive to give up writing is to be found in the experience that everything that happens and occurs cannot stand on its own since it is always also an index of what did not take place. Bartleby no longer repeats the written letter because the price of the affirmation of what took place is too high for him: it implies the rejection of everything that did not take place, of every potentiality that was not actualized.

Let us briefly compare what happens here in Agamben's scene of writing to Heidegger's account of the call of conscience. It is not unthinkable to interpret the empty call as a revocation rather than as a vocation, analogously to what I suggested earlier, in chapter 4, in relation to Heidegger's and Agamben's reading of Saint Paul. Yet, one should add to such an interpretation that in *Sein und Zeit*, the calling itself is not revoked or annulled. In this sense, Agamben's scene of writing goes one step further and introduces another focus. It is not said of Bartleby that he effaces texts that are already written. This would mean that he would aim to destroy what happened, but this kind of destructive force is not at work in Bartleby. In fact, Bartleby does not seem to participate in anything in the world at all. Thus, the experiment of decreation is not the act of unwriting all that has been written or destroying all that has happened: this would itself be one more act, albeit a destructive one. Deactualization is something else: Bartleby goes to the source of the problem; writing itself is "given up"; the actualization of writing itself is interrupted by the scribe who no longer writes and thus maintains his potentiality not to write.

The key to understanding this deactualization of what is and has occurred should therefore not be found in a destruction but, rather, in terms of the (non-)affirming of what is and what happened. In the context of his interpretation of why Bartleby gives up writing, it will come as no surprise that Agamben briefly refers to G. W. F. Leibniz and Friedrich Nietzsche since these two philosophers, despite their huge differences, both claim in their own way that *it is necessary to affirm what took place in the past,* as I explain below. The experiment of Bartleby offers an alternative to their conceptions of our *comportment* to the past; it does so by calling the past into question, as Agamben writes, by "re-calling it," that is, remembering *and* revoking it. The Dead Letter Office triggers such a revoking remembrance, which does not affirm what happened but reconsiders it. Agamben beautifully describes this type of remembrance, which he borrows from Benjamin: "Remembrance restores possibility to the past, making what happened incomplete and completing what never was. Remembrance is neither what happened nor what did not happen but, rather, their potentialization, their becoming possible once again."[65] This revoking remembrance makes what happened incomplete because it sees what happened as an index of what did not happen. Thus, remembrance is a comportment to the past that gives *potentiality* back to the past; that is, it considers what happened and what did not happen in light of their underlying potentiality, namely, that they can happen but can also not happen.

What is said here on the remembrance of the past in general can be found *mutatis mutandis* in Heidegger's attempt to remember the history of metaphysics in his notion of thought as *Andenken* or remembrance, as discussed in chapter 4. *Andenken* does not affirm or repeat what happened and how being was interpreted in metaphysics; rather, it gives potentiality back to the past since it places metaphysics in light of what *it did not think* or actualize in the course of its history. Together with *Vordenken, Andenken* understands metaphysics in light of its unthought and guides thinking toward an other beginning. Inspired by this Heideggerian conception of remembering, one might add that the comportment to what is or was, to what took place or takes place, as enacted by Agamben's Bartleby, could also be characterized as a form of *Verhaltenheit,* or restraint, in Heidegger's sense. In restraint, we do not simply affirm what we encounter or hear in a call addressed to us; rather, we *suspend* our judgment. Agamben suggests that this is the comportment par excellence that opens up the domain of potentiality. Hence, it is a comportment that allows us to withdraw from what is and what occurred to the *contingency* of its occurring. This comportment is crucial for understanding Agamben's place in the contemporary discussions on the event. This can be seen along two lines of thought, deepening our insight into Agamben's account of contingency and its accompanying comportment of (revoking) remembrance.

1. Bartleby's Formula. Like so many other discussions of *Bartleby, the Scrivener,* Agamben's interpretation also deals with the famous "formula" for which Bartleby became famous: "I would prefer not to." Like Gilles Deleuze, Agamben argues that this formula neither affirms nor negates anything in particular: it "hovers...between affirmation and negation, acceptance and rejection, giving and taking." Hence, it announces a zone of indistinction, as Agamben furthers Deleuze's reading of Bartleby: "the formula opens a zone of indistinction...between the potential to be (or do) and the potential not to be (or do)." Thus, Bartleby's formula "is the formula of potentiality."[66]

To judge whether or not this reading of Bartleby's formula makes sense, is left to the reader: Agamben's complicated strategy of substantiating it leads us past medieval theology, skeptic philosophy, and Deleuze, but it impresses more by erudition than by argumentative rigor. Nevertheless, I am interested in the fact that he reads the formula as expressing the comportment described above. This is why he characterizes it in terms of the skeptic suspension of judgment (*epochē*). In particular, and this is a very fortunate choice, he understands Bartleby's "I would prefer not to" in terms of the skeptic "*ou mallon*," meaning, "no more than," which forms the heart of their *epochē:* the one *no more than* the other; being *no more than* nonbeing.[67] This suspension that no more affirms than negates grants Bartleby's formula its particular comportment to what is or has occurred: it announces the potentiality as *the potential to no more be than not to be;* it announces the contingency of all that is and all that occurs.

Hence, despite Agamben's capricious interpretation of *Bartleby, the Scrivener,* his strategy is clear and brings us back to our main line of inquiry here in part 2. By reading a "no more than" in Bartleby's formula, Agamben can contrast it to Leibniz's principle of reason by rendering this principle in the following form: "'there is a reason for which something does rather than does not exist.'"[68] The comportment to what is and what occurred that Leibniz's principle expresses refers us back to a reason and a ground: only reason provides and grounds a "preference"—a "rather than," a being "more powerful"—of being over nonbeing. As soon as the principle of reason is suspended, the "rather than" loses its ground and reason and transforms into a "no more than." The experiment on being that is conducted in *Bartleby, the Scrivener* suspends the principle of reason and, thus, discloses the domain of the "no more than," of the "no preference," which is the domain of pure potentiality and absolute contingency.

2. *Contingency as Absolute.* Potentiality, Agamben notes, "creates its own ontology."[69] This ontology is the ontology he is looking for in one of the quotes I used as an epigraph to the introduction: "Until a new and coherent ontology of potentiality...has replaced the ontology founded on the primacy of actuality and its relation to potentiality."[70] Yet, what does it mean for ontology to have contingency as its absolute? His account of remembrance, of a "re-calling" of the past has one more important implication for this question. When ontology is based on absolute contingency, there are far-reaching consequences, as Agamben affirms: "If Being at all times and places preserved its potential not to be, the past itself could in some sense be called into question, and moreover, no possibility would ever pass into actuality or remain in actuality."[71] If being is absolutely contingent, that is, "at all times and places preserved its potential not to be," as this quote tells us, "no possibility would ever pass into actuality." Hence, Agamben discerns a *potentiality without actualization* in the notion of absolute contingency. Moreover, an ontology in which being preserves its potential not to be is an ontology in which the principle of the irrevocability of the past can no longer be maintained but needs to be suspended.

What does this latter suspension mean? The principle of irrevocability does not only resound in Shakespeare's *Macbeth*—"What's done cannot be undone"—but appears also in Aristotle's *Ethica Nicomacheia*, as Agamben points out.[72] There, Aristotle writes, "what is past is not capable of not having taken place."[73] The potential not to have taken place is denied to the past and even to God in his relation to the past, as Aristotle suggests, quoting Agathon: "For this alone is lacking even to God, / To make undone things that have once been done."[74] For Aristotle, this principle attests to a powerlessness with respect to the past that applies to God as well.

Yet, this principle is understood and affirmed in different ways throughout the history of philosophy. As noted above, Agamben brackets Leibniz and Nietzsche together as proponents of the idea that one should affirm the past, although they do it for different reasons. Leibniz does not acknowledge that the aforementioned ontological impotentiality of God with respect to the past is due to a weakness of God. Rather, he founds the principle of the irrevocability of the past in the principle of reason. For Leibniz, God does have access to all possible worlds, but God only singles out the best of these worlds. Because he chooses the best of all possible worlds, there is *no reason* for God to change his preference. Hence, for Leibniz's God, it is not a simple fact of the past with which the demiurge is confronted. Rather, every time he returns to "the pyramid of possible worlds," the demiurge takes delight in his own choice. Agamben's assessment of these passages from Leibniz's *Theodicy* is very telling: "It is difficult to imagine something more pharisaic than this demiurge, who contemplates all uncreated possible worlds to take delight in his own single choice. For to do so, he must close his own ears to the incessant lamentation that, throughout the infinite chambers of this Baroque inferno of potentiality, arises from everything that could have been but was not, from everything that could have been otherwise but had to be sacrificed for the present world to be as it is."[75] This quote indicates that the principle of the irrevocability of the past is not a simple given in Leibniz's metaphysics, but that it is grounded in the continuous repetition and affirmation of the divine judgment that "the present world" deserves to be singled out among all possible worlds.

Nietzsche, on the contrary, is not so much concerned with the divine comportment to the world and its past but, rather, with the human comportment to the past. Referring to the aforementioned passage from Aristotle's work on the irrevocability of the past,

Agamben interprets Nietzsche's account of an affirmation of the past: "The impossibility of 'wanting Troy to have been sacked,' of which Aristotle speaks in the *Nichomachean Ethics*, is what torments the will, transforming it into resentment." To avoid the dangers of resentment, stemming from a tormented will that wills something that was not, Nietzsche suggests to willingly embrace all that was. Only in this way can the spirit of revenge and resentment be avoided. Yet, as Agamben comments, "solely concerned with repressing the spirit of revenge, Nietzsche completely forgets the lamentations of what was not or could have been otherwise."[76] Agamben interprets Nietzsche's theory of the eternal return of the same in this light: by affirming what took place, the will wills it to take place again or repeat itself in the same way.

Hence, both Leibniz and Nietzsche indicate that the principle of the irrevocability of the past concerns first and foremost an *affirmative comportment* to the past, either in the form of the divine affirmation based on the principle of reason or in the form of the human affirmation based on the will. In both cases, such an affirmation may be said to *repeat* (rather than *regret*) the past since it ignores "the lamentations of what could have been but was not." By giving up copying, Bartleby refuses to repeat what was once written and suspends both reason and will. When Agamben writes that Bartleby's "experiment is only possible by calling into question the principle of the irrevocability of the past," then this "calling into question" concerns first and foremost *the affirmative comportment* with which this principle goes hand in hand in modern thought. Bartleby practices a restraint with respect to what is written in order to remember the past—not by affirming it and not by destroying it but by giving potentiality back to it: remembrance returns to the *contingency* of the past; it thinks what was as what could also not be, and what was not as what could be.

This, then, is what *Bartleby, the Scrivener* offers to ontology today, according to Agamben. It conducts an experiment on being in which remembrance is the practice that thinks being *in its contingency*—what is, in its potential to not-be, and what is not, in its potential to be. Hence, this remembrance does not simply remember what took place but, rather, remembers what could have been but was not. Exactly this remembrance allows us to think why the affirmation of existence and of what took place withdraws itself from the experience to which remembrance invites us: only by considering the past in its potentiality without actuality can we open our thought to what could have been and to what may be.

SEVEN

The Ethos of Contingency

"The negative knowledge of our mortality thus refers to
the positive knowledge of our possible rebirth."
—Quentin Meillassoux, *L'inexistence divine*

"Plato must himself resort...to myths, like the myth of Er the
Pamphylian returning from the kingdom of the dead."
—Alain Badiou, *Petit manuel d'inesthétique*

Throughout this study, I have argued that present-day philosophy is confronted with the task of answering the question of what ontology might be after ontotheology.[1] As I have argued, the core of this ontotheological constitution of metaphysics is found in the principle of reason and its quest for a unifying ground, as Heidegger puts it. Thus, the expression "after ontotheology" delineates a precise task for philosophy, namely, to think being in such a way that it offers an alternative to the two motives that hold ontotheology together: the primacy of unity as well as the primacy of ground or reason. Despite the different conceptions of the theological motive in ontotheology, as well as of the concepts of plurality and event that offer an alternative to ontotheology, one might say that in contrast to the *necessary, universal, and unifying ground,* which is the culmination point of the principle of sufficient reason, the suspension of this principle is concerned with creating the concept of a *contingent, singular, and pluralizing event.*

In addition to the two axes of plurality and event offering alternatives to unity and reason, respectively, I have argued from the outset of this study that a third axis needs to be taken into account as well. The philosophical comportment or disposition to the necessary, universal, and unifying ground is *theōria*. The inquiry into a contingent, singular, and pluralizing event requires another ethos of thought that allows it to think the event and its contingency. Throughout this study, I indicated different forms of this philosophical comportment. In this final chapter, I want to gather the most important results of this study in light of the questions that continuously accompanied my inquiries into plurality and event: what alternative comportment of thought do present-day ontologies introduce, and in which sense do they relate to the conceptions of the event to which they are related?

Deductive Fidelity and the Affirmation of Thought

The so-called speculative school has made a major contribution to the question of ontology today. In this study, I only discussed two representatives of this school: Badiou and Meillassoux. Based on the results of the previous chapters and despite the differences between Meillassoux and Badiou discussed in chapter 5, the comportment of their ontological thought may in both cases be called "speculative." Speculation is no longer *theōria* or contemplation in the ancient metaphysical sense of the word since it does not explore or posit a unified ground as the ultimate cause and principle of reality. Yet, in other senses, speculation does inherit certain aspects of the old *theōria*. This is why Badiou characterizes his own thought as "metaphysics without metaphysics," as noted in chapter 1. Although the adjective "speculative" probably does not have one univocal meaning when comparing its usage among its different representatives, it seems reasonable to say that based on the similarities between Badiou's and Meillassoux's accounts of thought, a thought is called speculative when it includes the following three dimensions.

First, speculative thought uses mathematics as either the main model for thinking or as a science that contributes significantly to the development of philosophical questions. Both Badiou's use of set theory to develop his ontology of multiplicities and Meillassoux's use of probability theory to account for the stability of the laws from physics are examples of this. As argued before, it might be commendable—as Badiou does—to reconsider the role and the place of mathematics in opposition to the Heideggerian dismissal of mathematics. Yet, although this reappraisal of mathematics guides especially Badiou's trajectory of multiplicity, event, and fidelity to develop an alternative to unity, ground, and *theōria*, no *intrinsic* connection exists in general between the reappraisal of mathematics and the task to develop an ontology after ontotheology.

Second, speculative thought has a taste for the absolute. I would interpret Badiou's "metaphysics without metaphysics" exactly in this sense: speculative thought remains metaphysics in its quest for an absolute, albeit this absolute is no longer an absolute, highest being, as Meillassoux explains. Behind this reappraisal of the absolute against the philosophies of finitude and relativity lurks the basic conviction that thought should be absolute to deserve the name of (first) philosophy. This is a Platonic motive in this school: thought should not presuppose but should inquire into that which is without presupposition. As I argued before, this dimension of speculative thought does concern the heart of the quest for an ontology after ontotheology: the principle of presupposition is yet another variant of the principle of reason; the philosophies of finitude, as far as they presuppose an empty presupposition, cannot absolve thinking from presuppositions. Therefore, this taste for the absolute and for the absolving dimension of thought is indeed *intrinsically* connected to a suspension (as Heidegger and Agamben suggest) or a straightforward rejection of the principle of reason (as Meillassoux proposes) that guides the contemporary reflections on event and contingency.

Third, Badiou's work has influenced the understanding of the adjective "speculative" in a third sense. Speculative thought arrives at its absolute by means of a primordial *affirmation of an axiom, hypothesis, or principle* from which a thought subsequently derives that has as its task deducing the consequences. Let me first recall how this dimension of speculative thought appears in Badiou's work, where it is developed most systematically, and subsequently indicate how it is not simply absent in Meillassoux's work. Meillassoux, however, has less tendency to embrace speculative thought in terms of a decision but insists on arguments; in his work, speculative thought returns in the form of his preference for principles.

For Badiou, the subject's fidelity describes the comportment toward the event that affirms that the event has taken place and follows the demand of the event to deduce and carry out its consequences. Fidelity, therefore, occurs in the domains in which events can happen, which according to Badiou are the domains of politics, love, art, and science. As I showed in chapter 1, his ontological project in *L'être et l'événement* can be understood in terms of such a fidelity, namely, deductive fidelity: it affirms the hypothesis "the one is not" and faithfully deduces the consequences of this hypothesis. Although this particular affirmation makes Badiou an heir to Heidegger's critique of ontotheology by developing an ontology of the many rather than of the one, he cannot account for the *necessity* of his own choice for the existence of the many in the form of set-theoretical "multiplicities." In this sense, the axiomatic choice for the hypothesis "the one is not" mirrors the hypothesis "the one is" from which ontotheology departs.

In chapter 3, I showed to what extent this particular deductive fidelity goes against the grain of Plato's dialogue *Parmenides*, to which Badiou refers in this context. Badiou's deductive fidelity, however, maintains one fundamental aspect of the dialectic method Parmenides teaches Socrates: it is the task of dialectics to deduce the consequences of a hypothesis. Yet, in another fundamental aspect, Badiou does not follow Parmenides. For the latter, it is not enough to hypothesize and deduce; as soon as one hypothesis is examined, its opposite should also be examined. Badiou, on the other hand, does not do this. Moreover, this difference with the *Parmenides* places the similarity in a different light. Even Badiou's deductions seem to be different from Parmenides' deductions. Throughout his deductions, whether they belong to the hypothesis "the one is" or to its negation, Parmenides examines the inconsistencies and contradictions to which both of these hypotheses lead. Therefore, all his deductions lead to the final conclusion of the dialogue, which implies that the interlocutors cannot reach a conclusion in the matter they examined: "Whether one is or is not, it and the others both are and are not, and both appear and do not appear all things in all ways, both in relation to themselves and in relation to each other."[2] Against the background of the ruthless examinations of Parmenides that do not shy away from any inconsistencies, the deductive fidelity of Badiou stands out as the deductions of a *faithful* one, of one who has always already *affirmed, from the outset*, the truth of its hypothesis: deductive fidelity does not find any fault with the hypothesis it is supposed to examine critically.

In this particular context, Badiou would probably defend himself by saying that set theory offers a *consistent* theory of the many; therefore, he does not come across a contradiction. Although this might explain why Badiou's account of the many does not suffer from the inconsistencies Parmenides comes across, this is nevertheless not a convincing response since Badiou himself does not maintain this set theoretical consistency throughout *L'être et l'événement:* the matheme of the event contradicts one of the axioms that is introduced to secure the consistency of set theory. Consequently, the project of *L'être et l'événement* is built upon an affirmation of this contradiction, out of which the dualism of being and event is born.

In my discussion of the relation between Badiou and Romano in chapter 5, I indicated the consequences of this focus affirmation for Badiou's conception of the human comportment to the event. Subjectivity and fidelity can only appear in and as the affirmation of the hypothesis "an event has taken place," and they are only concerned with the consequences of this event and not with its taking place or its contingency. This means that the event is always already presupposed for the human to be a subject, as Badiou calls it, or to be an *advenant*, as Romano claims. Thus, the human comportment to the event is marked by an *irreducible delay*.

In more general terms, this third dimension of speculative thought has important implications that can be seen most clearly against the background of the *Parmenides*. If thought indeed derives from a primordial affirmation of a hypothesis, principle, or axiom, thought necessarily passes by another possibility of thought, namely, the encounter with what *precedes* this decision. By departing from a primordial affirmation, it deprives itself of the possibility that "it might be otherwise." In contrast to a thought deriving from a primordial affirmation, the aporia Parmenides confronts at the end of the dialogue that carries his name indicates that the issue of the one and the many *must be left undecided*. More precisely, aporia means here that thought can neither affirm nor negate the existence of the one. Consequently, rather than affirming the hypothesis "the one is" or its negation, the *Parmenides* invites the reader to suspend his or her judgment; the dialogue ends in an *epochē* of the issue: neither affirmation nor negation. In chapter 3, I discussed in which sense this aporia indeed obstructs the *euporia* in Aristotle's sense—namely, to allow a passage from dialectical investigation to knowledge—but may be called a *euporia* in another sense, as Agamben's work indicates: by not deciding on the issue, and by suspending a decision, another realm is opened up, which Agamben interprets as the realm of contingency.

This announces a clear difference between two attitudes to the event, namely, affirmation and suspension or *epochē*. This difference is crucial for understanding how philosophers today conceive of the comportment to the event and the ethos of contingency. To put it in very basic terms, if we conceive of contingency as Meillassoux and Agamben do both in their own way as the potentiality-of-being-otherwise or the potentiality not to . . . , thought's affirmation of what happened or of what exists is always premature since contingency indicates that it can also be otherwise; if it is the task of thought to think contingency, it has to suspend affirmation (as well negation).

Affirmation plays a complex role in contemporary thought and tends to threaten the primacy of contingency by offering two examples. These examples are not straightforward and reflect perhaps some of my basic concerns more than offer strict and complete arguments.

The Quest for Principles

In chapter 5, I asked why Meillassoux does not offer us an account of a particular ethos of contingency that would capture his conception of thought. The answer to this question is actually quite straightforward: he does not do so because the subject matter of his thought—contingency—is not attuned to the speculative ethos of thought that he follows—entering the absolute by means of the speculative suggestion of a principle. In this particular sense, I discern a specific tension in Meillassoux's expression "the principle of unreason"—not to say that this expression seems to be a *contradictio in terminis*. The quest for *principles* is, I would say with Heidegger's analyses in *Der Satz vom Grund,* always a quest that depends on the principle of reason or ground since a quest for principles is the quest for the *archē* that offers us the ground to understand reality. This marks the expression "principle of unreason" with a specific tension: on the one hand, we have Meillassoux's adherence to the ethos of thought that looks for principles. This ethos belongs to the realm of metaphysics as guided by the principle of sufficient reason. On the other hand, we have Meillassoux's keen eye for the subject matter of contingency expressed in the word "unreason" and even more beautifully and convincingly grasped in the expression "potentiality-of-being-otherwise," which, however, requires another ethos of thought.

How do this tension and this preference for principles influence Meillassoux's discourse? By thinking the potentiality-of-being-otherwise, Meillassoux will never find himself in the same position as Badiou; rather than affirming any event, he aims to think what *can* take place, and all that is—the world as well as thought—may be otherwise. Nevertheless, his speculative comportment to this subject matter is an affirmation of the quest for principles in the form of the principle of unreason. This latter affirmation definitely does not have the Kierkegaardian or Sartrian undertones as it has in Badiou since Meillassoux's affirmation is always built upon argumentations. Nevertheless, *Après la finitude* may be understood as an effort to think the consequences of the principle of unreason.

Of course, as noted in chapter 5, *Après la finitude* offers an argument for why this principle of unreason should be maintained: it is the unacknowledged presupposition of all forms of correlationism. Although strong correlationism implicitly uses it, it does not explicitly affirm it. Due to this lack of affirmation, strong correlationism is caught up in the problems he describes. Therefore, only positing the principle of unreason and thinking from this point onward allows us to reach the absolute and nonpresupposed already at work in strong correlationism. Yet, one may be slightly concerned about the fact that this latter response in terms of the problems of strong correlationism does not immediately deal with the principle of reason itself, nor with the question of why philosophy needs principles and why principles are the only form of absoluteness open to thought. In particular, from the perspective of Platonic dialectic, one may wonder whether he truly and *critically* investigates the principle of unreason.

In this sense, his ingenious and striking account of probability theory to support the claim that the empirical stability of the laws of physics is not at odds with the principle of unreason, is perhaps symptomatic (but only symptomatic). He uses this account to show that the speculative principle of unreason can also be maintained in relation to what seems to disprove it immediately, namely, the stability of the laws of physics. However, his analysis only shows that this empirical stability *does not offer us a decisive argument* for either the principle of reason or the principle of unreason (since the empirical stability of physical laws is perfectly compatible with the principle of reason). Strictly speaking, this analysis leaves the issue of "principle of reason" or "principle of unreason" *undecided*. This is indicative of his mode of thinking, which proceeds from an affirmation of a certain principle and of a quest for principles in general. Moreover, this is in contrast to the critical examination of Socrates, who says, "when I have taken up this position, I run away for fear of falling into some abyss of nonsense and perishing."[3]

Interestingly enough, Meillassoux is highly aware of the strangeness of his arguments; yet, rather than fearing to fall into "some abyss of nonsense and perishing," he writes, "Philosophy is invention of strange forms of argumentation, necessarily bordering on sophistry, which remains its dark structural double."[4] Yet, I would add, exactly *because* philosophy's arguments border on sophistry, the Socratic fear of nonsense is a crucial philosophical impetus. This is why *Après la finitude*, demands (after the speculative postulate of the principle of unreason) a dialectical investigation that examines what the consequences are when the principle of unreason is not valid. To put it as a question: Why does Meillassoux not consider a third option, beyond positing or negating the principle of unreason? Why does he posit and affirm the principle of unreason rather than merely *suspending* the principle of reason? Does this choice really allow him to enter the realm of the absolute or does his negligence of the other option expose his blindness to the realm of an absolute to which the aporia grants access—the passage offered by what seems impassable? Let us not forget that Meillassoux displays an aversion to the aporia, given his strong affirmation of the principle of noncontradiction.

Coming back to the tension between the ethos of thought—a quest for principles—and the subject matter of Meillassoux's thought—potentiality-of-being-otherwise—I would suggest that there is also another way of doing justice to the philosophical, Platonic imperative to head for the absolute. Rather than thinking the absolute as another principle, as Meillassoux does in his adherence to a certain metaphysical motive and mode of thought, Agamben's interpretation of the absolute as the quest to absolve thought from all principles seems to be more helpful in this regard and more in line with the subject matter Meillassoux aims to think: since the concept of a principle or *archē* refers back to a ground and a reason for thought, the thought of contingency does not seem to allow for any principle.

The Presupposed Call

The second example shows that this primordial affirmation is not only operative in the speculative school but also in the hermeneutic-phenomenological school, albeit it less in the form of an affirmation of a first principle. In the previous chapters, I referred a number of times to the dispute between Agamben and Heidegger concerning the voice of conscience and the voice of being. This dispute can be interpreted as a dispute concerning a similar problematic—affirmation versus suspension—since Agamben's critique of Heidegger's conception of the call and the voice of conscience ultimately concerns the primordial affirmation from which such a thought departs. This thought does not consider the possibility that the voice *may not call*. In a gesture that resembles Plato's *Parmenides*, Agamben maintains that thought's quest for an absolute cannot be grounded in an affirmation or in a postulate since this affirmation can never think the impotentiality—the potential not to be—of what it affirms. In this sense, the absolution of thought—aiming to absolve from all presuppositions—can never depart from an affirmation, but requires an *epochē* and especially the suspension of the principle par excellence that affirms the reasonability of existence: a reason *exists* for all that is and happens.

This latter argument shows that the difference between a comportment of thought that departs from an affirmation and a comportment of thought that begins with the suspension of presuppositions concerns the subject matter of this thought itself: what is an ontology that does not presuppose the principle of reason? We will see in the next sections not only how Heidegger's work offers other motives that are more in line with this suspension by thought, but also how this difference between affirmation and suspension helps us to rethink the disharmony between Meillassoux's subject matter—contingency or a potentiality-of-being-other—and the comportment of thought toward it.

Nancy's Ellipsis: The Empty Preference for Being

Next to Badiou, it is Nancy whose work offers an important contribution to a rethinking of the problem of the one and the many in present-day continental thought. Unlike Badiou, Nancy's ontology does not simply affirm the primacy of the many over the one. He does not depart from the hypothesis that the one is not. Rather, as I explained in part 1, Nancy offers an alternative account of the *koinon,* of the in-common, such that it is not subsumed under the primacy of *hen,* the one. In his focus on being-in-common, Nancy affirms neither unity nor sheer multiplicity. In this sense, he indeed offers an alternative to Parmenides' aporia.

As I discussed in chapter 2, he models this *koinon* on his notion of *partage* or sharing. This notion of sharing is intimately connected to a conception of the *event.* Sharing-being is not a stable or fixated situation; rather, it is the very happening of being. Being takes place as sharing. As I noted in chapter 6, when discussing the figure of the touch and of contiguity, Nancy's account of the event of sharing offers also a particular conception of contingency. Moreover, as we saw in Nancy's account of the *Ion,* this sharing comes equipped with its own conception of sense or meaning, namely, of sense as significance and transmissibility.

When the event is thought first and foremost as the taking place of being as sharing, the proper comportment to the event (or being) is undergoing it and experiencing it *while it takes place.* The figure of the touch, as I discussed it in chapter 6, thus indicates that the human being is in the midst of the event's taking place—and the human being is always in this taking place because human existence is part of this taking place of being-in-common with other beings. Recalling Nancy's reading of the *Ion,* we may compare this comportment to the event to the way in which the rhapsode sings because he is taken up in an enthusiasm that simply works and touches (in) him.

In this conception, the comportment toward the event obviously cannot be a distanced theoretical view of it. The ethos of contingency is not to be found in an analogue of our sight but rather in an analogue of our touch. To touch or to be touched by an event does not require the affirmation of the hypothesis "the event has taken place," since we are already taken up in it. Rather, this comportment requires sensitivity in the sense of being-in-touch with what takes place, with the obviousness of the taking place of our being, as Nancy suggests.[5] In chapter 2, I already contrasted this to Badiou's account of the scintillating event and Heidegger's conception of authenticity. In the terminology of the previous section, one might say that Nancy does not recognize a realm of Badiou's truth or of Heidegger's authenticity that first needs to be affirmed before we have access to it.

Although Nancy denies the affirmation (as well as the scintillation) of such a realm *beyond* our everyday being-in-common, this does not mean that the comportment to the event he suggests can be understood in terms of suspension. The suspension of the realm of significance *to which our existence always already belongs* is unthinkable since it would require an interruption of the very taking place of our existence. Therefore, he understands the relation between sense and its suspension as follows: "That sense itself is infinitely suspended or in suspense, that suspension is its state or its very *sense* does not prevent but, rather, imposes the condition that there can be no possible gesture of the suspension of sense by means of which one could gain access to the origin of sense as to its end."[6] Sense is "infinitely suspended," Nancy writes, yet there is no suspension of sense. The latter means that our existence is always already entrusted to the taking place of sense. It is our abandonment to significance that implies that sense cannot be suspended. At the same time, the concept of sharing also implies that sense is never fully exhausted in a singular taking place. This, of course, brings us back to the central theme of abandonment as discussed in chapter 3 and developed further in chapter 6. The double gesture—there is no suspension of sense and sense is in suspense—characterizes abandonment. We only have access to sense because we *are* like one of those singular rings by which a magnetic force is transmitted, which Socrates describes in the *Ion;* this is how we are in-common, and in this sense, sense cannot be suspended. Yet, because this singular sharing (as one ring in a chain of rings) is our only access, sense remains in suspense for it comprises the transmissibility of *all* rings.

In chapter 3, I already offered a critique of this notion of abandonment. Now, after chapter 6, it is possible to offer a more comprehensive account of this critique. By his insistence on the very taking place of the event of being, Nancy affirms what one could call, lacking better terms, the very *positivity* of being or the preference for being. Significance as the taking place of being is the transmissibility or transitivity of being, and the nonsuspension of significance is the nonsuspension of this transitivity of being. Of course, Nancy cannot foresee or predict any limit or end to this transitivity. Moreover, sharing in this transmissibility is being-the-singular passage of this transitivity. Since such a passage presupposes a plurality of being-the-singular, the reach of this transitivity is always in suspense.

Yet, if no suspension of this transitivity is possible since we always are the passage of this transitivity, how can we relate to what *does not share* in this sharing or transitivity? In terms of the remembrance I discussed in the previous chapter, one may wonder whether "what could have been, but was not" can ever be included in such a transitivity of being. In more systematic terms, we may now make the following observation. If the contingency of being is understood in light of the figure of the touch, and if this contingency concerns the taking place of the transitivity of being, then the potentiality-of-being can only be understood in this framework as the potential to be in a very specific sense: being can only be transmitted to what *can be and will be* by this transmission. Yet, in contrast to Nancy's conception of contingency as touch, another conception of contingency exists: usually we call a being contingent *if it can also not be,* that is, if it can also *not* share in the transitivity of being.

Of course, this result need not surprise us since it confirms the conclusions we reached in the previous chapters: a thought that departs from the concept of *partage* will meet its limits when confronted with a *non-partage*. Yet, this analysis now allows us to phrase more precisely what kind of ethos of contingency speaks from Nancy's work. Despite his critique of philosophies that *affirm* what is not presented in our situation (as Badiou would say) or what is not given in our everyday existence (as Heidegger would say), Nancy does not reject affirmation itself. Badiou affirms the truth of the event *rather than* the situation we inhabit; Heidegger affirms authentic being *rather than* everydayness; if we now conceive contingency as that which can no more be than not be, Nancy's attention to *partage* as the transmissibility and transitivity of being in turn affirms what can be rather than what can not-be.

Nancy's difference between significance and signification can be understood with regard to the attitude of suspension: while suspending every particular signification, he does not suspend significance itself. Rephrased in terms of the principle of reason—"a reason exists why something exists rather than not"—means that Nancy suspends every particular reason. Yet, although he brackets "a reason exists why" by this suspension, he maintains the *rather than* in his affirmation of being over nonbeing. This leads to the following form of Leibniz's principle: "...something exists rather than not." Unlike Leibniz's version, this formulation no longer accounts for the "rather than" in terms of "a reason exists." The preference of being over nonbeing that this Nancyan version of Leibniz's principle expresses is grounded in an empty presupposition, a mere ellipsis. This remaining preference indicates that Nancy's suspension is only partial: he does not suspend the "rather than," although he leaves it in suspense, entrusted to the empty form of presupposition, symbolized by an ellipsis.

This partial suspension affirming the "rather than" and the preference of being over nonbeing leaves open another suggestion: a more thorough suspension than Nancy's might no longer exclude the potential not to be and lead to a more comprehensive comportment toward a contingency as introduced by Heidegger's possibility of the impossibility, Meillassoux's potentiality-of-being-otherwise, and Agamben's pure potentiality.

Epochē as Comportment

For a period of approximately two centuries, Plato's Academy adopted skepticism as a genuinely Platonic philosophy. As Cooper suggests in his introduction to *The Complete Works of Plato,* all dialogues "can sustain the skeptical reading" since Plato never speaks in his own name and therefore always leaves room for the idea that the points of view his protagonists adopts are not his own, thus inviting the reader to question rather than to affirm these points of view.[7] Yet, such a skeptic reading seems to be invited especially by dialogues such as the *Parmenides.* Parmenides' final conclusion, which I quoted above, summarizes beautifully the experience of aporia that his dialectic inquiry of the one and the many brings to those who are present. Thought cannot pass here and cannot pass judgment since the aporia leaves us with nothing but the impossibility to come to a conclusion.

To consider the impact of the shock such an aporia must present for thought, recall that Parmenides' method requires that we examine the hypothesis "the one is" as well as "the one is not." This implies that his method covers from the outset *all* options that are logically possible: the point of departure of this dialogue is the concatenation of all hypotheses under examination, which is in this case nothing less than the tautology "the one is or the one is not." Since a tautology is necessarily true—"what cannot not-be (true)"—the dialectic method seems to have secured its success from the outset. In light of this security, the aporia to which the dialectic investigation leads, namely, the negation of the tautology from which it departs, is a truly astounding and disturbing thought.

In logic, one may escape this aporia by suspending the principle of the excluded third or of noncontradiction. Three-valued logic adds a third value next to the values False and True. This third value may be interpreted as an intermediate between False and True. Therefore, it is sometimes denoted as "½" to indicate its place between 0 = False and 1 = True. This symbolization suggests that statements S with this truth-value ½ may be understood heuristically as "S may be true and S may be false." Consequently, statements such as "X exists" with this truth-value express "X may be as well as not-be." Moreover, in such a three-valued logic, the negation of tautology is the complement of 1, that is, $(0 \vee ½) = ½$. Hence, from a heuristic point of view, the negation of tautology to which the aporia of the *Parmenides* leads once the principle of the excluded third is suspended, is simply the *potentiality* of the one to exist *and* not to exist: "the one can be and the one can not-be."

In this framework, we may see how the suspension or *epochē* does not simply express our perplexity with regard to the aporia, but offers a passage—a *euporia*—of dealing with it without ignoring it. Once the principle of the excluded third is suspended, the suspension of judgment to which Parmenides' conclusion compels us opens up another passage in which a pure potentiality or contingency is announced of which the formula is "what no more exists than not."[8] Let me elaborate on this skeptical ethos of contingency in discussion about Meillassoux, Heidegger, and Agamben.

For Meillassoux, speculative thought posits the principle of unreason while maintaining—and actually proving, based on the principle of unreason—the principle of noncontradiction. Here, the difference between Heidegger's and Agamben's *suspension* of the principle of reason and of principles in general, Meillassoux's *affirmation* of the principle of unreason and of the ethos of thought to find principles is brought into the open. Whereas the former suspension invites thought to suspend the principle of the excluded third and, in this way, hears in the encounter with aporias the announcement of the potentiality-of-being-other, the latter positing necessitates the principle of noncontradiction.

In addition to this difference, it is important to note what Meillassoux's affirmation obscures. Whereas suspension offers a way for thought out of the aporias it encounters in its way, affirmation refers thought to a beginning *that is not thought*. In particular, it obscures the fact that thought never simply derives from a postulate; rather, in every situation in which thought's reasoning does not offer a passage and in which it is therefore possibly placed for a decision, thought encounters, experiences, and is confronted *first* with the task to think an *undecidability*, that is, to think a bifurcation point it cannot pass *by thinking*. If there is a necessity or urgency to decide or to pass, it is grounded in thought's encounter with an undecidable.

Heidegger's analysis of the difference between the first beginning of metaphysics, which culminates in the principle of reason, and the other beginning of thought that suspends this principle by turning into the event, may be interpreted as a response to these issues. As discussed in chapter 4, the notion of decision is also important for Heidegger, but for him thought does not depart from a decision. Rather, it first needs to think where the necessity of such a decision comes from. It needs to think the de-cision (*Ent-Scheidung*) that precedes every actual decision. In the context of the difference between the first and the other beginning in the *Beiträge*, it is such a decision setting apart the first and the second beginning. Consequently, thought itself cannot simply belong to one of these beginnings; it cannot only follow one of the two trajectories while neglecting or denying the other one. Rather, inceptual thinking (*das anfängliche Denken*) finds itself on the crossing of both beginnings and inaugurates a dispute or setting apart (*Auseinandersetzung*) between them.

Hence, for Heidegger, thought cannot neglect anything, but needs to think *both* beginnings. As *Andenken*, it remembers the first beginning and thinks its unthought. As *Vordenken*, it is a preparedness to prepare—rather than to choose and depart from this choice—the thought of the event. Whereas Badiou lets thought depart from a choice and a primordial affirmation, Heidegger introduces another motive (next to the motive of affirmation that is also present in his work); he insists that an aporia for thought, which presents itself here in the form of a bifurcation point, does not allow thinking to pass it by forcing the issue. For Heidegger, thinking does not invoke anything other than itself. Even in its confrontation with an aporia, it *thinks* the impossibility by which it is not granted a simple passage rather than forcing its way.

Although this aspect of thought to think the undecidability with which it is confronted seems to be absent in Meillassoux's speculative line of thought in *Après la finitude,* one may wonder what will happen when his readers will finally get access to his long-awaited but still unpublished study, *The Divine Inexistence.*[9] In chapter 5, I referred to his essay "Spectral Dilemma" on divine inexistence. In this essay, Meillassoux introduces the principle of unreason to rethink the aporia with which the examination of both hypotheses—"God exists" as well as "God does not exist"—confronts us. Although "Spectral Dilemma" introduces the question concerning the existence of God with a strong urgency—it arises from the concern of what will happen to the victims of violence and of how they can be done justice—this urgency does not lead Meillassoux to a hasty decision forcing the aporia by either affirming or negating God's existence. Rather, he respects the aporia and waits for another passage. In particular, he shows that the negation of the tautology "God exists or God does not exist" calls for a *third* option: God inexists, but *may come to exist*. Phrased in these terms, the principle of unreason neither corresponds to a choice of a thinker nor to the exploration of a reason by which one hypothesis is true rather than the other. Instead, in this version, the principle of unreason announces the potentiality that neither affirms nor negates the existence of God: it withdraws the actual existence of God in order to think God as potentiality: God can be and God can not-be. In this sense, the outlines of another ethos of contingency are also hidden in certain aspects of Meillassoux's work: thinking that restrains itself and does not force itself to pass judgment on the aporia it confronts.[10]

In chapter 3, I argued that the aporetic experience could be interpreted as part of a strategy to interrupt the normal course of the dialectical method. In its normal course, the dialectical argument would lead to a reasoned affirmation of one of the hypotheses—either the one is or the one is not. By interrupting it, as I suggested, the *Parmenides* becomes a dialogue in which the dialectic method itself is exemplified. By suspending this normal course, the dialectical method is not simply followed but rather exposed and made known. This displacement of the nonpassage of aporia into a new passage, a *euporia* as Agamben calls it, does not force its way out of the aporia but exposes the rule of dialectics. Moreover, it exposes the dialectic capacity *not* to reach a conclusion, as I wrote. Neither affirming nor negating, this new passage shows that the *epochē* itself is an intrinsic possibility of dialectic thought—as it is encountered in many of Plato's dialogues.

Based on my earlier reflections in this chapter, and my conclusion from chapter 3, the suspension at which the *Parmenides* arrives is a full suspension. It does not only suspend the presupposition of a reason for preferring one hypothesis over the other but also presupposes a will or a choice to ground such a preference; it even suspends the elliptical, empty presupposition "...something exists rather than not exist," which is the secret form of Nancy's abandonment. This suspension does not just disclose thought in an *exemplary* way, it does so by exposing potentiality: "The one can no more be than not-be."

Recall that Meillassoux's account of contingency stems from one concern, namely, "that thought can think what there must be when there is no thought."[11] If thought, in its speculative form, always requires a judgment on what is, it seems not unreasonable to claim that the aporia exactly describes the situation "when there is no (speculative) thought." By suspending judgment, thought that is no longer speculative thought "can think what there must be" in this situation: potentiality or contingency.

We encountered this restraint of thinking to pass judgment in chapter 4, when Heidegger introduced the basic mood of the other beginning as *Verhaltenheit*. Whereas *theōria* has wonder (*thaumazein*) as its basic mood, which corresponds to a certain distanced appreciation of what is, of a reality to which the philosophers themselves harmoniously belong despite their distance toward it, the other beginning corresponds to the shock that brings our abandonment of being into the open. Here, thinking no longer experiences a cobelonging to being since it finds this abandonment at its core. Consequently, it cannot simply affirm being. Nor can it simply negate being because such a negation belongs to the same logic of affirmation by affirming nonbeing.[12] Therefore, the mood of this thinking is necessarily a form of restraint; it holds itself back in front of any affirmation or negation; it maintains its hesitation and reservation in relation to any judgment.[13]

Moreover, this hesitation affects thinking profoundly as we can see in Heidegger's determination of both *Andenken* and *Vordenken*. Heidegger's as well as Agamben's conception of remembrance is clearly marked by such a hesitation in its relation to the past. The forgetfulness that remembrance aims to overcome does not concern facts or ideas that once were present but are now forgotten. Remembrance does not affirm what took place; rather, it gives potentiality back to the past, as Agamben writes. In addition, Heidegger's account of remembrance as thinking the unthought of metaphysics traces out this characteristic: remembrance does not affirm or reject the destiny of metaphysics but, rather, guides us to its provenance in the event. Thinking as *Vordenken* complements Heidegger's conception of remembrance and redirects our attention from the destiny of metaphysics to the event's destining itself and the simple concealment (its *lēthē*) it includes. Simple concealment is not simply nothing. Simple concealment is the domain of pure potentiality; it is the domain that holds being in reserve (*vor-enthalten*). Therefore, only a mood that is restrained and reserved, that suspends its judgment, can approach, announce, and tune in to this domain of simple concealment, pure potentiality, and absolute contingency.

Instead of an Epilogue: Another Parmenides, Another Ending

Although in his later dialogues Plato often introduces characters setting forth a doctrine rather than questioning them, many if not all dialogues end inconclusively. Yet, not all of them end in an aporia. Plato also explored other endings that leave the dialogue in abeyance as well. One of the most remarkable examples can be found at the end of the *Republic*. In its last book, Socrates aims to settle the ancient dispute between poetics and philosophy. To decide on this matter, one cannot be satisfied with listening to the songs of the poets and being placed under their spell: a dialogue between poets who chant and philosophers who argue cannot settle this dispute because they speak in a different language—the poetic language of song versus the prosaic language of argument; the language with meter versus the language without meter. Therefore, Socrates demands that not the poets themselves but rather the *philopoiētēs*, the friends of poetry, engage in this discussion. They should speak on behalf of poetry in the philosophical language of prose (*aneu metrou logon*).[14] Only in this way can friends of poetry come to its rescue and offer a convincing reason why poetry should be allowed to return from the exile to which Socrates bans poetry in the first pages of book 10.

To clarify why it is impossible for him to allow the poets themselves to engage in this conversation, Socrates states that if the *philopoiētēs* cannot give convincing arguments to defend poetry,

> My friend, even as men who have fallen in love, if they think that the love is not good for them, hard though it be, nevertheless refrain, so we, owing to the love [*erōs*] of this kind of poetry inbred in us by our education in these fine polities of ours, will gladly have the best possible case made out for her goodness and truth, but so long as she is unable to make good her defence we shall chant over [*epadontes*] to ourselves as we listen to the reasons that we have given as a countercharm [*epōdēn*] to her spell, to preserve us from slipping back into the childish love of the multitude; for we have come to see that we must not take such poetry seriously as a serious thing that lays hold on truth, but that he who lends an ear to it must be on his guard fearing for the polity in his soul and must believe what we said about poetry.[15]

In this beautiful rhetoric, the meaning of the word that forms the title of this dialogue, *politeia*, is doubled. In distinction to the *politeia*—polity, constitution, or republic—in which Socrates lives and which inspires its subjects to an erotic love for (Homer's) poetry, another *politeia* exists, namely, a polity of the soul that is threatened in its quest for justice by this erotic love for poetry. At first sight this doubling of meaning does not seem to threaten the clarity or univocity of what is said since it seems to be mastered fully by the one who expresses it: the meaning of *politeia* is doubled according to and in light of the distinction between philosophy and poetry to which Socrates' attention is drawn here. Yet, a more careful attention to book 10 of the *Republic* shows how this mastery slowly slips away in and by the movement of Socrates' prose.

For instance, the doubling of *politeia* also doubles the song [*epōdē*]. To overcome the spell the poetic song [*epōdē*] casts on all subjects of the republic, the philosopher introduces *another* song, a "counter-charm," to break the poetic enchantment. Within the limits of the above quote, one might argue that this doubling of the song simply generates a metaphor: whereas the poetic song is a song in the literal sense of the word, Socrates only uses "song" metaphorically for the philosopher because it means that "we listen to the reasons [*logos*] that we have given." This suggests that the literal meaning of the metaphorical *epōdē* is simply *logos*.

Yet, if we read on in the dialogue, such a clear-cut interpretation becomes more unlikely. In fact, the issue of justice cannot be settled by *logos* alone if *logos* is rendered as argument. The final stages of the dialogue make this perfectly clear: the *Republic* does not end with a reason or an argument; Socrates feels himself compelled, for the sake of argument, to conclude his *logos* with a genre that we would usually consider to be poetic. However, within the context of a dispute between philosophy and poetry, one should be careful not to move too fast to a conclusion.

The final stages of the *Republic* indicate that, ultimately, it is not *logos* in the sense of argument and reason that ignites philosophy's "counter-charm" by which the poetic enthusiasm is broken or interrupted. Rather, the *logos* with which Socrates concludes his speech is a story: the myth of Er. Although Socrates indeed uses the word *muthos* to characterize this tale, it is important to note that he first introduces it as an *apologos*, which means both tale and defense.[16] *Apologos* refers immediately back to the long citation I quoted above in which Socrates demands that poetry defend itself—*apologeomai*—not using the language of poetry but of prose. Hence, if we maintain the interpretation of *logos* as reason or argument, we end up with the following paradoxical or ironical composition: whereas Socrates demands that poetry defend itself by reason, the dialogue's exposition of the *logos* of justice does not find its conclusion in reason, but in Plato's own poetic production, a *muthos*.[17]

Obviously, such an ending of the dialogue complicates the distinction between philosophy and poetry. It renders the dispute between philosophy and poetry undecided since it shows that poetry has to account for itself using argument and, on the contrary, philosophy uses poetic means that simply cannot be translated in an argument or a reason. Yet, the recognition of this unsettling, deconstructive effect cannot be the endpoint of this analysis: this effect recognizes only what Plato wove into the composition of the dialogue, but it does not account for what happens here in this strange course of the dispute between philosophy and poetry. It seems as if we are in an analogous situation in which Heidegger finds himself in the *Beiträge* when he wants to characterize thinking in terms of the distinction between believing and knowing: in a certain respect thinking is (essential) knowing and not believing; yet, in another respect thinking is (essential) believing and not knowing. Analogously, the *logos* Socrates offers at the end of the *Republic* is in a certain sense not poetic; yet in another sense it is poetry because it employs *muthos*.

What is the particular role of this necessity of philosophical *logos* to interrupt its normal, argumentative course at the end of this dialogue, and to take its recourse to *muthos*? To capture what the final chord of the dialogue means, it should be interpreted in accordance with the task of philosophy set out in the long quote above, namely, to interrupt poetic enchantment and to offer *an other* song and another poetics from the one Homer offered Socrates. In this sense, the *muthos* at the end of the *Republic* can at best be another *muthos*, and that means a parody of a *muthos* in the Homeric sense of poetics. Nevertheless, this parody of *muthos* also interrupts the interpretation of *logos* as argument. One might say that this parody offers a *logos* in response to the clear-cut aporia that imposes itself on every interpretation that wants to judge whether the final myth is poetic or argumentative. Thus, in this *muthos* of Er, we encounter a "wholly other song" that does not decide on its own character.[18]

Nevertheless, despite this aporia and despite our inability to decide whether we should read it in a philosophical or poetical register, by offering a wholly other song, or what I called here a parody of *muthos* in the Homeric sense, the story still speaks.[19] In this sense, the end of the *Republic* is not a simple aporia since a mere aporia renders us baffled and speechless. The story, however, despite our incapacity to judge its character, speaks and thus offers another passage and another comportment for thought at the limits of its capacities. Thus, two questions impose themselves: What kind of speech is this that overcomes the speechlessness to which an aporia usually leads us? What does this story tell us, that is, which ontological experiment does this story offer us?

First, rather than characterizing the *logos* Socrates unfolds in book 10 of the *Republic* as a form of mere argument or as culminating in mere poetry, one should find another characterization for the discursive practice Socrates reveals. In line with the type of language he demands from the *philopoiētēs,* the friends of poetry—to speak in prose on poetry's behalf—I would like to suggest that Socrates speaks *in prose* on philosophy's behalf. Rather than a poetic myth in the Homeric sense of the word, the story of Er is a tale as well as a defense. Although it looks like a myth, it would be better to say that it both imitates and deviates from Homeric myth; in this sense it is a *parody* of myth. In particular, Socrates' myth of Er may be called a parody in a specific ancient meaning of the word with which "the classical world...was familiar," as Agamben argues in his essay "Parody."[20] He describes how at a certain period in ancient Greece, some rhapsodes of the Homeric poems no longer always recite the poems as they are supposed to do, letting "melody...correspond to the rhythm of speech." Yet, they also do not simply stop reciting. Rather, they introduce "discordant melodies," singing beside the song. This practice, Agamben claims, offers us a "more ancient meaning of the term" parody: "In the case of the recitation of the Homeric poems, when this traditional link is broken and the rhapsodes begin to introduce discordant melodies, it is said that they are singing *para tēn ōidēn,* against (or beside) the song.... According to this more ancient meaning of the term, then, parody designates the rupture of the 'natural' bond between music and language, the separation of song from speech.... Breaking this link liberates a *para*, a space beside, in which prose takes its place."[21]

A wholly other song can only be sung by singing "against (or beside) the song" in the first sense of the song. Plato's retelling of old myths may be characterized analogously. He never simply follows them, but he sings beside the song, changes them and parodies them in the exemplary sense Agamben suggests here: the parody of song interrupts the normal recitation but also "liberates a *para*, a space beside, in which prose takes its place." In this sense, to sing beside the song is neither mere reciting nor mere silence. Rather, it is the discursive practice that corresponds neither to the poetic spell nor to the philosophical argument, but rather to the other song for which both Plato and Agamben suggest the name "prose," words without meter. Socrates, as I would like to suggest, employs an analogous discursive practice at the end of the *Republic* when introducing a story. His *logos* is an *apologos* for philosophy that does not use argument, but imitates poetry by deviating from it; thus, it opens up a space for prose, which is a tale *and* a defense.

Second, to understand what the *apologos* tells us and what type of experiment on being it offers, let us first note that the tale tells an impossible story; it takes us beyond the limits of what can humanly be experienced or thought. The story takes us to the *topos daimonios*, the "mysterious region" to which the soul journeys after death.[22] Since nobody returns from his own death, this region indeed cannot be experienced. Therefore, the story requires the most remarkable messenger (*angelos*) possible: the soldier Er experiences *what cannot be experienced*.[23] Hence, the story does not forget the aporetic structure of the issue of justice and the impossibility of solving it in dialectics; rather, the aporetic structure is integrated into the tale's composition. The messenger Er is an exception to the rule or principle that governs the relation between the living and the *topos daimonios*. He goes to this place *and returns* to tell the living what takes place in this region. Note that the story itself introduces this rule or principle. In this sense, the story can only be understood coherently on the condition that we suspend the principles it announces itself when interpreting it.

While being there, Er learns that this mysterious region is the place where souls are judged for their lives. This suggests that every effort to expose the *topos daimonios* requires thought to comport itself accordingly, and this means to suspend judgment: since every judgment always already *presupposes* the realm in which judgments take place, only a thought that suspends and interrupts judging may hope not to take this region as a mere point of departure, but to expose it for what it is. Moreover, the *topos daimonios* is not only the region of judgment, it is also the region in which the souls choose their next life; it is a story on the possibility of the soul's rebirth. This region is the soul's version of Leibniz's pyramid of possible worlds. Yet, unlike Leibniz's demiurge that always affirms his own choice for the best of these worlds, a soul chooses differently each time, based on its experiences in its previous lives and the wisdom it gained (or forgot to gain) from them. This choice determines what happens in the next life. In this sense, the story paints a picture of the soul as something shared by many: the soul's ended lives left their traces and marks on it, and these traces and marks guide the soul toward the lives that are not yet given shape and are not yet born. The *topos daimonios* is thus the region in which the soul is not affirming the past lives when it remembers them and is guided by their traces: the soul is not doomed to repeat these past lives in the lives yet to come. Rather, in this mysterious region, remembrance makes the past lives possible again: it considers what happened in light of an utterly new, possible, and still formless life. Thus, the soul places its past lives in light of a pure potentiality, of the lives that can no more be than not be.

Along these lines, the story paints a particular picture of remembrance, structurally akin to the one Heidegger explores in his account of thought as *Andenken* and to the one Agamben explores in his essay on Bartleby. In fact, Heidegger explicitly affirms this in his reading of the tale of Er in his lecture course *Parmenides*.[24] Reading the final sentences of the story in which Er narrates that the soul has to traverse the Plain of Concealment (*Lēthē*) and drink from the water of the River of Carelessness (*Amelētos*) before entering a new life, Heidegger argues that this story does not think about (*Denken über*) something—it is nonphilosophical in this sense—but that it does remember (*Denken an*) something, namely, simple concealment (*lēthē*).²⁵ Thus, according to Heidegger, Plato tells a story on the inceptual dimension (*das Anfängliche*) of being and its intrinsic concealment.

One's soul is thus never one's own. What applies to Heidegger's *Ereignis* applies *mutatis mutandis* to the soul as the story unfolds it. The event by which we receive what is our own is also the moment of expropriation; similarly, the soul is expropriated from what receives it as its own: the story tells us that all human beings have to pass the River of Carelessness and drink from its water, which makes one forget "all things."²⁶ For all humans, the messenger tells us, their soul is a plurality of distinct lives sharing in one soul. There is no reason to read this in terms of the ontotheological version of the soul being an eternal substance that does not change. Not only does this story suspend the principle of reason forming the core of ontotheology and depends with its full weight on the possibility of the exception — Er is introduced as the exception to the rule that governs the relation between the living and the mysterious region — but the story also offers another interpretation of the soul. The sharing of plural lives is not something fixed but *takes place*, again and again, in utterly different ways, between consecutive lives, in the *topos daimonios*. In this region, the soul does not have a particular, eternal form. Rather, it has no form of its own at all except for the marks and traces left by its previous lives. Hence, even if there is a form of the soul, it is one that is historically formed by the sense of justice it acquired by living its lives. In itself, the soul is pure potentiality, pure matter, capable of adopting any form of life. Thus, the story tells us that although humans no longer remember this place because they drank from the water that makes them forget and thus always exist *after* the soul's inception, this mysterious place ruled by contingency is their beginning as well as their end; this is the place where the community with those who died and those who are not yet born takes place.

The story remembers the *topos daimonios* and turns the attention of those who read and listen to it to this place, relocating human life in its pure contingency. To say in the context of such a story that the soul is immortal, as Socrates does, is not establishing a fixed, eternal entity that will never disappear. Rather, the soul connects human life to the pure potentiality in which it is embedded. Whenever the story of Er is remembered and retold, it does not simply tell us what was, but it discloses how the mysterious region takes everything that occurred and all lives that are lived back to their pure potentiality.

NOTES

NOTES TO INTRODUCTION

1. Deleuze, *Logique du sens*, 210/179. Quoted in Badiou, *Deleuze*, 34. Throughout this book, page numbers refer to the original German and French sources unless indicated differently. Whenever I use an English translation, I first refer to the page number in the original language and then to the page number of the translation, as I did here.

2. This argument can be found in the contrast between Ricoeur's and Derrida's conceptions of the relation between poetic language and speculative language; see van der Heiden, "Announcement, Attestation, and Equivocity," 415–32.

3. Agamben, *Means without End*, ix.

4. Marchart, *Post-Foundational Political Thought*, 9.

5. See, e.g., Agamben's reflections on economics in relation to the theological dogma of the trinity (Agamben, *What Is an Apparatus?*, 10; Agamben, *The Kingdom and the Glory*, 53–65).

6. Agamben, *Homo Sacer*, 44.

7. The notion of ontotheology finds its origin in Kant, *Kritik der reinen Vernunft*, B659–B671, where it describes the form of theology that proceeds on the basis of a priori concepts alone and is concerned with the question of the existence of a highest being (*Urwesen*). As part of transcendental theology, ontotheology in distinction from cosmotheology is par excellence the example of the speculative use of theoretical reason since it seeks for synthetical a priori judgments concerning what lies beyond the realm of the a priori conditions of possible experience, to which theoretical reason should limit itself, according to Kant.

8. Nancy, *Être singulier pluriel*, 45/25; translation adapted.

9. As shown in Hägglund, *Radical Atheism*, and Watkin, *Difficult Atheism*.

10. It is important to distinguish the two different orientations to which the word "God" attunes us: a metaphysical one and a religious one. When it comes to the question of ontotheology, these two orientations are distinct, as Heidegger's comments already indicate. Whereas the metaphysical concept of God concerns the questions of principles and causes, the religious one concerns religious practices such as feasts, sacrifices, and prayers. This book deals with the former one alone. The relation of present-day thought to the latter is much more ambiguous and complex.

11. Heidegger, "Die onto-theo-logische Verfassung der Metaphysik," in *Identität und Differenz*, 51–79. As Heidegger puts it, "Wie kommt der Gott in die Philosophie?" (64).

12. Ibid., 63.

13. See "*die Wesung des Seyns*" (Heidegger, *Beiträge*, 74/59). Heidegger uses the expression "the beingness of being" as a translation of "*die* ousia *des* on" (Heidegger, *Wegmarken*, 378).

14. Heidegger, *Identität und Differenz*, 63. *Das Ganze* means in German "the whole" or "totality," *im Ganzen* also means "in general" and is synonymous to *im Allgemeinen*.

15. Heidegger, "Einleitung zu 'Was ist Metaphysik?,'" in *Wegmarken*, 365–83.

16. Heidegger, *Wegmarken*, 378.

17. Ibid., 378.

18. For the relationship between ontology and theology in Aristotle, see Höffle, *Aristotle*, 99–100.

19. Heidegger, "Was ist Metaphysik?," in *Wegmarken*, 365–66.

20. Ibid., 378–79.

21. Heidegger, *Identität und Differenz*, 63.

22. Heidegger, "Entwürfe zur Geschichte des Seins als Metaphysik," in *Nietzsche II*, 417. Translation is from Heidegger, *The End of Philosophy*, 55.

23. Heidegger, *Beiträge*, 63/51.

24. Ibid., 209/163.

25. The relation between *koinon* and *idea* returns a number of times, and each time it is used to determine the *Leitfrage* of metaphysics; see, e.g., Heidegger, *Beiträge*, 75, 116, 206, 209.

26. Heidegger, *Beiträge*, 32/28.

27. Heidegger, *Der Satz vom Grund*, 171.

28. Ibid., 42/27. Note that Kant also ranges this principle under the heading of ontotheological use of speculative reason; see Kant, *Kritik der reinen Vernunft*, B663–64.

29. Heidegger, *Der Satz vom Grund*, 43/28.

30. Note that this reference to the other beginning as completely other returns like a chorus in Heidegger's text; see, e.g., Heidegger, *Beiträge*, 9, 10, 28, 73.

31. Arendt, *The Human Condition*, 12–21.

32. Aristotle, *Metaphysics* 1072b24, in *Complete Works*, ed. Barnes. See also Höffle, *Aristotle*, 99–100.

33. Badiou, "Homage to Jacques Derrida," 43.

34. Arendt, *The Life of the Mind*, 200.

35. Arendt, *The Human Condition*, 324, and *The Life of the Mind*, 78.

Notes to Part 1

1. "For Nancy, touch remains the motif of a sort of absolute, irredentist, and postdeconstructive realism" (Derrida, *Le toucher*, 60/46). This characterization returns in the title of the second part of Gratton and Morin, *Jean-Luc Nancy and Plural Thinking*, 77, and is referred to and developed by Gratton, "The Speculative Challenge," 118.
2. See Bryant, Srnicek, and Harman *The Speculative Turn*.
3. Meillassoux, *Après la finitude*, 13–21.
4. Ibid., 18. See also Harman, *Towards Speculative Realism*, 2.
5. I will return to this issue in chapter 5. Note that also the critique on Badiou within this speculative turn concerns the issue of the Kantian distinction between *phenomena* and *noumena* that is traced in *Court traité* and *Logiques des mondes*; see, e.g., Johnston, "Phantom of Consistency," and van der Heiden, "Subjective Fidelity," 124–28.
6. Badiou, *Deleuze*, 69/44.
7. Badiou, "Metaphysics and the Critique," 190. Derrida, *Demeure*, 120/89.
8. Meillassoux, *Après la finitude*, 47; my translation.
9. Harman, *Towards Speculative Realism*, 112.
10. If these phenomena are examples of the absolutes that Meillasoux claims the strong model of correlationism does not make disappear from the philosophical scene, then one can only conclude the opposite of what Meillassoux argues, namely, that the oeuvres of the philosophers of this strong model do pretend to think these absolutes (Meillassoux, *Après la finitude*, 61). In part, chapter 6 will be devoted to this issue.
11. Heidegger, *Sein und Zeit*, 35.
12. Meillassoux, *Après la finitude*, 20/6.
13. Badiou, *L'éthique*, 44.
14. Nancy, *Être singulier pluriel*, 58/38.

Notes to Chapter 1

1. Badiou, *L'être et l'événement*, 41/31; my italics.
2. See Milbank's comments as quoted in Watkin, *Difficult Atheism*, 103.
3. Heidegger, *Der Satz vom Grund*, 23–24.
4. Badiou, *L'être et l'événement*, 267–81.
5. Badiou, *Le nombre et les nombres*, 20/9. See also Badiou's strong resistance against the way in which mathematics is understood in Peano arithmetic (ibid., 63–69). Badiou, *Court traité*, 39–54.
6. Plato, *Parmenides* 136a, in *Complete Works*, ed. Cooper.
7. Plato, *Republic* 511b, in *Complete Works*, ed. Cooper.
8. Badiou, *Court traité*, 33/39.
9. Ibid., 33/39.

10. Badiou, *Deleuze*, 31/19.
11. Badiou, *Court traité*, 33. Heidegger's quote: "The precedence of whatness brings the precedence of beings themselves in what they are. The precedence of beings establishes Being as *koinon* in terms of the *hen*. The eminent character of metaphysics is decided. The one as unifying unity becomes authoritative [*maßgebend*] for subsequent determinations of Being" (Heidegger, *Nietzsche II*, 417).
12. This discussion starts at the end of Plato, *Parmenides* 163b.
13. Badiou, *L'être et l'événement*, 43/34. This is why Badiou calls Plato "pre-Cantorian," since Cantor proposes a coherent way to think infinite multiplicities.
14. Plato, *Parmenides* 164d. Badiou, *L'être et l'événement*, 43–44/33–34.
15. Badiou, *L'être et l'événement*, 42/32.
16. Hallward, *Badiou*, 90.
17. Badiou, *Manifeste pour la philosophie*, 47/66.
18. This is an idea borrowed from Plato, *Republic* 607b.
19. Badiou, *L'être et l'événement*, 143/125.
20. Ibid., 143/125.
21. Ibid., 144.
22. Badiou quoted in Riera, "For an 'Ethics of Mystery,'" 79. I would like to thank the second referee of this manuscript for suggesting this essay to me: Riera quotes the same passage from Badiou, *Petit manuel d'inesthétique*, 36/19, although Riera removes the reference to the myth of Er in his quotation with an ellipsis. I've adapted the translation of Badiou's quote by replacing "to" with "from": Er returns *from* the kingdom of the dead in Plato's *muthos* at the end of *The Republic*.
23. Lacoue-Labarthe, *Heidegger*, 43–77.
24. Van der Heiden, "The Poetic Experience," 115; see also van der Heiden, "Reading Bartleby, Reading Ion."
25. Nancy, *Le partage des voix*. Nancy also follows a suggestion made by Heidegger, which makes clear that Heidegger's assessment of Plato is always ambiguous.
26. Heidegger, *Beiträge*, 15.
27. Sallis, *The Verge of Philosophy*, 85.
28. Heidegger, *Beiträge*, 24.
29. Badiou, *L'être et l'événement*, 35.
30. Ibid., 69/56. Note that the term "the void" is not foreign to Heidegger's work. He uses the notion "die Leere" especially in relation to the refusal and the withdrawal of being (Heidegger, *Beiträge*, §242).
31. Badiou, *L'être et l'événement*, 16/9.
32. Ibid., 67/54.
33. Badiou, "Metaphysics and the Critique," 183. Note that Badiou also writes that, despite being beyond the measure of our cognition, this being "can nonetheless be rationally demonstrated." I will come back to this point later.

34. Badiou, *L'être et l'événement*, 16/10.
35. Ibid., 68–69/55–56.
36. It stands out because it is the only existential axiom; the other ones are conditional.
37. Badiou, *Le Nombre*, 35/23.
38. Heidegger, *Beiträge*, 22.
39. Ibid., 382/302. I have replaced "emptiness" with "void" in the translation to emphasize the similarity in terminology with Badiou.
40. Badiou, *L'être et l'événement*, 16.
41. See also part 2 of this book and my discussion of Meillassoux therein.
42. Two of which are discussed in Badiou, *L'être et l'événement*, parts 6 and 7. See also Badiou, *Court traité*, 52–53.
43. Badiou, *Court traité*, 49–54.
44. Ibid., 54/56; my italics.
45. Bosteels, "Alain Badiou's Theory," 208–09n15.
46. Ricoeur, *Le conflit*, 23/18.
47. Ibid., 7/22.
48. Badiou, *L'être et l'événement*, 45/35.
49. I only discuss here the early Ricoeur; this issue receives a more subtle treatment in the later Ricoeur; see van der Heiden, "Announcement, Attestation, and Equivocity."
50. Deleuze, *Logique du sens*, 9–10.
51. Ibid., 292–307.
52. Deleuze refers to Derrida in *Logique du sens*, 296n2. The problem of simulacrum and mimesis also plays a huge role in Plato's *Sophist*, which is extensively discussed in Nancy, "*Le ventriloque*."
53. See, e.g., Heidegger's reflection on Hölderlin's words, "Giebt es auf Erden ein Maas? / Es giebt keines" (Heidegger, *Hölderlins Hymne "Der Ister,"* 205–06.)
54. Throughout this book, I will use "meaning" and "sense" as synonyms since both occur without any clear distinction as translations of the French word *sens*, especially in many of Nancy's texts.
55. Badiou, *Court traité*, 54.
56. Badiou, "L'écriture du générique: Samuel Beckett," in *Conditions*, 329–68. Since I'm mainly interested in the systematic role of event and nomination in Badiou's work, I will not discuss whether or not Badiou's reading does justice to Beckett. This question has already been treated extensively in the literature. See, for instance, how Gibson problematizes the development toward the event that Badiou discerns in Beckett's work as well as his tendency to focus on the event and the nomination of the event as a central theme in Beckett's work (Gibson, *Beckett and Badiou*, 217). Similarly, as Lecercle argues in reference to Gibson, "the 'poetics of nomination' is hardly central to the text as a whole" (*Badiou and Deleuze Read*, 136).
57. Badiou, *Conditions*, 349/269.

58. Van der Heiden, *Truth (and Untruth)*, 133.
59. I have discussed this extensively in ibid., 132–35.
60. Derrida, *Psyché*, 63–93.
61. Badiou, *Conditions*, 349–50/269.
62. Badiou, *Le Nombre*, 133/106.
63. Heidegger, *Parmenides*, 18.
64. Badiou, *L'être et l'événement*, 436/398.
65. Ibid., 437/399.
66. See Badiou, *Saint Paul;* Badiou, *Second manifeste*, 18.
67. An introduction to this issue can be found in Badiou, *Le fini et l'infini*.
68. Badiou, "Metaphysics and the Critique," 183.
69. Badiou, *Court traité*, 21/31.
70. As Badiou writes elsewhere, "the metaphorical God of Heidegger" ("Metaphysics and the Critique," 181). To see how complicated and multifaceted the theme of God and the divine is in Heidegger, see Derrida, *Foi et savoir*, 89–96, and Vedder, *Heidegger's Philosophy of Religion*.
71. Heidegger, *Beiträge*, 410.
72. Meillassoux, *Après la finitude*, 141/103; translation slightly adapted.
73. This set of all sets would, of course, be the set theoretical version of totality (see Badiou, *L'être et l'événement*, 49–59). Apparently the argument that excludes totality is so important that he repeats it in *Logiques des mondes*, 165–67.
74. Badiou, *L'être et l'événement*, 25/18.
75. Ibid., 53/42.
76. Ibid., 200.
77. In the literature, similar concerns arise concerning the strange relation between being and event, between ontology and subject. On the one hand, ontology excludes the event and, on the other hand, ontology only arrives as the practice of a subject. Does this not lead to a dualism, as Balibar claims in "'The History of Truth'"? Does it not imply that Badiou's thought derives from two incompatible points of departure, as Meillassoux suggests in "*Nouveauté et événement*"? Meillassoux's cutting argument basically runs as follows: if an event is needed for ontology to arrive whereas the category of the event can only be thought within ontology, does this not lead to two types of event: one preceding ontology and one as a result of an ontological investigation?
78. The technical background can be found in parts 7 and 8 of *L'être et l'événement*. Part 7 discusses the notions of generic and truth; part 8 discusses the notion of forcing. The notion of fidelity is introduced in part 5 at 232–39.
79. Badiou, *Saint Paul*, 56–57.
80. Badiou, *L'être et l'événement*, 259.
81. Ibid., 363–65/329–31.
82. Ibid., 432.
83. Ibid., 363–69.
84. Ibid., part 6.

85. Therefore, Badiou defines truth as such a generic set deriving from a procedure of fidelity (ibid., 369–74).
86. Ibid., 434.
87. Ibid., 435/397.
88. Recall that *T* was only a subset of *S* and not an element.
89. Badiou, *L'être et l'événement*, 416–18.
90. Badiou, "Metaphysics and the Critique," 190.
91. Badiou, *Second manifeste*, 18.
92. Whether or not *Logiques des mondes*, in which Badiou discusses the role of relations, solves this problem will be discussed in chapter 4.
93. Arendt's conception of dialogue and plurality, which I do not discuss in this book, offers an account of a dialogue that does not strive for consensus.
94. Badiou also refers to this issue: "In the absence of any temporality" (*L'être et l'événement*, 449/410).
95. Ibid., 437.
96. Badiou, *Second manifeste*, 21.
97. Ibid., 19.
98. Badiou's more complicated account of four subjective figures in *Logiques des mondes* does not solve this issue since here one is either a true subject of an event or simply in denial with respect to the event's having taken place.
99. Badiou, *Second manifeste*, 132. Note that Žižek criticizes Badiou for exactly this tendency to neglect the importance of death and negativity (Žižek, *The Ticklish Subject*, 145–51).
100. Badiou, *Second manifeste*, 106.

Notes to Chapter 2

1. The first epigraph is from Nancy, "*L'être abandonné*," in *L'impératif catégorique*, 139; trans. Brian Holmes as "Abandoned Being," in *The Birth to Presence*, 36. The second is from Nancy, *Être singulier pluriel*, xv.
2. Nancy, *Être singulier pluriel*, 58/38.
3. As Derrida writes, one cannot "choose the false [infinity] without giving homage to the superiority and the anteriority of the true [infinity]" (*L'écriture et la différence*, 176).
4. Nancy, *Le sens du monde*, 51–56. See also my discussion of Badiou's account of Cantor in chapter 1.
5. Nancy, *La pensée dérobée*, 19n1.
6. " '*Finitude*' désigne la *fin* de la présence comme être stable, permanent, disponible, impassible—comme chose donnée et comme figure dessinée, comme mythe constitué ou comme raison établie" (Nancy, *La pensée dérobée*, 19; my translation).
7. See the following beautiful comment made by Harman emphasizing the primacy of relatedness for every determination of beings: "There is no Pierre, no salt, and no lioness before they touch one another. The in-itself is a unified

whatever.... By contrast, Nancy's monad-free vision is one in which things gain determinacy only through mutual touch" (Harman, "On Interface," 100–01). I do not agree, though, with Harman's claim that this indifferent *whatever* "precedes this touch." For Nancy, the value of existence, of the "there is," is only given in and as ontological touching: being *is* being-with, as I will explain below. Here, a further reflection on the meaning of "whatever" might be helpful, as, for instance, Agamben does when he interprets the Latin *quodlibet ens* ("whatever being"): "*Quodlibet ens* is not 'being, it does not matter which,' but rather 'being such that it always matters' " (Agamben, *The Coming Community*, 1). Agamben's interpretation of *quodlibet ens* as "being such that it always matters" is, as always, very close to Nancy's concerns. In particular, as I will show, it is close to the concern of significance (*signifiance*)—that which always matters—which for Nancy is the primordial meaning of being that happens as touching. In this interpretation of the "whatever," the moment of significance is at work even in what sounds like pure indifference—"whatever."

8. Nancy, *Une pensée finie*, 48/27.

9. "L'infinitude, par conséquent, n'est pas une autre essence que celle de l'être fini: elle est l'existence même... comme partage de la finitude entre tous les existants" (Nancy, *La pensée dérobée*, 20; my translation).

10. Nancy, *Être singulier pluriel*, 83–84/61–62 ; my italics.

11. Ibid., 45/26. For a critique of Heidegger's account of *Mitsein* in *Sein und Zeit*, see Nancy, "The Being-With of Being-There."

12. Arendt, *The Human Condition*, 9.

13. Nancy, *Être singulier pluriel*, 82/60; translation adapted: the English translation misses the implicit reference here to Badiou's use of set theory and translates *la théorie des ensembles*—set theory—quite oddly as "the theory of togetherness." Agamben refers to a similar problem in Badiou's ontology when he discusses the role of "being an element," which the example would expose (Agamben, *The Coming Community*, 9–11).

14. Two texts of Nancy come to mind here: "*Le ventriloque*" and *Le partage des voix*. Some of the themes that play a role in these two texts return later in the short essay "*Répondre du sens*," in Nancy, *La pensée dérobée*, 167–77.

15. Derrida, *L'écriture et la différence*, 411.

16. Ibid., 427.

17. One might also refer to Agamben for a critique like that of Derrida and Nancy (Agamben, *Potentialities*, 44). See also van der Heiden, "Absolute Presupposition," 92–95.

18. For this and the following quotes in this paragraph, see Nancy, *Le partage des voix*, 17–21/213–15.

19. Ibid., 21/215.

20. Nancy, *L'oubli de la philosophie*, 40/29.

21. Nancy, *Le partage des voix*, 18/213–14; *L'oubli de la philosophie*, 41/29–30.

22. Nancy, *L'oubli de la philosophie*, 45/32.

23. Nancy, *Le sens du monde*, 21–22/10. See also Nancy, *L'oubli de la philosophie*, 31–33. In what follows, I use "significance" as translation of *signifiance*.
24. Nancy, *L'oubli de la philosophie*, 54/37.
25. Ibid., 88/58–59.
26. Nancy, *Le sens du monde*, 112/68–69.
27. Nancy, *La pensée dérobée*, 93.
28. As Nancy terms it, "*vidé de signification*" (*Être singulier pluriel*, 111).
29. Derrida, "*Préjugés*," in Derrida et al., *La faculté de juger*, 123.
30. Agamben, *Homo Sacer*, 51.
31. Nancy, "*L'être abandonné*," in *L'impératif catégorique*, 139–53; translated by Brian Holmes as "Abandoned Being," in Nancy, *The Birth to Presence*, 36–47.
32. Ibid., 141/36.
33. Ibid., 150/44.
34. Hamacher, "*Ou, séance*," 41.
35. To examine Plato's *agathōn*, see also Nancy, *Une pensée finie*, 94–95.
36. Nancy, *Le sens du monde*, 84/51.
37. Sallis, *The Verge of Philosophy*, 24. See also Nancy, *La pensée dérobée*, 19–20; and Nancy, *La communauté désoeuvrée*, 17.
38. Nancy, *Le sens du monde*, 85/51.
39. Ibid., 86/51.
40. Nancy, *Le sens du monde*, 88/52.
41. Ibid., 88/52.
42. Agamben, *The Coming Community*, 68.
43. Nancy, *L'oubli de la philosophie*, 32–33/23.
44. Heidegger, *Sein und Zeit*, 37; Heidegger, *Ontologie*, 9–14.
45. Heidegger, *Unterwegs zur Sprache*, 115. He also uses the notion of *Kundgabe* and explains it as *Eröffnung* in this book (210). As Nancy writes on Heidegger's interpretation of *hermēneuein*: Heidegger, "who, offering its oldest meaning as its newest, understood it as the meaning of the transmission of a message, of the announcement of news and of its forwarding by a carrier. The messenger is not the signification of the message, nor is he its interpreter" (Nancy, *L'oubli de la philosophie*, 88–89/59).
46. Nancy, *Le partage des voix*, 46/227.
47. This reinterpretation of hermeneutics as speaking on behalf of the other is of crucial importance to contemporary thought and can be traced clearly in the work of Derrida and Agamben as well (see van der Heiden, *De stem van de doden*).
48. Plato, *Ion* 534b. Translations are taken from the Loeb Classical Library edition.
49. Although the notion of abandonment is not used frequently in *Le partage des voix*, it occurs in at least two ways: first to describe how Heidegger abandons (classical) hermeneutics; second, it is used to describe the way in which we "participate" in the form of *partage*, to which we are abandoned. In this latter sense, abandonment is used in the technical sense of the word to which I refer here.

50. Plato, *Ion* 534b, 533d.

51. This relation between "ban" and the divine voice seems to be based on the etymological relation of the German *bannan* and the Indo-European root **bhā* to which Nancy refers (Nancy, *L'impératif catégorique*, 151). As Benveniste writes: "this root **bhā*, which in the vocabulary of the Indo-European expressed this strange, extra-human power of the word, from its first awakening in the human infant to its collective manifestations, which were non-human in virtue of their being depersonalized and were regarded as the expression of a divine voice" (*Indo-European Language and Society*, 413).

52. Nancy, *La pensée dérobée*, 167; my translation. Thus, Nancy understands *hermēneia* as "making him speak" (*Le partage des voix*, 57/232).

53. Nancy, *Le partage des voix*, 69/237–38.

54. Plato, *Ion* 534c.

55. Nancy, *Le partage des voix*, 83/244.

56. Ibid., 68

57. Nancy, *La pensée dérobée*, 174.

58. Ibid., 174.

59. Ibid., 173.

60. Agamben, *Means without End*, 10; see also 59, 96. Elsewhere, Agamben puts it in terms of transmissibility: "how can there be a tradition not simply of a *traditum* but of openness itself, transmissibility itself?" (Agamben, *Potentialities*, 105). Note that Nancy refers himself to this usage of communicability by Agamben (Nancy, *Le sens du monde*, 177).

61. Nancy, *Le sens du monde*, 19.

62. Nancy, *Être singulier pluriel*, 19/2.

63. Nancy, *Le sens du monde*, 184/118.

64. Ibid., 178/114.

65. For a more critical reading of *Le partage des voix* in relation to the role of understanding, see Naas, "Urania"

66. Agamben, *The Coming Community*, 67.

67. Plato, *Ion* 534c.

68. Nancy, *Le partage des voix*, 66/236.

69. Ibid., 79/242.

70. Gadamer, *Wahrheit und Methode*, 390.

71. Nancy, *Être singulier pluriel*, 110/87. Another way of understanding con-sensus is offered in Agamben's "The Friend," in *What Is an Apparatus*, 25–37. As Agamben argues, Aristotle's notion of the friend should be understood as an ontological term since friendship is founded in the experience of con-senting the existence of the friend. This sensing together and affirmation of the friend's existence is not based on the participation in a common subject matter or substance. Consequently, to con-sent (which translates Aristotle's *sunaisthanesthai*) should not be understood as a consensus, as Agamben emphasizes (37). Friendship, as it functions from the classical conception of philosophical dialogue onward, is thus not a striving toward consensus, but only toward a con-division of existence to which the experience of con-senting corresponds.

72. Agamben, *Means without End*, 99.
73. Nancy, *Être singulier pluriel*, 20/2.
74. Ibid., 74/53; Nancy, *La communauté désoeuvrée*, 17.
75. Nancy, *La communauté désoeuvrée*, 71.
76. Badiou, *Court traité*, 54/56. To emphasize it once more, *partage* does not mean that some thing or good can be shared or exchanged. From the ontic perspective of beings, goods, or things, *partage* is also "strictly speaking unshareable" (Nancy, *La vérité de la démocratie*, 33).
77. Agamben, *Potentialities*, 37; *Language and Death*, 18.
78. Agamben, *Potentialities*, 37.
79. Also on this point one might find a close affinity between Agamben and Nancy. Agamben opposes exposition to supposition and presupposition (Agamben, *The Coming Community*, 28, 67).
80. Nancy, *Le sens du monde*, 19/2.
81. As Agamben also writes, "it is not the presupposition of a being but its exposure" (*The Coming Community*, 96).
82. Heidegger, *Sein und Zeit*, 241–46.
83. Ibid., 250.
84. Although he does not reject the theme of being-toward-death, it is clear that for him this cannot be distinguished from being-toward-life and, ultimately, should be understood as being-toward-existence and being-toward-the-world; see Nancy, *Le sens du monde*, 54–56.
85. Heidegger, *Hölderlins Hymne "Der Ister,"* 80. For a more detailed account of Heidegger's account of *Auseinandersetzung*, see van der Heiden, "*De toe-eigening.*"
86. Singularity is derived from the "ultra-one" from which the event results (see Badiou, *L'être et l'événement*, 211/189).
87. This is the case because the generic set is by definition a subset of the situation; see Ibid., 373.
88. Univocity is Deleuze's alternative, according to Badiou (Badiou, *Deleuze*, 31–47).
89. Aristotle, *Metaphysics* 1003a33–35, in *Complete Works*, ed. Barnes.
90. Agamben, *Means without End*, 99.
91. See van der Heiden, *Truth (and Untruth)*, 142–54, 197–204.
92. Nancy, *La communauté désoeuvrée*, 84/34.
93. Nancy, *Être singulier pluriel*, 99/76.
94. Ibid., 105/81.

Notes to Chapter 3

1. This also guides Badiou in his recent reading of Plato; see Badiou, *La République de Platon*, 9–10, as well as in *Second manifeste*, 119–30.
2. Badiou, *Court traité*, 32–33.
3. Plato, *Republic* 511b.

4. Plato, *Parmenides* 128d, in *Complete Works*, ed. Cooper.
5. Ibid., 130d.
6. Ibid., 135d, 136a; my italics.
7. Badiou, *Logiques des mondes*, 15–16.
8. Badiou, "Metaphysics and the Critique," 183.
9. Badiou, *Second manifeste*, 97/83. See van der Heiden, "The Scintillation," 93–109.
10. Heidegger, *Der Satz vom Grund*, 24/16.
11. See, for instance, Badiou, *Second manifeste*, 123–24; quotation at 139.
12. Badiou, *Logiques des mondes*, 481–88, 493–97.
13. For all these remarks, see Badiou, *L'être et l'événement*, 17–21.
14. Badiou, *L'être et l'événement*, 25.
15. Badiou, *Logiques des mondes*, 529/508; my italics. The notion of the trace of the event in *Logiques des mondes* will be discussed in chapter 4.
16. Agamben, *The Coming Community*, 10.
17. Agamben, *Signature of All Things*, 18.
18. Badiou, *Manifeste pour la philosophie*, 18.
19. Similarly, *Logiques des mondes* is a fidelity to the axiom that "there are only bodies and languages, except that there are truths" (Badiou, *Logiques des mondes*, 12/4).
20. Meillassoux, "*Nouveauté et événement*," 39–64.
21. Badiou, *Second manifeste*, 139.
22. Badiou, *La République de Platon*, 13.
23. Ibid., 13. See also Badiou, *Second manifeste*, 119–20. Recall that the notion of incorporation describes the notion of fidelity in *Logiques des monde*: the human being becomes a subject when it incorporates the procedure of being faithful to a truth.
24. Badiou, *La République de Platon*, 359–61.
25. Badiou, *Second manifeste*, 119, 123.
26. This is even more clear in *Logiques des mondes*, where the basic axiom from which this book departs states that truths exist beyond that which is: "There are only bodies and languages, except that there are truths" (Badiou, *Logiques des mondes*, 12/4).
27. Plato, *Parmenides*, 130d.
28. Agamben, *Potentialities*, 43–45. For a more elaborate account of the relation between Agamben and Gadamer, see van der Heiden, "Absolute Presupposition."
29. Agamben, *Potentialities*, 35.
30. Ibid., 45.
31. *Logiques des mondes* develops other subjective figures next to the faithful subject. Although these other figures consist in denying and obscuring the event, they only affirm that a comportment to the event is always based on the presupposition of the event's having taken place, even if these subjective figures do not recognize this (Badiou, *Logiques des mondes*, 86–87, and the whole of book 1).

32. Plato, *Parmenides* 166c.
33. Agamben, *Potentialities*, 217
34. Badiou, *L'être et l'événement*, 44.
35. Agamben, *Remnants of Auschwitz*, 65.
36. Ibid., 65; my italics.
37. Plato, *Parmenides* 136c, 137a.
38. See Heidegger's discussion of the terms "aporia" and "*euporia*" in relation to Aristotle's conception of dialectics in *Grundbegriffe der aristotelischen Philosophie*, 158–61. There he writes, "Das *telos* ist das *euporein*, das Gut-Hindurchkommen. *Aporia* ist nicht selbst ein *telos*, sondern sie steht im Dienste eines bestimmten Durchlaufens" (160).
39. Agamben uses the term "*euporia*" in this way in relation to "aporia" in *Potentialities*, 217–18.
40. Ibid., 113; my italics.
41. Agamben, *Homo Sacer*, 49–62.
42. As Agamben writes, "*Being in force without significance (Geltung ohne Bedeutung)*: nothing better describes the ban that our age cannot master than Scholem's formula for the status of law in Kafka's novel" (ibid., 51).
43. Ibid., 58.
44. Ibid., 49. Agamben quotes here Derrida, *La faculté de juger*, 123.
45. Agamben, *Homo Sacer*, 54.
46. Plato, *Phaedrus* 230d–e. For a longer discussion of Derrida's reading, see van der Heiden, *Truth (and Untruth)*, 97–101.
47. Derrida, *La dissémination*, 80/71; my italics.
48. Agamben, *Homo Sacer*, 58. Immediately after this note Agamben analyzes Nancy's concept of the ban.
49. Agamben, *Homo Sacer*, 55.
50. Agamben, *Potentialities*, 115.
51. Note that Agamben also discusses this theme of the voice and its intrinsic negativity in relation to Heidegger's account of the voice of conscience, and one may perhaps extend this analysis to the voice of being. This voice is always presupposed but exactly because of this never exposed as such (Agamben, *Language and Death*, 59).
52. Agamben, *Language and Death*, 33–34; Agamben, *End of the Poem*, 63–65; Augustine, *De trinitate*.
53. Agamben, *Language and Death*, 39.
54. This is most clearly in Agamben's analysis of the letter (*grammē*) and the structure of the trace that mark Derrida's thought: these notions demonstrate the presuppositional structure of metaphysics but do not overcome it. Their importance would already be traceable in Plotinus's *Enneads* as well as in Plato's idea of the Good as being beyond essence; see Agamben, *Language and Death*, 39–40.
55. Ibid., 53; my italics.
56. Agamben, *Potentialities*, 33.

57. One might argue that these analyses also prefigure the theme of inoperativeness when Heidegger notes that we have an experience of language itself at those moments in which we cannot find the word for something. Apparently, only when the normal usage of language breaks down do we have a chance of experiencing language itself (Heidegger, *Unterwegs zur Sprache*, 161).

58. Agamben, *Potentialities*, 35.

59. Agamben, *The Coming Community*, 2. Similarly, he writes, "The transcendent, therefore, is not a supreme entity above all things; rather, the pure transcendent is the taking-place of every thing" (14–15).

60. Agamben, *Potentialities*, 32.

61. Agamben makes this connection himself; see *Signature of All Things*, 22–23 and *The Coming Community*, 97.

62. Nancy, *Le partage des voix*, 59.

63. Plato, *Republic* 607e–608a. I will return to this passage in my final considerations in chapter 7.

64. To a certain extent this is affirmed by Nancy himself: whereas there is a suspension of meaning in the sense of signification, there is "no suspension of sense" in the sense of significance (Nancy, *Le sens du monde*, 36/18).

65. Agamben, *Homo Sacer*, 61–62.

66. McCall, *Melville's Short Novels*, 21.

67. Agamben, *Homo Sacer*, 48.

68. Agamben, *Potentialities*, 268. Also note that Ion, as the rhapsode of Homer, always performed an already existing and fixed text.

69. McCall, *Melville's Short Novels*, 9.

70. Socrates' ironic example of the poet Tynnichus from Chalcis indicates clearly that the poet's potential *presupposes* enthusiasm: "The best evidence for this account is Tynnichus from Chalcis, who never made a poem anyone would think worth mentioning, except for the praise-song everyone sings, almost the most beautiful lyric-poem there is, and simply, as he says himself, 'an invention of the Muses'" (Plato, *Ion* 534d–e).

71. Berkman, *L'effet Bartleby*, 162. For a more extensive account of the relation between rhapsode and scribe, see also van der Heiden, "Reading Bartleby, Reading Ion," 92–108.

Notes to Part 2

1. Marion, *De surcroît*, 37/31; translation slightly adapted.

2. "Der Grund heißt Gott als die erste seiende Ursache alles Seienden" (Heidegger, *Der Satz vom Grund*, 42/27).

3. Meillassoux, *Après la finitude*, 46/57.

NOTES TO CHAPTER 4

1. Heidegger explicitly uses the term "das Revolutionäre" in this context (Heidegger, *Grundprobleme der Philosophie*, 37). Translation for Badiou epigraph is mine. Original reads: "On a envie de dire: 'écoutez, si cette pensée est encore tout entière à venir, revenez nous voir quand au moins un morceau en sera venu!'" (Badiou, "L'offrande réservée," 16).
2. Heidegger, *Der Satz vom Grund*, 43/28.
3. "Die Vorlesung 'Der Satz vom Grund' ist ein Versuch Sein in das Ereignis zu erörtern" (Heidegger, *Der Satz vom Grund*, 191); my translation; I follow Bret Davis's suggestion in *Country Path Conversations*, 111, to translate *erörtern* as "to emplace through discussion."
4. Heidegger, *Der Satz vom Grund*, 20/13.
5. Ibid., 46.
6. Ibid., 51. The English translation chooses to translate *Vorstellen* as "cognition." I will consistently render it as "representation."
7. Ibid., 60/40, 53/35.
8. Ibid., 53/35.
9. Ibid., 58/38.
10. Ibid., 59.
11. Ibid., 66, 69, 73; see also Heidegger, *Beiträge*, 64.
12. Since "leap" is not only *Sprung* in German but also, albeit less common, *Satz*, the expression *der Satz vom Grund* can also be translated as "the leap (away) from the ground" (ibid., 80).
13. Ibid., 79/53.
14. Ibid., 77/52, 72/48.
15. Heidegger, *Beiträge*, 12–13/12–13.
16. Ibid., 205.
17. Heidegger, *Beiträge*, 262/206, 9/9.
18. Ibid., 59/48.
19. Heidegger, *Der Satz vom Grund*, 88; Heidegger, *Beiträge*, 81–82.
20. Heidegger, *Beiträge*, 173.
21. Heidegger, *Der Satz vom Grund*, 88/60.
22. Heidegger, *Beiträge*, 172–73/135–36. Note that Heidegger's German is passive here: "muß zugespielt/hinübergespielt werden."
23. The translators of both the *Beiträge* and *Grundprobleme der Philosophie* translate *Besinnung* as "reflection." I will use both "reflection" and "contemplation."
24. Heidegger, *Grundprobleme der Philosophie*, 35–41/34–39.
25. Ibid., 35–36/34.
26. Ibid., 43/40. This quote may also problematize Badiou's idea of Heidegger suturing philosophy to poetics: in addition to the poet, he also mentions the architect, the thinker, and the statesman as being involved in the creative and formative moments in history.

27. Heidegger, *Der Satz vom Grund*, 89.
28. Ibid., 91.
29. "Wo der letzte Rest der Verbergung des Seins schwindet..." (Heidegger, *Der Satz vom Grund*, 95).
30. Agamben, *Language and Death*, 39.
31. For what follows, see Heidegger, *Zur Sache des Denkens*, 50.
32. Heidegger, *Grundprobleme der Philosophie*, 41/39. The above comments leave the critical questions concerning the voice of conscience and the voice of being that Agamben raises with respect to Heidegger's thought unaffected, so I will return to them later. Moreover, Agamben acknowledges that Heidegger's thought does not fully belong to this negative structure of metaphysics, as I will discuss in chapter 6.
33. Heidegger, *Der Satz vom Grund*, 132/89; my italics.
34. Ibid., 140.
35. Ibid., 165.
36. As Heidegger writes, "Der Ab-grund ist die ursprüngliche Wesung des Grundes" (Heidegger, *Beiträge*, 379). Hence, reason and ground are refused to us. Heidegger continues the quote, "Sofern der Grund auch und gerade im Abgrund noch gründet und doch nicht eigentlich gründet, steht er in der Zögerung" (380).
37. "Das Seyn ist grundlos und kennt deshalb kein Warum. Das Seyn ist, indem es ist: reines Er-eignis" (Heidegger, *Das Ereignis*, 121).
38. They do appear: *Andenken* appears only in quotation, whereas *Vordenken* is used twice (Heidegger, *Beiträge*, 506–07, 19, 437).
39. Ibid., 26/23.
40. Ibid., 31/26.
41. Heidegger, *Hölderlins Hymne "Der Ister,"* 80/65. Note that the English translation offers "encounter" as a translation of *Auseinandersetzung*. For a description of Heidegger's conception of Hölderlin's translation, see van der Heiden, "De toe-eigening."
42. Heidegger, *Grundprobleme der Philosophie*, 12/12.
43. Heidegger, *Beiträge*, 187.
44. Ibid., 58/47.
45. Ibid., 57/46. "Die ursprüngliche Zueignung des ersten Anfangs (und d. h. seine Geschichte) bedeutet das Fußfassen im anderen Anfang. Dieses vollzieht sich im Übergang von der Leitfrage... zur Grundfrage" (171).
46. In this sense, as Heidegger writes, thinking "fragt schon aus diesem her" (ibid., 171).
47. Ibid., 15/15.
48. Heidegger, *Grundprobleme der Philosophie*, 162–63.
49. Ibid., 184/159 .
50. Heidegger, *Beiträge*, 15/14–15. Yet, as Heidegger also writes, the basic mood of inceptual thinking must have multiple names because every name is borrowed from tradition and is thus marked by the way it is used in the first beginning (Heidegger, *Beiträge*, 22). This also means that *Verhaltenheit* as a term

should be heard in its plurality of meanings in order to do justice to the originary moment of every beginning—in this case, inceptual thinking. In what follows, I will maintain *Verhaltenheit* as the name for comportment (since it is related to terms that express comportment in general in German), but I will also point out different instances of meaning in *Verhaltenheit*.

51. Heidegger, *Beiträge*, 15/14.
52. Ibid., 15, 62.
53. Ibid., 229/180. See also Heidegger, *Grundprobleme der Philosophie*, 124–25.
54. Heidegger, *Grundprobleme der Philosophie*, 181/156.
55. Ibid., 12/12.
56. Heidegger, *Beiträge*, 107.
57. Nancy, *Le sens du monde*, 34/17.
58. Ibid., 35/18.
59. Ibid., 33–34n1/175n19. One might add to this the similarity Nancy discerns between Badiou and Heidegger on the motive of the scintillation of the event: the event receives its grandeur from its difference from the "grayness" of the world and "the insignificance of the everyday" (Nancy, *Être singulier pluriel*, 28/10).
60. See van der Heiden, "Subjective Fidelity," 124–28.
61. I explained *in extenso* how this works in *L'être et l'événement* in chapter 1. A similar transgression of the law that a set cannot be an element of itself appears in *Logiques des mondes*, 413/391. The only difference is that the transgression of this law gives rise to a different typology of change.
62. The function of appearing is defined by a function $Id(x, y)$ that adds to two element x, y in a set S a value in the transcendental T of the world to which S belongs; the value in T measures the identity of x and y. By definition, existence is the self-identity, $Id(x, x)$, of an element x in S. Since it follows from the definition of the transcendental that it has both a minimal and a maximal value, it makes sense to talk about elements of S that exist minimally or maximally. Since existence is derived from the function of appearing, a maximal existence can also be called a scintillating event. For the definitions of appearing and existence, see Badiou, *Logiques des mondes*, 257–61. The algebraic details of the transcendental are discussed in book 2, section 3.
63. Badiou, *Logiques des mondes*, 285/269.
64. Ibid., 417.
65. Ibid., 529/507. See also van der Heiden, "The Scintillation."
66. See also van der Heiden, "The Scintillation."
67. Badiou, *L'être et l'événement*, 233/211.
68. Badiou, *Logiques des mondes*, 529/508.
69. Nancy, *Le sens du monde*, 59/35.
70. An analysis of Heidegger's conception of truth helps to fully determine the value and meaning of Nancy's interpretation of Heidegger's phrase that truth penetrates the event. Clearly, Nancy's comments tend toward the equation of truth and presence. Yet, Heidegger's conception of truth does not allow such an

equation, as I have argued in van der Heiden, *Truth (and Untruth)*, chapter 2. This implies that it is not too difficult to find a "third resource" in Heidegger, beyond "constitutive self-evidence" and "inaugural decision," as Nancy suggests. In fact, this third resource can already be found in the concept of truth.

71. Badiou, *Logiques des mondes*, 68/60. Hence, what formally distinguishes the faithful subject from the obscure and the reactive subject is exactly the negation sign in front of the sign for the trace of the event, ε, that appears in the formulas for the obscure and reactive subject.

72. See Badiou, *Logiques des mondes*, 61, 65, 68.

73. Heidegger, *Beiträge*, 88.

74. Ibid., 88/70.

75. See, for instance, Agamben, *Potentialities*, 245.

76. Ibid., 259.

77. As I discussed in chapter 1 in relation to Nancy, Heidegger uses here the terminology "das Bringen von Botschaft und Kunde" (Heidegger, *Unterwegs zur Sprache*, 122). Recall that Angelus Silesius refers to the Greek *angelos*, which Agamben strikingly describes as "the messenger...who performatively announces an event" (Agamben, *Potentialities*, 257).

78. Heidegger, *Der Satz vom Grund*, 140.

79. Critchley, *Faith of the Faithless*, 183–94.

80. Badiou, *Saint Paul*, 50/47. For Heidegger, this critique concerns comportment toward God: not theoretical speculation as in Aristotle, but another comportment toward God announces itself here (Heidegger, *Phänomenologie des religiösen Lebens*, 97). In chapter 4 of *Faith of the Faithless*, Critchley reads these Pauline lectures mainly as "experiments on political theology," as the subtitle of the book indicates. Yet, they are also concerned with the more fundamental philosophical question of ontology. In what follows, I will place everything in this ontological light—this is an important difference from Critchley's reading.

81. This is a second aspect in which my reading is different from Critchley's. For him, the main point seems to be to show that the different contemporary readings of Paul share a "crypto-Marcionism"—by which he applies the basic thesis of Taubes's *Die politische Theologie des Paulus* to the present-day readings of Paul: "My other concern is with the way in which a certain ultra-Paulinism asserts itself in figures like Agamben, Heidegger, and Badiou that might lead one to conclude that the contemporary return to Paul is really a return to Marcion" (Critchley, *Faith of the Faithless*, 195). Yet, I will show that paying attention to the differences between (in particular) Badiou and Heidegger gives us some important clues as to the differences in their ontological projects.

82. Badiou, *Saint Paul*, 5/4.

83. Ibid., 85/81.

84. "The present study takes up the center of Christianity: the eschatological problem. Already at the end of the first century the eschatological was covered up in Christianity. In later times one misjudged all original Christian concepts.

In today's philosophy, too, the Christian concept-formations are hidden behind a Greek view" (Heidegger, *Phänomenologie des religiösen Lebens*, 104/73).

85. Ibid., 98–105. Although Heidegger obviously does not use the term *Ereignis* in the same strong sense as in his later work, he does speak of the event of the parousia: "Das Ereignis der Parusie" (Heidegger, *Phänomenologie des religiösen Lebens*, 112; see also 149).

86. In fact, Heidegger also places the Resurrection in light of this second coming because the parousia is also the day when the deceased believers will be resurrected with him (Heidegger, *Phänomenologie des religiösen Lebens*, 115, 152–53). Badiou, on the contrary, places the resurrection of the dead in light of Christ's Resurrection (Badiou, *Saint Paul*, 47–48).

87. Heidegger, *Phänomenologie des religiösen Lebens*, 102.

88. This is why Heidegger writes that the enactment (*Vollzug*) of life that stems from this comportment prevails in Paul's letters over the specific coherence of occurrences that might take place at a certain moment in the future (Heidegger, *Phänomenologie des religiösen Lebens*, 114).

89. Quoted in ibid., 79/112.

90. The title of this subsection is a quote from Critchley, *Faith of the Faithless*, 177–78.

91. Ibid., 177.

92. Ibid., 178.

93. Badiou, *Saint Paul*, 50/47.

94. Ibid., 105/98.

95. Ibid., 11/11.

96. Critchley, *Faith of the Faithless*, 178.

97. Heidegger, *Phänomenologie des religiösen Leben*, 117–20. The title of Agamben's reading, *The Time that Remains*, refers to 1 Corinthians 7:29, which immediately precedes the occurrences of the *hōs mē* in Paul's letter. For his account of the *hōs mē*, see Agamben, *The Time that Remains*, 23–25.

98. Heidegger, *Phänomenologie des religiösen Lebens*, 112, 116, 148. As Heidegger emphasizes, the Greek term *schēma tou kosmou* does not refer to an objective order of the world or cosmos for Paul. Rather, it concerns the human comportment to the world, as he explains in reference to Romans 12:2 in which Paul incites the believers "not to be conformed to this world" (120/86).

99. Ibid., 120/86.

100. Agamben, *The Time that Remains*, 34.

101. Heidegger, *Phänomenologie des religiösen Lebens*, 116/83; my italics.

102. Ibid., 117/84.

103. Ibid., 121.

104. Heidegger, *Sein und Zeit*, 267.

105. One might also connect this theme to the notion of *Ruf* and *Anruf* in *Sein und Zeit* (Critchley, *Faith of the Faithless*, 184).

106. Agamben, *The Time that Remains*, 23; my italics.

107. Ibid., 97.

108. Ibid., 26.
109. Badiou's Paul in this sense is indeed the opposite of Bartleby, as suggested by Berkman, *L'effet Bartleby*, 169–71. Badiou writes of Bartleby's behavior as betrayal (Badiou, *Logiques des mondes*, 422). As we shall see in chapter 6, for Agamben, Paul is comparable to Bartleby.
110. Agamben, *The Time that Remains*, 25.
111. Badiou, *Court traité*, 54.
112. Heidegger, *Wegmarken*, 52/43–44.
113. Hence, faith is the presupposition of theology that cannot be explained or grasped by theology: "Theology can only render faith more difficult, that is, render it more certain that faithfulness cannot be gained through the science of theology, but solely through faith" (ibid., 56/46). Yet, while faith does not need philosophy, theology does need it because it is a science: "If faith does not need philosophy, the *science* of faith as a *positive* science does" (61/50).
114. This example is also discussed in Derrida, *Foi et savoir*, no. 48.
115. "Der Glaube hat im Denken keinen Platz" (Heidegger, *Holzwege*, 372).
116. Heidegger, *Beiträge*, 368–70/291–92.
117. "Die *Fragenden* dieser Art sind die ursprünglich und eigentlich Glaubenden" (ibid., 369).
118. Ibid., 369–70/292.
119. In this sense, I fully agree with Critchley when he writes, "Agamben owes much more to Heidegger's reading of Paul than to Benjamin. I do not know—although one may guess—the reason why Agamben tries to play down his debt to Heidegger" (Critchley, *Faith of the Faithless*, 166).
120. Agamben, *The Time that Remains*, 134.
121. As opposed to what Critchley claims, it is not so much a question of ontology generally, but rather of propositional attitudes and an Aristotelian ontology that is rejected by Agamben (see Critchley, *Faith of the Faithless*, 163–64).
122. Agamben, *The Time that Remains*, 129; my italics. He also refers to this passage at 41.
123. Agamben, *End of the Poem*, 65–66.
124. This difference is lost on Critchley in his discussion of the Pauline words, "You are not your own": all depends on the question of whether the expropriation of the position one holds gives pure potentiality back or not (Critchley, *Faith of the Faithless*, 181).
125. Badiou, *Logiques des mondes*, 536/514.
126. Agamben, *Language and Death*, 54–62. As he notes, Heidegger's analysis of the voice of conscience traces "*another Voice*" in Dasein (59), which Heidegger also calls "an *alien* voice" (Heidegger, *Sein und Zeit*, 277). Agamben finds a similar structure in Heidegger's use of "the voice of being" in the epilogue to *Was ist Metaphysik?* (Heidegger, *Wegmarken*, 307; Agamben, *Language and Death*, 60).

NOTES TO CHAPTER 5

1. Marion, *De surcroît*, 46–48.
2. Ibid., 47/40; my italics.
3. This is immediately borrowed from Heidegger: death is the "*unüberholbare Möglichkeit,*" the "possibility not to be bypassed" (Heidegger, *Sein und Zeit*, 251/232).
4. Marion, *De surcroît*, 48/40.
5. Ibid., 48/41. The translation has been slightly adapted: in accordance with the translation of Romano's *L'événement et le monde*, I translate *événementiel* as "eventual."
6. Romano, *L'événement et le monde*, 106.
7. For this and the following comments on Heidegger, see Romano, *L'événement et le monde*, 26–33.
8. Derrida, *Apories*, 61–80.
9. "La naissance est l'événement selon lequel l'être même est donné ou advient" (Romano, *L'événement et le monde*, 33).
10. Ibid., 32/20.
11. Ibid., 33. This hermeneutics is also called "evential hermeneutics" ("*herméneutique événementiale,*" at 34).
12. Ibid., 58/41, 59/42. He refers explicitly to Leibniz's principle and the "first and last *ratio* for the world" (57/40) it aims to find.
13. Ibid., Ibid., 56/39, 55/38, 60/42, 59/42, 62/44, 177.
14. Ibid., 186.
15. Ibid., 170.
16. Ibid., 186. "C'est pourquoi il exclut principiellement toute causalité" (173).
17. Ibid., 172.
18. Ibid., 176.
19. Similarly, since the event temporalizes time, it is older than time. Therefore, as an absolute beginning, it can only be understood as the beginning of time itself; consequently, it appears always later than itself (see ibid., 186).
20. Ibid., 174. In *L'événement et le monde*, Romano illustrates the same structure of delay in the appearance of an event in relation to our "principal decisions" (68). Such a decision is also an event, but we are never contemporaneous with them: the decision is not simply taken in the dateable present we associate with it. In this present, in which the decision "declares itself," it appears as already having taken place: "when a decision transpires [*intervenir*] or, more accurately, 'breaks out' [*se déclarer*] the event has already taken place 'long before.'"
21. Ibid., 174, 186; see also 176.
22. Ibid., 175.
23. Ibid., 178; see also Marion, *De surcroît*, 39.
24. Romano, *L'événement et le monde*, 72/51; see also 75.

25. Ibid., 85/61.
26. Ibid., 85, 88.
27. Ibid., 89/64.
28. Ibid., 85, 86.
29. Ibid., 86/62. Clearly, the work of art as the opening and the beginning of a new world is also an important theme in Heidegger's work: "A beginning, on the contrary, always contains the undisclosed abundance of the unfamiliar and extraordinary, which means that it also contains strife with the familiar and ordinary" (Heidegger, *Holzwege*, 64; translation from Heidegger, *Poetry, Language, Thought*, 74).
30. Romano calls this "the world in its *evential* sense" (Romano, *L'événement et le monde*, 89).
31. Ibid., 115/84.
32. See ibid., 119. To indicate that it is not the impossible in an absolute sense (since it reconfigures a horizon), but only with respect to the understanding's project, he calls this possibilization of the event "im-possibility" (121).
33. Ibid., 96–97.
34. "Ce qui pouvait apparaître comme condition (l'être-au-monde) apparaît ici conditionné en retour" (ibid., 99).
35. Ibid., 101/73.
36. Ibid., 103/75, 106/77.
37. Ibid., 206/153.
38. Ibid., 111/81; my italics.
39. Heidegger, *Sein und Zeit*, 161/150; Romano, *L'événement et le monde*, 85, 231/172.
40. Marion, *De surcroît*, 52/44.
41. Shakespeare, *Macbeth*, 5.1.68.
42. The work of Hannah Arendt, probably the first thinker of birth and beginning in the context of hermeneutic phenomenology, convincingly shows that in relation to this irrevocability and irremediability, we cannot limit ourselves to an account of the comportments of understanding or fidelity; rather, the irrevocability of human action demands the comportment of forgiveness (Arendt, *The Human Condition*, 236–43).
43. Meillassoux, *Après la finitude*, 149/108. I added the italics on "other" in accordance with the original.
44. Meillassoux criticizes this dualism in "*Nouveauté et événement*," as I discussed briefly in chapter 1.
45. Meillassoux, *Après la finitude*, 150/176.
46. See Harman, *Quentin Meillassoux*, 92–97, and Meillassoux, "Excerpts from *L'inexistence divine*," 176. Since the manuscript is not yet published, it still remains to be seen exactly which role it will receive in the final version. Nevertheless, it indicates once more a certain affinity with Heidegger's insistence on thinking the contingency of being.
47. Meillassoux, *Après la finitude*, 54/39; I altered the English translation ("being-otherwise") to capture the reference to Heidegger's *Seinkönnen*.

48. Ibid., 18/5.
49. Ibid., 20.
50. Ibid., 24/9.
51. Ibid., 32/14.
52. Heidegger, *Sein und Zeit*, 227/208.
53. Ibid., 154/144.
54. Meillassoux, *Après la finitude*, 37/26.
55. Ibid., 22/8; translation adapted.
56. Ibid., 61/44.
57. Ibid., 46/33; translation adapted.
58. Ibid., 40.
59. Ibid., 47/34, 50–52.
60. Ibid., 54/39; translation adapted.
61. Ibid., 55/40, 56/41.
62. Ibid., 53.
63. Badiou develops this point in terms of the development of multivalued or nonclassical logics in which the principle of the excluded third does not apply; these logics are of crucial importance to Badiou's enterprise as well. Consequently, the question of this principle is not simply an issue in relation to the hermeneutic-phenomenological school (Badiou, *Logiques des mondes*, 180–82/167–69).
64. Badiou, *Saint Paul*, 45.
65. Agamben, *The Time that Remains*, 52–53. Note that Agamben addresses this issue already in the opening pages (3–5).
66. Meillassoux, *Après la finitude*, 47/34, 50/36.
67. Ibid., 73/53.
68. I will discuss this further in chapter 6.
69. Meillassoux, *Après la finitude*, 77/56, 50/36, 77/57.
70. To a certain extent, this also follows from his account of ancestrality: in relation to the past the "common" relation to the physical laws remains fixed, but in relation to the future we can only say that their stability is probable and subject to an absolute contingency.
71. Meillassoux, *Après la finitude*, 85/62.
72. Ibid., 85/62.
73. Heidegger, *Sein und Zeit*, 255–58.
74. Ibid., 258/238.
75. Ibid., 264/244.
76. "Die eigenste, unbezügliche und unüberholbare Möglichkeit beschafft sich aber das Dasein nicht nachträglich und gelegentlich im Verlaufe seines Seins. Sondern, wenn Dasein existiert, ist es auch schon in diese Möglichkeit geworfen" (ibid., 251).
77. See, for instance, Heidegger, *Das Ereignis*, 27.
78. Meillassoux, *Après la finitude*, 66.
79. Ibid., 98.
80. "Das Ereignis übereignet den Gott an den Menschen, indem es diesen dem Gott zueignet" (Heidegger, *Beiträge*, 26).

81. Meillassoux, *Après la finitude*, 87.
82. Heidegger, "*Zeit und Sein,*" in *Zur Sache des Denkens*, 3–66.
83. Meillassoux, "Spectral Dilemma," 263.
84. Ibid., 265.
85. See also Meillassoux, "Excerpts from *L'inexistence divine*," 192.
86. Meillassoux, "Spectral Dilemma," 268, 271. He writes, "From this point on, God must be thought as *the contingent, but eternally possible, effect of a Chaos unsubordinated to any law*" (274).
87. Ibid., 268.
88. Heidegger, *Beiträge*, 409/324.
89. Ibid., 382/302. I have replaced "emptiness" with "void."

Notes to Chapter 6

1. Agamben, *Potentialities*, 45. I quoted this passage fully in chapter 3.
2. See the difficult essay by Agamben, "**Se:* Hegel's Absolute and Heidegger's *Ereignis*," in *Potentialities*, 116–37.
3. Derrida, *Le toucher*, 245–79.
4. I will not go into detail here, but Derrida's analysis of Nancy beautifully indicates the tension in Nancy's work in this respect. On the one hand, Nancy favors the touch and its immediacy. On the other hand, in distinction to, for instance, Chrétien, as Derrida shows, Nancy emphasizes a "technical contingency," that is, a touch that cannot exist without technological prostheses. Yet such a technical dimension of every contact contaminates the purity and the immediacy presupposed in the touch (Derrida, *Le toucher*, 314/278).
5. Meillassoux, *Après la finitude*, 50.
6. Heidegger suggests that the abandonment of being is an event, "the least visible and experienceable," and that it is "the most hidden and most proper ground, and the essence" of nihilism (Heidegger, *Grundfragen der Philosophie*, 185/160).
7. See Heidegger, *Identität und Differenz*, 53–56; quoted and discussed in Agamben, *Potentialities*, 132.
8. Heidegger, "*Zeit und Sein,*" in *Zur Sache des Denkens*, 3–66; I focus on 49–51. This is partly inspired by Agamben's references in "**Se*: Hegel's Absolute and Heidegger's *Ereignis*," in *Potentialities*, 116–37.
9. Heidegger, *Zur Sache des Denkens*, 9. The following quote establishes this connection between giving and destining most explicitly: "Ein Geben, das nur seine Gabe gibt, sich selber jedoch dabei zurückhält und entzieht, ein solches Geben nennen wir das Schicken" (12).
10. Heidegger, *Der Satz vom Grund*, 95.
11. Heidegger, *Zur Sache des Denkens*, 50; quoted in Agamben, *Potentialities*, 130.
12. Agamben, *Potentialities*, 117; see also Agamben, *Homo Sacer*, 61.
13. Agamben, *Homo Sacer*, 59.

14. Heidegger, *Zur Sache des Denkens*, 50/40–41.
15. Agamben, *Homo Sacer*, 60; my italics.
16. Agamben, *Homo Sacer*, 60.
17. Agamben, *Homo Sacer*, 60–61.
18. Heidegger, *Zur Sache des Denkens*, 50/41; quoted in Agamben, *Potentialities*, 130.
19. Ibid., 50.
20. Van der Heiden, *Truth (and Untruth)*, 28–45. The difference between *pseudos* and *lēthē*, which I introduce there, may also be understood in the terms I develop here: *pseudos* is a negative concealment since it refers to a preceding realm of unconcealment, whereas *lēthē* is not negative because it does not presuppose another realm.
21. Agamben, *Potentialities*, 131. For Heidegger, *lēthē* is also a simple concealment; see the following telling quote: "Das entziehende und sich entziehende Verbergen ist für die Griechen das Einfachste alles Einfachen" (Heidegger, *Parmenides*, 189).
22. Heidegger, *Parmenides*, 176.
23. "Wo völlige, und das ist maß-lose Vergessung, und das ist Verbergung, waltet, kann diese nicht einmal Wesensgrund des Menschenwesens sein, weil sie überhaupt keine Entbergung zuläßt und so der Unverborgenheit den Wesensgrund vorenthält" (ibid., 183).
24. He uses *vor-enthaltende* (ibid., 189).
25. Heidegger, *Beiträge*, 99/79.
26. Agamben, *Potentialities*, 133. Agamben also simply follows the logic Heidegger develops in the *Beiträge* in which thought moves from wonder as the basic mood—or *archē*, as Agamben calls it—of philosophy to its own *habitus* or comportment to think the event, its "*se*."
27. See van der Heiden, *Truth (and Untruth)*, where I show that Derrida and Ricoeur often criticize the ontological impact of Heidegger's work in the name of the issue of language.
28. Nancy, "*Hors colloque*," 524.
29. Agamben, *Potentialities*, 177–84; Agamben, *Homo Sacer*, 44–48.
30. Agamben, *Potentialities*, 244. The quote is from Aristotle.
31. Ibid., 246, 253.
32. Ibid., 249. In *The Coming Community*, Agamben hints at another conception of creation (which would coincide with his conception of existence), in which creation is not understood in an ontotheological, but rather in the following terms: "Creation—or existence—...is rather the impotence of God with respect to his own impotence, his allowing—being able to *not* not-be—a contingency to be" (*The Coming Community*, 32). This strange expression "being able to not not-be" is also used in Agamben's chapter on Bartleby to describe the excellence of the pianist Glenn Gould "who can *not* not-play" (37). To not not-be is not the same as to be. Rather, this formulation expresses the excluded third or the remnant of to be and to not-be. For Agamben, this excluded third

is pure potentiality itself, that is, the potential to be and the potential not to be (*dunamis mē einai*).

33. Agamben, *Homo Sacer*, 47.
34. Agamben, "On Potentiality," in *Potentialities*, 177–84; Aristotle, *Metaphysics* 1047a24–26; Translation from the Loeb Classical Library edition. The translation from Barnes, *Complete Works of Aristotle*, vol. 2, is virtually the same: "And a thing is capable of doing something if there is nothing impossible in its having the actuality of that of which it is said to have the capacity."
35. Agamben, *Potentialities*, 264. A similar translation can be found in Agamben, *Homo Sacer*, 45–46, and in the essay "On Potentiality," in *Potentialities*, 183.
36. Agamben, *Potentialities*, 264–65.
37. Agamben, *Homo Sacer*, 46; Agamben, *Potentialities*, 183. A slightly different formulation can be found in Agamben, *The Coming Community*, 36.
38. Agamben suggests this relation to Hegel's *Aufhebung* in another context himself (*The Time that Remains*, 99).
39. Agamben, *Homo Sacer*, 44.
40. Aristotle, *De Anima* 417b7–b9.
41. Agamben, *Homo Sacer*, 46.
42. Agamben, "Bartleby, or On Contingency," in *Potentialities*, 243–71.
43. For this and what follows, see Aristotle, *Metaphysics* 1074b34–1075a3.
44. See also his comments on matter in relation to Plotinus (Agamben, *Potentialities*, 216–19). A thought of contingency or potentiality is a truly materialistic conception of being since it thinks being as pure matter.
45. Heidegger, *Beiträge*, 99/79.
46. Agamben, *Homo Sacer*, 58.
47. Heidegger, *Sein und Zeit*, 38.
48. For this prefiguration, see chapter 4.
49. Heidegger, *Sein und Zeit*, 243–44.
50. Ibid., 262/242.
51. Derrida, *Apories*, 124.
52. Heidegger, *Phänomenologie des religiösen Lebens*, 63, 118–20.
53. Agamben, *The Time that Remains*, 34.
54. For thrown possibilities, see Heidegger, *Sein und Zeit*, 144.
55. Heidegger, *Sein und Zeit*, 267.
56. To which Agamben also objects (*The Time that Remains*, 34).
57. Heidegger, *Sein und Zeit*, 275/254.
58. Ibid., 277. Agamben speaks of "another voice" (*Language and Death*, 59).
59. The possibility of hearing this voice is explicitly mentioned: "Dem Gewissensruf entspricht ein mögliches Hören" (Heidegger, *Sein und Zeit*, 269).
60. Agamben, *Potentialities*, 259.
61. Ibid., 260.
62. Ibid., 254.
63. McCann, *Melville's Short Novels*, 34.

64. Agamben, *Potentialities*, 269.
65. Ibid., 267.
66. Ibid., 255, 256.
67. Ibid., 256.
68. Ibid., 258. This inquiry into the principle of reason by Leibniz and the necessity to bracket exactly the reason or the "why" in order to think being refers to Heidegger's questions in the introduction to *Was ist Metaphysik*. One might even understand Agamben's reflections here as a response to Heidegger's remark that it is time "for thinking through the lecture 'What Is Metaphysics?,'... from its end, for once—from *its* end and not from some imaginary end" (Heidegger, *Wegmarken*, 383/290), since *Was ist Metaphysik* concludes with a reference to Leibniz's question, "Why are there beings at all, and why not far rather Nothing?" (Heidegger, *Wegmarken*, 122/96). This is reminiscent of Deleuze's reading of Bartleby in "Bartleby, ou la formule," in *Critique et clinique*, 89–114. Deleuze refers implicitly to the same formulation of Leibniz's principle and indicates that Bartleby reverses it as follows: "Je préférais rien plutôt que quelque chose" (Deleuze, *Critique et clinique*, 92). See also Agamben, *The Coming Community*, 104–05.
69. Agamben, *Potentialities*, 259.
70. Agamben, *Homo Sacer*, 44.
71. Agamben, *Potentialities*, 261.
72. Ibid., 262.
73. Aristotle, *Ethica Nicomacheia* 1139b10, in *Complete Works of Aristotle*, 2:1799.
74. Quoted by Agamben, *Potentialities*, 262.
75. Ibid., 266.
76. Ibid., 267.

Notes to Chapter 7

1. For the epigraph by Alain Badiou, *Petit manuel d'inesthétique*, 36/19, I adapted the translation and replaced "to" with "from" because Er returns *from* the kingdom of the dead.
2. Plato, *Parmenides* 166c, in Cooper, *Plato*, 397.
3. Ibid., 130d.
4. Meillassoux, *Après la finitude*, 103/76.
5. Nancy, *Le sens du monde*, 36.
6. Ibid., 36/18–19.
7. Cooper, *Complete Works of Plato*, xxiv. For the importance of this speaking for the other in (particular fragments of) Plato's dialogues and present-day philosophy, see van der Heiden, *De stem van de doden*.
8. The opening sentence of Agamben, *The Coming Community*, 1, reads: "The coming being is whatever being."

9. Parts of this study are published in English translation as "Excerpts from *L'inexistence divine*," added as an appendix to Harman, *Quentin Meillassoux*, 175–238.

10. As Harman suggests, this problematic might also lead to an "ethics of regret" (*Prince of Networks*, 176) in Meillassoux's thought, which would yet be another aspect of an ethos of contingency.

11. Meillassoux, *Après la finitude*, 50/36.

12. Nihilism in this sense is the secret accomplice of ontotheology, as both Heidegger and Agamben argue.

13. This is exactly the hesitation that is opened up by the suspension of the principle of reason, as Heidegger suggests: "Sofern der Grund auch und gerade im Abgrund noch gründet und doch nicht eigentlich gründet, steht er in der Zögerung" (*Beiträge*, 380).

14. Plato, *Republic* 607d, in Cooper, *Plato*, 1212. Note that prose, or "words without metre" (*aneu metrou logon*), is an expression that mirrors Gorgias's definition of poetry as "words having metre" (*logon echonta metron*) (see Steele, *Missing Measures*, 113).

15. Plato, *Republic* 607e–608a. I take the translation from the Loeb edition here because it focuses more sharply on the reference to song that Socrates introduces. The translation from Cooper, *Plato*, 1212 reads:

> However, if such a defense isn't made, we'll behave like people who have fallen in love with someone but who force themselves to stay away from him, because they realize that their passion isn't beneficial. In the same way, because the love of this sort of poetry has been implanted in us by the upbringing we have received under our fine constitutions, we are well disposed to any proof that it is the best and truest thing. But if it isn't able to produce such a defense, then, whenever we listen to it, we'll repeat the argument we have just now put forward like an incantation so as to preserve ourselves from slipping back into that childish passion for poetry which the majority of people have. And we'll go on chanting that such poetry is not to be taken seriously or treated as a serious undertaking with some kind of hold on the truth, but that anyone who is anxious about the constitution within him must be careful when he hears it and must continue to believe what we have said about it.

16. Plato, *Republic* 614b. See also Heidegger, *Parmenides*, 145.

17. Plato, *Republic* 608d.

18. See chapter 4. This expression is obviously borrowed from Heidegger's *Beiträge*.

19. As Heidegger suggests about this myth, "Das folgende Wort ist ein behütendes Wort, das der Zudringlichkeit des geläufigen Erklärens widersteht und streng genommen nur in seiner eigenen Wesensgestalt gesagt und gehört warden darf" (*Parmenides*, 146). Hence, this myth is a word that should be heard in its own tone of voice and should not be understood as a philosophical explanation.

20. Agamben, *Profanations*, 39.

21. Ibid., 39–40.
22. Plato, *Republic* 614c.
23. Ibid., 614d. For the fact that this region indeed cannot be experienced, see 621a.
24. Heidegger, *Parmenides*, 130–93. "*Der* muthos *gipfelt in der Sage vom Feld der* lēthē" (185). For a more critical reading, see van der Heiden, *De stem van de doden*, 277–84.
25. Heidegger, *Parmenides*, 190.
26. Plato, *Republic* 621a.

Bibliography

Agacinski, Sylviane, ed. *Mimesis des articulations.* Paris: Flammarion, 1975.

Agamben, Giorgio. *The Coming Community.* Translated by Michael Hardt. Minneapolis: University of Minnesota Press, 1993.

———. *The End of the Poem: Studies in Poetics.* Translated by Daniel Heller-Roazen. Stanford, CA: Stanford University Press, 1999.

———. *Homo Sacer: Sovereign Power and Bare Life.* Translated by Daniel Heller-Roazen. Stanford, CA: Stanford University Press, 1998.

———. *Infancy and History: On the Destruction of Experience.* Translated by Liz Heron. London: Verso, 2007.

———. *The Kingdom and the Glory: For a Theological Genealogy of Economy and Government.* Translated by Lorenzo Chiesa (with Matteo Mandrini). Stanford, CA: Stanford University Press, 2011.

———. *Language and Death: The Place of Negativity.* Translated by Karen E. Pinkus and Michael Hardt. Minneapolis: University of Minnesota Press, 1991.

———. *The Man without Content.* Translated by Georgia Albert. Stanford, CA: Stanford University Press, 1998.

———. *Means without End: Notes on Politics.* Translated by Vincenzo Binetti and Cesare Casarino. Minneapolis: University of Minnesota Press, 2000.

———. *Potentialities: Collected Essays in Philosophy.* Translated by Daniel Heller-Roazen. Stanford, CA: Stanford University Press, 1999.

———. *Profanations.* Translated by Jeff Fort. New York: Zone Books, 2007.

———. *Remnants of Auschwitz: The Witness and the Archive.* Translated by Daniel Heller-Roazen. New York: Zone Books, 2002.

———. *The Signature of All Things: On Method.* Translated by Luca D'Isanto with Kevin Attell. New York: Zone Books, 2009.

———. *The State of Exception*. Translated by Kevin Attell. Chicago: University of Chicago Press, 2005.

———. *The Time that Remains: A Commentary on the Letter to the Romans*. Translated by Patricia Dailey. Stanford, CA: Stanford University Press, 2005.

———. *What Is an Apparatus? and Other Essays*. Translated by David Kishik and Stefan Pedatella. Stanford, CA: Stanford University Press, 2009.

Arendt, Hannah. *The Human Condition*. Chicago: University of Chicago Press, 1998.

———. *The Life of the Mind*. London: Harcourt, 1978.

———. *Men in Dark Times*. New York: Harcourt, 1968.

Aristotle. *The Complete Works of Aristotle*. The Revised Oxford Translation. 2 vols. Edited by Jonathan Barnes. Princeton, NJ: Princeton University Press, 1995.

———. *Aristotle: Metaphysics, Books I–IX*. Translated by Hugh Tredennick. Cambridge, MA: Harvard University Press, 1933.

Augustine. *The Trinity (De trinitate)*. Translated by Edmund Hill. New York: New City Press, 1991.

Badiou, Alain. *Abrégé de métapolitique*. Paris: Seuil, 1998.

———. *Conditions*. Paris: Seuil, 1992. Translated by Steven Corcoran as *Conditions*. London: Continuum, 2008.

———. *Court traité d'ontologie transitoire*. Paris: Seuil, 1998. Translated by Norman Madarasz as *Briefings on Existence: A Short Treatise on Transitory Ontology*. Albany: State University of New York Press, 2006.

———. *Deleuze: "La clameur de l'être."* Paris: Hachette Littératures, 1997. Translated by Louise Burchill as *Deleuze: The Clamor of Being*. Minneapolis: University of Minnesota Press, 2000.

———. *De quoi Sarkozy est-il le nom*. Paris: Seuil, 2007.

———. *L'éthique: Essai sur la conscience du mal*. Caen: Nous, 2003.

———. *L'être et l'événement*. Paris: Seuil, 1988. Translated by Oliver Feltham as *Being and Event*. Continuum: London, 2005.

———. *Le fini et l'infini*. Paris: Bayard, 2010.

———. "Homage to Jacques Derrida." In *Adieu Derrida*, edited by Costas Douzinas, 34–46. New York: Palgrave, 2007.

———. *L'hypothèse communiste*. Paris: Nouvelles Editions Lignes, 2009.

———. *Logiques des mondes: L'être et l'événement 2*. Paris: Seuil, 2006. Translated by Alberto Toscano as *Logics of Worlds: Being and Event II*. London: Continuum, 2009.

———. *Manifeste pour la philosophie*. Paris: Seuil, 1989. Translated by Norman Madarasz as *Manifesto for Philosophy*. Albany: State University of New York Press, 1999.

———. "Metaphysics and the Critique of Metaphysics." *Pli* 10 (2000): 174–90.

———. *Le nombre et les nombres*. Paris: Seuil, 1990. Translated by Robin Mackay as *Number and Numbers*. Cambridge: Polity Press, 2008.

———. "*L'offrande réservée*." In *Sens en tous sens: Autour des travaux de Jean-Luc Nancy*, edited by F. Guibal and J.-C. Martin, 13–24. Paris: Galilée, 2004.

———. *Petit manuel d'inesthétique*. Paris: Seuil, 1998. Translated by Alberto Toscano as *Handbook of Inaesthetics*. Stanford, CA: Stanford University Press, 2005.

———. *La République de Platon*. Paris: Fayard, 2012.

———. *Saint Paul: La foundation de l'universalisme*. Paris: Presses Universitaires de France, 1997.

———. *Second manifeste pour la philosophie*. Paris: Flammarion, 2010. Translated by Louise Burchill as *Second Manifesto for Philosophy*. Cambridge: Polity Press, 2011.

Badiou, Alain, and Slavoj Žižek. *L'idée du communisme*. Paris: Nouvelles Editions Lignes, 2010.

Balibar, Etienne. "'The History of Truth': Alain Badiou in French Philosophy." *Radical Philosophy* 115 (2002): 16–28.

Benveniste, Émile. *Indo-European Language and Society*. Translated by Elizabeth Palmer. London: Faber and Faber, 1973.

Berkman, Gisèle. *L'effet Bartleby: Philosophes lecteurs*. Paris: Hermann, 2011.

Berkman, Gisèle, and Danielle Cohen-Levinas, eds. *Figures du dehors: Autour de Jean-Luc Nancy*. Nantes: Cécile Defaut, 2012.

Bernet, Rudolf. "The Traumatized Subject." *Research in Phenomenology* 30 (2000): 160–79.

Bosteels, Bruno. "Alain Badiou's Theory of the Subject: Part I, The Recommencement of Dialectical Materialism?" *Pli* 12 (2001): 200–29.

Brassier, Ray. "Presentation as Anti-Phenomenon in Alain Badiou's *Being and Event.*" *Continental Philosophy Review* 39 (2006): 59–77.

Brogan, Walter. "The Parting of Being: On Creation and Sharing in Nancy's Political Ontology." *Research in Phenomenology* 40 (2010): 295–308.

Bryant, Levi, Nick Srnicek, and Graham Harman, eds. *The Speculative Turn: Continental Materialism and Realism.* Victoria: Re-press, 2011.

Calarco, Matthew, and Steven DeCaroli, eds. *Giorgio Agamben: Sovereignty and Life.* Stanford, CA: Stanford University Press, 2007.

Calcagno, Antonio. *Badiou and Derrida: Politics, Events and Their Time.* London: Continuum, 2007.

Clemens, Justin, Nicholas Heron, and Alex Murray, eds. *The Work of Giorgio Agamben: Law, Literature, Life.* Edinburgh: Edinburgh University Press, 2008.

Critchley, Simon. *The Faith of the Faithless: Experiments in Political Theology.* London: Verso, 2012.

———. *Infinitely Demanding: Ethics of Commitment, Politics of Resistance.* London: Verso, 2007.

Deleuze, Gilles. *Critique et clinique.* Paris: Minuit, 1993.

———. *Différence et répétition.* Paris: Presses Universitaires de France, 1968. Translated by Paul Patton as *Difference and Repetition.* London: Athlone Press, 1994.

———. *Logique du sens.* Paris: Minuit, 1969. Translated by Mark Lester, with Charles Stivale, as *Logic of Sense.* New York: Columbia University Press, 1990.

Delpech-Ramey, J. "An Interview with Slavoj Žižek: 'On Divine Self-Limitation and Revolutionary Love.'" *Journal of Philosophy and Scripture* 1, no. 2 (2004): 32–38.

Derrida, Jacques. *Apories.* Paris: Galilée, 1996.

———. *Demeure: Maurice Blanchot.* Paris: Galilée, 1998. Translated by Elizabeth Rottenberg as *Demeure: Fiction and Testimony.* Stanford, CA: Stanford University Press, 2000.

———. *La dissémination.* Paris: Seuil, 1972.

———. *L'écriture et la différence.* Paris: Seuil, 1967. Translated by Alan Bass as *Writing and Difference.* London: Routledge, 2001.

———. *Foi et savoir: Les deux sources de la "religion" aux limites de la simple raison*. Paris: Seuil, 2000.

———. *Psyché: Inventions de l'autre*. Paris: Galilée, 1987.

———. *Le toucher, Jean-Luc Nancy*. Paris: Galilée, 1998. Translated by Christine Irizarry as *On Touching—Jean-Luc Nancy*. Stanford, CA: Stanford University Press, 2005.

Derrida, Jacques, Vincent Descombes, Garbis Kortian, Philippe Lacoue-Labarthe, Jean-François Lyotard, and Jean-Luc Nancy. *La faculté de juger*. Paris: Minuit, 1985.

Devisch, Ignaas. *Wij: Jean-Luc Nancy en het vraagstuk van de gemeenschap in de hedendaagse wijsbegeerte*. Leuven: Peeters, 2003.

Douzinas, Costas, ed. *Adieu Derrida*. New York: Palgrave, 2007.

Durantaye, Leland de la. *Giorgio Agamben: A Critical Introduction*. Stanford, CA: Stanford University Press, 2009.

Gadamer, Hans-Georg. *Wahrheit und Methode. Hermeneutik I. Collected Works*, vol. 1. Tübingen: Mohr Siebeck, 1999.

Gibson, Andrew. *Beckett and Badiou: The Pathos of Intermittency*. Oxford: Oxford University Press, 2007.

Gillespie, Sam. *The Mathematics of Novelty: Badiou's Minimalist Metaphysics*. Melbourne: Re-press, 2008.

Gratton, Peter. "The Speculative Challenge and Nancy's Post-Deconstructive Realism." In *Jean-Luc Nancy and Plural Thinking: Expositions of World, Ontology, Politics, and Sense*, edited by Peter Gratton and Marie-Eve Morin, 109–25. Albany: State University of New York Press, 2012.

Gratton, Peter, and Marie-Eve Morin, eds. *Jean-Luc Nancy and Plural Thinking: Expositions of World, Ontology, Politics, and Sense*. Albany: State University of New York Press, 2012.

Grondin, Jean. "La thèse de l'herméneutique sur l'être," *Revue de métaphysique et de morale*, 52, no. 4 (2006): 469–81.

Guibal, Francis, and Jean-Clet Martin, eds. *Sens en tous sens: Autour des travaux de Jean-Luc Nancy*. Paris: Galilée, 2004.

Hägglund, Martin. *Radical Atheism: Derrida and the Time of Life*. Stanford, CA: Stanford University Press, 2008.

Hallward, Peter. *Badiou: A Subject to Truth*. Minneapolis: University of Minnesota Press, 2003.

Hallward, Peter, ed. *Think Again: Badiou and the Future of Philosophy*. London: Continuum, 2004. This is a partial translation of Ramond, *Alain Badiou: Penser le multiple*.

Hamacher, Werner. "Ou, séance, touche de Nancy, ici." In *On Jean-Luc Nancy: The Sense of Philosophy*, edited by Darren Sheppard, Simon Sparks, and Colin Thomas, 40–63. London: Routledge, 1997.

Harman, Graham. "On Interface: Nancy's Weights and Masses." In *Jean-Luc Nancy and Plural Thinking: Expositions of World, Ontology, Politics, and Sense*, edited by Peter Gratton and Marie-Eve Morin, 95–107. Albany: State University of New York Press, 2012.

———. *Prince of Networks: Bruno Latour and Metaphysics*. Melbourne: Re-press, 2009.

———. *Quentin Meillassoux: Philosophy in the Making*. Edinburgh: Edinburgh University Press, 2011.

———. *Towards Speculative Realism: Essays and Lectures*. Winchester: Zero, 2010.

Heidegger, Martin. *Beiträge zur Philosophie (Vom Ereignis)*. GA 65. Frankfurt: Klostermann, 2003. Translated by Richard Rojcewicz and Daniela Vallege-Neu as *Contributions to Philosophy (Of the Event)*. Bloomington: Indiana University Press, 2012.

———. *Country Path Conversations*. Translated by Bret A. Davis. Bloomington: Indiana University Press, 2010.

———. *Das Ereignis*. GA 71. Frankfurt: Klostermann, 2009.

———. *Der Satz vom Grund*. GA 10. Frankfurt: Klostermann, 1997. Translated by Reginald Lilly as *The Principle of Reason*. Bloomington: Indiana University Press, 1991.

———. *The End of Philosophy*. Translated by Joan Stambaugh. Chicago: University of Chicago Press, 2003.

———. *Erläuterungen zur Hölderlins Dichtung*. GA 4. Frankfurt: Klostermann, 1981.

———. *Grundbegriffe der aristotelischen Philosophie*. GA 18. Frankfurt: Klostermann, 2002.

———. *Grundfragen der Philosophie. Ausgewählte "Probleme" der "Logik."* GA 45. Frankfurt: Klostermann, 1992. Translated by Richard Rojcewicz and André Schuwer as *Basic Questions of Philosophy: Selected "Problems" of "Logic."* Bloomington: Indiana University Press, 1994.

---. *Hölderlins Hymne "Der Ister."* GA 53. Frankfurt: Klostermann, 1984. Translated by William McNeill and Julia Davis as *Hölderlin's Hymn "The Ister."* Bloomington: Indiana University Press, 1996.

---. *Holzwege.* GA 5. Frankfurt: Klostermann, 1982.

---. *Identität und Differenz.* GA 11. Frankfurt: Klostermann, 2006.

---. *Kant und das Problem der Metaphysik.* GA 3. Frankfurt: Klostermann, 1991.

---. *Nietzsche II.* Stuttgart: Neske, 1998.

---. *Ontologie (Hermeneutik der Faktizität).* GA 63. Frankfurt: Klostermann, 1988.

---. *Parmenides.* GA 54. Frankfurt: Klostermann, 1982.

---. *Phänomenologie des religiösen Lebens.* GA 60. Frankfurt: Klostermann, 1995. Translated by Matthias Fritsch and Jennifer Anna Gosetti-Ferencei as *The Phenomenology of Religious Life.* Bloomington: Indiana University Press, 2004.

---. *Poetry, Language, Thought.* Translated by Albert Hofstadter. New York: Harper and Row, 1971.

---. *Sein und Zeit.* Tübingen: Niemeyer, 2001. Translated by Joan Stambaugh as *Being and Time.* Albany: State University of New York Press, 1996.

---. *Unterwegs zur Sprache.* Stuttgart: Klett-Cotta, 2003.

---. *Wegmarken.* GA 9. Frankfurt: Klostermann, 1976. Edited by William McNeill as *Pathmarks.* Cambridge: Cambridge University Press, 1998.

---. *Zur Sache des Denkens.* GA 14. Frankfurt: Klostermann, 2007. Partly translated by Joan Stambaugh as *On Time and Being.* New York: Harper and Row, 1972.

Heiden, Gert-Jan van der. "The Absolute Presupposition of Language: Agamben Reading Gadamer." In *Hermeneutics and the Humanities: Dialogues with Hans-Georg Gadamer,* edited by Madeleine Kasten, Herman Paul, and Rico Sneller, 92–109. Leiden: Leiden University Press, 2012.

---. "Announcement, Attestation, and Equivocity: Ricoeur's Hermeneutic Ontology between Heidegger and Derrida." *American Catholic Philosophical Quarterly* 85, no. 3 (2011): 415–32.

---. "The Poetic Experience of Language and the Task of Thinking: Derrida on Celan." *Philosophy Today* 53, no. 2 (2009): 115–25.

———. "Reading Bartleby, Reading Ion: On a Difference between Agamben and Nancy." *International Yearbook for Hermeneutics* 12 (2013): 92–108.

———. "The Scintillation of the Event." *Symposium: Canadian Journal of Continental Philosophy* 12, no. 2 (2008): 93–109.

———. *De stem van de doden: Hermeneutiek als spreken namens de ander*. Nijmegen: Vantilt, 2012.

———. "Subjective Fidelity in an Objective Phenomenology: On Badiou's Logic of Appearance." In *Investigating Subjectivity: Classical and New Perspectives*, edited by Gert-Jan van der Heiden, Karel Novotny, Inga Römer, and László Tengelyi, 115–31. Leiden: Brill, 2011.

———. "De toe-eigening van het oorspronkelijke en het eigene. Derrida's kritische vragen bij Heideggers begrip van vertaling." *Tijdschrift voor Filosofie* 71, no. 2 (2009): 305–29.

———. *The Truth (and Untruth) of Language: Heidegger, Ricoeur, and Derrida on Disclosure and Displacement*. Pittsburgh: Duquesne University Press, 2010.

Höffle, Otfried. *Aristotle*. Translated by Christine Salazar. Albany: State University of New York Press, 2003.

Johnston, Adrian. "Phantom of Consistency: Alain Badiou and Kantian Transcendental Idealism." *Continental Philosophy Review* 41 (2008): 345–66.

Kant, Immanuel. *Kritik der reinen Vernunft*. Werkausgabe, vol. 4. Edited by Wilhelm Weischedel. Frankfurt: Suhrkamp, 1968.

Lacoue-Labarthe, Philippe. *Heidegger: La poétique du poème*. Paris: Galilée, 2002.

Lecercle, Jean-Jacques. *Badiou and Deleuze Read Literature*. Edinburgh: Edinburgh University Press, 2010.

Livingston, Paul M. "Agamben, Badiou, and Russell." *Continental Philosophy Review* 42 (2009): 297–325.

Marchart, Oliver. *Post-Foundational Political Thought: Political Difference in Nancy, Lefort, Badiou and Laclau*. Edinburgh: Edinburgh University Press, 2007.

Marion, Jean-Luc. *De surcroît: Études sur les phénomènes saturés*. Paris: Presses Universitaires de France, 2001. Translated by Robyn Horner and Vincent Berraud as *In Excess: Studies of Saturated Phenomena*. New York: Fordham University Press, 2002.

McCall, Dan, ed. *Melville's Short Novels*. New York: Norton, 2002.

Meillassoux, Quentin. *Après la finitude: Essai sur la nécessité de la contingence*. Paris: Seuil, 2006. Translated by Ray Bassier as *After Finitude: An Essay on the Necessity of Contingency*. London: Continuum, 2008.

———. "Excerpts from *L'inexistence divine*." Translated by Graham Harman. Appendix to *Quentin Meillassoux: Philosophy in the Making*, by Graham Harman, 175–238. Edinburgh: Edinburgh University Press, 2011.

———. "*Nouveauté et événement*." In *Alain Badiou: Penser le multiple*, edited by Charles Ramond, 39–64. Paris: L'Harmattan, 2002.

———. "Spectral Dilemma." In *Collapse: Philosophical Research and Development IV*, edited by Robin Mackay, 261–75. Falmouth: Urbanomic, 2008.

Miller, Adam S., "An Interview with Alain Badiou: 'Universal Truths and the Question of Religion.'" *Journal of Philosophy and Scripture* 3, no. 1 (2005): 38–42.

Mills, Catherine. *The Philosophy of Agamben*. Stocksfield: Acumen, 2008.

Naas, Michael. "Urania—The Only *Real* Muse?" In *Internationales Jahrbuch für Hermeneutik 3*, edited by Günter Figal, 1–22. Tübingen: Mohr Siebeck, 2004.

Nancy, Jean-Luc. "The Being-With of Being-There." *Continental Philosophy Review* 41 (2008): 1–15.

———. *The Birth to Presence*. Translated by Brian Holmes et al. Stanford, CA: Stanford University Press, 1993.

———. *La communauté désoeuvrée*. Paris: Christian Bourgois, 1986.

———. *Corpus*. Paris: Métailié, 2006.

———. *La création du monde: Ou la mondialisation*. Paris: Galilée, 2002. Translated by François Raffoul and David Pettigrew as *The Creation of the World or Globalization*. Albany: State University of New York Press, 2007.

———. *Le discours de la syncope: I. Logodaedalus*. Paris: Flammarion, 1976. Translated by Saul Anton as *The Discourse of the Syncope: Logodaedalus*. Stanford, CA: Stanford University Press, 2008.

———. "L'Être abandonné." In *L'impératif catégorique*, 139–53. Translated by Brian Holmes as "Abandoned Being," in Nancy, *The Birth to Presence*, 36–47.

———. *Être singulier pluriel.* Paris: Galilée, 1996. Translated by Robert D. Richardson and Anne E. O'Byrne as *Being Singular Plural.* Stanford, CA: Stanford University Press, 2000.

———. *L'expérience de la liberté.* Paris: Galilée, 1988.

———. "Hors colloque." In *Figures du dehors: Autour de Jean-Luc Nancy,* edited by Gisèle Berkman and Danielle Cohen-Levinas, 519–38. Nantes: Cécile Defaut, 2012.

———. *L'impératif catégorique.* Paris: Flammarion, 1982.

———. *L'oubli de la philosophie.* Paris: Galilée, 1986. Translated by François Raffoul and Gregory Recco as "The Forgetting of Philosophy," in *The Gravity of Thought,* 5–71. New Jersey: Humanities Press, 1997.

———. *Le partage des voix.* Paris: Galilée, 1982. Translated as "Sharing Voices," in *Transforming the Hermeneutic Context: From Nietzsche to Nancy,* edited by Geyle Ormiston and Alan D. Schrift, 211–59. Albany: State University of New York Press, 1990.

———. *La pensée dérobée.* Paris: Galilée, 2001.

———. *Une pensée finie.* Paris: Galilée, 1990. Partially translated by Simon Sparks et al. as *Finite Thinking.* Stanford, CA: Stanford University Press, 2003.

———. "Philosophie sans conditions." In *Alain Badiou: Penser le multiple,* edited by Charles Ramond, 65–79. Paris: L'Harmattan, 2002.

———. *Le poids d'une pensée.* Grenoble: Presses Universitaires de Grenoble, 1991. Translated by François Raffoul and Gregory Recco as "The Weight of a Thought," in *The Gravity of Thought,* 73–84. New Jersey: Humanities Press, 1997.

———. *Le sens du monde.* Paris: Galilée, 1993. Translated by Jeffrey S. Librett as *The Sense of the World.* Minneapolis: University of Minnesota Press, 1997.

———. "Le ventriloque." In *Mimesis des articulations,* edited by Sylviane Agacinski, 271–338. Paris: Flammarion, 1975.

———. *La vérité de la démocratie.* Paris: Galilée, 2008.

Plato. *Plato: Complete Works.* Edited by John M. Cooper. Indianapolis: Hacking, 1997.

———. *Plato: Republic.* Vol. 2, books 6–10. Translated by Christopher Emlyn-Jones and William Preddy. Cambridge, MA: Harvard University Press, 2013.

———. *Plato: Statesman, Philebus, Ion*. Translated by Harold North Fowler and W. R. M. Lamb. Cambridge, MA: Harvard University Press, 1925.

Raffoul, François. "La création du monde." In *Figures du dehors: Autour de Jean-Luc Nancy*, edited by Gisèle Berkman and Danielle Cohen-Levinas, 227–44. Nantes: Cécile Defaut, 2012.

Ramond, Charles, ed. *Alain Badiou: Penser le multiple*. Paris: L'Harmattan, 2002.

Ricoeur, Paul. *Le conflit des interprétations: Essais d'herméneutique*. Paris: Seuil, 1969. Translated by Kathleen McLaughlin as *The Conflict of Interpretations*. London: Continuum, 2004.

———. *Du texte à l'action: Essai d'herméneutique II*. Paris: Seuil, 1986.

Riera, Gabriel. "Fidelity and the Law: Politics and Ethics in Badiou's *Logiques des mondes*." *Cardozo Law Review* 29 (2008): 2319–31.

———. "For an 'Ethics of Mystery': Philosophy and the Poem." In *Alain Badiou: Philosophy and Its Conditions*, edited by Gabriel Riera, 61–85. Albany: State University of New York Press, 2005.

Riera, Gabriel, ed. *Alain Badiou: Philosophy and Its Conditions*. Albany: State University of New York Press, 2005.

Risser, James. *The Life of Understanding: A Contemporary Hermeneutics*. Indianapolis: Indiana University Press, 2012.

Romano, Claude. *L'événement et le monde*. Paris: Presses Universitaires de France, 1998.

———. *L'événement et le temps*. Paris: Presses Universitaires de France, 1999.

Rooden, Aukje van. "L'Intrigue dénouée: Politique et literature dans une communauté sans mythes." PhD diss., University of Tilburg, 2010.

Sallis, John. *The Verge of Philosophy*. Chicago: University of Chicago Press, 2008.

Schürmann, Reiner. *On Being and Acting: From Principles to Anarchy*. Bloomington: Indiana University Press, 1987.

Sheppard, Darren, Simon Sparks, and Colin Thomas. *On Jean-Luc Nancy: The Sense of Philosophy*. London: Routledge, 1997.

Statkiewicz, Max. *Rhapsody of Philosophy: Dialogues with Plato in Contemporary Thought*. University Park: The Pennsylvania State University Press, 2009.

Steele, Timothy. *Missing Measures: Modern Poetry and the Revolt against Metre*. Fayetteville: University of Arkansas Press, 1990.

Taubes, Jakob. *Die politische Theologie des Paulus*. Edited by Aleida Assmann and Jan Assmann. Munich: Wilhelm Fink, 1993.

Tho, Tzuchien. "The Consistency of Inconsistency: Alain Badiou and the Limits of Mathematical Ontology." *Symposium* 12, no. 2 (2008): 70–92.

Torfing, Jacob. *New Theories of Discourse: Laclau, Mouffe and Žižek*. Oxford: Blackwell, 1999.

Vedder, Ben. *Heidegger's Philosophy of Religion: From God to the Gods*. Pittsburgh: Duquesne University Press, 2007.

Watkin, Christopher. "A Different Alterity: Jean-Luc Nancy's 'Singular Plural.'" *Paragraph* 30 (2007): 50–64.

———. *Difficult Atheism: Post-Theological Thinking in Alain Badiou, Jean-Luc Nancy and Quentin Meillassoux*. Edinburgh: Edinburgh University Press, 2011.

Žižek, Slavoj. *The Ticklish Subject: The Absent Center of Political Ontology*. London: Verso, 1999.

INDEX

abandonment, notion of, 78–83, 85, 124–25, 235–36, 243–44; and absolution, 231–39; Agamben and, 122–27, 245–47; and being, 155, 279–80, 312n6; Heidegger and, 78, 251–52; Nancy and, 92, 94, 127, 227, 230–31, 273; in Nancy's *Le partage des voix*, 87, 122, 297n49
Ab-Grund. *See* abyss (*Ab-Grund*)
Ableben, 188
absence, 37, 40, 47, 180, 215; *Ab-Wesen*, 150; hermeneutics and, 78–79
absolute, the, 6, 26, 58, 75, 226, 264; Agamben and, 225, 231, 270; Badiou and, 38, 50–51; contingency as, 258–61; for Hegel and Heidegger, 231–32, 235; infinite, totality, 51–55; metaphysics and, 211–13
absolute beginning, 186–204, 217, 309n19
absolute being, 26, 211, 225
absolute contingency, 204–22, 258, 280
absolute finitude, 73
absolute thought, 232–33
absolution, 226, 228, 231–39
Absprung (leap away from the ground), 142
abyss (*Ab-Grund*), the, 150–51, 246
action. *See* praxis
actuality and potentiality, 118, 240–41, 243–48, 255
actualization, 247, 253
advenant, the, 135, 189–200, 202, 217; after the event, 266
advent, 138–39, 156, 185, 206, 217; event and, 158–59, 166–67
affirmation, 164, 267, 270–71
after the event, 160, 172, 203, 266
Agamben, Giorgio, 2, 4–7, 24, 35, 137, 231; and "being together," 98; and abandonment, 122–26, 233, 236–37; and Aristotle, 93, 117; and *euporia*, 126, 267; and Heidegger, 233, 239, 247–53, 270, 313n26, 315n68; and Kafka, 251, 301n42; and language, 88–89, 114; and Leibniz, 216, 255–58; and Melville's *Bartleby the Scrivener*, 253–61, 286, 308n109, 313n32, 315n68; and metaphysics, 128, 147–48; and Nancy, 122, 127, 131, 147, 233, 299n79; and outside as threshold, 82; and parody, 284–85; and Plato, 102–03, 114–21, 125, 129–30; and presupposition, 182–83; and principle of irrevocability, 258–59; and pure potentiality, 166–67, 240–61, 275; and remembrance, 8, 256–57, 280, 286; and St. Paul, 172, 174, 176, 180–81; and the principle of reason, 264; and the remnant, 214–15
Agamben, Giorgio, works by: "Bartleby, or On Contingency," 240–41, 243, 247, 253–58, 286; *The End of the Poem*, 182; "The Friend," in *What Is an Apparatus*, 298n71; *Homo Sacer*, 122, 131, 234–35, 241–42, 251–52; *Means without End*, 98; "Parody," 284–85; "On Potentiality," 241; *Remnants of Auschwitz*, 117; "*Se*," 233; *The Signature of All Things*, 109; *The Time that Remains*, 181–82; "The Tradition of the Immemorial," 121, 126
agathōn, 80–83 123, 127, 129
alētheia, 156
Allgemeine, 10, 13, 15
always-already, the, 191
analogy, 44–47, 93, 97–100
Anaximander's Fragment, 178
ancestrality, 208–09, 215, 224, 311n70

331

Andenken (memory), 145–46, 149–53, 166, 277, 280; and remembrance, 256, 286
announcement, 84, 89, 162–69
anticipation, 196. See *Vordenken*
anupotheton, 102–03, 112–13, 116–18, 121, 129, 225. See also Plato
aporetic experience, 278–79
aporia, 123, 267, 270, 275–76, 279–80, 283–84; and *euporia*, 119–20, 122, 267, 301n38
appearance, 158, 162, 192
appearing, 26–27, 160, 164, 173
appropriation, 82, 139, 197, 237, 239; event of, 15, 165, 220–21; inceptual thinking and, 152–53. See also *Ereignis*; expropriation
Aquinas, 11–12
archai, 83
archē, 16, 32, 103, 117, 268, 270
Arendt, Hannah, 18–20, 73, 96, 310n42
Aristotle, 2, 35, 70, 98, 117, 248; and dialectics, 120; and divine thought, 241–42, 244–45; and metaphysics, 11–12, 18, 93; and the past, 259–60. See also Aristotle, works by
Aristotle, works by: *Metaphysics Lambda*, 12, 97–98, 117–18, 241, 244, 247; *Nichomachean Ethics*, 258–60; *Peri Psuchē*, 240, 242
as if (supposition), 66
atemporality, 65–66
atheism, 9
attestation, 19–20
attitude, 7–8
Augustine, 126–27
Auseinandersetzung, 94–96, 152–53
authentic death, 218
authenticity, 249–51, 272
authentic potentiality-of-being, 249–51
axiom, the, 52–53, 63–65, 103–14, 160; and the decision, 20–34; Heidegger and, 30, 106
axiomatic decision, 20–34, 42, 75, 92, 106, 113
axioms, 55, 173

Badiou, Alain, 1–5, 8–9, 50, 90–91, 99, 199, 263–66; and the axiomatic decision, 20–34, 42, 75, 92, 106, 113; and Bartleby the scrivener, 308n109; and Cohen's version of set theory, 59–61; and dialectics, 104–05; and the event, 138, 164, 168–69, 200, 203, 227–28, 230; and the excluded third, 311n63; and fidelity, 8, 121, 295n85; and Gödel, 58–59, 62; and Heidegger, 158, 239; and Meillassoux, 206, 264; and metaphysics, 25–26, 97, 147; methodology of, 136–37; and Nancy, 96, 157–58; and Plato, 33, 101–03, 112–14, 117; and Ricoeur, 45; and St. Paul, 169–70, 172–73, 177; and subjectivity, 191–92, 266; and the trace, 192, 223; and universal man, 214–15. See also Badiou, Alain, works by
Badiou, Alain, works by: *Court traité*, 44, 113, 177; "*L'écriture du générique: Samuel Beckett*," 47; *L'être et l'événement*, 30–31, 42, 52–53, 55, 62–63, 67–68, 103, 105, 107, 111–12, 117, 159–61, 163, 173, 204–05, 265–66, 305n61; "Homage to Jacques Derrida," 20; *Logiques des mondes*, 31, 66–67, 106, 111–12, 159–65, 172–73, 295n98, 300nn23, 26, 31; *Manifeste pour la philosophie*, 111; *Petit manuel d'inesthétique*, 35; *La République de Platon*, 113; *Saint Paul*, 214; *Second manifeste pour la philosophie*, 96, 113
ban, the, 243, 245–47, 298n51
Bartleby the scrivener, 121–32
Beckett, Samuel, 47, 49
before the event, 137, 189, 203
beginnings, 142–46, 153, 155, 165. See also first beginning (*der erste Anfang*); other beginning (*der andere Anfang*)
being, 2–4, 8–12, 15, 17, 45–49, 97; abandonment of (*Seinsverlassenheit*), 36–38, 78–79, 147, 234; actualization of, 246; Agamben and, 98, 122–26; appropriation of, 220–21; and the event, 29–30, 57–58, 114, 189–92, 205, 294n77; Heidegger and, 33, 139, 142–43, 234, 292n11; index of, 40–42; Nancy and, 28, 92, 271–75; and reason, 148–51; and thinking, 18–21, 145–46
being-as, 98, 100
being-at-work, 118
being-exposed-to, 95

being-in-common, 72–73, 88–90, 121, 271–73
being-in-the-world, 189, 196, 198
being-in-touch, 229, 272
beingness of beings (*Seiendheit des Seienden*), 9
being-one-with-the-other, 98, 100
being-on-the-threshold, 83, 122–23
being-other, 95
being-out-of-touch, 229
being-outside, 122
being-outside-ourselves, 89–90
being-present, 36
being-the-singular, 273
being-the-what-that-was, 93
being-together (*être-ensemble*), 73, 98–100
being-toward, 78–83, 86–87, 94, 95, 121–24, 127, 130; -death, 95, 169, 175, 248, 252, 299n84; -existence, 299n84; -life, 299n84; -the-other, 89–90; -the-world, 299n84
being-with (*Mitsein*), 72–73, 95, 121, 188, 296n7
being-with-one-another, 92–93
Beiträge zur Philosophie (Vom Ereignis) (Heidegger), 13–15, 165, 179, 222, 234, 239; experience of being 36–37, 39; inceptual thinking, 152–55; and *Notlosigkeit*, 37, 41, 78, 156, 184; and *Der Satz vom Grund*, 139–40, 142–47, 151–54, 170–71; and thinking, 277, 283
believing, 177–84, 283
belonging, 76, 78–83, 109
Betrachtung, 144–45
birth, 138–39, 197, 217; Badiou and, 156, 193; Heidegger and, 196, 217; Marion and, 187–88; Meillassoux and, 217; Romano and, 185, 193, 196, 198, 223
Bosteels, Bruno, 44

Cantor, Georg, 53–55
causality. *See* principle of causality
choice (*Wahl*), 165
Christ-event, the, 170, 176–77, 182
Christian experience of life, 10, 169–72, 174–75, 177–78
co-belonging (*Zugehörigkeit*), 50, 151, 210
communicability and transmissibility, 88–89, 128–30

comportment (*Haltung*), 7, 29–30, 164–65, 174–75, 256–57, 310n42; epochē as, 275–80; to an event, 167–70, 177, 223, 227. *See also* human comportment to the event
concealment, 147, 150, 235–37, 280. *See also* lēthē
conscience. *See* voice of conscience
consensus, 43, 65, 90–92
contemplation, 7–8, 144, 146
contingency, 4–8, 14–18, 21, 237–39, 267–74; as absolute, 258–61; and the event, 136, 138–39, 165–68, 173; excess, origin, and, 198–204; experience of, 183, 220–24; Meillassoux and, 24, 204–06, 216–18, 226, 279, 316n10; necessity and, 212; as the potentiality-of-being-other, 215–18; as potential-not-to-be, 247; and pure potentiality, 240–61; as touch, 228–29. *See also* absolute contingency
conviction, 19–20, 170
correlationism, 25, 72, 207–15, 220, 232, 235
correlationists, 141, 207–13, 215, 231
creation, 145, 240, 243, 254
creator, 11, 240–41, 243, 254
Critchley, Simon, 169–70, 172–73, 177, 306nn80, 81, 308n119, 308n121, 308n124

Dasein, 44, 135, 178, 182, 187–90; authenticity and inauthenticity, 249–52; and being-in-the-world, 196, 198; and death, 94–95, 171, 219, 248; and potentiality-of-being, 155, 175, 253
deactivation, 148. *See also* inoperativeness
dead letters, 254–56
death, 217–18, 309n3; and Dasein, 94–95, 171, 219, 248–49; Heidegger's analysis of, 171, 175, 186–88
decision, 20, 59, 61–63, 68, 277; Badiou's axiomatic, 30–34, 41–43, 54–56, 75, 92; and the event, 162, 165–67
declaration, 19, 55, 162–70, 177; Badiou and, 50, 67, 76, 115, 161
deconstruction, 1–2, 20, 123, 239
decreation, 253–61

deductive fidelity, 263–71
Deleuze, Gilles, 23–24, 46–47, 97–98, 257, 315n68
Denken (thinking), 148, 151, 178, 213, 277, 286–87. *See also Andenken* (memory); thinking (*Denken*); thought; *Vordenken*
Der Satz vom Grund (Heidegger), 134–35, 139, 167–68, 268; and the *Beiträge*, 139, 142–47, 151–54, 170–71; and St. Paul, 170–71; and thinking, 148–49
Derrida, Jacques, 9, 41, 46, 48, 108, 122–28, 201–02; Agamben and, 115, 127–28; Badiou and, 20, 26, 64, 66; and hermeneutics, 23–24, 69; and Kafka's parable *Vor dem Gesetz*, 79, 122–23, 251; and language, 110, 289n2, 313n27; and meaning, 2–3, 74–75, 124; and metaphysics, 147–48; and trace, 159, 301n54; and the wholly other, 213. *See also* Derrida, Jacques, works by
Derrida, Jacques, works by: *Apories,* 248; "La pharmacie de Platon," 123–24; *Le toucher, Jean-Luc Nancy,* 228, 312n4
Descartes, René, 11
desire, 77, 81–82, 87
destiny (*Geschick*), 150–51, 232
dialectical argument, 278–79
dialectical thought, 119–21
dialectic method, 275–76
dialectics, 32–33, 42–43, 103–06, 112–13, 265
dialogue, 96, 99–103; Nancy and, 84–85, 90–92, 103, 119–20, 227
Dieudonné, Jean, 107
disappearance, 37, 40, 49, 63–64, 216–17; of last remainder, 146, 232
divine *dunamis*, 88, 241–42
divine scribe, the, 240–47, 253–55
divine thought, 241–42, 244–45
divine voice, 86, 87, 182, 298n51
dying (*Sterben*), 188

Eigentlichkeit, 250
Einheit. See unity (*Einheit*)
Einstellung, 18–19
Einverständnis, 91
enthusiasm, 85–87, 90, 121–32, 180–82, 272

Entzug. See withdrawal (*Entzug*)
epistemology, 45
epochē, 139, 224, 236, 257, 267; as comportment, 271, 275–80; suspension of judgment on existence, 4, 6, 8–9, 21
Er. *See* myth of Er
Ereignis, notion of, 72, 143, 151, 153, 236–38, 287; and the event, 15, 139; Meillassoux and, 210, 219–20. *See also* Appropriation
Ereignung. See appropriation
Eros. *See* Platonic *erōs*
es gibt, 207–08, 231
ethos, 7–8, 18–21, 106
Euclidean and non-Euclidean geometry, 63–65
euporia, 117, 120–22, 126, 276, 279; and *aporia*, 119–20, 122, 267, 301n38
event, 1–21, 114–15, 155–63, 169, 231–39; axiom and, 31, 109; for Badiou, 29–32, 54, 66–67, 74, 96, 103, 106–08, 264; of birth as origin, 198–200; contemporary thinkers and, 23–24, 230; delay and, 309n20; for Heidegger, 143, 172–73, 186; naming of, 55–58, 293n56; Nancy and, 89–90, 205; nothingness and, 172; phenomenon of, 133–37; remainder of, 225–31; Romano and, 188–97; situation and, 49–50, 59, 67–68; subject and, 56, 64; suspension of the principle of reason and, 246; turning to, 232–33, 235; understanding, 194, 202–03; unhistorical, 232, 235–36, 238
evential birth, 198
evential understanding, 194–95
example, the, 109–11, 115, 120, 129–31
excess, 81–82, 198–204
excess-of-one, 96
excluded third, the. *See* principle of the excluded third
exemplarity, 11, 106–12, 115, 165
existence, 43–44
ex nihilo, 206
experience (*Erfahrung*), 51
exposition, 93–96, 152
expropriation (*Enteignis*), 220, 237, 287. *See also* appropriation

factical (*faktisch*), 188
facticity, 84, 212, 217–19, 249

faith, 19, 169–84, 308n113
faithful subject, the, 300nn23, 31, 306n71. *See also* fidelity
fidelity, 56–58, 115, 203, 227, 263–71, 300n23; Badiou and, 32, 170, 177, 222–23; and exemplarity, 106–13
finitude, 200, 212, 235, 238, 264, 295n6; concept of, 70–71; and infinity, 36, 50, 51–62
first beginning (*der erste Anfang*) of thought, 14–15, 142–43, 147, 151–54, 166–68, 232
first beginning of metaphysics, 277
first philosophy, 1–9, 19–20
first principle, 32–33, 53, 119, 270
forcing, 55–66, 110
fundamental question (*Grundfrage*), 9, 14
future, the, 191, 193
future anterior, 50, 59–60, 66, 110, 194

Gadamer, Hans-Georg, 2, 43, 48, 69, 83–84, 91, 114–15
Galois, Évariste, 107–09, 111
Gedächtnis, 145
generality (*das Allgemeine*), 13, 15
generic set, the, 96, 112, 197, 299n87; and forcing, 55–62; and infinity, 50–51, 200
Geschick, 145–47, 149–50
gift, 135; and being, 231, 236; Nancy and, 81, 87; refusal as, 36, 155
givenness, 230–31, 236–37; of the world, 207–08, 212
glossolalia, 181–83
God, 9, 15–18, 125, 259, 289n10; Aquinas and, 11–12; Badiou and, 53; Heidegger and, 139, 306n80; and Leibniz's principle of sufficient reason, 134; Meillassoux and, 211, 220–22, 278
Gödel, Kurt, 58–59, 62
good, the, 80–82, 112
ground (*Grund*), the, 12, 33, 149–51, 216, 246; leap away from, 14–18, 142; primacy of, 262–64; reason and, 304n36
guiding question (*Leitfrage*), 9–10, 14, 147

Haltung, 18–19
Harman, Graham, 26, 295n7
Hegel, G. W. F., 70, 235, 242, 255–56

Heidegger, Martin, 7, 188–89, 193, 213, 286, 310n29; Agamben and, 233, 247–53, 270, 313n26; and axiom, 30, 106; Badiou and, 31, 33–34, 40, 158, 185; and beyng, 139–56; and choice (*Wahl*), 165; as correlationist, 207–11; *Ereignis*, 139, 231, 235; and God, 134; and the hermeneutic-phenomenological school, 23–24; and language, 48, 98, 313n27; Hölderlin and, 153; legacy of, 9–22; Meillassoux and, 185, 205–06, 210, 223; and metaphysics, 5, 26–27, 62–63, 67, 148; methodology of, 136–37; Nancy and, 71–73, 156–59, 233; and principle of reason, 140–41, 216, 264, 275, 277; and St. Paul, 170–77, 182, 307nn88, 98; and the event, 138, 168–69, 228, 230; and withdrawal, 51–52. *See also* Heidegger, Martin, works by
Heidegger, Martin, works by: *Das Anaximander-Fragment*, 178; "Einleitung zu 'Was ist Metaphysik?'" 10; "Entwürfe zur Geschichte des Seins als Metaphysik," 12–13; *Grundprobleme der Philosophie*, 153; *Identität und Differenz*, 210; *Kritik der reinen Vernunft*, 25; "Die onto-theo-logische Verfassung der Metaphysik," 9; *Parmenides* (lecture course), 237, 286; *Phänomenologie und Theologie*, 178; "*Der Satz vom Grund*" (lecture), 143; *Unterwegs zur Sprache*, 84, 128; "Was ist Metaphysik?" 11; *Was ist Metaphysik*, 315n68; "*Zeit und Sein*" (lecture), 147, 220, 232–33, 236–37, 239. *See also Beiträge zur Philosophie (Vom Ereignis)*; *Der Satz vom Grund*; *Sein und Zeit*
hen, the one, 78–87, 92–93, 271
hermēneia, 91
hermēneuein, 36, 74, 83–85, 115, 130, 297n45
hermēneus, 87
hermeneutic-phenomenological school of thought, 48, 62–63, 135–37, 206, 270; correlation and, 207–15; and speculative school of thought, 7, 23–30, 36–37, 50. *See also*

Derrida, Jacques; Heidegger, Martin; hermeneutics; Nancy, Jean-Luc
hermeneutics, 1–3, 7, 66–67, 167, 185, 239, 297n47; Badiou's ontology in discussion with, 34–62; classical, 69–70, 74–78, 101–02, 110; language and, 114–15; and mathematics, 200, 205; as *partage*, 78–87; and Romano's *advenant*, 189, 192–94. *See also* Hermeneutic-phenomenological school of thought
Hermes, 88
highest being, the, 18, 21
hint (*Wink*), the, 158–62, 222
historical confrontation, 153
historical consideration (*historische Betrachtung*), 144–45
historical dialogue (*geschichtliche Zwiesprache*), 152–53, 178
historical reflection (*geschichtliche Besinnung*), 144–45
history, 25, 28, 72, 101, 166, 235–36; end of, 235–36, 238; of the event, 232–34; of metaphysics, 10–11, 13, 18, 142, 144–53, 216, 256; of philosophy, 33–35, 43–44, 240–41, 259
Hölderlin, Friedrich, 95–96, 152–53
Homer, 86–87, 91, 125, 130–31, 283–84
hōs mē structure, 172, 174–76, 182–83, 219, 248
human comportment to the event, 193, 196, 203–04. *See also* comportment
human existence, 188, 200
human voice, 181–82
Husserl, Edmund, 25, 229
hypothesis, 16, 31–32, 225–26, 228, 253; Badiou and, 47, 53, 113–21; Nancy and, 271–72; in the *Parmenides*, 34, 45, 102–06, 113–21, 264–67, 275, 278–79

idea, the, 42–43, 46, 66–67, 74–75, 106, 113. *See also* Platonic idea
impotential, the, 241–42, 270–71
impotentiality, 247–53
inauthenticity, 249–51
inceptual thinking, 151–55, 165, 179, 304n50
in-common (*koinon*), 13–15, 71–72, 89–90
incorporation, 96, 112–14, 163, 300n23

infinite, the, 51–56, 112, 200
infinity, 51–52, 55, 63, 68–71, 197, 200, 295n3
inoperativeness, 121, 126, 148
inspiration, poetic, 86
interpretation, 50, 80, 84, 131, 151–52; and meaning, 74–75, 77–78; and nomination, 36, 47–50
interpretations, 3, 44–45
Ion, the rhapsode. *See* Plato, works by, *Ion*
irrevocability. *See* principle of irrevocability

Jaeger, Petra, 139
judgment, 279–80, 286

Kafka, Franz: parable *Vor dem Gesetz*, 79–80, 83, 122–23, 125, 251
Kant, Immanuel, 25, 45, 70, 133, 289n7; and the absolute, 72; experience (*Erfahrung*), 51; Meillassoux and, 27, 207; and speculative thought, 210–11
knowledge (*epistēmē*), 90
koinon, 10, 12–15, 71–72, 89–90, 271; without *hen*, 73, 78–87, 92–93

Lacan, Jacques, 47
lack of want (*Not der Notlosigkeit*), 78. *See also Notlosigkeit*
language, 2–3, 59–60, 124, 126–28; Heidegger, and, 152–53, 239, 302n57, 313n27; of the situation, 56–59, 62, 74, 110
leap, 142–56, 168
leap-away-from (*Absprung*), 144, 151, 168
Leibniz, Gottfried Wilhelm von, 16, 257–59, 274–75; and the principle of irrevocability, 259, 260; and the principle of sufficient reason, 15–16, 134–35, 140, 216, 315n68; and the pyramid of possible worlds, 286
lēthē, 236–37, 280, 286–87, 313nn20, 21. *See also* concealment
Levinas, Emmanuel, 82, 159, 197, 213
logos, 2, 18–19, 149–50, 216, 282–83, 285

making-possible, 195–96, 202
Marchart, Oliver, 4
Marion, Jean-Luc, 133–36, 157, 206, 227; and death, 186–87, 201–02
mathematical thought, 31, 40–42

mathematics, 30–32, 101–03, 205, 209; Badiou and, 43–44, 47, 51–53, 108, 264; and dialectics, 42–43, 105; and poetics, 36, 49; speculative thought and, 263–64; subjectivity in light of, 61–68
matheme, the, 34–35
meaning, 74–79, 81–82, 84, 197; and abandonment, 94, 123; horizon of, 198–99, 200, 202; and sense, 88–89, 194, 293n54
Meillassoux, Quentin, 8–9, 27, 50, 135, 230, 276–77; and contingency, 6–7, 220–23, 238–39, 252, 279; and the event, 111, 185–86; and facticity, 212, 217–19; and Heidegger, 141, 218–23, 236, 239; methodology of, 136–37; and speculative thought, 23–24, 26, 31, 147, 204–22, 63–64. *See also* Meillassoux, Quentin, works by
Meillassoux, Quentin, works by: *Après la finitude*, 25, 205–07, 210, 219, 221, 224, 235, 268–70, 278; *The Divine Inexistence*, 278; *L'inexistence divine*, 206, 310n46; "*Nouveauté et événement*," 294n77; "Spectral Dilemma," 221, 278
Melville, Herman: *Bartleby, the Scrivener*, 131, 240, 247; Agamben and, 253–61, 286, 308n109, 313n32, 315n68
memory (*Andenken*), 145–46, 149–53, 166, 277, 280; and remembrance, 256, 286
messenger, 285, 287, 297n45; Silesian, 141, 306n77
metaphor, 48, 97, 99, 110
metaphysical thought, 11, 38, 233
metaphysics, 4, 11, 18, 71, 97, 135; and the absolute, 211–13; Agamben and, 128, 148; and classical hermeneutics, 74–78; history of, 142–51, 153; Heidegger and, 9–10, 13–14, 39, 143–44; and mathematics, 63, 65–66; as ontotheology, 16, 36, 98, 138; philosophers and, 20, 26, 124–25, 205–06, 211; and presupposition, 93–94
moment, the, 191
multiplicity, 29–30, 45–46, 93, 97, 226–27, 264
myth of Er, 35, 282–87, 292n22, 316n19

naming, 39–40, 50, 56–58, 63, 67, 163
Nancy, Jean-Luc, 2–4, 15, 70, 125–31, 136, 230; and abandonment of being, 80, 227–28, 233–34; and Agamben, 122, 147, 233, 299n79; and Badiou, 96, 157–58, 161, 274; and Derrida, 228, 312n4; and ellipsis, 271–75; and Heidegger, 156, 188, 239, 297n45, 305n70; and hermeneutics, 23–24, 69, 101–03; and phenomenology, 157, 186; and Plato, 35–36, 78–83, 116, 182, 240; and Plato's *agathoñ*, 82, 87, 123; and plurality, 6, 28; and the inoperative community, 121, 126; and the unlimited, 46–47. *See also* Nancy, Jean-Luc, works by; *partage*
Nancy, Jean-Luc, works by: *La communauté désoeuvrée*, 126; "L'être abandonné," 80, 126; *Être singulier pluriel*, 92; *L'oubli de la philosophie*, 81; *Le partage des voix*, 75, 83–84, 126; *Le sens du monde*, 80–81, 94
natural sciences, 208–09
Nietzsche, Friedrich, 255–56, 259–60
nomination, 47–50, 60–61
non-being of the one, 30
noncontradiction. See principle of noncontradiction
Notlosigkeit, 37, 41, 78, 156, 184
noumena and *phenomena*, 25, 207

one (*hen*), the, 12–13, 33–34, 51, 71–72, 100
oneness, 30, 33–34, 51, 71–72, 114, 199; and plurality, 12–14
origin, excess, and contingency, 198–204
originary faith, 179–80
other beginning, the, 14–17, 142–46, 149–54, 165–66, 237, 277–80
other, the, 197, 100
otherness, notion of, 27
outside, notion of, 82

Parmenides, 104–05, 119–20, 210–11. *See also* Plato, works by, the *Parmenides*
parody, 284–85
parousia, 170–76, 182, 307n85, 307n86
partage, 93, 122, 227, 271–74, 297n49, 299n76; concept of, 36, 73–74, 83–84, 86–88

past, the, 145, 160–61, 197, 209, 217, 256; being-the-what-that-was, 93; immemorial, 159, 187, 192; irrevocability of, 258–60; primacy of, 137; remembrance and, 144–45, 158, 280, 286
Pauline faith, 180, 182–83
perfection, question of, 11–12
phenomena and *noumena*, 25, 207
phenomenality, 27, 162
phenomenological gaze, the, 156–57
phenomenology, 24, 38, 135, 165, 178, 203; and death, 186–87; of the event, 156–58, 198; of otherness, 27
phenomenon, evental, 187
philosophy, 18, 35, 178, 207; and poetry, 44, 90–91, 130–31, 280–83
Pindar, 152
pistis, Pauline notion of, 177–78
Plain of Concealment (*Lēthē*), 286–87
Plato, 33, 35, 77–83, 98, 225; and *agathoñ* and *erōs*, 82–83, 87; dialogues of, 30, 90, 280–83. *See also* Anupotheton; Myth of Er; Parmenides; Plato, works by
Plato, works by: *Ion*, 36, 73–74, 84–91, 130–31, 181–82, 272, 302n68; *Meno*, 85; the *Parmenides*, 6, 14, 30–34, 46, 103–06, 113–21, 265–67, 275, 278–79; *Phaedrus*, 123–25; *Republic*, 74, 112–13, 115, 130–31, 280–85; *Sophist*, 85; *Symposium*, 74–75, 85; *Theaetetus*, 85
Plato's Academy, 275
Platonic dialectic, 269
Platonic *erōs*, 81–82
Platonic idea, 78, 112–14, 129–30. *See also* idea, the
plurality, 3–4, 6, 17, 23–24, 43; analogy, unlimitedness, and, 44–47; Badiou and, 27, 29–30, 34; Nancy and, 28, 36, 70, 73, 92–97, 188; and oneness, 12–14; remainder of, 225–31. *See also* twofold plurality
pluralizing: of beginnings, 17; of being, 226–27
poem, the, 34–35
poet, the, 85–87, 130–31, 152–53, 180–82; and enthusiasm, 89–90, 125, 302n70. *See also* rhapsode, the
poetic thought, 38, 41–42, 44, 49, 76, 289n2
poetics, 49, 205, 281–83, 303n26

poetry and philosophy, 35, 86, 90–91
politics, 4, 19–20, 177
possibility, 167, 172, 187, 195–96
possibility-of-being-otherwise, 216
possible, notion of, 156
posterior world, 194–95, 203
post-evental situation, 59–62, 110, 159–60, 190
postulate, 269–70, 277
potential, 132, 169–70, 257
potentiality, 118, 240–49, 252–56, 267, 314n44; Agamben and, 166–67, 176, 216, 237–38, 258; of the scrivener, 121–32
potentiality-of-being, 206, 218, 248, 273–74; Dasein and, 175–76, 196, 219, 253
potentiality-of-being-not, 230
potentiality-of-being-other, 212, 215–18, 276–77
potentiality-of-being-otherwise, 21, 137, 187, 206, 217–18, 230, 239, 252, 267–70
potential-not-to-be, 247
praxis, 4, 8, 20–21, 111–12, 114
pre-evental world, 190
preparation of the other beginning, 149, 151, 155, 159, 166
presence, 37, 71, 157, 162, 201; metaphysics of, 36, 40, 67
present, 50, 140, 145, 167, 171–72, 232; -at-handness (*Vorhandenheit*), 209; co-, 174; the (eternally), 41; figure of the world, 175, 180; world, 176, 259. *See also* being-present
present-at-handness (*Vorhandenheit*), 209
presupposed call, the, 270–71
presupposition, 6, 93–94, 115, 183, 225, 268, 271, 279; Agamben and, 121, 124–26, 128–29, 184, 233; of meaning, 78, 81; principle of, 226, 228, 264; problem of, 114–16. *See also* principle of presupposition
presuppositional form, 181–84
primary substance (*protēousia*), 98
principle of causality, 212, 247
principle of the excluded third, 214–15, 276, 311n63, 313n32
principle of irrevocability, 258–60, 310n42
principle of noncontradiction, 118, 213–15, 270, 276–77
principle of presupposition, 226, 228, 264

principle of sufficient reason, 80,
    134–37, 143, 204, 216, 264;
    and abandoned being, 80; and
    causality, 247; and concealment
    of being, 146–47; culmination
    point of, 262; Heidegger, 40–42,
    139–41, 145, 277; Leibniz's, 14–17,
    139–40, 257–58, 274–75, 315n68;
    Meillassoux and, 135, 185, 206,
    211, 268–69; primacy of, 262–63;
    Romano and, 189–90; and sovereign
    actualization, 245–46; suspension of,
    6–8, 151, 189–90, 216, 224, 287
principle of unreason, 210, 215–16,
    224, 268–70, 276–78
principles, quest for, 267–70
prior world, 194
probability theory, 269
proclamation, 20, 162–63
propriation, 237. *See also* appropriation
protē ousia, 93–94, 98
pure potentiality, 252–53, 280,
    286–88, 313n32; and contingency,
    240–61, 276

ratio, 149–51, 216. *See also logos*
reason (*Grund*), 16–17, 142, 149–51,
    304n36
refusal (*Versagung, Verweigerung*) of
    being, 36–37
relatedness, 72, 295n7
remainder, 16, 115–16, 121, 146, 148;
    of faith, 177; of plurality, 225–31,
    232
remembrance, 256, 260–61, 273–74,
    280, 286
representation (*Vorstellung*), 140–41
resemblance and analogy, 97–100
resoluteness, 19, 170
restraint (*Verhaltenheit*), 154–55,
    237–38, 248, 256, 260, 279–80
resurrection of Christ, 170–76, 182,
    307nn85, 86
retrieval (*Wiederholung*), 148
revocation, 253–61
rhapsode, the, 85–90, 121–32,
    181–82, 284. *See also* poet, the
Ricoeur, Paul, 65, 86, 91, 289n2,
    313n27; and being-as, 98; *Le
    conflit des interprétations*, 44, 70;
    hermeneutics, 43–48, 69, 75; Nancy
    and, 83–84
Riera, Gabriel, 35

Romano, Claude, 135–37, 157,
    185, 194–95, 206; and the event,
    188–97, 201, 203, 222–23,
    227–28, 230; and the hermeneutic-
    phenomenological school, 7, 24. *See
    also* Romano, Claude, works by
Romano, Claude, works by: *L'événement
    et le monde*, 188, 309n20;
    L'événement et le temps, 188;
    "L'événement ou le phénomène
    advenant," 186

Schickende, das, notion of, 150
Schickungen, notion of, 150
Schleiermacher's hermeneutics, 48
Scholem, Gershom, 122, 301n42
scintillating event, the, 204, 223, 272,
    305n62
scintillation, 156–69, 183, 305n59;
    without genesis, 192
Sein und Zeit (Heidegger), 14, 72, 84,
    169; Agamben and, 247–49, 255;
    death in, 94–95, 171, 175, 186;
    Dasein, 94, 198; Meillassoux and,
    208–09, 218–19; phenomenology
    in, 27, 36; and potentiality, 206,
    247, 253; Romano and, 7, 188, 191.
    See also Dasein
Seinkönnen, 206
Seinsgeschick, 151
sense and signification, 88–89, 92,
    194–96, 200–02, 272–73
set theory, 40, 65–66, 294n73, 305n61;
    Badiou and, 43, 52–60, 107–09,
    117, 197, 266, 296n13
sharing, 90–96, 227, 271, 287; of
    being, 47, 92, 229; of voices, 87, 99,
    116, 130. *See also partage*
significance, 194–95; (*signifiance*), 83,
    88, 127, 274, 2956n7, 302n64. *See
    also* meaning; sense
signification, 49, 74–80, 83, 86–88,
    125, 131, 302n64
Silesian messenger, the, 140–42
Silesius, Angelus, 140–41, 306n77
simil and *simul*, 98–100
simulacrum, 46, 98–99
singularity, 14–18, 95, 164
situation, 56–59, 62, 64, 67–68; Badiou
    and, 39–40, 48–49, 160, 173
Socrates, 32, 85–91, 103–04, 116, 273,
    284; and enthusiasm, 130–31; and
    the idea of the Good (*agathōn*), 80;

and nonsense, 269; and *periagōgē* of the soul, 113; Phaedrus and, 123–24
soul, 286–88
sovereign ban, 243, 245
speaking in tongues. *See* glossolalia
speculative school of thought, 23–28, 46–47, 69–70, 238–39, 263; and the event, 7, 135–36; and the hermeneutic-phenomenological school of thought, 23, 36–37, 50, 102, 210, 270. *See also* Badiou, Alain; Deleuze, Gilles; Meillassoux, Quentin
speculative thought, 263–66
speech, 199, 142, 284–85
Spinoza, Baruch, 12, 51
Sterben, 188
St. Paul, 180–83, 306n81, 307nn88, 98, 308n109; and *hōs mē* structure, 175–76, 248; letters of, 169, 214, 250; meontology of, 172–76
strong correlationism, 212–13, 268–69, 291n10
subject, the, 26–32, 55–68, 96, 177, 187, 200; and the event, 106–08, 113–14, 160–64, 167, 169, 191–92, 217
subjective fidelity, 62–63, 134, 205, 265–66
subjectivity, 62–68, 206
subtraction (*soustraction*), 39–42
sufficient reason. *See* principle of sufficient reason
supposition, 78, 93, 182. *See also* presupposition
suspension, 139–40, 267, 270–73, 275, 279

temporal dimensions, 190–93
theia moira, 86–87, 91
theōria, 7–8, 18–21, 41, 263–64
thinking (*Denken*), 115, 142–45, 166, 179–80, 182
thought, 20, 146, 277, 314n44; absolute, 232–33; dialectical, 119–21; divine, 241–42, 244–45; fidelity and affirmation of, 263–71; mathematical, 31, 40–42; metaphysical, 11, 38, 233; poetic, 38, 41–42, 44, 49, 76, 289n2; speculative, 263–66. *See also* first beginning (*der erste Anfang*) of thought; hermeneutic-phenomenological school of thought; speculative school of thought; thinking (*Denken*)
threshold, 82–83, 95
tonality, 140–43
totality, 51–55
touch, 228–30, 272–74, 291n1, 312n4
trace, 159–64, 168, 192–93, 204, 301n54, 306n71
transcendent, the, 125, 302n59, 305n62
transitivity of being, 273–74
transmissibility, 88–89, 128, 298n60
truth, 32, 113, 200, 272; of the event, 57–59, 62–63, 157–59, 173; Heidegger and, 208–09, 305n70
twofold plurality, 36, 42–47

understanding, 193–97, 200–03, 222–23, 227
unhistorical event, the, 232, 235–36, 238
unifying ground, 9–21, 135–36
unity (*Einheit*) of being, 12, 136, 262, 264
universalism, 164, 169
univocity, 97, 299n88
unlimitedness, 44–47
unmoved mover, the, 244
unreason. *See* principle of unreason

veil (*Nebel*), 141
veiled speech, 124
veiling, 236
Verenden, 188
Verhaltenheit, 154–55, 238, 248, 256, 279, 304n50
vita activa (*bios politikos*), 19–20
vita contemplativa (*bios theōrētikos*), 19–20
voice of being, 181–84, 270, 304n32
voice of conscience, 249–55, 270, 301n51, 304n32, 308n126
void, 36–42, 49, 50, 57, 68, 224, 292n30
Vordenken, 148–49, 151–52, 166–67, 220, 256, 277

wholly other, the, 212–13, 219–22
Wink, 158–62, 222
wisdom (*sophia*), 74
withdrawal (*Entzug*), 36–42, 51–52, 68, 146, 177, 233
writing, 123–25, 241, 254–55